DATE DUE		

AFRICAN-AMERICAN WRITERS

Philip Bader

Facts On File, Inc.

Note on Photos

Many of the illustrations and photographs used in this book are old, historical images. The quality of the prints is not always up to current standards, as in some cases the originals are from old or poor-quality negatives or are damaged. The content of the illustrations, however, made their inclusion important despite problems in reproduction.

African-American Writers

Copyright © 2004 by Philip Bader

Facts On File, Inc.
132 West 31st Street
New York NY 10001

Library of Congress Cataloging-in-Publication Data

Bader, Philip, 1969–
    African-American writers / Philip Bader.
       p. cm.—(A to Z of African Americans)
    Includes bibliographical references (p.) and indexes.
    ISBN 0-8160-4860-6 (acid-free paper)
    1. American literature—African American authors—Bio-bibliography—Dictionaries.
    2. African American authors—Biography—Dictionaries. 3. African Americans in
    literature—Dictionaries. 4. Authors, American—Biography—Dictionaries. I. Title.
    II. Series.
    PS153.N5B214 2004
    810.9'96073'003—dc21   2003008699

Facts On File books are available at special discounts when purchased in bulk quantities for businesses, associations, institutions, or sales promotions. Please call our Special Sales Department in New York at (212) 967-8800 or (800) 322-8755.

You can find Facts On File on the World Wide Web at http://www.factsonfile.com

Text design by Joan M. Toro
Cover design by Nora Wertz

Printed in the United States of America

VB Hermitage 10 9 8 7 6 5 4 3 2 1

This book is printed on acid-free paper.

CONTENTS

LIST OF ENTRIES

ACKNOWLEDGMENTS

I would like to express my gratitude to several individuals whose material and moral support have sustained me through the many months that went into the writing of this book. I owe a considerable debt to Dr. R. Kent Rasmussen, a scholar of considerable repute, a generous mentor, and a good friend. Without Dr. Rasmussen's consistent encouragement and cogent advice, I could not have written this book.

To Michelle Murphy and Andrea Miller, I owe my thanks for their gracious assistance in reading and commenting on the early manuscript.

My thanks to Charlotte Sumrow Pirch for supplying crucial research materials. I would also like to acknowledge a host of friends and family, whose love and support I cherish profoundly, and whose forbearance amid difficult months of work I could never adequately repay.

Finally, to all at Facts On File, and in particular my editor, Nicole Bowen, I thank you for your patience and professionalism and for the opportunity to take part in a work that has proved to be deeply enriching.

INTRODUCTION

For more than two centuries, black authors have explored traditional genres such as poetry, drama, short fiction, novels, and essays. They have produced histories and scientific studies. They have worked as journalists, editors, screenwriters, and educators. Black authors have written science fiction, fantasy, mysteries, travel books, diaries, and songs. Black writers have argued their humanity, raged against social injustice, and celebrated the rich cultural traditions of African and African-American life. From their roots in the early years of enslavement in America, black writers have achieved the highest honors available to any author, regardless of culture, color, or creed. On August 25, 1746, Lucy Terry, a young slave woman of 16, wrote a ballad commemorating the ambush of a white family by Native Americans in Massachusetts. On December 7, 1993, Toni Morrison, a woman from a northeastern Ohio steel town, addressed an audience in Norway upon receiving the Nobel Prize in literature.

African-American history began with the arrival of 20 African indentured servants in the colonial settlement of Jamestown, Virginia, in 1619. Indentured servitude soon gave way to slavery, and more than a century would pass before the first known African-American author, Lucy Terry, recorded a skirmish between Native Americans and colonial settlers in the poem "Bars Fight." The development of a national market for slavery during the 17th and 18th centuries brought Africans in increasing numbers to the shores of America as an inexpensive source of labor.

The African-American literary tradition arose in part from a desire to challenge the assumptions of race and culture that have dominated American society from the colonial era to modern times. A principal justification for the enslavement of Africans and the perpetuation of the institution of slavery hinged on a belief in the cultural and intellectual inferiority of people of African descent that was evidenced by a lack of anything that might be construed as literature or art, at least according to Western, Eurocentric concepts. The writings of such authors as Jupiter Hammon and Phillis Wheatley soon gave the lie to such arguments and represented acts of revolution that sparked more than two centuries of literary innovations and a growing national awareness of the contributions of black Americans to American culture and art.

The earliest writings by African Americans, written and published during the colonial era, introduced many of the themes and issues that would preoccupy succeeding generations: the right to live in freedom, under the same laws and with the same opportunities as other Americans. Throughout history, black authors have consistently explored the political dimensions of literature and its ability to effect social change. African-American writers have also provided an essential framework for shaping cultural identity and solidarity. Through the various eras and movements of the African-American literary tradition, including the early nationalist and antislavery movements of the 18th and 19th centuries, the cultural awakening in Harlem during the 1920s and 1930s, the rise of protest and black nationalist literature during the mid-20th century, and the considerable critical and popular success, particularly by women, in the late 20th and early 21st centuries, black authors have returned to the roots of their cultural heritage, preserved in the songs and stories of their ancestors.

The 150 authors covered in this book represent the vast diversity of backgrounds and styles through the centuries. Their works have left an indelible mark on the literary landscape of American culture and preserved a heritage far older than the institutions of American slavery and the cultural repression that followed in its wake.

In selecting writers for this book, the author looked to the major voices within African-American literature through the eras that have marked its development. Early authors such as Lucy Terry, Phillis Wheatley, Jupiter Hammon, Olaudah Equiano, David Walker, William Wells Brown, and Harriet Jacobs established a foundation for the development of a literary tradition. While their writing reflected the literary conventions of their times, it also expanded the boundaries of those conventions to provide a platform for voicing opposition to the systematic disenfranchisement of African Americans, whose rights were denied by a young nation founded on the principles of freedom and equality for all people. However, it should be kept in mind that the classifications outlined here represent only general categories by which to evaluate common themes and trends across several generations of authors.

Early African-American writings contradicted the racial, scientific, and religious biases used to support slavery. Prior to the Civil War, increasing numbers of slaves and former slaves learned to read and write. Their descriptions of the brutal realities of slave life galvanized growing numbers of white Americans and free African Americans who opposed slavery, while also offering hope to those still in bondage. Firsthand depictions of slave life gave rise to a new genre in American literature, the slave narrative. No greater example of the power and influence of these narratives can be found than the *Narrative of the Life of Frederick Douglass* (1845). Douglass's narrative presented an unequivocal indictment of the dehumanizing impact of slavery on slave and slaveholder alike. He also revealed the liberating power of education—the power of words—by which African Americans could effectively confront and refute their oppressors.

Douglass's influence was felt among the numerous black writers who emerged prior to and following the Civil War. After the war, emancipated slaves struggled to find their way in a society that had finally abolished slavery but that had yet to accept them as equals. The works of such authors as Henry Walton Bibb, Sarah Forten, Frances Ellen Watkins Harper, Harriet E. Wilson, William Cooper Nell, Victor Séjour, and James Monroe Whitfield continued to address the needs of the black community in its early years of freedom and further extended the narrative and thematic scope of African-American literature.

At the turn of the 20th century, W. E. B. DuBois emerged as one of the first writers to locate African-American life within a broader historical context. His landmark work, *The Souls of Black Folk* (1903), and the numerous sociological studies that followed, provided the philosophical foundation for what came to be known as the New Negro movement. It revealed a cultural heritage independent of slavery and linked to the grandeur of Africa's ancient and storied past. A tribute given to DuBois upon his retirement from the National Association for the Advancement of Colored People (NAACP) summed up his artistic and intellectual contributions to African-American literature and culture: "He created, what never existed before, a Negro intelligentsia, and many who have never read a word of his writings are his spiritual disciples and descendants."

DuBois's many literary descendants, and those of his contemporaries Alain Locke and James Weldon Johnson, were soon to emerge during the Harlem Renaissance period, a cultural and literary revival of unparalleled energy. In the 1920s and 1930s black authors, artists, and musicians began to explore their cultural roots in an outpouring of creativity that unabashedly celebrated the beauty and richness of African-American life. Authors such as Langston Hughes, Arna Bontemps, Zora Neale Hurston, and Sterling Brown established new methods of literary expression, drawn in part from African and African-American folk traditions and conditioned by the challenges of modern urban life and the persistence of racial prejudice and oppression. The Harlem Renaissance also saw an unprecedented increase in works by women such as Jessie Redmon Fauset, Nella Larsen, Ann Petry, Anna Julia Cooper, and many others.

While literary works by black writers found wide critical and popular support, particularly during the Harlem Renaissance, racial discrimination remained an essential aspect of American life. In the 1940s and 1950s the works of such authors as Richard Wright, Ralph Ellison, James Baldwin, Gwendolyn Brooks, Adrienne Kennedy, and Lorraine Hansberry portrayed the uncertainty and alienation that characterized the lives of many African Americans in the segregated Jim Crow South and in the urban slums of the North. Wright's *Native Son* (1940), Ellison's *Invisible Man* (1952), Baldwin's *Go Tell It on the Mountain* (1953), and Hansberry's *A Raisin in the Sun* (1959) addressed the intolerable social and physical conditions under which many African Americans suffered and inspired numerous works of protest fiction. Like the slave narratives of the previous century, protest works focused attention on the dehumanizing and schizophrenic nature of American racism. These works also fueled the growing and largely

nonviolent Civil Rights movement of the mid-20th century.

During the turbulent 1960s and 1970s, many African-American writers saw little hope for a voluntary shift in American assumptions of race, and their creative focus became more ethnocentric. Authors such as LeRoi Jones (later known as Amiri Baraka), Larry Neal, Hoyt Fuller, Addison Gayle, Jr., Carolyn M. Rodgers, and other early architects of the Black Arts Movement began to articulate a new literary aesthetic—a black aesthetic that more accurately reflected the social and political realities of modern African-American life. Closely aligned politically and ideologically with the Black Power movement and galvanized by the murders of social activists Martin Luther King, Jr., and Malcolm X, Black Arts authors such as Don L. Lee (later known as Haki R. Madhubuti), Ed Bullins, Nikki Giovanni, Sonia Sanchez, and Mari Evans decried racial injustice and often demonstrated in their writing an open hostility toward white society and its power structures. The Black Arts Movement was community based, highly political, and reaffirmed in new ways the cultural traditions preserved by previous generations of authors during the Harlem Renaissance.

Despite its considerable influence, many judged the Black Arts Movement to be too narrow in its artistic focus. This was particularly true among women, whose writing increasingly addressed gender as well as racial discrimination. Ntozake Shange's play *for colored girls who have considered suicide/when the rainbow is enuf* (1974) and Alice Walker's epistolary novel *The Color Purple* (1982) generated some controversy among male authors for what was perceived as negative literary portraits of African-American men. Nonetheless, works by women continued to capture the imaginations of contemporary critics and readers of all cultural backgrounds by emphasizing the varied roles of women as mothers, daughters, and wives, and, in a broader sense, the cultural and historical archivists of the past.

One of the most celebrated authors in modern American and African-American literature, Toni Morrison popularized what has come to be known as the neo-slave narrative, in which modern authors use the context of slavery as a political and creative framework for their fiction. Margaret Walker's *Jubilee* (1966) is regarded as the earliest example of the genre. Others include Ernest J. Gaines's *The Autobiography of Miss Jane Pittman* (1971), Octavia Butler's *Kindred* (1979), Sherley Anne Williams's *Dessa Rose* (1986), and Charles R. Johnson's *Middle Passage* (1990). In 1987, Morrison published the Pulitzer Prize–winning *Beloved* (1987), one of the most acclaimed examples of the neo-slave narrative and a classic of contemporary American fiction. Morrison's reputation reached the ultimate height in 1993 when she received the Nobel Prize in literature, an event that demonstrated the limitless possibilities for African-American writers and the impact that writings by black authors have had in America and throughout the world.

Ai
(Florence Anthony)
(1947–) poet, novelist, educator

Best known for her dramatic monologues, in which she often adopts the personae of political, historical, and cultural icons, Ai has earned numerous accolades for the complex and often violent imagery that fills her poetry. "I find it very exciting to become other people," Ai stated in a 2000 interview with *Radcliffe Quarterly* about her use of characters, real and invented. "I don't think of them as masks for myself. They're my characters; they're not me." Also the author of an unpublished novel and a distinguished professor of literature, Ai has been the recipient of an American Book Award, a National Book Award, and the Academy of American Poets' Lamont Prize.

Born Florence Anthony on October 21, 1947, in Albany, Texas, Anthony later adopted the pseudonym Ai, which means love in Japanese. "I should not, for all eternity, have to be identified with a man who was only my stepfather," Ai has explained about the changing of her name. Her racial heritage includes African-American, Choctaw, and Irish ancestry on her mother's side, and Japanese from her father. Raised in Arizona, Las Vegas, and San Francisco, Ai returned to Tucson to attend the University of Arizona, from which she graduated in 1969 with a bachelor's

degree in Japanese. There she met New York University professor and poet Galway Kinnell, who encouraged her to enroll in the writing program at the University of California at Irvine. She completed the program in 1971.

Ai published her first collection of poems, *Cruelty*, in 1973. Employing her own version of the dramatic monologue, Ai assumed the identities of unconventional and sometimes disturbing characters, and addressed issues such as abortion, suicide, and child abuse. *Cruelty* drew serious critical attention, and Ai was awarded a Guggenheim Fellowship and a Radcliffe (now Bunting) Fellowship, both in 1975.

Ai's use of dramatic monologues grew increasingly more complex in her later published collections, which included *Killing Floor* (1979), *Sin* (1986), *Fate: New Poems* (1991), *Greed* (1993), and *Vice: New and Selected Poems* (1999). Poems in these volumes gave dramatic voice to a host of disparate characters, including a child murderer, a black participant in the Los Angeles riots of 1992, and such historical figures as Gen. George Custer, J. Edgar Hoover, and President Lyndon B. Johnson.

By adopting the identities of fictional and historical characters, Ai provides different and highly imaginative perspectives on issues of race, gender, politics, and civil rights. Critics have often balked at the graphic imagery of her poems while also praising her courage in dealing with difficult subject matter in direct and compelling language. Her numerous literary honors include several literary fellowships, the Academy of American Poets' Lamont Prize in 1978 for *Killing Fields,* the American Book Award in 1987 for *Sin,* and the National Book Award for her 1999 collection *Vice: New and Selected Poems.* In 2003 Ai published *Dread,* her seventh volume of poetry.

In addition to poetry, Ai has completed an unpublished novel, *Black Blood,* which explores African-American ancestry in the context of interracial marriage. Also a distinguished professor of literature and creative writing, Ai has served as poet-in-residence at Wayne State University and George Mason University, as writer-in-residence at Arizona State University, and as a visiting professor at the University of Colorado at Boulder. She became a tenured professor at Oklahoma State University in 1999 and began extensive research into her Native American cultural heritage. In 2002 Ai was given the Mitte Chair in Creative Writing at Southwest Texas State University.

Further Reading

Ai. *Dread.* New York: W. W. Norton and Co., 2003.
———. *Greed.* New York: W. W. Norton and Co., 1993.
———. *Vice: New and Selected Poems.* New York: W. W. Norton and Co., 1999.
Andrews, William L., Frances Smith Foster, and Trudier Harris, eds. *The Concise Oxford Companion to African American Literature.* New York: Oxford University Press, 2001.
Russell, Sandi. *Render Me My Song: African-American Women Writers from Slavery to the Present.* New York: St. Martin's Press, 1991.

Ai accepts the National Book Award for poetry in 1999 during ceremonies held in New York City. *(AP/Wide World Photos)*

Andrews, Raymond
(1934–1991) *novelist*

In his four novels, all set in the fictional Muskhogean County, Georgia, and in his personal memoir, Raymond Andrews exhibited a rich gift for storytelling and for capturing the extraordinarily repressive social milieu of the rural South before the civil rights era. He was born near Madison, Georgia, on June 6, 1934, one of 10 children of George and Viola Andrews. His parents were sharecroppers, and he helped work the farm until the age of 15, when he moved to Atlanta. He attended Washington High School in that city and later served four years in the U.S. Air Force. Following his discharge, he moved to New York City and took a job with KLM Royal Dutch Airlines that allowed him to travel widely in the United States and Europe.

In 1975 Andrews published his first writing, an article on baseball that appeared in *Sports Illustrated.* The following year, he released an excerpt from the novel *Apalachee Red* in the journal

Artaxia, and Dial Press published the full novel in 1978, earning Andrews the first ever James Baldwin Prize for Fiction. Two more novels, *Rosiebelle Lee Wildcat* and *Baby Sweet's,* followed in 1980 and 1983, respectively, composing a trilogy about life in the fictional Muskhogean County.

Patterned on Morgan County, Georgia, where Andrews was born, Muskhogean County is a microcosm of African-American life in the rural South before the civil rights era. The narrative in *Apalachee Red* begins with the arrest and imprisonment of Big Man Thompson in 1918 for a crime he did not commit and continues to document a host of other injustices. Law enforcement officials routinely terrorize the black community. Wealthy whites exploit black workers and, through rape or intimidation, sexually abuse black women. In addition, the black community of Apalachee is polarized by intraracial tension between Light Town and Dark Town. Into this volatile environment comes Apalachee Red, a native of Muskoghean County. The son of a wealthy white landowner, John Morgan, and one of his black domestics, Red returns to Apalachee unexpectedly on Thanksgiving Day in 1945 to assume his birthright and to exact revenge for the wrongs his family has suffered.

Rosiebelle Lee Wildcat, the second book in Andrews's Muskhogean trilogy, was inspired by Andrews's own grandmother and recounts the exploits of Rosiebelle Lee, a mixed-race beauty, and further documents the racial tensions among its inhabitants. The trilogy's final book, *Baby Sweet's,* focuses on the intermingling of whites and blacks in Baby Sweet's brothel during the course of one day, July 4, 1966.

Supporting himself through the 1970s and 1980s with a number of temporary jobs, Andrews continued to write. He published his memoir, *The Last Radio Baby,* in 1990, wherein he describes his childhood and adolescence in Morgan County, Georgia. *Jessie and Jesus and Cousin Clare,* his fourth and final novel, appeared in 1991. Also set in the town of Apalachee, the two-part novel traces the lives of three women whose treachery wreaks havoc in their own lives and those of the inhabitants of Apalachee.

On November 26, 1991, just after the release of his fourth novel, Raymond Andrews took his own life, cutting short a remarkable literary career. He had been working on a fifth novel, *99 Years and a Dark Day,* at the time of his death. Widely considered one of the most gifted authors of his generation, Andrews exhibited an amazing gift for storytelling and created some of the most memorable characters in African-American literature. His Muskhogean trilogy stands as a remarkable achievement in regional southern literature, and American literature in general, drawing deserved comparisons to William Faulkner and his Yoknapatawpha County novels.

Further Reading

Andrews, Raymond. *The Last Radio Baby: A Memoir.* Atlanta, Ga.: Peachtree Publishers, 1990.

Andrews, William L., Frances Smith Foster, and Trudier Harris, eds. *The Concise Oxford Companion to African American Literature.* New York: Oxford University Press, 2001.

Contemporary Black Biography. Volume 4. Detroit, Mich.: Gale Research, 1993, 1–4.

Folks, Jeffery J. "Trouble in Muskhogean County: The Social History of a Southern Community in the Fiction of Raymond Andrews." *Southern Literary Journal* 30, no. 2 (spring 1998): 66.

Angelou, Maya
(Marguerite Johnson, Marguerite Annie Johnson)
(1928–) *poet, novelist, essayist autobiographer, screenwriter, director, actor, playwright, children's fiction writer, educator*

Maya Angelou's creative achievements span numerous genres and disciplines. Her poetry and prose have earned National Book Award and Pulitzer Prize nominations. She received an Emmy nomination in 1977 for her role in the television adaptation of ALEX HALEY's *Roots*. Angelou is also one of only two poets to have recited their poetry at a presidential inauguration. An internationally acclaimed author, poet, actor, director, and educator, Angelou is one of the most vital and compelling voices in contemporary American and African-American literature. "In all my work, in the movies I write, the lyrics, the poetry, the prose, the essays," Angelou explained in a 1990 interview for *Paris Review*, "I am saying that we may encounter many defeats—maybe it's imperative that we encounter the defeats—but we are much stronger than we appear to be, and maybe much better than we allow ourselves to be."

Maya Angelou was born Marguerite Johnson on April 4, 1928, in St. Louis, Missouri, one of two children born to Vivian Baxter and Bailey Johnson. After her parents divorced, Marguerite and her brother, Bailey, moved to Stamps, Arkansas, to live with their paternal grandmother, Ann Henderson, who owned and operated a general store and owned several rental properties. At age eight, Marguerite returned with Bailey to St. Louis to live with her mother, an engaging and charismatic socialite, and her mother's boyfriend, Mr. Freeman. While living in her mother's home, Marguerite was sexually abused and raped by Freeman, who was subsequently murdered by her uncles after her testimony during Freeman's trial for these crimes.

Shattered by these traumatic experiences, and believing that her words had contributed to Freeman's death, Marguerite refused to speak for several years. She moved back to her grandmother's home in Stamps and became an avid reader, finding solace in a world that required no spoken words. Over time, and with the help of an elderly friend, Bertha Flowers, whom she later described as "one of the few gentlewomen I have ever known" and someone who "has remained throughout my life the measure of what a human being can be," Marguerite began to speak again.

Living in the pre–civil rights South, Marguerite soon became aware of the limitations that racism and sexism imposed on her. She graduated from Lafayette Training School, where she was frequently reminded that she could expect a future with no legitimate intellectual pursuits. She left the increasingly hostile racial prejudice of Stamps at her grandmother's behest, moving in 1940 to San Francisco, California, to live with her mother and new stepfather. There, she attended George Washington High School and studied theater, music, and dance at the California Labor School. She also mounted a lengthy and successful campaign to become San Francisco's first black female streetcar conductor. Subsequently, her unexpected pregnancy at the age of 17, and the birth of her son, Guy, in 1945, compelled her to reexamine the direction of her life.

In the early years of motherhood, she struggled to cope with the enormous responsibility of caring for her son while also trying to mature as an individual. She found work wherever she could, as a cook, a waitress, a dancer, and a chauffeur. She also worked briefly as a brothel madam and prostitute, and suffered a short dependence on drugs. After the kidnapping of her son, whom she had left in the care of a friend, and who was returned shortly after, she began to overcome the confusion and misdirection of this period in her life, due in large part to the support of her mother and brother.

During the early 1950s, she worked in a record store in San Francisco, where she met her first husband, an Italian ex-sailor named Tosh Angelou. In 1953, after the failure of her marriage, she found work at a popular San Francisco nightclub and became a popular singer and dancer. She adopted the stage name Maya Angelou and, to her surprise, was invited to join the cast of an international tour of George Gershwin's *Porgy and Bess* that visited 22 countries in Europe and Africa from 1954 to 1963. A growing need to become involved with the Civil Rights movement, and her long absence from her son, convinced Angelou to leave the tour early and return to the United States.

In 1959, Angelou moved to New York City and supported herself by performing in nightclubs,

Maya Angelou recites her poem "On the Pulse of the Morning" at Bill Clinton's presidential inauguration on January 20, 1993. *(AP/Wide World Photos)*

including the famed Apollo Theater in Harlem. She also appeared in two dramatic productions, Jean Genet's *The Blacks,* with actor James Earl Jones, and *Cabaret for Freedom,* an off-Broadway production that she wrote, directed, and starred in. She also participated in the Harlem Writers Guild and met novelists JOHN OLIVER KILLENS and JAMES BALDWIN, who encouraged her burgeoning interest in writing.

While in New York, Angelou met the civil rights leaders Martin Luther King, Jr., and Malcolm X, and served briefly as the northern coordinator of the Southern Christian Leadership Conference. She also led a march on the United Nations in protest of worldwide racial oppression. After meeting and falling in love with African activist Vusumzi Make, she moved with him and her son to Cairo, where she worked as an associate editor at the English-language newspaper *Arab Observer.* When her relationship with Make ended in 1962, Angelou moved to Ghana and found work in the University of Ghana's School of Music and Dance, and as a reporter for the *Ghanian Times* and editor for the *African Review.*

Angelou returned to the United States in 1966 and began to focus on her writing. During the next few years she served as a lecturer at the University of California at Los Angeles, and authored a 10-part television series on African influences in American life, as well as a play, *The Least of These* (1966). With the encouragement of author James Baldwin, who suggested that she write about her past, Angelou decided to write her autobiography.

In a series of six volumes published between 1971 and 2002, Angelou traced the events of her life, from childhood to her return from Africa in the late 1960s. *I Know Why the Caged Bird Sings* (1970), nominated for a National Book Award, relates the details of her difficult childhood in St. Louis and Stamps, and ends with the birth of her son in San Francisco. *Gather Together in My Name* (1974) and *Singin' and Swingin' and Gettin' Merry Like Christmas* (1976) chronicle her struggles as a single mother, her success as a singer and dancer, and her extensive travels as a cast member in *Porgy and Bess. The Heart of a Woman* (1981) and *All God's Children Need Traveling Shoes* (1986) describe her life in New York and Africa. The sixth volume, *A Song Flung up to Heaven* (2002), covers the years between 1964 and 1968.

Apart from their value as a record of the cultural and familial influences that have shaped Angelou as an individual, as an author, and as a mother, Angelou's autobiographical writings also serve as an example for others. "All my work, my life, everything is about survival," she explained in Claudia Tate's *Black Women Writers at Work* (1983). Critics generally praised her first book, *I Know Why the Caged Bird Sings*, which Angelou later adapted for television, above all others for its sensitive depiction of her traumatic childhood and her emphasis on the role that family and community can play in individual healing. A common thread among all her autobiographical writings, however, is Angelou's brilliant command of language and the lyrical quality of her prose.

In addition to her best-selling autobiographies, Angelou has published several volumes of poetry. Her first collection, *Just Give me a Cool Drink of Water 'fore I Diiie* (1971), earned a Pulitzer Prize nomination. Angelou's other published collections include *Oh Pray My Wings Are Gonna Fit Me Well* (1975), *And Still I Rise* (1978), *Shaker, Why Don't You Sing?* (1983), *I Shall Not Be Moved: Poems* (1990), and *A Brave and Startling Truth* (1995).

Angelou married writer and cartoonist Paul Du Feu in 1973. That year, she also starred in her first Broadway play, *Look Away,* for which she received a Tony Award nomination. Angelou's considerable achievements in the performing arts also include the writing and directing of several plays, including *Ajax* (1974, adapted from the play by Sophocles), *Encounters* (1974), *And Still I Rise* (1976, adapted from her poem), and *King* (1990, adapted from the book by Lonne Elder III). In 1998 she directed her first feature film, *Down in the Delta,* starring Alfre Woodard. Angelou is the first African-American woman to join the Director's Guild, and she has written, produced, directed, and starred in numerous theatrical, film, and television productions. In 1977 she earned an Emmy nomination for her starring role in Alex Haley's television miniseries *Roots.*

Having lectured and taught at several universities in the United States during the 1970s, Angelou was given a lifetime appointment at Wake Forest University in North Carolina as Reynolds Professor of American Studies in 1981. Perhaps one of the proudest moments of

Angelou's remarkable career came in 1993, when President Bill Clinton asked her to recite a poem for his inauguration. "On the Pulse of Morning," written specifically for the event, captured the spirit of Angelou's lifelong efforts toward cultural and spiritual renewal, while also challenging the new president to embrace that vision for the United States and for the world.

Angelou's contributions to American and African-American literature and culture comprise a vast array of creative endeavors in theater, music, television, and film. She has published autobiographies, poetry, plays, screenplays, essays, short fiction, children's fiction, and, in 2002, an exclusive line of greeting cards for Hallmark. An internationally acclaimed author, social activist, and educator, Angelou has been awarded more than a dozen honorary degrees from various U.S. universities. Her poetry has been featured in films (*Poetic Justice*, 1993), recited at the United Nations, and recorded for commercial release, for which Angelou received a 1994 Grammy Award for best spoken-word album.

Maya Angelou is among the most popular and visible contemporary African-American authors. While the unflinching optimism of her autobiographical and poetic works has resonated with people of all colors and ethnicities, Angelou's articulation of the challenges facing black women in a society imbued with racism and sexism, and her celebration of the unique strengths and achievements of black women, have remained particularly poignant. In 2000 President Clinton awarded Angelou the National Medal of Art, one of numerous honors that she has attained during her prestigious career.

Further Reading

Angelou, Maya. *The Complete Collected Poems of Maya Angelou.* New York: Random House, 1994.

———. *Even the Stars Look Lonesome.* New York: Random House, 1997.

———. *I Know Why the Caged Bird Sings.* New York: Random House, 1970.

Lupton, Mary Jane. *Maya Angelou: A Critical Companion.* Westport, Conn.: Greenwood Press, 1998.

Williams, Mary E., ed. *Readings on Maya Angelou.* San Diego, Calif.: Greenhaven Press, 1997.

Attaway, William
(William Alexander Attaway)
(1911–1986) *novelist, playwright, short story writer, songwriter, screenwriter*

A versatile and gifted author of novels, a play, short fiction, songs, and scripts for television and film, William Attaway was one of the earliest African Americans to write for television and film. Though often eclipsed by his more acclaimed contemporaries, such as RICHARD WRIGHT and LANGSTON HUGHES, Attaway was heralded as one of the finest chroniclers of the Great Migration, a period in the early 20th century during which multitudes of African-American families fled the poverty and racism of the South for the hope of a better life in the urban North.

William Alexander Attaway was born on November 19, 1911, in Greenville, Mississippi, the son of William S. Attaway, a physician and founder of the National Negro Insurance Association, and Florence Parry Attaway, a schoolteacher. As a child, Attaway moved with his family to Chicago, Illinois, as part of the Great Migration, which would later form the subject of his best-known novel, *Blood on the Forge* (1941). Encountering the poetry of Langston Hughes as a high school student, and discovering that Hughes was black, Attaway began to consider a career as a writer. His earliest works were plays written for his sister's amateur theatrical group. After his graduation from high school, Attaway attended the University of Illinois in Urbana. The death of his father interrupted his studies, and he spent two years traveling in the West and writing.

Attaway returned to Chicago and completed his bachelor's degree at the University of Illinois in 1936. He also saw the production of his first play, *Carnival*, produced at the University of

Illinois in 1935. Also in 1935, Attaway became involved with the Federal Writers' Project, where he met and befriended Richard Wright. Attaway moved to New York City following his graduation and held several odd jobs to support his writing, while also earning a role in George S. Kaufman and Moss Hart's *You Can't Take It with You.*

He completed his first novel, *Let Me Breathe Thunder,* in 1939. The novel depicts the experiences of two white migrant workers, Step and Ed, who befriend an abandoned Mexican child named Hi-Boy while traveling in the West. The novel follows the three travelers through desperate circumstances as they struggle to survive, and chronicles the moral downfall of the innocent Hi-Boy, who suffers as other characters in the novel do from an association with Step and Ed. *Let Me Breathe Thunder* received mixed reviews, with some critics favorably comparing it in language and theme to the works of John Steinbeck.

With the help of a grant from the Julius Rosenwald Fund, Attaway began work on his second novel, *Blood on the Forge,* published in 1941. Considered his most accomplished work, *Blood on the Forge* chronicles the lives of three brothers, Big Mat, Chinatown, and Melody Moss, who leave their life as sharecroppers in Kentucky when Big Mat assaults a white overseer who insulted his mother. The brothers move north to Pennsylvania in search of a better life. They find work in a steel mill, but life in the industrialized North begins to tear them apart. Critics praised the realism of Attaway's depictions of the racial and spiritual struggles that confronted rural blacks in the North. In an unfamiliar setting and forced to work like machines in the steel mill, where they had to compete with American-born whites, European immigrants, and other blacks for employment, the three brothers find disaster where they hoped to discover prosperity.

Despite the overwhelming critical success of *Blood on the Forge,* Attaway never published another novel. He published the short story "Death of a Rag Doll" in 1947, but soon turned his attention to music and film writing. During the 1950s, he wrote and arranged songs for his friend the renowned singer Harry Belafonte, and he published two books on American popular music, *The Calypso Songbook* (1957) and *I Hear America Singing* (1967). He also wrote scripts for radio, television, and film, including a screen adaptation of Irving Wallace's *The Man,* about the first African-American president, which was finally rejected by producers, and the script for *One Hundred Years of Laughter,* the American Broadcasting Company's television special about African-American humor. Attaway also participated in the Civil Rights movement, joining the march on Selma, Alabama, in 1965 to support voting rights for African Americans.

Attaway spent more than a decade living in Barbados with his wife, Frances Settele, and their two children, before settling in California in his final years to work on a script for *The Atlanta Child Murders* (1985). William Attaway died of heart failure on June 17, 1986, in Los Angeles, California. Attaway's literary legacy rests primarily on his novel *Blood on the Forge,* which has been called the finest depiction of the Great Migration era in American literature. Overshadowed somewhat by the overwhelming success of his contemporary and friend, Richard Wright, Attaway still retains an important place among African-American writers of the early 20th century; the reprinting of *Blood on the Forge* in 1993 has brought renewed critical and popular attention to his writings.

Further Reading

Andrews, William L., Frances Smith Foster, and Trudier Harris, eds. *The Concise Oxford Companion to African American Literature.* New York: Oxford University Press, 2001.

Attaway, William. *Blood on the Forge.* New York: Doubleday, 1941. Reprint, New York: Anchor Books, 1993.

Morgan, Stacy I. "Migration, Material Culture, and Identity in William Attaway's *Blood on the Forge* and Harriette Arrow's *The Dollmaker.*" *College English* 63 (July 2001): 712.

B

Baldwin, James
(James Arthur Baldwin)
(1924–1987) *essayist, novelist, poet, playwright, educator, civil rights activist*

Among African-American writers and social leaders of the 20th century, perhaps none have articulated the painful legacy of slavery and racism in modern America better than James Baldwin. An internationally acclaimed author of essays, novels, plays, and poetry, Baldwin is best known for his eloquent and finely crafted essays and his autobiographical novel *Go Tell It on the Mountain* (1953). Baldwin's writings reshaped the language of racial protest during the 1950s and 1960s and have continued to inspire generations of black authors and activists.

James Arthur Baldwin was born on August 2, 1924, to Berdis Emma Jones, who delivered him out of wedlock at Harlem Hospital in New York. Baldwin's mother later married David Baldwin, a factory worker and puritanical lay preacher in a storefront church in Harlem, who Baldwin later described as "certainly the most bitter man I have ever met." Baldwin's childhood in Harlem was characterized by poverty, racism, and resentment by his stepfather, whose physical and psychological abuse shattered the boy's self-esteem.

As a student at Public School 24 in Harlem, Baldwin soon impressed his teachers with his intelligence, and they encouraged him to read and write. He began to frequent the local public library, eventually claiming to have read every one of its books, and developed a passion for film and drama. Baldwin attended Frederick Douglass Junior High School and received further encouragement from poet COUNTEE CULLEN, a French teacher at the school and founder of its literary club. Baldwin edited the school newspaper, the *Douglass Pilot,* to which he also contributed a short story and several essays.

Confronted by the emotional, physical, and sexual turmoil of adolescence, Baldwin retreated into Christianity at the age of 14 and became a youth minister at the Fireside Pentecostal Assembly. Having suspended his growing literary ambitions, Baldwin devoted himself passionately to the church, earning the respect and support from his congregations that had been missing in his home life.

At age 17, Baldwin had become disenchanted with the church, which he perceived as stifling his creative and intellectual development. He would later claim that "whoever wishes to become a truly moral human being . . . must first divorce himself from all the prohibitions, crimes, and hypocrisies of the Christian church," a position that was influenced in large part by the attitudes and actions of his stepfather.

Baldwin attended DeWitt Clinton High School and served as editor in chief of the school

James Baldwin poses for a photo during a visit to the United States in 1982. *(AP/Wide World Photos)*

newspaper, the *Magpie,* which published three of his short stories. Following his graduation in 1942, Baldwin found work with a construction company and held several other odd jobs to help support his family. He was also influenced during this period by his friendship with Beauford Delaney, a Greenwich Village artist who remained a mentor and father figure until Delaney's death in 1979.

After the death of his stepfather in 1943, Baldwin moved to Greenwich Village and devoted himself more fully to his writing. He began work on a novel and made the acquaintance of novelist RICHARD WRIGHT, who recommended Baldwin for a Eugene Saxton Fellowship, which was awarded in 1945. Baldwin published his first professional writing, a review of Maxim Gorky's *Best Short Stories,* in the *Nation* in 1947. His first essay, "The Harlem Ghetto," appeared in *Commonwealth* the following year.

By 1948 Baldwin could no longer tolerate the racial bigotry that he had suffered for most of his life. With the help of a Rosenwald Fellowship, he decided to sail for Europe, where he felt that he could live and write more freely. His departure from the United States also signaled a shift in his personal life, when he cancelled plans for an impending marriage and from that time forward embraced his homosexuality personally and publicly.

With the exception of brief periods of travel throughout Europe and Africa, and visits to the United States as a lecturer and civil rights activist, Baldwin spent the remainder of his life in France. In 1953 he published his first novel, *Go Tell It on the Mountain.* Set primarily in a storefront church, the novel captured in painful and compelling detail many of Baldwin's experiences as an adolescent, in the church and in his stepfather's home. "It was an attempt to exorcise something," Baldwin explained about his writing of the novel, "to find out what happened to my father, what happened to all of us."

The success of *Go Tell It on the Mountain,* which has remained one of his most widely acclaimed works, established Baldwin as a major American author. His next work, the play *The Amen Corner,* also focused on his early life, in particular his relationship to his stepfather, and serves as a powerful indictment of the church and its role in the lives of African Americans. Baldwin described his main character, Sister Margaret, in this way: "Her sense of reality is dictated by the society's assumption, which also becomes her own, of her inferiority. Her need for human affirmation, and also for vengeance, expresses itself in her merciless piety."

Though produced by OWEN DODSON in 1955 as a student production at Howard University, Baldwin's *The Amen Corner* would not reach Broadway until 1965, when it opened at the Ethel Barrymore Theatre in New York. It remains one of his most frequently produced dramatic works. Baldwin's other plays include *Blues for Mister Charlie* (1964), *One Day, When I Was Lost: A Sce-*

nario *Based on the Autobiography of Malcolm X* (1972), and *A Deed from the King of Spain* (1974).

Baldwin published his second novel, *Giovanni's Room*, in 1956. The novel depicts a brief but intense love affair between a white American tourist, David, and a bartender, Giovanni, whom David meets in Paris while awaiting the arrival of his fiancée. David eventually denies his homosexuality and abandons Giovanni, whose life is ultimately destroyed by the loss. "It is not so much about homosexuality," Baldwin said of the novel, "it is what happens if you are so afraid that you finally cannot love anybody." *Giovanni's Room*, which was later adapted for the stage, received generally positive reviews upon its publication and has since come to hold an important place in African-American and gay and lesbian literature.

Over the next several years, Baldwin published five more novels: *Another Country* (1962), *Tell Me How Long the Train's Been Gone* (1968), *If Beale Street Could Talk* (1974), *Just above My Head* (1979), which earned an American Book Award nomination, and *Harlem Quartet* (1987). Though regarded favorably by many critics, particularly for their autobiographical content and their explication of America's impoverished perspectives on racial and sexual identity, Baldwin's novels never matched the widespread critical and popular success of his essays.

Notes of a Native Son (1955), Baldwin's first essay collection, included works previously published in numerous magazines and literary journals and marked the inception of his reputation as a leading American essayist. Some of the included essays, particularly "Everybody's Protest Novel" and "Many Thousands Gone," also brought controversy. His critique of racial stereotypes in American literature, which included an examination of difficulties he identified in Richard Wright's novel *Native Son* (1940), led to a falling out with Wright, who had been a mentor and friend of many years.

Baldwin's most celebrated collection of essays, *The Fire Next Time*, was published in 1963 and reflected a maturity in his themes and tone. "My Dungeon Shook: Letter to My Nephew on the One Hundredth Anniversary of the Emancipation," the first of two essays in the collection, is a lengthy epistle addressed to his nephew, James, in which Baldwin explains how racism has shaped his personal and family life. Baldwin exhorts his young namesake to remain free of racial bigotry and to help make America "what America must become." In his second essay, "Down at the Cross: Letter from a Region in My Mind," Baldwin continues to explore the nature of American racism and warns that continued racial oppression will invariably lead to violence.

A landmark work in its passionate articulation of the causes and conditions of racial strife in America, *The Fire Next Time* has come to be regarded as one of Baldwin's most powerful works. His other collections of essays include *Nobody Knows My Name: More Notes of a Native Son* (1961), *No Name in the Street* (1972), *The Devil Finds Work* (1976), *The Evidence of Things Not Seen* (1985), and *The Price of the Ticket: Collected Nonfiction 1948–1985* (1985). Baldwin also collaborated on the publication of two dialogues, *A Rap on Race* (1971, with anthropologist Margaret Mead) and *A Dialogue* (1973, with poet NIKKI GIOVANNI).

After more than 10 years in Europe, Baldwin returned to the United States in 1957 and toured the South to witness the violence and oppression that African Americans suffered in their fight for civil rights. His experiences during this period and during his return in the 1960s formed the basis of numerous essays and lectures. Though Baldwin was not a central figure in the movement for civil rights, his growing reputation as a writer brought added visibility to the struggle.

In addition to essays, plays, and novels, Baldwin also produced an acclaimed body of short fiction, published throughout his early career and collected in *Going to Meet the Man* (1965). "Sonny's Blues," Baldwin's most famous short story, is set against the economic hardships and rampant racism of life in Harlem during the 1940s and 1950s, and depicts the turbulent relationship between two brothers, whose individual characters and perspectives create divisions between them, but who ultimately learn to accept each other.

The murders of three friends, Medgar Evers, Martin Luther King, Jr., and Malcolm X, during the 1960s led to Baldwin's further despair at American institutionalized racism and precluded any hope of a permanent return from abroad. In the late 1970s and 1980s, Baldwin accepted several teaching appointments that included short stints at the University of Massachusetts at Amherst, Bowling Green State University, Mount Holyoke College, and the University of California at Berkeley. James Arthur Baldwin died of cancer on November 30, 1987 (some sources say December 1), at his home in St. Paul de Vence in southern France.

One of the 20th century's most eloquent and influential voices for racial justice, James Baldwin provided an intensely personal perspective on the legacy of hatred and oppression in the lives of African Americans. His assertion that "all art is a kind of confession" informs all of his literary work. In recognition of his considerable achievements in literature, and as a testament to their regard for him as an honorary citizen, the French government designated James Baldwin a Commander of the Legion of Honor in 1986.

Further Reading

Baldwin, James. *The Fire Next Time.* New York: Dial, 1963.

———. *Go Tell It on the Mountain.* New York: Knopf, 1953.

Campbell, James. *Talking at the Gates: A Life of James Baldwin.* Berkeley: University of California Press, 1991.

Miller, D. Quentin, ed. *Re-Viewing James Baldwin: Things Not Seen.* Philadelphia, Pa.: Temple University Press, 2000.

Bambara, Toni Cade
(Miltona Mirkin Cade)
(1939–1995) *short story writer, novelist, editor, essayist, screenwriter*

A critically acclaimed author of short fiction, novels, essays, and documentary film scripts, Toni Cade Bambara combined a distinguished career as a writer with an unflagging commitment to social and community causes, particularly those that focused on the physical and spiritual well-being of women. "I am about the empowerment and development of our sisters and the community," she explained in Claudia Tate's *Black Women Writers at Work* (1983). "That sense of caring and celebration is certainly reflected in the body of my work." A two-time American Book Award winner, Bambara also earned an Academy Award for her work on the 1986 documentary film *The Bombing of Osage Avenue.*

Toni Cade Bambara was born Miltonia Mirkin Cade on March 25, 1939, in the Harlem section of New York City, where she lived until age 10. Her mother, Helen Brent Henderson Cade, who had grown up in the days of the Harlem Renaissance, strongly encouraged her daughter's natural creativity. "She gave me permission to wonder, to dawdle, to daydream," Bambara said of her mother's early influence. Bambara's later direction as a writer also owed something to the fiery orators on Speaker's Corner in Harlem, where her mother took her to listen to the impassioned speeches of unionists, Pan-Africanists, communists, and Temple People, as Black Muslims were known at that time.

Cade attended public schools in New York, New Jersey, and in the South before enrolling at Queens College in New York, where she received her bachelor's degree in theater arts and English in 1959. As an undergraduate, she won the Peter Pauper Press Award in 1958 and Queens College's John Colden Award for fiction in 1959. She also published her first short story, "Sweet Town," in *Vendome* magazine in 1959. After graduation,

Cade worked as an investigator for the New York State Department of Welfare and traveled to Europe to study at the École de Mime Etienne Decroux in Paris, France.

Upon her return to the United States, Cade worked at Metropolitan Hospital as a recreation director in the psychiatric ward. She also served as program director of Colony Settlement House in Brooklyn. In 1964 she completed her master's degree at the City College of New York (now the City University of New York) and joined the college's Search for Education, Elevation, and Knowledge (SEEK) program as an English instructor. Though not yet devoted full time to a career as a writer, Bambara published several stories during this time in magazines and journals such as *Redbook, Prairie Schooner,* and the *Massachusetts Review.*

Until 1969 Bambara published under the name of Toni Cade. She added Bambara to her name in 1969 after discovering the name written on a sketchbook in a trunk owned by her great-grandmother. That year, she also accepted a position as an assistant professor at Rutgers University's Livingston College and began to devote more attention to writing. She edited two important anthologies: *The Black Woman* (1970), an influential collection of writing by authors such as TONI MORRISON, NIKKI GIOVANNI, ALICE WALKER, and AUDRE LORDE; and *Tales and Stories for Black Folks* (1971), a collection of short stories by various professional and student writers that emphasized the importance of family and community in understanding and preserving one's cultural heritage.

Bambara published her first collection of short stories, *Gorilla, My Love,* in 1972. Comprising 15 stories written between 1950 and 1970, and a humorous caveat entitled "A Sort of Preface," *Gorilla, My Love* displays Bambara's talent for rich, musical language. Critics also praised the depth and diversity of Bambara's characters, whose experiences reveal the enormous emotional and physical support that can exist within a strong, loving community. Bambara's second collection of stories, *The Seabirds Are Still Alive* (1977), reflects the influence of her travels in Cuba in 1973, where she met with the Federation of Cuban Women, and her visit to Vietnam in 1975 as a guest of the Women's Union. The 10 stories in *The Seabirds Are Still Alive* also explore the role of community in the preservation of individual identity, particularly in the face of racial and gender inequities.

After earning wide critical acclaim for her short fiction, Bambara published her first novel, *The Salt Eaters,* in 1980. An experimental novel with an unconventional narrative structure, *The Salt Eaters* is set in the town of Clayborne,

Toni Cade Bambara devoted much of her time to developing the talents of young African-American writers. *(© Joyce Middler)*

Georgia, and explores the history of the community through the relationship of its two primary characters: Velma Henry, a fiery civil rights activist who has suffered an emotional breakdown that led her to attempt suicide, and Minnie Ransom, a spiritual healer and leader of the community. In vivid and sometimes surreal images, the novel examines how communities can reshape past, present, and future events to promote physical and emotional healing. Perhaps her best known and most critically acclaimed work, *The Salt Eaters* won the American Book Award and the Langston Hughes Society Award, both in 1981.

Bambara had left Rutgers University in 1974 to move with her daughter to Atlanta, Georgia. During the late 1970s, Bambara devoted herself to several community programs, helping to found the Southern Writing Collective of African American Writers, and often holding writing workshops in her home. She also held several visiting professorships at Stephens College in Columbia, Missouri, Atlanta University, and Spelman College. Bambara was awarded several citations of merit from the cities of Detroit (1989) and Atlanta (1989) for her commitment to community arts and social programs.

Bambara had an enduring interest in film and the performing arts. "I've always considered myself a film person," she told Claudia Tate in *Black Women Writers at Work* (1983). Bambara wrote the screenplays for several television documentaries in the 1970s, and served as writer and narrator for film documentaries on Malcolm X, John Coltrane, and Cecil B. Moore in the 1980s. In 1986 Bambara wrote and narrated Louis Massiah's documentary film *The Bombing of Osage Avenue*, about the police bombing of the Philadelphia headquarters of the militant Pan-African organization MOVE in 1985, which resulted in the deaths of 11 people. The film won an Academy Award in 1986 for Best Documentary Film.

Bambara published a final collection of stories, *Raymond's Run: Stories for Young Adults*, in 1989. In 1993 she was diagnosed with colon cancer, but she refused to let her health stand in the way of her creative work. She teamed up once again with filmmaker Louis Massiah on the film documentary *W. E. B. Du Bois: A Biography in Four Voices*, released in early 1995, which features an interview with Bambara that offers an intimate portrait of her personal history and her unique literary vision. Toni Cade Bambara succumbed to cancer on December 9, 1995, in New York.

One of the most celebrated and respected African-American authors of the late 20th century, Toni Cade Bambara helped focus attention on the vital role that communities play in the formation and preservation of personal and group identity. She also fought for expanded social and political roles for women at a time when many civil rights groups overlooked such roles. "When I look back at my work with any little distance," she explained in a 1982 interview, the two characteristics that jumped out at her were "the tremendous capacity for laughter, but also a tremendous capacity for rage." Two posthumously published works by Bambara, edited by novelist Toni Morrison, who also edited Bambara's early works while at Random House, have added to the legacy of her life and writing. *Deep Sightings and Rescue Missions: Fiction, Essays, and Conversations* was released in 1996; and the novel *Those Bones Are Not My Child*, set against the series of child murders in Atlanta from 1979 to 1981, appeared in 1999.

Further Reading

Bambara, Toni Cade. *Deep Sightings and Rescue Missions: Fiction, Essays, and Conversations.* New York: Pantheon Books, 1996.

———. *The Salt Eaters.* New York: Random House, 1980. Reprint, New York: Vintage, 1992.

———. *Those Bones Are Not My Child.* New York: Pantheon Books, 1999.

Tate, Claudia, ed. *Black Women Writers at Work.* New York: Continuum, 1983.

Baraka, Amiri
(LeRoi Jones, Everett Leroy Jones, Imamu Amiri Baraka)
(1934–) *playwright, poet, essayist, screenwriter, short story writer, educator*

An influential and prolific author whose writing spans numerous genres, Amiri Baraka has played a central role in shaping the political focus of African-American literature since the 1960s. Critics have identified individual phases in Baraka's literary career, from his early inspiration by predominantly white Beat poets, to his later interest in Black Nationalism and marxism. Despite his political fluctuations, Baraka has remained consistent in the theme of his writing. Often polemical, abrasive, and controversial, Baraka's plays, poetry, essays, screenplays, and short fiction convey his outrage at a society that he sees as sanctioning and even encouraging racism. The recipient of numerous literary awards, including an Obie Award for best off-Broadway play, an American Book Award, and the Langston Hughes Medal for outstanding contribution to African-American literature, Baraka was also instrumental in the formation of the Black Arts Repertory Theatre/School in New York, and he helped define the artistic principles of the Black Arts Movement.

Born Everett Leroy Jones on October 30, 1934, in Newark, New Jersey, Amiri Baraka grew up in a middle-class home. His father, Coyt Everett Jones, was a postal worker, and his mother, Anna Lois Jones, was a social worker. Young Jones attended McKinley Junior High School and Barringer High School, then a college preparatory academy. An exceptionally bright student, he had begun to write in his childhood, creating comic strips and composing short stories. Jones earned a scholarship to Rutgers University, where he enrolled in 1951. Feeling isolated on a predominantly white campus, he transferred to the traditionally black Howard University, in Washington, D.C., where he studied with the renowned poet and literary critic STERLING BROWN. When his interest in music began to interfere with his studies, Baraka left the university and joined the U.S. Air Force, spending his two-year stint primarily in Puerto Rico.

While in the air force, Jones began to read extensively, devouring works by such authors as Ernest Hemingway, Franz Kafka, and Marcel Proust. He also began writing poetry. Just prior to the end of his tour of duty, Jones was accused of communist sympathies and dishonorably discharged in 1957. He moved to New York's East Village, where the Beat movement was gaining momentum. In 1958 he married Hettie Cohen, a white intellectual and editor at *Partisan Review,* with whom he had two daughters. Also in 1958, Jones and Cohen founded the journal *Yugen,* in which they published works by struggling East Village writers, including Allen Ginsberg, Gregory Corso, and Jack Kerouac. To create further opportunities for unknown writers and artists, Jones coedited *Floating Bear,* an underground newspaper, and cofounded the American Theater for Poets in 1961.

Jones's earliest poetry, collected in *Preface to a Twenty-Volume Suicide Note* (1961) and *The Dead Lecturer* (1964), reveals both the roots of his interest in the avant-garde Beat movement, as well as his growing disenchantment with the movement's apolitical ideals. His shift in political focus was inspired in part by his trip to Cuba in 1960, where he met the Communist leader Fidel Castro and numerous young writers and social activists. Jones wrote of his experiences in Cuba in the essay "Cuba Libre," which won the Longview Award for best essay in 1961.

By the early 1960s Baraka had become a leader among the artists and writers of the East Village. The overwhelming success of his first play, *Dutchman* (1964), both confirmed his exalted place among avant-garde intellectuals and signaled his shift toward Black Nationalism. Winner of the 1964 Obie Award for best off-Broadway play, *Dutchman* depicts an ideologically and physically violent meeting between a young middle-class black man named Clay and Lula, a young white intellectual, on a subway. In addition to *Dutchman*, Jones wrote and produced three additional plays in 1964. *The Baptism*, which explores conventional American attitudes toward salvation, debuted at the Writer's Stage Theatre, and *The Slave* and *The Toilet* appeared at St. Mark's Playhouse.

Jones moved to Harlem in 1965 and severed ties with his old associates in the East Village as well as his wife and two children, a decision that was influenced in part by the assassination of Malcolm X in 1964. Devoting his creative and political energies toward a more aggressive Black

Amiri Baraka, shown here in 1965, was named poet laureate for the state of New Jersey in 2001. *(Library of Congress)*

Nationalism, he founded the short-lived but influential Black Arts Repertory Theatre/School in 1965, and he wrote several militant anti-white plays, including *Experimental Death Unit #1* (1965), *Jello* (1965), *A Black Mass* (1965), and *Arm Yourself, or Harm Yourself* (1965). Jones also published his only novel, the experimental *The System of Dante's Hell*, in 1965. A year later, he returned to his native city of Newark, New Jersey, and established the Spirit House Players. That year he also married a black woman, Sylvia Robinson (later known as Amina Baraka), with whom he has five children, and changed his name to Imamu Amiri Baraka.

In addition to his involvement with the Black Arts Repertory Theatre/School and the Spirit House Players, organizations that helped promote the works of such writers as LARRY NEAL and ED BULLINS, Baraka also helped found the Black Community Development and Defense Organization, the Congress of African Peoples (convened in Atlanta, Georgia, in 1970), and the National Black Political Convention (convened in Gary, Indiana, in 1972). Baraka was arrested during the Newark race riots of 1967 for unlawful possession of firearms, convicted, and sentenced before the ruling was finally overturned on appeal. During this tumultuous period, Baraka wrote several plays, including *Great Goodness of Life (A Coon Show)* (1967), *Madheart* (1967), *Slave Ship: A Historical Pageant* (1967), *The Death of Malcolm X* (1969), *Bloodrites* (1970), *Junkies Are Full of (Shhh . . .)* (1970), and *A Recent Killing* (1973).

While devoting much of his time to political concerns in the early 1970s, including his support of Kenneth Gibson during his successful 1970 bid to become Newark's first black mayor, Baraka continued to work on several literary projects. He published two collections of poetry, *Black Magic* (1969) and *It's Nation Time* (1970), featuring poems that were heavily steeped in Black Nationalist ideology. In 1974, Baraka attended the Sixth Pan-African Congress at Dar es Saalam, Tanzania. His experiences there and his growing disillusionment with American political structures precipitated a change in focus during the late 1970s toward a marxist perspective. Baraka exhibited his ideological shift in plays such as *Sidnee Poet Heroical* (1975, later published as *The Sydney Poet Heroical*), *S-1* (1976), *The Motion of History* (1977), and *What Was the Relationship of the Lone Ranger to the Means of Production?* (1979).

Baraka served as a visiting professor at Yale University in New Haven, Connecticut (1977–78), and George Mason University in Washington, D.C. (1978–79). In 1980 he joined the faculty of the State University of New York at Stony Brook. The previous year, Baraka had been arrested after a dispute with his wife. While serving his sentence under house arrest in Harlem, he wrote *The Autobiography of LeRoi Jones* (1983). Baraka also wrote several more plays, including *At the Dim'cracker Convention* (1981), *Weimar* (1981), *Money: A Jazz Opera* (1982), and *Primitive World: An Anti-Nuclear Jazz Musical* (1984).

Baraka accepted a visiting professorship at Rutgers University in 1988, but became embroiled in a very public and controversial dispute with the university two years later, claiming that Rutgers had denied him the opportunity for tenure. Baraka issued an inflammatory statement in which he compared the university's faculty to the Ku Klux Klan and the Nazi Party. During much of the 1990s, Baraka performed his poetry throughout the country, reading at universities, festivals, and jazz clubs, often with the accompaniment of jazz musicians. His plays from this period include *The Life and Life of Bumpy Johnson* (1991), *General Hagz Skeezag* (1992), *Meeting Lillie* (1993), and *The Election Machine Warehouse* (1996).

Throughout his prolific career as a playwright, Baraka also wrote influential collections of poetry, essays, and short fiction. Among his best-known later collections of poetry are *Transbluesency: The Selected Poems of Amiri Baraka/LeRoi Jones (1961–1995)* and *Funk Lore: New Poems, 1984–1995* (1996). Baraka's political and musical

essays, published over the last four decades in journals such as the *Nation, Downbeat,* and the *Saturday Review,* have been collected in numerous volumes, including *Home: Social Essays* (1966), *Black Music* (1968), *Raise, Race, Rays, Raze: Essays Since 1965* (1971), and *Daggers and Javelins: Essays, 1974–1979* (1984).

No stranger to cultural and political criticisms of his life and work, Baraka again found himself at the center of controversy in 2002 over his poem "Somebody Blew Up America," inspired by the World Trade Center attack on September 11, 2001. The controversy began when Baraka recited the poem, which includes the lines "Who knew the World Trade Center was gonna get bombed / Who told 4000 Israeli workers at the Twin Towers / To stay home that day," at the Geraldine R. Dodge Poetry Festival in September 2002.

Baraka, who had published the poem almost a year earlier, had been named New Jersey's poet laureate on August 28, 2002. His recital of the poem in September sparked a national debate about the allegedly anti-Semitic elements in the poem, and prompted New Jersey's governor to seek Baraka's resignation from the position. In his response to the allegations, Baraka defended his position as being critical of Israel rather than being anti-Semitic, and claimed that the controversy grew out of a misinterpretation and misreading of his poem. He also refused to resign his post. In response, the New Jersey State Senate voted to abolish the poet laureate position.

Amiri Baraka has distinguished himself in a variety of genres. He is a prolific playwright, poet, and essayist. He has published one novel, *The System of Dante's Hell* (1965), and he has written several screenplays, including a 1967 adaptation of his play *Dutchman.* His short fiction has been collected in *Tales* (1967) and *The Fiction of LeRoi Jones/Amiri Baraka* (2000), and he coedited the influential Black Arts anthology *Black Fire: An Anthology of Black Writing* (1968). Baraka's writing has won the Obie Award, an American Book Award (in 1984, for *Confirmation: An Anthology of African-American*

Women), a lifetime achievement award from the Before Columbus Foundation, and the Langston Hughes Award from the City College of New York.

Throughout his numerous shifts in political and social ideology, Baraka has remained committed to the preservation of black culture and identity. Perhaps more than any other writer, Baraka promoted and popularized the artistic principles of the Black Arts Movement through his own writing and through his assistance to other authors of that period. Though some of his artistic and political rhetoric has sometimes put him at odds with critics, peers, and the general public, Baraka has remained an important and influential figure in the history and development of African-American literature.

Further Reading

Baraka, Amiri. *The LeRoi Jones/Amiri Baraka Reader.* New York: Thunder's Mouth Press, 1999.

Watts, Jerry Gafalio. *Amiri Baraka: The Politics and Art of a Black Intellectual.* New York: New York University Press, 2001.

Woodard, K. Komozi. *A Nation within a Nation: Amiri Baraka (LeRoi Jones) and Black Power Politics.* Chapel Hill: University of North Carolina Press, 1999.

Beckham, Barry
(Barry Earl Beckham)
(1944–   ) *novelist*

Though his reputation as a novelist rests primarily on only two books, Barry Beckham has earned critical acclaim for his innovative exploration of the physical and emotional challenges facing African Americans in an uncaring and openly hostile white society. His characters reflect, in their violent and unpredictable behavior, the frustration inherent in their struggle to achieve and maintain a sense of personal and cultural identity.

Beckham was born on March 19, 1944, to Clarence and Mildred Williams Beckham in Philadelphia. The family moved to Atlantic City,

New Jersey, when Beckham was nine. He was a good student, serving as senior class president in high school and later enrolling at Brown University in 1962, where he studied English. Under the influence of the novelist John Fowles, one of his professors, Beckham began writing his first novel, *My Main Mother,* as a senior at Brown. Following his graduation, Beckham studied briefly at Columbia Law School before accepting a job in public relations with Chase Manhattan Bank.

My Main Mother was published in 1969 to largely positive reviews. It tells the story of Mitchell Mibbs, a troubled but gifted black youth who relates, in one evening, the events that led him to murder his mother. The product of a debilitating and alienating home life that invites comparisons to the protagonists in RICHARD WRIGHT's *Black Boy* and JAMES BALDWIN's *Native Son*, Mitchell is estranged from his mother, Pearl, who abandons him to pursue a singing career in New York and who cruelly manipulates his uncle Mervin Pip, the only father figure in Mitchell's life. Unable to cope with his mother's indifference, Mitchell poisons her. Beckham's use of vivid imagery in the novel underscores Mitchell's isolation and resignation to the forces, both social and familial, that disrupt an otherwise promising future.

The themes of alienation and powerlessness figure prominently in Beckham's second novel, *Runner Mack*, published in 1972. Scholars have noted Beckham's indebtedness to RALPH ELLISON's *Invisible Man*, particularly in Beckham's application of broader developments in African-American history to the specific events in the life of his protagonist, Henry Adams. Moving north from Mississippi to become a professional baseball player, Henry soon finds himself at the mercy of forces beyond his control. Unable to purse his baseball career, he finds employment at the Home Manufacturing Company and later is drafted by the army to fight in the Alaskan War, a bizarre parody of the Vietnam War in which he is forced to kill seals and caribou. In the army, he meets Runner Mack, and the two desert their posts to initiate a plot to bomb the White House and wrest control of the government from white society. The plot fails when only a handful of black revolutionaries decide to participate. Runner Mack commits suicide, and the novel ends with Henry standing in the path of a speeding truck. The novel was nominated for the National Book Award in 1972 and was widely praised for its depiction of the brutal realities of modern urban life in general and the obstacles faced by African Americans in their search for identity in an increasingly absurd and hostile society.

After successful careers in business with Chase Manhattan Bank and Western Electric, Beckham became a professor of English at Brown University in 1970 and the director of its graduate program in creative writing in 1980. He left Brown in 1987 and taught at Hampton University, in Washington, D.C., for two years before retiring to devote more time to his publishing company, Beckham Publications Group, founded in 1984. In addition to his two novels, Beckham published a play, *Garvey Lives!*, that was produced in Providence, Rhode Island, in 1972, and *Double Dunk,* a biography of the playground basketball legend Earl Manigault. In 1982 he published the first edition of *The Black Student's Guide to Colleges,* which he regularly updates, and has continued to promote educational opportunities for black students through workshops at high schools throughout the United States. In his forthcoming educational guidebooks, which he will release under the name of *Urban Student Guide...,* Beckham extends the scope of his research to address the needs of Latino-, Asian-, and Native American students.

Further Reading

Andrews, William L., Frances Smith Foster, and Trudier Harris, eds. *The Concise Oxford Companion to African American Literature.* New York: Oxford University Press, 2001.

Beckham, Barry. *Runner Mack.* Washington, D.C.: Howard University Press, 1983.

Draper, James P. *Black Literature Criticism.* Vol. 1. Detroit, Mich.: Gale Research, 1992, 152–171.

Bennett, Gwendolyn
(Gwendolyn Bennetta Bennett, Gwendolyn Bernette Bennett, Gwendolyn Bennett Jackson, Gwendolyn Bennett Crosscup)
(1902–1981) *poet, journalist*

Though considered by many to be a minor literary figure during the Harlem Renaissance, Gwendolyn Bennett earned the respect of her contemporaries, including LANGSTON HUGHES and COUNTEE CULLEN, as well as that of the earlier generation of African-American writers, among them JAMES WELDON JOHNSON. Her lively and lyrical poems celebrated African-American life on both physical and emotional levels.

Bennett was born on July 8, 1902, in Giddings, Texas, at a time when the state of Texas refused official birth certificates to African Americans. Her parents, Joshua and Mayme Bennett, came from middle-class backgrounds and were well educated, and the family moved frequently in the early years of Bennett's life. They lived in Nevada, where her parents worked as teachers on a local American Indian reservation until 1907, and then relocated to Washington, D.C., where Bennett's father studied law. When the marriage failed, Bennett continued her nomadic existence with her father, who was unwilling to give his ex-wife custody of their daughter. Bennett and her father lived for many years in various cities in Pennsylvania before settling in Brooklyn, New York.

Despite the disruption in her education caused by frequent moves, Bennett excelled, first at Central High School in Harrisburg, Pennsylvania, and later at the Brooklyn Girls High School, where she became the first African American elected to the school's literary and dramatic societies. She would go on to write the lyrics to her senior class graduation song and the commencement speech. Following her graduation in 1921, she enrolled in fine arts classes at Columbia University and later at the Pratt Institute, intending to pursue a career in graphic arts. She also began writing poetry.

Her first published poem, "Heritage," appeared in *Opportunity* in 1923, and she designed the cover for an issue of the *Crisis* that same year. She became acquainted with many leading figures in the Harlem Renaissance, who encouraged her to continue writing, and she worked briefly with WALLACE THURMAN and Langston Hughes on the failed journal *Fire!!* In 1924 she left New York to teach at Howard University, in Washington, D.C., where she earned a scholarship to study art in Paris for a year. She published two short stories, "Tokens" and "Wedding Day," based on her experiences in Paris, which depicted the lives of African-American expatriates who remained in France following World War I.

Bennett's poetry evokes a sense of pride in African-American culture. In her poem "Heritage," she describes her desire to "feel the surging / Of my sad people's soul / Hidden by a minstrel-smile." In "Hatred," published in 1927, she confronts the racial hatred of her people with a hatred of her own that is "Like a dart of singing steel" and solemn "As pines are sober."

Upon her return to New York in 1926, she was encouraged by James Weldon Johnson to write a regular column for *Opportunity*. She began writing "The Ebony Flute," a literary and social column that kept readers apprised of new publications by African-American writers and of opportunities for struggling writers. The column flourished until 1928, when it was discontinued. Bennett had married Alfred Joseph Jackson, a physician, in 1927, and the two moved in 1928 to Florida, where Alfred hoped to establish his own medical practice. Bennett found the intense segregation and racial hatred of the South too oppressive and convinced her husband to return to New York in 1932.

Upon her return, she found New York in the grip of the Great Depression, and work was difficult to find. Following the death of her husband, Bennett found work in one of President Franklin Delano Roosevelt's New Deal programs, the Works Progress Administration's Federal Arts Pro-

ject. She worked with the sculptor Augusta Savage, eventually replacing her as the director of the Harlem Community Art Center in 1939. Soon after, Bennett became a casualty of the post–World War II "red scare" and was suspended and later removed as director on the basis of her alleged left-wing political convictions. She worked briefly as the director of the George Washington Carver School, a manual arts school, and later at the Consumers Union in Mount Vernon, New York, with the poet HELENE JOHNSON.

After remarrying, Bennett withdrew from public and artistic life, and she spent the rest of her life as a homemaker and antiques dealer in Kutztown, Pennsylvania, with Richard Crosscup. On May 30, 1981, a little more than a year after Richard's unexpected death, Gwendolyn Bennett died of congestive heart failure. Though she never published a collected volume of her poetry, Bennett was acclaimed by her fellow authors for her unselfconscious and lively celebration of African heritage and an artistic vision that was equal to many of her more prolific and celebrated contemporaries.

Further Reading

Andrews, William L., Frances Smith Foster, and Trudier Harris, eds. *The Concise Oxford Companion to African American Literature.* New York: Oxford University Press, 2001.

Cullen, Countee, ed. *Caroling Dusk.* New York: Carol Publishing Group, 1993.

Gates, Henry Louis, Jr., and Nellie Y. McKay, eds. *The Norton Anthology of African American Literature.* New York: W. W. Norton, 1997.

Bibb, Henry Walton
(1815–1854) *autobiographer*

Best known for his vivid account of slave life in Kentucky, New Orleans, and Arkansas, and his subsequent escape to freedom, Henry Walton Bibb never achieved the literary or political stature of his contemporary FREDERICK DOU-

GLASS. However, he is credited with producing one of the most detailed and truthful accounts of slave life ever published.

Bibb was born in Shelby County, Kentucky, in 1815, the eldest son of a slave, Mildred Jackson, and a Kentucky state senator, James Bibb. At an early age, Henry witnessed the sale of his brothers and sisters to other slave owners, and his first wife was forced into prostitution by her owner. "A poor slave's wife," he writes, "can never be true to her husband contrary to the will of her master." After repeated attempts to escape, and brutal punishments for his disobedience, he succeeded in 1837, only to be recaptured six months later when he returned to rescue his family.

In 1842, having left his wife and daughter behind, Bibb arrived in Detroit, Michigan, and became active in the abolitionist movement. He lectured on the horrors of slavery and worked for the Detroit Liberty Association, a political party promoting abolition. On a lecture tour to Boston, he met Mary Miles, and the two were married in 1848. He published his autobiography, *The Life and Adventures of Henry Bibb: An American Slave,* in 1849. Though it was initially received with considerable skepticism, after an extensive investigation into the details of Bibb's narrative sponsored by the Liberty Association, his work was vindicated, and he became, along with Frederick Douglass and WILLIAM WELLS BROWN, one of the leading African-American activists in the abolitionist movement.

Following the passage of the Fugitive Slave Act of 1850, whereby escaped slaves living free in nonslaveholding states could be apprehended and returned to slavery, Bibb fled to Canada with his wife Mary. There, he and Josiah Henson, also an escaped slave, created the Refugees' Home Colony on 2,000 acres of land near Windsor, Ontario, which provided ex-slaves with vocational training. Bibb also started the first African-American newspaper in Canada, *Voice of the Fugitive.* Bibb spent the remaining years of his life in Canada. He established the North American Convention of Col-

ored People, an organization opposed to the repatriation of African Americans to Africa. Instead, he advocated their immigration to the safety of Canada. Henry Bibb died in 1854.

Bibb was a gifted orator in the cause of abolition, and his autobiography added an eloquent and disturbing perspective on the conditions of slave life to the growing literary tradition of the slave narrative. In addition, his documentation of the folklore among slaves, particularly "conjuring," or the casting of spells, provided insight into the significance of the supernatural in early African-American culture, a theme that would appear frequently in the literature of later generations of African-American writers.

Further Reading

Andrews, William L. *To Tell a Free Story: The First Century of Afro-American Autobiography.* Urbana-Champaign: University of Illinois Press, 1989.

Bibb, Henry. *The Life and Adventures of Henry Bibb: An American Slave.* Madison: University of Wisconsin Press, 2000.

Cooper, Afua. "The Fluid Frontier: Blacks and the Detroit River Region." *Canadian Review of American Studies* 30, no. 2 (2000): 129.

Davis, Charles, and Henry Louis Gates, Jr. *The Slave's Narrative.* New York: Oxford University Press, 1991.

Bonner, Marita Odette
(Marieta Bonner Occomy, Joseph Maree Andrew)
(1899–1971) *essayist, short story writer, playwright*

A contemporary of ZORA NEALE HURSTON, NELLA LARSEN, and ANN PETRY, Marita Odette Bonner brought her own unique vision to the tradition of Harlem Renaissance literature. Her stories and plays, appearing frequently in the pages of *Opportunity* and the *Crisis* between 1924 and 1941, addressed racial and gender conflicts among African Americans of diverse economic and social backgrounds living in crowded and ethnically mixed urban settings.

Bonner was born in Boston, Massachusetts, on June 16, 1899, to Joseph and Mary Anne Bonner, and educated in the public schools of Brookline, a suburb of Boston. The only child among her three siblings to survive childhood, she excelled in music, writing, and the German language, and later attended Radcliffe College, majoring in English and comparative literature. Following her graduation in 1922, she moved to Washington, D.C., and taught at the Bluefield Colored High School.

In Washington, she met the playwright GEORGIA DOUGLAS JOHNSON, whose celebrated "S" Street Salon became a gathering place for several writers and artists of the Harlem Renaissance movement. Encouraged by LANGSTON HUGHES and ALAIN LOCKE, among others, Bonner began her writing career in 1925, with the publication of the story "Hands" in *Opportunity*. That same year, she published her acclaimed essay "On Being Young—A Woman—and Colored," which was awarded the *Crisis* prize for best essay.

In these early works, and in the numerous short stories that followed, Bonner examined the limited opportunities afforded African Americans in white-dominated but ethnically diverse urban settings. She also emphasized the particular difficulties faced by women who struggled with racial as well as gender prejudice.

Bonner published three plays: *The Pot-Maker: A Play to Be Read*, in 1927, *The Purple Flower*, in 1928, and *Exit, an Illusion: A One-Act Play*, in 1929. Though never produced in her lifetime, these plays were highly regarded and influential among her contemporaries in the Harlem Renaissance. Bonner employed several innovations, including second-person narrative and surrealistic allegory, in portraying characters who confront their personal limitations within a broader environment of racial injustice and addressing a potentially violent reaction to continued racial oppression by white society. *The Purple Flower* was awarded the *Crisis* prize for best drama in 1928.

Bonner married William Almy Occomy, an accountant, in 1930 and moved to Chicago. She also shifted her literary focus to Frye Street, a fictional neighborhood in Chicago's Black Belt, where communities comprising numerous ethnicities struggled to exist in a debilitating and racially tense urban environment. Notable among the Frye Street stories are the trilogy "Triple Triad on Black Notes" and the two-part story "Tin Can," which won a literary prize in 1933.

In 1941 Bonner published her last short story, "One True Love," in which she returned to the theme of the "double bind" experienced by African-American women that she developed in "On Being Young—a Woman—and Colored." For the next 30 years, Bonner devoted herself to raising her three children and returned to teaching, first at Phillips High School in Chicago and, from 1950 to 1963, at the Doolittle School, assisting mentally handicapped children. She died on December 6, 1971, from injuries sustained in an apartment fire.

In 1987 Beacon Press published *Frye Street and Environs: The Collected Works of Marita Bonner*, which included five previously unpublished works. The collection generated renewed interest in her writing, which had gone largely unnoticed in the years following her death. Bonner was one of the best-educated and most versatile authors to come out of the Harlem Renaissance. Her exploration of the profound impact of racial, economic, and environmental pressures on the inner and outer lives of her characters remains a fundamental theme in African-American literature.

Further Reading

Andrews, William L., Francis Smith Foster, and Trudier Harris, eds. *The Concise Oxford Companion to African American Literature*. New York: Oxford University Press, 2001.

Brown-Guillory, Elizabeth, ed. *Wines in the Wilderness: Plays by African American Women from the Harlem Renaissance to the Present*. Westport, Conn.: Greenwood Press, 1990.

Flynn, Joyce, and Joyce Occomy Stricklin, eds. *Frye Street and Environs: The Collected Works of Marita Bonner Occomy.* Boston, Mass.: Beacon Press, 1987.

Musser, Judith. "African American Women and Education: Marita Bonner's Response to the 'Talented Tenth.'" *Studies in Short Fiction* 34, no. 1 (winter 1997): 73.

Bontemps, Arna
(Arnaud Wendell Bontemps)
(1902–1973) *poet, novelist, short story writer, editor, librarian*

A central figure in the cultural and literary movement known as the Harlem Renaissance, Arna Bontemps wrote in a variety of genres. He published poetry, novels, short fiction, children's fiction, biography, and history. He also edited several influential literary anthologies. Though his critical reputation rests in large part on his acclaimed historical novel, *Black Thunder* (1936), and his prolific writings for children, Bontemps played a significant role in shaping the direction and themes of African-American literature in the mid-20th century by emphasizing the proud history of African and African-American cultural heritage. Bontemps also contributed to the legacy of African-American literature in his work as a librarian at Fisk University, where he helped assemble one of the most respected collections of books by black authors in the United States, and at Yale University, where he served as the curator of the JAMES WELDON JOHNSON collection.

Arna Bontemps was born Arnaud Wendell Bontemps on October 13, 1902, in Alexandria, Louisiana. His mother, Maria Caroline Bontemps, worked as a schoolteacher, and his father, Paul Bismark Bontemps, was a second-generation stone- and brickmason, lay minister, and jazz trombonist. Bontemps moved with his family to Los Angeles, California, at age three, and came under the influence of his great-uncle Joe Ward, called Uncle Buddy, a dissolute but kindhearted

Arna Bontemps, shown here in 1939, was named an honorary consultant in American cultural history in 1972. *(Library of Congress)*

man who regaled him with folk stories about life in Louisiana. From Uncle Buddy, Bontemps learned about the rural roots of his racial heritage and developed a love for storytelling.

In contrast to Uncle Buddy, Bontemps's father insisted that his son try to assimilate into white mainstream life. The conflict between his father and Uncle Buddy made a deep impression on Bontemps. "In their opposing attitudes toward roots," he wrote in 1963, "my father and my great-uncle made me aware of conflict in which every educated American Negro, and some who are not educated, must somehow take sides." Compelled by his father to attend a white boarding school and later Pacific Union College, an Adventist college, Bontemps took his own side in the debate over cultural roots. He graduated from Pacific Union College in 1923 and left for New York City the following year to pursue a literary career.

Bontemps arrived in Harlem in the autumn of 1924. "Full of golden hopes and romantic dreams," he explained in his 1963 collection of poetry, *Personals,* "I had come all the way from Los Angeles . . . to hear the music of my taste, to see serious plays, and God willing, to become a writer." Bontemps accepted a teaching position at Harlem Academy, an Adventist school, and spent his free time writing poetry. His published poems earned several literary prizes, including the Poetry Prize from the *Crisis* magazine in 1926, and the Alexander Pushkin Poetry Prize in 1926 and 1927. Bontemps married Alberta Johnson in 1926, and the first of their six children was born in 1927. Bontemps also completed his first novel, *Chariot in the Sky,* though it was never published.

Living in New York City at the height of the Harlem Renaissance, Bontemps became acquainted with many of the leading African-American writers and scholars of the time. He had befriended the poet LANGSTON HUGHES shortly after his arrival in 1924, and the two developed a lifelong friendship that produced numerous literary collaborations. Bontemps also maintained friendships with such notable authors as COUNTEE CULLEN, CLAUDE McKAY, RUDOLPH FISHER, and WALLACE THURMAN, whom he had first met while living in Los Angeles. In 1931 Bontemps published his first novel, *God Sends Sunday,* to mixed critical reviews. The novel depicts the exploits of Little Augie, a character based on his great-uncle, who rises to fame as a jockey and later falls into a life of poverty and physical hardship.

In 1932 Bontemps won an award from the National Urban League's *Opportunity* magazine for his short story "A Summer Tragedy," a moving tale of an elderly couple worn out by their lives as sharecroppers. That same year, Bontemps collaborated with Langston Hughes on the successful children's novel *Popo and Fifina: Children of Haiti*

(1932). Bontemps published another children's book, *You Can't Pet a Possum,* in 1934. Bontemps had reluctantly moved to Huntsville, Alabama, in 1931, to assume a teaching position at Oakwood Junior College. There, he soon experienced difficulties with administrators over his research for a new novel. Ordered to burn an impressive collection of books by African-American authors, Bontemps instead chose to resign. He moved back to California to finish his research for his next novel, *Black Thunder,* at his father's home in Los Angeles.

Black Thunder, published in 1936, was a greater critical than popular success. In his review of the novel, RICHARD WRIGHT called it "the only novel to deal forthrightly with the historical and revolutionary traditions of the Negro people." In *Black Thunder,* Bontemps dramatized the events surrounding a historical but unsuccessful slave revolt by Gabriel Prosser in Virginia during the 1800s. Critics praised the depth of Bontemps's characters, white and black, and his extensive use of historical sources.

Bontemps moved to Chicago, Illinois, in 1935 to assume the position of principal at Shiloh Academy. He published his second children's book, *Sad Faced Boy,* in 1937. From 1938 to 1942 Bontemps worked as an editorial supervisor to the Federal Writers' Project, part of President Franklin D. Roosevelt's depression-era Works Progress Administration. He also published four more books: *Drums at Dusk* (1939), a historical novel about the 18th-century black revolution in Santo Domingo; *Father of the Blues,* a biography of blues legend W. C. Handy (1941); *Golden Slippers: An Anthology of Negro Poetry for Young Readers* (ed., 1941); and *The Fast Sooner Hound* (1942), a children's tale that he coauthored with Jack Conroy.

In 1943 Bontemps received his master's degree from the University of Chicago's Graduate School of Library Science and accepted the position of head librarian and professor at Fisk University in Nashville, Tennessee, where he remained until 1966. During his tenure, the Fisk University library became a leading center of research for African-American history and literature. These years were also a prolific period for Bontemps as a writer. In 1946 he collaborated with Countee Cullen on a musical, *St. Louis Woman,* a controversial but successful adaptation of his novel *God Sends Sunday.* In 1948 Bontemps published his award-winning *The Story of the Negro,* a young-adult history of African Americans from ancient Egypt to the 20th century. He also collaborated again with Langston Hughes on three anthologies of literature by and about African Americans: *The Poetry of the Negro* (1949), *The Book of Negro Folklore* (1959), and *American Negro Poetry* (1963).

The critical failure of his third adult novel, *Drums at Dusk* (1939), convinced Bontemps to focus more exclusively on children's literature; during the 1940s and 1950s, he produced a wealth of fiction, history, and biography for young readers. His books for children included *We Have Tomorrow* (1945), *They Seek a City* (1945, with Jack Conroy), *Slappy Hooper: The Wonderful Sign Painter* (1946, with Jack Conroy), *Sam Patch* (1951, with Jack Conroy), *Chariot in the Sky: A Story of the Jubilee Singers* (1951), *The Story of George Washington Carver* (1954), *Lonesome Boy* (1955), *Frederick Douglass: Slave, Fighter, Freeman* (1959), *One Hundred Years of Negro Freedom* (1961), *Famous Negro Athletes* (1964), *Great Slave Narratives* (ed., 1969), *Hold Fast to Dreams* (ed., 1969), *Free at Last: The Life of Frederick Douglass* (1971), and *Young Booker: Booker T. Washington's Early Days* (1972). Bontemps also published his only collection of poetry, *Personals,* in 1963.

After his retirement from Fisk University in 1966, Bontemps held distinguished teaching positions at the University of Illinois at Chicago Circle (1966–69), and at Yale University (1969–70), where he also served as the curator for the James Weldon Johnson Collection at the Beinecke Library. He returned to Fisk University in 1970 and served as writer-in-residence until 1973. In his final years, Bontemps published *The Harlem Renaissance Remembered* (1972), a collection of literary reminiscences of the celebrated authors and literary figures of that era, many of whom he had

known personally. He also published a collection of his short fiction, *The Old South: "A Summer Tragedy" and Other Stories from the Thirties* (1973). Arna Wendell Bontemps died of a heart attack on June 4, 1973, in Nashville, Tennessee.

In his novels, poetry, short fiction, and children's literature, Bontemps consistently challenged racial prejudice and celebrated the unique contributions made by African Americans to the literature and history of the United States. Modern reprints of many of Bontemps's children's books continue to enrich the lives of new generations of children; and two previously unknown books, *The Pasteboard Bandit,* a collaborative work with Langston Hughes, and *Bubber Goes to Heaven,* were published in 1997 and 1998, respectively. On July 8, 2003, the Dance Theater of Harlem debuted *St. Louis Woman: A Blues Ballet,* adapted from Bontemps and Cullen's 1946 musical collaboration *St. Louis Woman.* Among the many honors he received during his lifetime was an appointment as honorary consultant in American Cultural History to the Library of Congress in 1973.

Further Reading

Alvarez, Joseph A. "The Lonesome Boy Theme as Emblem for Arna Bontemps's Children's Literature." *African American Review* 32 (spring 1998): 23.

Andrews, William L., Frances Smith Foster, and Trudier Harris, eds. *The Concise Oxford Companion to African American Literature.* New York: Oxford University Press, 2001.

Bontemps, Arna. *Black Thunder: Gabriel's Revolt, Virginia, 1800.* New York: Macmillan, 1936; reprinted, Boston, Mass.: Beacon Press, 1992.

Nichols, Charles H. *Arna Bontemps–Langston Hughes Letters, 1925–1967.* New York: Dodd, Mead, 1980.

Bradley, David
(David Henry Bradley, Jr.)
(1950–) *novelist, essayist, educator*

David Bradley earned critical acclaim for two novels, *South Street* and *The Chaneysville Incident,* both published before the author was 35. The latter novel received the PEN/Faulkner Award in 1982. Also for many years a distinguished professor of creative writing, he remains a frequent contributor of stories, essays, and reviews to numerous periodicals, including the *New York Times Book Review,* the *New York Arts Journal, Esquire,* and the *Southern Review.*

Bradley was born in the predominantly white rural community of Bedford, Pennsylvania, on September 7, 1950 to David Bradley, Sr., a minister, and Harriette Marie Bradley, a local historian. Following his graduation from high school, Bradley was named the Benjamin Franklin National Achievement and Presidential Scholar. He graduated summa cum laude from the University of Pennsylvania in 1972 and received his M.A. degree from the University of London in 1974.

Following his return to the United States, Bradley published his first novel, *South Street,* which he had begun as an undergraduate at the University of Pennsylvania. Set in three locations along Philadelphia's South Street, the novel tells the story of a young poet, Adlai Stevenson Brown, who frequents Lightnin' Ed's Bar. Using street vernacular and shifting narrative perspectives, Bradley presents life in the South Street ghetto through the eyes of the hustlers, prostitutes, alcoholics, and preachers who live there. The novel was inspired by Bradley's own experiences in the South Street Bar as a college student and was well received by critics, who praised its original and humane portrayal of the grim realities of life in depressed urban centers.

Bradley wrote four versions of his second novel, *The Chaneysville Incident,* before finally publishing it in 1981. The novel was inspired by a story that Bradley had heard from his mother in Bedford about 13 escaped slaves who preferred to be killed rather than return to slavery. Blending historical fact with fiction, Bradley created a complex narrative spanning several generations wherein a cynical college professor, John Washington, confronts his past and ultimately heals the familial and cultural rifts in his life.

Bradley's depiction of John Washington's search for his true identity, an identity that has been fractured by a separation from his ancestry and from what John calls his "home ground," earned him national recognition as a writer of great depth and fueled comparisons to the work of JAMES BALDWIN, RALPH ELLISON, and TONI MORRISON. The novel was awarded the PEN/Faulkner award and the American Academy and Institute of Arts and Letters grant for literature in 1982.

In addition to his writing, Bradley also maintained a distinguished career as a professor of English at the University of Pennsylvania, San Diego State University, and Temple University, where he served from 1977 to 1996. His abiding interest in history and civil rights led to his coeditorship of *The Encyclopedia of Civil Rights in America,* published in 1998, and he has continued to publish reviews, essays, and numerous interviews in which he discusses his goals and methods as a writer. *The Chaneysville Incident* remains a modern classic of African-American literature and holds a place among masterworks, including Ralph Ellison's *Invisible Man* and RICHARD WRIGHT's *Native Son.*

Further Reading

Andrews, William L., Frances Smith Foster, and Trudier Harris, eds. *The Concise Oxford Companion to African American Literature.* New York: Oxford University Press, 2001.

Appiah, Kwame Anthony, and Henry Louis Gates, Jr. *Africana: The Encyclopedia of the African and African American Experience.* New York: Basic Civitas Books, 1999.

Bradley, David, Jr. *The Chaneysville Incident.* New York: HarperCollins, 1990.

Gates, Henry Louis, Jr., and Nellie Y. McKay. *The Norton Anthology of African American Literature.* New York: W. W. Norton, 1997.

Braithwaite, William
(William Stanley Beaumont Braithwaite)
(1878–1962) *poet, critic, editor*

A respected poet and critic, William Stanley Braithwaite helped reinvigorate interest in poetry in the United States, particularly that of African-American writers, in the early 20th century. While recognizing the power of verse to address political and racial issues, he remained committed to its ability to transmit universal truths that transcended racial lines.

Braithwaite was born in Boston on December 6, 1878. The son of Emma DeWolfe and James Smith Braithwaite, William enjoyed a prosperous and cultured upbringing; following the death of his father, however, he was forced to abandon his education at the age of 12 to help support his family. He found work as a typesetter at a publishing company, Ginn & Co., in Boston, where he developing a passion for 19th-century romantic poetry, particularly the works of John Keats and William Blake. Inspired by the lyricism of the romantics, Braithwaite began writing his own poems.

In 1903 Braithwaite married Emma Kelly, with whom he would have seven children, and began publishing his first poems in the *Atlantic Monthly* and *Scribner's.* He produced his first volume of poetry, *Lyrics of Life and Love,* in 1904 and acknowledged his debt to John Keats in poems such as "Keats Was an Unbeliever" and "On a Pressed Flower in My Copy of Keats." A second volume of poetry, *House of Falling Leaves,* followed in 1908.

Braithwaite became a regular columnist for the *Boston Transcript* in 1906. He celebrated the poetry of white and African-American poets in his columns, and he brought attention to the works of numerous young African-American writers such as PAUL LAURENCE DUNBAR, JAMES WELDON JOHNSON, COUNTEE CULLEN, and CLAUDE McKAY. Braithwaite also published several anthologies of older verse, including *The Book of Elizabethan Verse.* After a failed attempt to create a magazine of American poetry in 1912, Braithwaite began work on his *Anthology of Magazine Verse.* Published annually, his anthology collected poetry previously published in other journals and magazines and included critical commentaries and biographical details of the authors.

By including the work of young African-American poets with that of such popular white authors as Robert Frost and Amy Lowell, Braithwaite brought their work to a larger audience. Inclusion in his anthology soon became a coveted distinction, and Braithwaite earned considerable acclaim as a critic of uncommon skill. His insistence that poetry remain racially neutral and avoid polemics also generated criticism from some contemporary black critics and writers.

In 1918 Braithwaite received the Spingarn Medal, the highest honor awarded by the National Association for the Advancement of Colored People, for his contribution to literature. He continued to publish his *Anthology of Magazine Verse* until 1929. During the lean years of the Great Depression, he took a teaching position at Atlanta University in 1935 and taught literature for the next 10 years. Following his retirement from teaching in 1945, Braithwaite moved to Harlem and began work on his *Selected Poems,* published in 1948, as well as a book on the Brontës. He died in 1962.

As an editor and poet, William Stanley Braithwaite created a prolific body of work, including three volumes of poetry, several anthologies of English and American verse, the novel *A Fragment Wrenched from the Life of Titus Jabson* (1924), a collection of short stories titled *Frost on the Green Leaf* (1928), and his autobiography, *The House under Arcturus,* published in 1941. Though aesthetically at odds with the younger generation of African-American writers, many of whom he assiduously promoted, Braithwaite earned their respect. Countee Cullen dedicated his *Caroling Dusk: An Anthology of Verse by*

Black Poets (1972) to Braithwaite, "whom those who know him," wrote Cullen, "delight to honor."

Further Reading

Andrews, William L., Frances Smith Foster, and Trudier Harris, eds. *The Concise Oxford Companion to African American Literature.* New York: Oxford University Press, 2001.

Appiah, Kwame Anthony, and Henry Louis Gates, Jr. *Africana: The Encyclopedia of the African and African American Experience.* New York: Basic Civitas Books, 1999.

Gates, Henry Louis, Jr., and Nellie Y. McKay, eds. *The Norton Anthology of African American Literature.* New York: W. W. Norton, 1997.

Brooks, Gwendolyn
(Gwendolyn Elizabeth Brooks)

(1917–2000) *poet, novelist, essayist, autobiographer*

Acclaimed by critics for the depth and precision of her poetic language, Gwendolyn Brooks was the first African-American writer to receive a Pulitzer Prize, awarded in 1950 for her poetry collection *Annie Allen.* Known primarily as a poet, Brooks also published novels, essays, and a two-volume autobiography. She was the recipient of numerous literary honors during a writing career that spanned six decades, including the Poetry Society of America's Frost Medal, a Lifetime Achievement Award from the National Endowment for the Humanities, and the First Women Award from the National First Ladies Library.

Gwendolyn Elizabeth Brooks was born on June 17, 1917, in Topeka, Kansas, the daughter of David Anderson Brooks, a janitor, and Keziah Corrine Brooks, a schoolteacher. Shortly after her birth, the family moved to Chicago, Illinois, where Brooks was raised and spent most of her life. During her childhood, Brooks's parents encouraged her early literary ambitions, providing books for her to read and relieving her of many household duties. Brooks read widely in her father's set of Harvard Classics and particularly enjoyed the works of PAUL LAURENCE DUNBAR and L. M. Montgomery's *Anne of Green Gables* books. She also composed plays for her mother's Sunday school class. Brooks published her first poem at age 13 in *American Child* magazine.

At age 16, Brooks met the celebrated Harlem Renaissance poets LANGSTON HUGHES and JAMES WELDON JOHNSON, both of whom encouraged her to develop her writing and served as literary mentors. Brooks drew particular inspiration from Hughes. "The words and deeds of Langston Hughes were rooted in kindness, and in pride," she wrote in her autobiography *Report from Part One* (1972). Hughes convinced her "that a black poet need not travel outside the realm of his own experience to create a poetic vision and write successful poetry."

As a high school student, Brooks regularly contributed poems to the *Defender,* a black daily newspaper in Chicago, and developed a local reputation as a poet. She majored in English at Wilson Junior College and graduated in 1936, after which she found employment with the Youth Council of the National Association for the Advancement of Colored People (NAACP). In 1939 she married Henry Lowington Blakely, Jr., himself an aspiring writer and fellow employee at the NAACP, with whom she had two children.

Brooks continued to hone her poetic skills in the early 1940s by attending a workshop with her husband, conducted on Chicago's South Side by Inez Cunningham Stark. There Brooks became acquainted with the work of major contemporary poets and submitted her own poems for review by the workshop. In 1943 she received the Midlands Writers Conference poetry award. Two years later, Brooks published her first book of poetry, *A Street in Bronzeville* (1945), which brought her national critical acclaim.

In *A Street in Bronzeville,* Brooks created a complex and personal portrait of urban black life as she had witnessed it growing up in Chicago.

Poems such as "The Mother" and "Kitchenette Building" provide intimate and compelling portraits of the daily struggle for survival in African-American urban communities, and a group of 12 well-crafted sonnets in the latter half of the collection address the prejudiced treatment of African Americans in the U.S. military during and after World War II.

The critical success of *A Street in Bronzeville* brought Brooks several national honors, including her selection by *Mademoiselle* magazine as one of 10 "Women of the Year" in 1945. She was also awarded a prestigious Guggenheim Fellowship in 1946. Brooks's second book of poetry, however, exceeded all expectations. Written as a poetic sequence that depicts the experiences of its protagonist, Annie Allen, through the various stages of her maturity, *Annie Allen* (1949) became the first book by an African-American author to win a Pulitzer Prize.

Now a nationally acclaimed poet, Brooks took on the challenge of writing her first and only novel, *Maud Martha* (1953), which, like her previous poetry, chronicles the life and maturity of its young black protagonist, set against the Great Depression and post–World War II eras. The short narrative, consisting of loosely configured scenes in Maud Martha's life, was largely overlooked by critics, many of whom praised its lyrical prose but judged it a minor work within the tradition of the African-American novel.

Brooks's next book of poetry, *The Bean Eaters* (1960), was published at the height of the Civil Rights movement and reflected a shift in her creative focus toward specific racial issues. Some of the poems, in particular "In Honor of David Allen Brooks, My Father," revealed the poignant language and sophisticated poetic constructions of her early work.

In 1967 Brooks attended the Second Black Writers' Conference at Fisk University, where she was impressed by the passion of young writers such as JOHN OLIVER KILLENS and AMIRI BARAKA and their emphasis on poetic works rooted in and directed toward African-American culture. Her interest in a more radical social perspective was evident in her next collections of poetry, *In the Mecca* (1968), which won the Anisfield-Wolf Award, and *Riot* (1969), her first book to be published after her move to Randall Dudley's all-black publishing company, Broadside Press, as well as in *Family Pictures* (1970), *Black Street: Joe Frazier and Muhammad Ali* (1971), *Aloneness* (1971), *Aurora* (1972), and *Beckonings* (1975). "Anything I write," Brooks said of her change in artistic focus, "is going to issue from a concern with and interest in blackness and its progress."

Brooks was named Illinois poet laureate in 1968 and devoted much of her time outside of writing to the encouragement of young writers. She visited schools, community centers, and prisons, and established poetry prizes with her own funds. She also taught at several universities, including the City University of New York (1971). In 1972 she published *Report from Part One: An Autobiography,* consisting of reminiscences of her life in Chicago and her early work as a poet. A second volume, *Report from Part Two,* was published in 1996.

Brooks continued to explore her unique vision of black life through verse in volumes such as *Black Love* (1981), *To Disembark* (1981), *The Near-Johannesburg Boy and Other Poems* (1986), *Blacks* (1987), *Winnie* (1988), and *Children Coming Home* (1991). A final volume, *In Montgomery,* was published posthumously in 2001. Brooks also wrote children's books, among which are *Bronzeville Boys and Girls* (1956), *The Tiger Who Wore White Gloves* (1974), and *Very Young Poets* (1983). In the 1990s Brooks served as professor and writer-in-residence at Chicago State University, which established the Gwendolyn Brooks Center for Black Literature and Creative Writing in 1993. Shortly after being diagnosed with cancer, Gwendolyn Elizabeth Brooks died on December 3, 2000, in Chicago, Illinois.

During a writing career that included several landmark achievements, Gwendolyn Brooks became the first African-American recipient of the Pulitzer Prize and the first to serve as a poetry consultant to the Library of Congress. Her other literary honors include fellowships from the Guggenheim Foundation and the National Academy of Poets, and a Lifetime Achievement award from the National Endowment for the Humanities in 1989. In 1995 President Bill Clinton awarded Brooks the National Medal of Art. "I believe that we should all know each other," Brooks said in an interview with *Jet* magazine shortly before her death, "we human carriers of so many pleasurable differences."

Further Reading

Brooks, Gwendolyn. *Blacks.* Chicago, Ill.: David Company, 1987.

———. *To Disembark.* Detroit, Mich.: Third World Press, 1981.

Bryant, Jacqueline K. *Gwendolyn Brooks'* Maud Martha: *A Critical Edition.* Detroit, Mich.: Third World Press, 2002.

Kent, George E. *A Life of Gwendolyn Brooks.* Lexington: University Press of Kentucky, 1990.

Madhubuti, Haki R., ed. *Say That the River Turns.* Detroit, Mich.: Third World Press, 1987.

Wright, Stephen Caldwell, ed. *On Gwendolyn Brooks: Reliant Contemplation.* Ann Arbor: University of Michigan Press, 2001.

Brown, Claude

(1937–2002) *autobiographer, essayist*

With the publication of his autobiography, *Manchild in the Promised Land,* and its realistic and troubling account of black urban life, Claude Brown helped invigorate the growing debate on civil rights in the 1960s. Brown depicted the despair and brutality of life in Harlem in vivid detail, but his work also speaks to the hope that exists within the African-American community for transcending the constraints of such socially and racially oppressive environments.

Claude Brown was born on February 23, 1937, the son of Henry Lee, a railroad worker, and Ossie Brock Brown, a domestic. His parents had migrated from South Carolina in 1935, hoping to find better economic opportunities in the north. Brown received an early education in Harlem street life. At age eight he was stealing and fighting as a member of the Buccaneers, a Harlem street gang. His long record of truancies from school resulted in numerous expulsions. After several trips to the New York City juvenile detention center, Brown was sent to the Wiltwyck School, a reform school for delinquent youths. There, Dr. Ernest Papanek, who would become a lifelong mentor and friend, supervised him.

After two years at Wiltwyck, Brown returned to Harlem, where he soon became involved again in the violence and criminal activity of the streets. During an attempted robbery, he received a near-fatal gunshot wound to the stomach. He was sentenced to a second trip to reform school, this time in the more hardened Warwick School for Boys, where he served three terms. Upon his release in 1953, Brown returned briefly to theft and drug dealing before deciding to leave the streets and finish high school at night. He moved to Greenwich Village at 17 and worked several odd jobs, including playing jazz, to pay his way.

In 1959 Brown enrolled at Howard University, in Washington, D.C., and worked part-time as a postal clerk. He also began submitting short stories and essays to the intellectual and non-paying journals *Dissent* and *Commentary.* At Howard University, Brown studied under TONI MORRISON, who read and critiqued some of his early writing. Under the encouragement of Ernest Papanek, his early mentor from Wiltwyck, Brown published an essay on Harlem life in *Dissent,* after which a representative from the publisher Macmillan negotiated a deal for a book-length account of his life in Harlem.

Brown married Helen Jones, a telephone operator, in 1961, and he finished his autobiography two years later. *Manchild in the Promised Land* was published in 1965, and the book was an instant critical success. Brown's honesty in relating the details of his early life in Harlem, and his astute social commentary on urban problems facing African-American families throughout America, struck a chord with readers. Following this early success as a writer, he published several essays in such periodicals as *Esquire,* the *New York Times Magazine,* and *Life.*

After earning his degree in government and business from Howard University in 1965, Brown studied law briefly at Stanford University before transferring to Rutgers. During this period, he also wrote and lectured on poverty, juvenile justice, and social reforms. He published his second book, *The Children of Ham,* in 1976. The book describes the activities of a group of teenagers in Harlem who encourage each other, despite considerable obstacles, to remain free of drugs and stay in school. Though it conveyed an important message to inner-city youth, *The Children of Ham* never achieved the critical or popular success of its predecessor.

For the remainder of his life, Brown continued to support social reforms and devoted much of his time to youth mentoring programs in Harlem and New Jersey as well as to prison outreach programs. *Manchild in the Promised Land* became a modern classic, selling more than 4 million copies and ranking as the second-best-selling book published by Macmillan, behind *Gone with the Wind.* Translated into 14 languages, the book remains required reading in many schools across America. Claude Brown died of lung cancer on February 2, 2002, in New York City.

Further Reading

Andrews, William L., Frances Smith Foster, and Trudier Harris, eds. *The Concise Oxford Companion to African American Literature.* New York: Oxford University Press, 2001.

Brown, Claude. *Manchild in the Promised Land.* New York: Simon and Schuster, 1999.

Horowitz, Irving Louis. "Seeing through a Manchild's Eyes." *Chronicle of Higher Education* 48 (April 12, 2002): B5.

Brown, Sterling
(Sterling Allen Brown)
(1901–1989) *poet, literary critic, editor, educator*

A renowned poet, critic, and editor of some of the most influential anthologies and historical studies of African-American literature and folklore, Sterling Brown served for 40 years as a distinguished professor of literature at Howard University, in Washington, D.C. Brown was committed, in his teaching and writing, to the celebration of folk traditions and to counteracting the misconceptions and stereotypes associated with African Americans in mainstream white literature and society. His writing has earned numerous literary honors, including fellowships and prizes, and Brown was named the poet laureate of the District of Columbia in 1984.

Sterling Allen Brown was born on May 1, 1901, in Washington, D.C., the son of a writer and distinguished professor of religion, Sterling Nelson Brown, and Adelaide Allen Brown. He grew up in a comfortable middle-class home, graduated with honors from the prestigious Dunbar High School, and received his bachelor's degree from Williams College. As an undergraduate, Brown was elected to the academic honor society Phi Beta Kappa and became the only student in his class to graduate with highest honors in English. He also won Williams College's Graves Prize for his essay "The Comic Spirit in Shakespeare and Molière." In 1923 Brown graduated from Harvard University with a master's degree in English.

From 1923 to 1929 Brown held teaching positions in numerous black colleges in the South, including Virginia Seminary and College (1923–26), Lincoln University (1926–28), and Fisk University (1928–29). Brown's years of living and teaching in rural African-American communities throughout the South, where he collected folktales and developed a love of jazz and blues, played an important role in shaping the direction of his writing.

Brown's first major poem, "Roland Hayes," was published in the National Urban League's literary magazine *Opportunity* in 1925, and won second prize in that year's poetry contest. In 1927 he won *Opportunity*'s first prize for his poem "When de Saints Go Ma'ching Home." With the publication of his first collection of verse, *Southern Road* (1932), Brown established himself as one of the most significant folk poets of the Harlem Renaissance. Drawing on the dialects, folktales, and unusual characters with whom he had become acquainted during his years in the South, Brown created a portrait of African-American life in *Southern Road* that captured the profound humor, intelligence, and dignity of black folk culture.

Among the many vibrant characters that appear in the poems of *Southern Road,* Slim Greer stands out as one of the most memorable. Brown included three poems about Greer in *Southern Road* ("Slim Greer," "Slim Lands a Job?" and "Slim in Atlanta"). Two additional poems ("Slim in Hell" and "Slim Hears 'the Call'") appeared in later collections of his verse. Brown's Slim Greer poems draw on and expand the figure of the trickster found in the oldest oral traditions of African culture and African-American folklore. "The Slim Greer poems," writes John Edgar Tidwell in *The Oxford Companion to African American Literature,* "represent the principal concern in nearly all of Brown's work: reclaiming the humanity of African Americans to insure the completion of selfhood."

Brown began teaching in 1929 at Howard University, where he would remain for the next 40 years. Unable to find a publisher for his second collection of poetry, *No Hiding Place,* Brown turned his attention to literary criticism. He was awarded a prestigious Guggenheim Fellowship in 1937, which allowed him to complete two important scholarly collections, *The Negro in American Fiction* and *Negro Poetry and Drama,* both published in 1937. An important study of the ways in which African Americans had typically been portrayed in American literature, Brown's *The Negro in American Fiction* identified several images (among them what he called "The Contented Slave," "The Comic Negro," and "The Exotic Primitive") that contributed to the misrepresentation and misunderstanding of black culture.

With Arthur P. Davis and Ulysses Lee, Brown edited *The Negro Caravan* in 1941, the most comprehensive collection of black writing of its time and a work that many scholars consider one of the most important literary anthologies in African-American history. *The Negro Caravan* helped showcase the rich literary talents of African-American writers and their significant contributions to American literature.

Brown served as editor on Negro affairs for the Federal Writers' Project, a part of President Franklin D. Roosevelt's depression-era Works Progress Administration. He also conducted research for the Carnegie-Myrdal Study of the Negro in 1939. In addition to his lengthy tenure as a distinguished professor at Howard University, Brown also held visiting professorships at the University of Illinois, the University of Minnesota, the New School for Social Research, Sarah Lawrence College, and Vassar College.

In 1969 Brown reluctantly retired from Howard University after 40 years of service. In 1974 he published a revised edition of his landmark *Southern Road,* which renewed critical and popular interest in his poetry and led to the publication of his second volume of poetry, *The Last Ride of Wild Bill, and Eleven Narrative Poems* (1975). Five years later, poet MICHAEL S. HARPER edited *The Collected Poems of Sterling A. Brown* (1980), which combined poems from Brown's two published volumes as well as his unpublished collection *No Hiding Place.* During his final years Brown gave frequent lectures and poetry readings across the United States. He was awarded the Lenore Marshall Poetry Prize in 1982 and was named poet laureate of the District of Columbia in 1984. Sterling Allen Brown died in Takoma Park, Maryland, on January 13, 1989.

The recipient of numerous literary awards and fellowships, Sterling Brown earned national recognition as a poet, literary scholar, and educator for his contributions to American literature. His dedication to the folk roots of African-American literature, and his more than 40 years of service as an educator and literary historian, helped prepare a foundation in the mid-20th century for future academic programs devoted to American and African-American studies. For Brown, his greatest legacy was the many students he helped train, among whom were poet and playwright AMIRI BARAKA, and Leopold Senghor, the future president of Senegal in West Africa.

Further Reading

Brown, Sterling A. *The Collected Poems of Sterling A. Brown.* New York: Harper and Row, 1980. Reprint, Evanston, Ill.: Triquarterly Books, 1996.

Gates, Henry Louis, Jr., and Nellie Y. McKay, eds. *The Norton Anthology of African American Literature.* New York: W. W. Norton, 1997.

Hill, Patricia Liggins, general editor. *Call and Response: The Riverside Anthology of the African American Literary Tradition.* New York: Houghton Mifflin, 1998.

Brown, William Wells
(ca. 1814–1884) *novelist, historian, playwright, poet*

With the publication of *Clotel; or, the President's Daughter* in 1853, William Wells Brown became the first African American to publish a novel. His literary career would continue to be marked by a series of landmarks. Despite his tireless efforts as an antislavery lecturer in the United States and Europe, Brown found time to author the first drama, the first travel book, and the first military history to be published by an African American.

Brown employed his gifts as a writer primarily for the cause of abolition, but scholars also credit him with the creation of characters and themes that remain central to the African-American literary tradition.

He was born in about 1814, on a plantation near Lexington, Kentucky. His mother was a slave known only as Elizabeth, and his father is thought to have been the half brother of his master. Aside from his work as a house slave and field hand, William was frequently hired out during his boyhood and teenage years to work in larger cities, primarily in and around St. Louis, Missouri. He spent a year as a handyman for the slave trader James Walker, during which he made frequent trips by steamship between the slave markets in St. Louis and New Orleans.

On his return to his master's plantation in 1832, he discovered that he was to be sold. He decided to escape with his mother, but the two were eventually captured. He was subsequently sold in 1833, and he successfully escaped on New

William Wells Brown is generally considered to be the first African-American novelist. *(Library of Congress)*

Year's Day in 1834, while on a trip to Cincinnati with his new master's family. Traveling by night to Cleveland, he received assistance from Wells Brown and his wife, Quakers to whom Brown paid tribute by adopting the husband's name. (Previously he had been known only as William.) During the next nine years, Brown married a free African-American woman, with whom he had two children, and he worked on a steamboat on Lake Erie and as a conductor for the Underground Railroad in New York.

In 1843 Brown joined the Western New York Anti-Slavery Society and began lecturing throughout New England and parts of Canada. He moved to Boston, Massachusetts, in 1847 and published his first book, *Narrative of William W. Brown, a Fugitive Slave, Written by Himself.* Brown's autobiography was an immediate success, running through three American and four British printings in less than three years. Now an internationally known author, Brown traveled to Europe to attend a peace conference in Paris and to lecture on abolition in England. He also began to attend lectures on medicine. While maintaining a rigorous speaking schedule, he also published two more books. In 1852 he published *Three Years in Europe, or Places I Have Seen and People I Have Met,* the first travel book written by an African American. The following year, he published *Clotel; or, the President's Daughter,* the first African-American novel.

Brown's novel chronicles the life of Clotel, whose mother, Currer, was one of Thomas Jefferson's slaves in her youth, and whose children were fathered by him. Currer, Clotel, and her younger sister Althesa are eventually separated and sold to different masters, and the bulk of the narrative describes their attempts to reunite and their eventual fates. During the 1860s Brown published three additional versions of the novel. *Clotel: Miralda, or the Beautiful Quadroon* appeared in 16 serialized installments in the *Anglo-African* from 1860 to 1861. *Clotelle: A Tale of the Southern States* was published in an abridged version in 1864. Brown's third version, *Clotelle, or the Colored Hero-*

ine (1867), included four additional chapters that carried the story through the end of the Civil War.

Having remained in Europe following the passage of the Fugitive Slave Act of 1850, whereby escaped slaves living in the North could be captured and returned to their masters, Brown returned to the United States in 1854 after friends purchased his freedom. In 1855 he published a second memoir, *The American Fugitive in Europe,* and a historical study, *St. Domingo: Its Revolution and Its Patriots,* before achieving another literary first for an African American with the publication of his play *The Escape, or a Leap for Freedom* in 1858. The story of a slave couple, Melinda and her husband, who escape to Canada, the play depicts the brutal realities of life under slavery, particularly the sexual abuse of female slaves. Melinda is relentlessly pressured to become her master's mistress, a circumstance that prefigures the sexual predations of Dr. Flint in HARRIET ANN JACOBS's *Incidents in the Life of a Slave Girl* (1861).

During the 1860s Brown authored two important volumes of history. *The Black Man: His Antecedents, His Genius, and His Achievements* (1863) and *The Negro in the American Rebellion* (1867), the first work of military history relating to African Americans, highlighted the historical and cultural contributions of African Americans. A more ambitious and comprehensive volume of African-American history, *The Rising Son; or, the Antecedents and Advancement of the Colored Race,* published in 1874, contained sketches of the lives of prominent African Americans. Brown published his final book, *My Southern Home,* in 1880. This third memoir included further details of his life as a slave and observations of southern life during Reconstruction. William Wells Brown died at his home, outside Boston, Massachusetts, on November 6, 1884.

A relentless advocate of abolition, William Wells Brown maintained a busy lecture schedule for more than 40 years. His literary achievements brought him international recognition, and his *Narrative of William W. Brown* was second in popularity only to his contemporary FREDERICK DOUGLASS's *Narrative of the Life of Frederick Douglass* (1845). As a conductor in the Underground Railroad, Brown was responsible for bringing dozens of escaped slaves to freedom. He was a literary pioneer, a practicing physician, and an eloquent defender, in his books and speeches, of the rights of African Americans, whose life and legacy continues to inform the African-American literary tradition.

Further Reading

Brown, William Wells. *Clotel, or The President's Daughter.* Armonk, N.Y.: M. E. Sharpe, 2001.

———. *The Travels of William Wells Brown, including the Narrative of William Wells Brown, a Fugitive Slave, and the American Fugitive in Europe, Sketches of People and Places Abroad.* New York: Markus Weiner Publications, 1991.

Fabi, M. Giulia. "The 'Unguarded Expressions of the Feelings of Negroes': Gender, Slave Resistance, and William Wells Brown's Revisions of Clotel." *African American Review* 27, no. 4 (winter 1993): 639.

Gates, Henry Louis, Jr., and Nellie Y. McKay, eds. *The Norton Anthology of African American Literature.* New York: W. W. Norton, 1997.

Bullins, Ed
(Edward Bullins, Kingsley B. Bass, Jr.)
(1935–   ) *playwright, essayist, novelist*

A powerful voice in contemporary African-American theater, Ed Bullins gained critical attention during the 1960s as a visible and outspoken member of the Black Arts Movement. Concerned specifically with the creation of plays for a black audience, Bullins earned wide critical acclaim from white reviewers and audiences in the 1970s, during which he won three Obie Awards for distinguished playwriting and fellowships from the Guggenheim and Rockefeller foundations.

Edward Bullins was born on July 2, 1935, in Philadelphia, the son of Bertha Marie Bullins, a civil servant, and Edward Bullins. Reared primarily by his mother, Bullins attended public school in North Philadelphia, where as a junior-high student he became involved with an inner-city street gang called the Jet Cobras and suffered a near-fatal knife wound in a street fight. Bullins dropped out of Franklin High School in Philadelphia to join the U.S. Navy, serving from 1952 to 1955. He moved to California in 1958 and attended Los Angeles City College from 1961 to 1963, during which he founded *Citadel*, a campus literary magazine, and began to write.

In 1963 Bullins moved to San Francisco and began writing plays. Influenced by the emerging Black Nationalist movement, he became involved with community theater organizations such as Black Arts/West and the Black Student Union of San Francisco State College (now University), and cofounded Black House of San Francisco with fellow playwright Marvin X.

Bullins's first major production opened on August 5, 1965, at the Firehouse Repertory Theater, where he presented a program of three plays: *How Do You Do?, Dialect Determinism,* and *Clara's Ole Man.* Also in 1965 Bullins became Minister of Culture for the Black Panther Party, a position he held until 1967, when a dispute with party leader Eldridge Cleaver compelled him to leave the organization.

In 1967 Bullins moved to New York at the request of Robert MacBeth, director of the New Lafayette Theater in Harlem. Bullins's first New York production, *The Electronic Nigger,* premiered on February 21, 1968, and ran for 96 performances, establishing him as a major voice, along with AMIRI BARAKA and LARRY NEAL, of the Black Arts Movement. *The Electronic Nigger* won the 1968 Drama Desk–Vernon Rice Award. Bullins remained with the New Lafayette Theater until its demise in 1972 and produced nearly a dozen plays, including a controversial adaptation of Albert Camus's *The Just Assassins* in 1969 called *We Righteous Brothers,* under the pseudonym of Kingsley B. Bass, Jr. Bullins also served as editor of the journal *Black Theatre.*

Ed Bullins poses for a photo at his office in Harlem, New York City, in 1971. *(AP/Wide World Photos)*

In the 1970s Bullins gained a wider audience and critical appeal with Obie Award–winning productions of *In New England Winter* (1971), *The Fabulous Miss Marie* (1971), and perhaps his most acclaimed play, *The Taking of Miss Janie* (1975), which also won a New York Drama Critics Circle Award. In addition to teaching at Fordham University, Columbia University, Bronx Community College, and Manhattan Community College, Bullins also served as playwright-in-residence at the American Place Theatre and a writing coordinator for the New York Shakespeare Festival from 1975 to 1982.

Bullins returned to California in the early 1980s and established the Bullins Memorial Theatre, named in honor of a son, Edward, Jr., who died in an automobile accident. He also lectured at several universities and colleges, including the University of California at Berkley and Antioch College, where he later received his bachelor's degree in liberal studies. In 1994 he completed his M.F.A. degree in playwriting at San Francisco State University.

After a prolific period of playwriting during the 1960s and 1970s, during which he became one of the preeminent advocates of Black Arts ideology, Bullins has produced only a handful of plays during his later career, including *A Teacup Full of Roses* (1989), *Salaam, Huey Newton, Salaam* (1990), *American Griot* (1991, with Iris Açkamoor), and the critically acclaimed *Boy X Man* (1997). In addition to plays, Bullins has published a collection of his early short fiction, *The Hungered Ones: Early Writings*, and a novel, *The Reluctant Rapist* (1973).

Bullins's drama is characterized by its insistence on non-European cultural and political frames of reference. Employing what he has called the "secret language used in Black theater," which draws on such elements as African religion, jazz and blues, and urban street culture, Bullins adopts a fundamentally radical political perspective intended primarily for black audiences. His characters struggle to survive in crumbling urban centers and contend with the ambivalence and racism of mainstream white American culture. Ultimately, Bullins's drama is concerned with the expression and preservation of a uniquely black vision of culture and art.

In 1995 Ed Bullins was appointed professor of theater at Northeastern University, in Boston, Massachusetts. Several of his plays, beginning with *In the Wine Time* (1968), form a series of proposed plays in what Bullins calls the Twentieth Century Cycle, a chronicle of the black man in America. The seventh in the series, *Boy X Man*, was produced in Boston in 1997. The play depicts a middle-aged man's return to his native Philadelphia and his confrontation with the memories of his past, initiated by the death of his mother.

Ed Bullins is widely considered to be one of the most influential and acclaimed contemporary American playwrights. The author of more than 50 published and unpublished plays, Bullins has earned prestigious fellowships from the Guggenheim Foundation (1971, 1976); the Rockefeller Foundation (1968, 1970, 1973); and the National Endowment for the Arts (1974). He is also the recipient of the New York Drama Critics Circle Award and three Obie Awards for distinguished playwriting.

Further Reading

Adjaye, Joseph K., and Adrianne R. Andrews, eds. *Language, Rhythm, and Sound: Black Popular Cultures into the Twenty-first Century.* Pittsburgh: University of Pittsburgh Press, 1997.

Bullins, Ed. *Five Plays: Goin' a Buffalo; In the Wine Time; A Son, Come Home; The Electronic Nigger; Clara's Ole Man.* New York: Bobbs-Merrill, 1969.

———, ed. *New Plays from the Black Theatre: An Anthology.* New York: Bantam Books, 1969.

Hay, Samuel A. *Ed Bullins: A Literary Biography.* Detroit, Mich.: Wayne State University Press, 1997.

Butler, Octavia
(Octavia Estelle Butler)
(1947–) *novelist, short story writer*

Octavia Butler is one of only a few African-American science fiction writers, and the only African-American woman to earn popular and critical acclaim predominantly in the genre of science fiction. Her writing has earned science fiction's top literary honors, including the Nebula Award, the Hugo Award, and the Locus Award.

Octavia Estelle Butler was born on June 22, 1947, in Pasadena, California. Her father, Laurice Butler, died during her infancy, and her mother, Octavia, supported the family by working as a domestic. Often accompanying her mother to work, Butler witnessed the racial and economic indignities common to the African-American working poor, particularly women. Class, gender, and racial inequalities would play a central role in her writing.

Butler began writing as a child, creating stories that would eventually provide the framework for her larger novels. She attended Pasadena City College, where she won a short story contest during her first semester, and later studied at California State University at Los Angeles. After attending a class at the Screenwriters Guild taught by the renowned science fiction author Harlan Ellison, Butler spent six weeks at the Clarion Science Fiction Writers' Workshop in Pennsylvania. Her first published story appeared in the science fiction anthology *Clarion* in 1970.

In 1976 Doubleday published *The Patternmaster*, the first of five novels in Butler's Patternist series. The other volumes include *Mind of My Mind* (1977), *Survivor* (1978), *Wild Seed* (1980), and *Clay's Ark* (1984). Historical and apocalyptic in scope, the Patternist novels cover a broad time frame and numerous settings, from 17th-century West Africa and the transatlantic slave trade to 23rd century California. Butler uses familiar science fiction conventions, such as interplanetary travel, extraterrestrial life-forms, and human genetic mutations, in her compelling exploration of the interactions between the Patternists, a race of telepathic humans, the mutes (who have no telepathic powers), and the mutant Clayarks, humans stricken by a virus that alters their physical appearance and abilities.

During her work on the Patternist series, Butler published *Kindred* (1979), a novel that combines elements of science fiction, fantasy, and the more traditional slave narrative form. Dana Franklin, an African-American writer living in Los Angeles in 1976, finds herself transported back in time to antebellum Maryland. There, she discovers that her life is linked to that of a young slave owner's son, Rufus Weylin, whom she must protect in order to preserve her existence in 20th-century Los Angeles. As she moves back and forth through time, Dana discovers details of her family history that were previously unknown.

Also an accomplished short fiction writer, Butler has won numerous awards for her stories and novellas. "Speech Sounds" (1983), a story about the aftermath of a world virus that attacks the language center of the brain, won the Hugo Award for best science fiction story in 1984. *Bloodchild* (1984), in which human males are compelled by an alien race to give birth to their offspring, won all three major science fiction honors for best science fiction novella in 1985, including the Hugo, Nebula, and Locus awards. Butler was nominated for a third Hugo Award for her novella *The Evening and the Morning and the Night*, published in *Omni* magazine in 1987.

In her Xenogenesis series (*Dawn: Xenogenesis*, 1987; *Adulthood Rites*, 1988; *Imago*, 1989), Butler envisions a postapocalyptic world where humans must rely on a race of aliens, the Oankali, and their ability to control genetic mutations, to preserve the human race. *Parable of the Sower* (1995) and *Parable of the Talents* (1998) begin a new, ambitious series of novels in which a young girl, Lauren Olamina, tries to restore order to a crumbling and violent society by creating a new religious philosophy called Earthseed. In *Parable of the Sower*, Lauren leaves the ruins of her home and begins to attract others to her fledgling religion, which teaches that "God is change." *Parable of the Talents* traces Lauren's initial success in establishing her Earthseed community and its eventual suppression as Lauren and her followers are imprisoned in concentration camps and separated from their children. Butler was awarded a prestigious MacArthur Fellowship in 1995, in part for her considerable achievement in *Parable of the Sower*, which was nominated for a Nebula Award in 1996. *Parable of the Talents* won the 1999 Nebula Award for best science fiction novel.

Butler has earned international acclaim as a science fiction writer and received every major award given in that genre. Her ability to reconfigure traditional racial, gender, and power struggles has also added a new dimension to the tradition of African-American literature. "Every story I write adds to me a little, changes me a little," says Butler, "forces me to reexamine an attitude or belief." Butler's novels and stories compel her readers to effect similar adjustments of attitude and belief by addressing contemporary issues of racial and gender inequalities in unique and sometimes startling ways. In 2000 Octavia Butler received the PEN Center West Lifetime Achievement Award in recognition of her substantial literary contributions.

Further Reading

Butler, Octavia. *Blood, and Other Stories*. New York: Seven Stories Press, 1995.

———. *Parable of the Talents*. New York: Seven Stories Press, 1998.

Gates, Henry Louis, Jr., and Nellie Y. McKay, eds. *The Norton Anthology of African American Literature*. New York: W. W. Norton, 1997.

Mehaffy, Marilyn, and AnaLouise Keating. "'Radio Imagination': Octavia Butler on the Poetics of Narrative Embodiment." *MELUS* 26, no. 1 (spring, 2001): 45.

Raffel, Burton. "Genre to the Rear, Race and Gender to the Fore: The Novels of Octavia E. Butler." *Literary Review* 38 (April, 1995): 454.

Chesnutt, Charles W.
(Charles Waddell Chesnutt)
(1858–1932) *short story writer, novelist, biographer, essayist*

Often referred to as the father of the modern African-American novel, Charles Waddell Chesnutt was the most influential African-American fiction writer of the late 19th and early 20th centuries. His stories, novels, and essays provided realistic depictions of African-American life during the antebellum and postbellum eras, free of the racial stereotypes so frequently reinforced by white writers of those periods. Chesnutt's writing challenged deep-seated racial assumptions, and many issues addressed in his works, including miscegenation, intraracial prejudice, and the folk traditions of African-American culture, would be taken up by later generations of writers.

Born on June 20, 1858, in Cleveland, Ohio, Charles Waddell Chesnutt was the son of free African-American parents, Andrew and Ann Marie Chesnutt, who had moved from North Carolina to Ohio to escape the increasing hostility toward free men and women of color in the South prior to the Civil War. In 1866 Andrew returned with his family to Fayetteville, North Carolina, where young Charles grew up. Chesnutt attended the Howard School, an all-black facility established by the Freedmen's Bureau in 1865. Faced with the need to help support his family, Chesnutt arranged to work as a student teacher at the Howard School, which allowed him to study and earn money. Two years later, he moved to Charlotte, North Carolina, to work as a full-time teacher. He returned to Fayetteville in 1877 and became the assistant principal, and later principal, of Howard School.

Chesnutt married Susan Utley Perry, a fellow teacher, in 1878. He also began a period of rigorous self-study, becoming proficient in the German and French languages, mathematics, and stenography. In 1883 Chesnutt left Howard School to find more lucrative work in New York City. He worked briefly as a stenographer and journalist on Wall Street before accepting a position as a clerk for the Nickel Plate Railway Company in Cleveland, Ohio, where his wife and four children joined him in 1884. Chesnutt later became a stenographer in the office of the railway's lawyer, where he studied law and eventually passed the Ohio bar.

At age 14, Chesnutt had published his first short story in a weekly Fayetteville African-American newspaper. His first national literary success came with the publication of his story "The Goophered Grapevine" in the *Atlantic Monthly* in 1887, the first of several stories to feature the character Julius MacAdoo. These stories, which also include "Po' Sandy" (1888), "The Conjurer's Revenge" (1899), and "Dave's Neckliss" (1899), were later collected with others and published in 1899 as *The Conjure Woman*. Chesnutt published a second volume of stories, *The Wife of His Youth and Other Stories of the Color Line*, in 1900, which included stories about the intraracial prejudices against light-skinned African Americans.

Chesnutt's short fiction, particularly the stories in *The Conjure Woman*, was praised by critics for its innovative structure and its mixture of realism and fantasy. Drawing on African-American folk traditions and dialects, Chesnutt depicted the physical and psychological hardships suffered by African Americans who, like Julius MacAdoo in "The Goophered Grapevine," demonstrated remarkable strength and ingenuity in the face of overwhelming suffering, in order to preserve their lives and their communities.

In light of his growing literary success, Chesnutt abandoned his stenography business, which he had established in 1890, and devoted himself exclusively to writing. He published his first novel, *The House behind the Cedars*, in 1900. The novel depicts a tragic love story wherein two light-skinned African-American siblings, John and Rena, decide to pass for white. John's attempt is immediately successful, while Rena's true identity is discovered by the man she loves, and she is devastated by his rejection of her.

Chesnutt's second novel, *The Marrow of Tradition*, was published in 1901 and drew its plot from the Wilmington, North Carolina, race riot of 1898. Both novels received generally favorable reviews, and *The Marrow of Tradition* was praised for its disturbing examination of contemporary attitudes toward race in the post–Civil War South. Despite his moderate critical success, Chesnutt's novels sold poorly. A third novel, *The Colonel's Dream* (1905), fared no better. To ensure the financial stability of his family, Chesnutt reopened his stenography business.

In the last 25 years of his life, Chesnutt published only a handful of short stories and essays. Though commercial success as a writer eluded him, Chesnutt remained a favorite of African-American readers throughout his life. He was awarded the

Spingarn Medal by the National Association for the Advancement of Colored People in 1928 for his contributions to African-American literature. Chesnutt published his final work, the autobiographical essay "Post-Bellum, Pre-Harlem," in 1931, wherein he summarized his career as a writer and the general state of African-American literature. Charles Waddell Chesnutt died in Cleveland, Ohio, on November 15, 1932.

Despite Chesnutt's modesty regarding his literary achievements, African-American scholars have shown a steadfast interest in his works. Three previously unpublished novels, *Mandy Oxendine* (1997), *Paul Marchand, F.R.C.* (1999), and *The Quarry* (1999), have brought Chesnutt's work to a new generation of readers and have renewed scholarly interest in his accomplishments as a novelist. He is considered by many to have inaugurated the tradition of the short story in African-American literature, and he is widely acknowledged for establishing literary themes that have remained the focus of African-American authors to this day.

Further Reading

Carmian, Karen. "Charles Chesnutt: Crossing the Color Line." *Canadian Review of American Studies* 25, no. 2 (1995): 95.

Chesnutt, Charles Waddell. *Conjure Tales and Stories of the Color Line.* New York: Penguin, 2000.

———. *Stories, Novels, and Essays.* Library of America, 131. New York: Library of America, 2002.

Gates, Henry Louis, Jr., and Nellie Y. McKay, eds. *The Norton Anthology of African American Literature.* New York: W. W. Norton, 1997.

McWilliams, Dean. *Charles W. Chesnutt and the Fictions of Race.* Athens: University of Georgia Press, 2002.

Childress, Alice

(1916–1994) *playwright, novelist, screenwriter, essayist, editor*

An award-winning dramatist and novelist, Alice Childress began her career in theater as an actor with the American Negro Theatre (ANT) in New York. She later wrote, directed, and produced plays for the ANT as her creative focus shifted toward writing. The first African-American woman to have a play professionally produced on Broadway, and the first woman to receive an Obie Award for best off-Broadway play, Childress has also distinguished herself in other genres, earning a National Book Award nomination for her 1973 young adult novel, *A Hero Ain't Nothin' but a Sandwich,* which she later adapted successfully into an award-winning screenplay. "I concentrate on portraying have-nots in a have society," Childress has said about the focus of her writing, "those seldom singled out by mass media, except as source material for derogatory humor and/or condescending clinical, social analysis."

Born on October 12, 1916, in Charleston, South Carolina, Alice Childress spent her early years living in poverty. She moved to Harlem at age five to live with her grandmother, Eliza Campbell, who nurtured young Childress's creative aspirations. In Harlem's Salem Church, where her grandmother was a member, Childress learned about the social and racial struggles with which African Americans, particularly women, were forced to contend. "We went to Wednesday night testimonials," Childress explained in a 1987 interview. "Now that's where I learned to be a writer. I remember how people, mostly women, used to get up and tell their troubles to everybody."

Childress became a voracious reader, spending much of her time in the public library. She graduated from Julia Ward Junior High School, and attended Wadleigh High School for three years, but dropped out after the deaths of her mother and grandmother in the early 1930s. Left on her own to care for her only daughter after the failure of her first marriage, Childress worked several odd jobs, including positions as a domestic, an assistant machinist, and an insurance agent. In 1940 Childress joined the inaugural staff of Harlem's American Negro Theatre (ANT), an association that would last for 11 years, during

which Childress served as a writer, actor, and director of the ANT. She also played roles in numerous ANT productions, including the 1944 Broadway production of *Anna Lucasta,* in which she costarred with Ossie Davis, Ruby Dee, and Sidney Poitier.

In 1949 Childress wrote her first play, *Florence,* and established her reputation as a promising playwright. Set in a segregated train station, *Florence* uses a conversation between two women, one black and one white, to explore the subtle and unexpected ways that racism can be manifest. Other plays followed, including *Just a Little Simple* (1950), an adaptation of LANGSTON HUGHES's novel *Simple Speaks His Mind,* and *Gold through the Trees* (1952), the first play by a black woman to be professionally produced. Childress's growing success as a playwright allowed her to help improve working conditions and compensation for other black actors and stage workers by instituting union contracts in off-Broadway productions. In the 1950s Childress also wrote a series of monologues about African-American life from the perspective of a young female domestic, originally published as "Conversations from Life" in Paul Robeson's newspaper *Freedom,* and as "Here's Mildred" in the *Baltimore Afro-American.* The monologues were later published in book form as *Like One of the Family: Conversations from a Domestic's Life* (1956).

Childress's next play, *Trouble in Mind,* which she directed and starred in, opened off-Broadway in 1955 at the Mews Theatre in New York City. The play addressed the poor working conditions and the racism that many black actors suffered at the hands of white directors and producers. *Trouble in Mind* earned Childress an Obie Award in 1956 for best off-Broadway play, the first Obie given to a woman. In 1957 Childress married musician Nathan Woodward, who had composed music for some of her dramatic productions.

In 1966 Childress produced one of her most controversial plays, *Wedding Band: A Love/Hate Story in Black and White,* at the University of

Michigan in Ann Arbor. The play depicts a marriage between a white baker and a black seamstress in South Carolina during the World War I era, and highlights the overwhelming racial prejudice that divides the two lovers. Originally intended as a Broadway production, *Wedding Band* did not appear on Broadway until 1972. Childress also adapted the play for a television production by the American Broadcasting Company (ABC) in 1973. Her next projects included a television production of *Wine in the Wilderness: A Comedy-Drama* (1969); *The Freedom Drum: Martin Luther King at Montgomery, Alabama* (1969, also produced as *Young Man Martin Luther King*); two one-act plays, *String* (1970, adapted from the story "A Piece of String," by Guy de Maupassant) and

Mojo: A Black Love Story (1970); and the dramatic musical *Sea Island Song* (1977), with music written by her husband, Nathan Woodward.

With the publication of her first novel, *A Hero Ain't Nothin' but a Sandwich* (1973), Childress shifted her focus toward a young adult audience and toward the writing of fiction. A gritty and forthright look at the issue of teenage addiction, the novel depicts the life of a young heroin addict, Benjie, and includes the narrative perspectives of the people who shape his immediate environment, including family, friends, and even the pusher who supplies his drugs. The novel earned a National Book Award nomination in 1974 and was named by the *New York Times* as one of its Outstanding Books of the Year. Because

Alice Childress, shown here in 1991, became the first female recipient of the Obie Award for best off-Broadway play. *(Ray Grist)*

of its controversial subject matter, *A Hero Ain't Nothin' but a Sandwich* was banned repeatedly by several libraries until 1983, when a court injunction returned the book to library shelves. Childress also wrote the screenplay for the successful 1977 film adaptation of the novel, which starred Cicely Tyson and Paul Winfield.

Childress's other works for children include the plays *When the Rattlesnake Sounds* (1975) and *Let's Hear It for the Queen* (1976), and the young adult novel *Rainbow Jordan* (1981). Her other novels include *A Short Walk* (1977), *Many Closets* (1987), and *Those Other People* (1989). *Moms: A Praise Play for a Black Comedienne*, Childress's tribute to the life of Jackie "Moms" Mabley, was produced in 1987. In addition to writing, Childress lectured frequently on issues relating to the African-American theater and served as a visiting scholar at the Radcliffe Institute for Independent Study (now the Mary Ingraham Bunting Institute). Alice Childress died from cancer on August 14, 1994, in Queens, New York.

A pioneer in American theater in the 1940s and 1950s, Alice Childress provided a foundation for the work of several African-American women playwrights who followed her, including LORRAINE HANSBERRY, NTOZAKE SHANGE, and ADRIENNE KENNEDY. Childress was the first African-American woman to have a play produced on Broadway and the first woman to win an Obie Award. In her plays and novels, she celebrated the lives and hopes of middle-class African Americans in their struggles against racism and their pursuit of social and economic justice.

Further Reading

Andrews, William L., Frances Smith Foster, and Trudier Harris, eds. *The Concise Oxford Companion to African American Literature*. New York: Oxford, 2001.

Brown-Guillory, Elizabeth. *Wines in the Wilderness: Plays by Women from the Harlem Renaissance to the Present*. Westport, Conn.: Greenwood Publishing Group, 1990.

Childress, Alice. *A Hero Ain't Nothin' but a Sandwich*. New York: Coward, McCann, 1973. Reprint, New York: Puffin, 2000.

Jennings, La Vinia Delois. *Alice Childress*. New York: Twayne Publishers, 1995.

Cleage, Pearl
(Pearl Michelle Cleage, Pearl Lomax, Pearl Cleage Lomax)
(1948–) *playwright, novelist, essayist, poet, short story writer, journalist, editor*

An acclaimed author of plays, novels, essays, poetry, and short fiction, Pearl Cleage has called herself "an African-American Urban Nationalist Feminist Warrior." Concerned with issues of urban and cultural renewal, Cleage's writing reflects her abiding interest in the power of black women to revitalize their families and communities.

Pearl Michelle Cleage was born on December 7, 1948, in Springfield, Massachusetts, one of two daughters born to Albert Buford Cleage, a clergyman, and Doris Graham Cleage, a schoolteacher. Cleage grew up in West Detroit, Michigan, where her father preached in Presbyterian and Congregationalist churches until founding his own church, the Pan African Orthodox Christian Church. Influenced by Black Nationalism, Albert Cleage eventually changed his name to Jaramogi Abebe Agyemen. Cleage acknowledged the influence of her father's cultural and political convictions. "By the age of eight or nine," she wrote in a 1991 essay, "I understood clearly that slavery and racism had created a complex set of circumstances that impacted daily on my life as an African-American."

Cleage attended high school in Detroit and discovered that her light complexion placed her in what she has described as a "racial subgroup that is both punished and rewarded for the genes it shares with its former masters." In 1966 Cleage enrolled at Howard University, in Washington, D.C., where she studied playwriting. After a brief courtship, she married Michael Lomax, a Georgia politician with whom she had one daughter, and completed her bachelor's degree in drama and playwriting at Spelman College, in Atlanta, in 1971.

While balancing the demands of motherhood with her stressful career during the early 1970s as director of communications for the city of Atlanta, and as the press secretary for Maynard Jackson, Atlanta's first African-American mayor, Cleage also began to write poetry. Her first collection of poems, *We Don't Need No Music,* was published by Dudley Randall's Broadside Press in 1971. By 1976 Cleage had left her job in city government and began working as a freelance writer, journalist, and writer/interviewer for *Ebony Beat Journal,* an Atlanta television talk show.

Cleage had begun writing drama as a student at Howard University, where her first plays were produced in the late 1960s. In 1983 Cleage became playwright-in-residence at the Just Us Theatre Company in Atlanta, where *puppetplay* (1983), a surrealistic one-act play featuring two women and a male marionette, caught the attention of drama critics. Her first off-Broadway production, *Hospice,* debuted at the New Federal Theatre in 1983.

In 1992 Cleage's *Flyin' West* debuted at the Alliance Theater Company in Atlanta. The story of four female runaway slaves who settle in the historically black community of Nicodemus, Kansas, during the 1890s, *Flyin' West* established Cleage as a nationally known playwright and an important voice in contemporary African-American theater. "On the surface it's about homesteaders, pioneers," she explained in an interview with *American Visions.* "But it's also a way to talk about contemporary issues, like race, gender, class, feminist issues." Her other critically acclaimed plays include *Chain* (1992), *Late Bus to Mecca* (1992), *Blues for an Alabama Sky* (1995), and *Bourbon at the Border* (1997).

In addition to her theatrical productions, Cleage has also published collections of poetry,

Known initially as a playwright, Pearl Cleage has also distinguished herself as a gifted novelist. *(Barry Forbus)*

essays, and short fiction. In 1997 she published her first novel, *What Looks Like Crazy on an Ordinary Day,* which became an Oprah Winfrey Book Club selection in 1998. The novel depicts a black professional woman's return to her native Michigan home and her confrontation with her past. Cleage's other novels include *I Wish I Had a Red Dress* (2002) and *Some Things I Thought I'd Never Do* (2003).

Pearl Cleage has earned national recognition as a playwright, poet, essayist, and author of short fiction and novels. She has also served as a regular contributor for the *Atlanta Tribune,* and her essays and poems have appeared in the *African American Review,* the *New York Times Book Review,* and the *Journal of Black Poetry.* In 1986 she joined the faculty of Spelman College as an instructor of creative writing, and in 1991 became Spelman's playwright-in-residence. An outspoken feminist,

Cleage in her writing explores the daily challenges that confront African-American women, though she is concerned more with the activities than the titles of feminism. "I'm less interested in what people call themselves than in what they do," she explained in a *Los Angeles Times* interview. "If they are working in neighborhoods, raising their children and struggling to build positive relationships with women and men, then I call that a feminist."

Further Reading

Cleage, Pearl. *The Brass Bed and Other Stories.* Detroit, Mich.: Third World Press, 1991.
———. *Deals with the Devil, and Other Reasons to Riot.* New York: Ballantine, 1993.
———. *What Looks Like Crazy on an Ordinary Day: A Novel.* New York: Avon Books, 1997.
Giles, Frieda Scott. "The Motion of Herstory: Three Plays by Pearl Cleage." *African American Review* 31 (winter 1997): 709.

Cliff, Michelle

(1946–) *novelist, short story writer, poet, essayist, educator*

Born in Jamaica and educated in the United States and England, Michelle Cliff has experienced the differences of race and class in a variety of cultural contexts. Her novels, short fiction, poetry, and essays explore the inherent ambiguity in the lives of individuals and communities that have been marginalized by colonialism, racism, and gender and sexual prejudice. "In my writing I am concerned most of all with social issues and political realities," Cliff has stated, "and how they affect the lives of people."

Michelle Cliff was born on November 2, 1946, in Kingston, Jamaica. At the age of three, Cliff moved to New York with her family and grew up primarily among other West Indian immigrants. At the age of 10, Cliff returned to Jamaica and attended Kingston's St. Andrews High School

for Girls. An early interest in writing, influenced by her reading of *The Diary of Anne Frank* as a child, was discouraged by her parents, who humiliated Cliff by seizing her personal diary and reading portions to other family members. "That incident really shut me down as a writer," she recalled in a 1994 interview.

Cliff received her bachelor's degree in European history from Wagner College in New York in 1969, after which she served as an editor for W. W. Norton. In 1971 she enrolled at the Warburg Institute in London; she received a master's degree in comparative literature in 1974. Cliff returned to New York and resumed her work as an editor for W. W. Norton until 1979, at which time she resigned to pursue her renewed interest in writing.

From early childhood, Cliff balanced her time between the United States and Jamaica, where she often returned to spend her summers. The differences in culture and attitudes toward race between her native Jamaica and other regions in which she studied and worked would provide a rich and painful source of material for her writing.

In her first published book, *Claiming an Identity They Taught Me to Despise* (1980), Cliff explores in a series of prose poems the difficulty of growing up on the margins of society in New York and Jamaica, where the legacy of colonialism has created a complex class system based on color. In poems such as "Notes on Speechlessness," "Obsolete Geography," and "The Laughing Mulatto (Formerly a Statue) Speaks," Cliff links the suppression of cultural and sexual identity with a denial of speech. The inability to integrate personal and cultural identity would remain a major theme in her fiction writing.

In her first novel, *Abeng* (1984), Cliff depicts the relationship between Clare Savage, a light-skinned girl, and her friend Zoe, who has a darker complexion, as each struggles with issues of race, class, and sexual identity while growing up in the complex social structure of colonial Jamaica. The character of Clare returns in Cliff's second novel, *No Telephone to Heaven* (1987), as she travels to Jamaica as an adult to confront her past in a society that systematically deprives individuals of their racial heritage. *Free Enterprise* (1993), Cliff's third novel, explores the relationship between two African-American women who aid John Brown during his 1859 raid on Harpers Ferry.

Cliff's other works include *The Land of Look Behind: Prose and Poetry* (1985), and two collections of short stories, *Bodies of Water* (1990) and *The Store of a Million Items: Stories* (1998). Like her novels, Cliff's short fiction examines the lasting effects of racial and cultural prejudice in Jamaica and the United States and the ways that individuals react to such oppression in their personal lives.

An important voice in the growing body of Afro-Caribbean and Caribbean-American literatures, Cliff has also maintained a distinguished teaching career, with academic appointments at such institutions as New York's New School University; Trinity College, in Hartford, Connecticut; and the University of California at Santa Cruz. As a writer and educator, Michelle Cliff focuses on the racial and political oppression of all colonized people, from Africa and the Caribbean to the enduring legacy of oppression for African Americans. "I have experienced colonialism as a force first-hand," Cliff has stated. "Thus colonialism—and the racism upon which it is based—are subjects I address in most of my writing."

Further Reading

Adisa, Opal Palmer. "Journey into Speech—A Writer between Two Worlds: An Interview with Michelle Cliff." *African American Review* 28 (summer 1994): 273.

Cliff, Michelle. *Abeng.* Trumansburg, N.Y.: Crossing Press, 1984.

———. *No Telephone to Heaven.* New York: E. P. Dutton, 1987.

———. *The Store of a Million Items: Stories.* Boston, Mass.: Houghton Mifflin, 1998.

Clifton, Lucille
(Thelma Lucille Sayles)
(1936–   ) *poet, children's fiction writer, essayist, autobiographer*

A three-time Pulitzer Prize nominee and National Book Award winner, Lucille Clifton has earned numerous critical and popular accolades for her poetry, memoirs, and children's fiction. Clifton's writing explores the dynamic relationship between personal and cultural identity. "The proper subject of poetry is life," Clifton explained in a 1993 National Public Radio interview.

Lucille Clifton was born Thelma Lucille Sayles on June 27, 1936, in Depew, New York, one of three children born to Samuel and Thelma Moore Sayles. She grew up in a working-class household that included her grandparents and several uncles. Among these, her great-grandmother Caroline Sale Donald played a central role in her emotional and creative development. Born in Africa and brought to America as a slave, Caroline escaped to the North as a young girl. Many of Clifton's poems and children's stories owe their inspiration to the life of her great-grandmother.

During her early childhood, she moved with her family to Buffalo, New York, where she grew up and attended public schools. Her interest in writing was inspired in part by her parents, who were both great readers, and particularly her mother, who also wrote poetry. At age 16, she left Buffalo to attend Howard University, in Washington, D.C., on a full scholarship provided by her church.

At Howard, she studied under such notable professors and writers as A. B. Spellman, playwright and poet OWEN DODSON, and STERLING BROWN. Her classmates included AMIRI BARAKA and TONI MORRISON (then Chloe Wofford). She decided to study drama, and she appeared in the premiere performance of JAMES BALDWIN's play *The Amen Corner* in 1954. She returned to New York in 1955 and enrolled at Fredonia State Teachers College. There she joined a community of students, one of whom was ISHMAEL REED, who met to read and perform plays, and she began to write poetry.

Following her graduation in 1958, she married Fred James Clifton, with whom she would have six children over the next seven years. While balancing her time between her family and her job as a clerk for the New York State Department of Employment, she also began to focus on her writing. In 1969 Clifton sent some of her poems to ROBERT HAYDEN, who in turn submitted them to a literary competition for unknown writers. Clifton won the competition, and that year her first collection of poems, *Good Times,* was published by Random House.

Lucille Clifton attends a reception in New York prior to her acceptance of the 2000 National Book Award for poetry. *(AP/Wide World Photos)*

The poems in *Good Times* reflect the abiding interests of all Clifton's writing: a strong sense of family, a keen and proud awareness of her African-American heritage, and the coexistence of great suffering and great joy in urban African-American communities. Selected by the *New York Times* as one of the best books of 1969, *Good Times* established Clifton's reputation as a major American poet.

In 1970 Clifton published her first children's book, *Some of the Days of Everett Anderson,* about the life of a young African-American boy. In succeeding volumes featuring the young protagonist, Clifton documents the changes in Everett's family and personal life. Other volumes in this successful and award-winning series include *Everett Anderson's Christmas Coming* (1971), *Everett Anderson's Year* (1974), *Everett Anderson's 1-2-3* (1977), *Everett Anderson's Nine Month Long* (1978), *Everett Anderson's Goodbye* (1988), which won the Coretta Scott King Award from the American Library Association, *Everett Anderson's Friend* (1993), and *One of the Problems of Everett Anderson* (2001).

Clifton's books for children provide lessons in cultural diversity, racial heritage, and family life, in order to help children understand the world. In *All Us Come 'cross the Water* (1973), she explores the connection between Africa and African-Americans. Oriented particularly toward African-American children, Clifton's children's books also feature characters of other ethnicities. *Sonora Beautiful* (1981) features a young white girl as its protagonist. Her other works for children include *The Boy Who Didn't Believe in Spring* (1973), *The Lucky Stone* (1979), and *The Times They Used to Be* (2000).

From 1971 to 1974 Clifton served as poet-in-residence at Coppin State College, in Baltimore, Maryland, during which time she published *Good News About the Earth* (1972) and *An Ordinary Woman* (1974). Her stature as a poet was confirmed in 1974 when she was named poet laureate of the state of Maryland. In 1980 she was nominated for a Pulitzer Prize for her fourth collection of poetry, *Two-Headed Woman.* Following the death of her husband in 1984, Clifton joined the faculty of the University of California at Santa Cruz. She published two additional volumes of poetry in 1987, *Good Woman: Poems and a Memoir, 1969 to 1980* (also nominated for a Pulitzer Prize), and *Next: New Poems.*

In 1989 Clifton returned to Maryland and received an appointment as professor of literature and humanities at St. Mary's College. Clifton received her third Pulitzer Prize nomination in 1991 for *Quilting: Poems, 1987–1990.* Her other collections of poetry include *The Book of Light* (1993), *Selected Poems* (1996), *The Terrible Stories* (1996), a National Book Award nominee, and *Blessing the Boats: New and Selected Poems, 1988–2000* (2000), which won the National Book Award. Clifton has also published a prose autobiography, *Generations: A Memoir* (1976), which was reprinted in *Good Woman: Selected Poems and a Memoir.*

A nationally acclaimed author of poetry, memoirs, and children's fiction, Lucille Clifton has been hailed as one of the finest poets of the 20th century. In 1998 she was appointed Blackburn Professor of Creative Writing at Duke University in Durham, North Carolina. She has performed her poetry for audiences across the United States. In her poems and stories, Clifton celebrates the bonds of family, community, and racial heritage, in a voice that is distinctly black and female. "I am a black woman poet," Clifton has stated, "and I talk like one."

Further Reading

Clifton, Lucille. *Blessing the Boats: New and Selected Poems, 1988–2000.* Rochester, N.Y.: BOA Editions, 2000.

———. *Good Woman: Poems and a Memoir, 1969–1980.* Rochester, N.Y.: BOA Editions, 1987.

———. *The Terrible Stories: Poems.* Rochester, N.Y.: BOA Editions, 1996.

Glaser, Michael S. "I'd Like Not to Be a Stranger in the World." *Antioch Review* 58 (summer 2000): 310.

Coleman, Wanda
(Wanda Evans)
(1946–   ) poet, short story writer, novelist

In her citation for Wanda Coleman's Lenore Marshall Poetry Prize, awarded in 1999, poet Marilyn Hacker described Coleman as a poet "whose angry and extravagant music . . . has been making itself heard across the divide between West Coast and East, establishment and margins, slams and seminars, across the too-American rift among races and genders . . . for two decades." An award-winning poet, Coleman is also an accomplished short fiction writer, and she won an Emmy for her writing on the daytime drama *Days of Our Lives* in 1976.

Born Wanda Evans on November 13, 1946, in Los Angeles, California, she was raised by her parents, George and Lewana Evans, in the Watts section of Los Angeles. She began writing poetry as an adolescent and published her earliest poetry in local newspapers. The Watts riot of 1965, in which 34 people, mostly black, lost their lives, highlighted the racial tensions and depressed economic conditions of Los Angeles's inner cities, and it helped fuel the national debate on civil rights. The plight of the urban poor, particularly women, would also become a central theme in her poetry and prose.

After attending college in Los Angeles for two years, Evans served as writer-in-residence at Studio Watts from 1968 to 1969. She published her first short story, "Watching the Sunset," in *Negro Digest* in 1970. Married with two children by the age of 20, Coleman was compelled to balance her career as a writer with the needs of her family. She worked several jobs, including stints as a waitress, medical secretary, proofreader, Peace Corps recruiter, and staff writer for NBC's *Days of Our Lives,* for which she won an Emmy for best writing in a daytime drama in 1976.

In 1977 Black Sparrow Press published Coleman's first volume of poetry, the chapbook *Art in the Court of the Blue Fag.* Established in the 1960s as a literary source for noncommercial, avant-

Wanda Coleman has electrified audiences across the nation with her spoken-word performances, often with the accompaniment of jazz musicians. *(George Evans)*

garde writers such as Charles Bukowski, whose poetry was an early inspiration for Coleman, Black Sparrow Press has remained Coleman's principal publisher. Her poetry collections *Mad Dog Black Lady* (1979) and *Imagoes* (1983) expanded her growing regional success to a national audience, and she was awarded fellowships from the National Endowment for the Arts in 1981 and the Guggenheim Foundation in 1984. Coleman also earned wide acclaim as a performance poet, combining elements of jazz and blues rhythms with the vivid depictions of the violence and poverty so frequently a part of life in Los Angeles's racially polarized urban communities.

Heavy Daughter Blues: Poems and Stories 1968–1986, published in 1987, included several of Coleman's short stories in addition to her poems. Other volumes of verse and prose followed, including a collection of short stories, *A War of Eyes and Other Stories* (1988), which solidified her reputation as a respected writer of fic-

tion; *African Sleeping Sickness: Stories and Poems* (1990), which won the Harriette Simpson Arnow Prize for fiction; and *Hand Dance* (1993). Coleman also published several autobiographical and journalistic pieces about her experiences in Los Angeles in the 1996 collection *Native in a Strange Land: Trials and Tremors.*

Shifting between moments of resignation and rage, Coleman's *Bathwater Wine* (1998), which received the Lenore Marshall Poetry Prize in 1999, provides a poignant look at the poet's personal life. She writes of her adolescence in the lengthy and atmospheric "Dreamwalk." In "American Sonnet 35," a continuation of a series of poems begun in earlier collections, she describes the frustration of unrealized ambitions: "usta be young usta be gifted—still black."

In 1999 Coleman published her first novel, *Mambo Hips and Make Believe,* in which she chronicles the relationship between two women from diverse racial and economic backgrounds. Tamala and Erlene, both of whom dream of becoming writers, confront the personal and physical obstacles that stand between them and the realization of their goals. Following the publication of her chapbook memoir *Love-ins with Nietzsche,* published in 2000, Coleman released her most acclaimed volume of poetry, *Mercurochrome: New Poems* (2001), which was a finalist for the 2001 National Book Award. This collection features several portraits of family members, including one of her son, whose untimely death from cancer is memorialized in the poem "Christening." In the poem "Essay on Language," Coleman decries the "bloodless banal crap" that she finds typical of much contemporary poetry. One of the sections of *Mercurochrome,* entitled "Retro Rogue Anthology," features a series of fascinating "imitations and transliterations," as Coleman calls them, of several renowned American poets, most of them white.

A passionate and dynamic poet, as well as a novelist, short story writer, and an Emmy Award–winning television writer, Wanda Coleman has also distinguished herself as a powerful spoken word performer. Incorporating jazz and blues to complement her words, she has amazed audiences with the energy and conviction of her verse. Sometimes overlooked by critics because of her unconventional style, Coleman has continued to challenge critics and readers alike with the depth and force of her vision as a writer and her uncompromising approach to racial and gender equality.

Further Reading

Andrews, William L., Frances Smith Foster, and Trudier Harris, eds. *The Concise Oxford Companion to African American Literature.* New York: Oxford University Press, 2001.

Coleman, Wanda. *Mercurochrome: New Poems.* Santa Rosa, Calif.: Black Sparrow Press, 2001.

———. *Native in a Strange Land: Trials and Tremors.* Santa Rosa, Calif.: Black Sparrow Press, 1996.

Gates, Henry Louis, Jr., and Nellie Y. McKay, eds. *The Norton Anthology of African American Literature.* New York: W. W. Norton, 1997.

Cooper, Anna Julia
(Anna Julia Haywood Cooper)
(1858–1964) *essayist, educator*

During the late 19th century, when early American feminists such as Susan B. Anthony fought for greater social and political equality for women in the United States, Anna Julia Cooper courageously challenged those who refused to include African-American women within the debate on gender equality. Finding that feminist leaders were largely concerned only with the needs of white women, Cooper became the voice of dispossessed black women in her only book-length work, *A Voice from the South by a Black Woman of the South,* which remains a seminal text of American feminism.

Cooper was born Anna Julia Haywood on August 10, 1858, in Raleigh, North Carolina. Her mother, Hannah Stanley Haywood, was one of hundreds of slaves owned by George Washington Haywood, whom Cooper believed to have been her father. Following the end of the Civil War and the coming of emancipation, Cooper earned a place in St. Augustine's Normal School and Collegiate Institute, a training school for teachers, where she distinguished herself as an exceptionally gifted student. She graduated to the level of student teacher by the age of eight and faced severe opposition when she expressed a desire to study mathematics and science, courses of study that were traditionally reserved for male students.

Cooper left St. Augustine's in 1877 to marry George Cooper, a former slave and fellow student. Following her husband's death two years later, she enrolled as a sophomore in Oberlin College in Ohio in 1881. She received her undergraduate degree in 1884 and a graduate degree in mathematics four years later. While finishing her graduate degree, she began teaching at Wilberforce University and later returned to St. Augustine's for a year as an instructor. Cooper moved to Washington, D.C., in 1887, where she accepted a position as a Latin and mathematics teacher at Washington High School, later renamed Dunbar High School after the nationally celebrated African-American poet PAUL LAURENCE DUNBAR.

During her 38 years as a teacher at the nation's preeminent African-American secondary school, Cooper played an essential role in shaping its academically rigorous curriculum. She emphasized the need for African Americans, particularly women, to seek college degrees and to study physical sciences and liberal arts during an era where black students were primarily encouraged to pursue vocational training. Objecting to the work of BOOKER T. WASHINGTON and his successful Tuskegee Normal and Industrial Institute in Alabama, whose curricula stressed economic independence through vocational training, Cooper insisted that African Americans should have unrestricted access to higher education.

Equal educational opportunities for African Americans, and the full enfranchisement of

African-American women in the fight for gender equality, became two central themes in Cooper's acclaimed collection of essays, *A Voice from the South by a Black Woman of the South,* published in 1892. A monumental work that many modern critics cite as the touchstone of contemporary black feminist theory, *A Voice from the South* attempted to fill a void in the national debate on race, in which there has been "no word from the Black Woman," as Cooper states in her preface. In 1893 Cooper addressed a largely white audience at the World's Congress of Representative Women in Chicago, Illinois. Her address, under the title "I Speak for the Colored Women of the South," reiterated the importance of not overlooking the claims of African-American women in the pursuit of equality.

In 1901 Cooper was appointed principal of M Street High School, as Washington High School was subsequently named. She devoted herself to maintaining a curriculum that would ensure her students the opportunity to compete for positions in the best schools in the country. By 1906, however, her efforts created conflict with the local school board, and after refusing to modify her program, she was fired. She was later rehired, though only as a teacher, and would remain there until her retirement in 1929. In 1914 she began postgraduate studies at Columbia University in French literature and history. She was invited in 1924 to finish her degree at the Sorbonne in Paris, from which she received her Ph.D. in 1925. Her dissertation, on French attitudes toward slavery, was published in France in 1925.

Following her retirement from M Street High School, ultimately renamed Dunbar High School, Cooper served as president of Frelinghuysen University in Washington, D.C., a night school for working African Americans. She also continued to write, publishing two short works, *Legislative Measures Concerning Slavery in the United States* (1942) and *Equality of Races and the Democratic Movement* (1945). In 1951 she edited the two-volume collection *Life and Writings of the Grimké*

Family. Anna Julia Cooper died on February 27, 1964, at the age of 105.

A remarkable scholar, author, activist, and pioneering feminist, Anna Julia Cooper devoted her life to the social and political advancement of African-American women. She was a fearless educator who stressed the centrality of higher education as a means of empowerment. At the Pan-African Conference in London in 1900, organized in part by the eminent sociologist and scholar W. E. B. DuBOIS, she was one of only a few women invited to speak. Her defense of the power and dignity of women to effect social and moral change in *A Voice from the South* has continued to inform modern black feminist theory, and elements of her thought can be found in the work of many contemporary African-American authors, including TONI MORRISON and ALICE WALKER.

Further Reading

Alexander, Elizabeth. "'We Must Be about Our Father's Business': Anna Julia Cooper and the In-Corporation of the Nineteenth Century African American Woman Intellectual." *Signs: Journal of Women in Culture and Society* 20, no. 2 (winter 1995): 336.

Cooper, Anna Julia. *A Voice from the South.* New York: Oxford University Press, 1988.

Gates, Henry Louis, Jr., and Nellie Y. McKay, eds. *The Norton Anthology of African American Literature.* New York: W. W. Norton, 1997.

Johnson, Karen Ann. *Uplifting the Women and the Race: The Lives, Educational Philosophies and Social Activism of Anna Julia Cooper and Nannie Helen Burroughs.* New York: Garland Publishing, 2000.

Cooper, J. California
(Joan California Cooper, Joan Cooper, Juan Andres Correa Guzman)
(unknown–   ) *novelist, short story writer, playwright, essayist*

J. California Cooper first gained national attention as a playwright, earning an award as Black

Playwright of the Year in 1978. Also the author of novels, short stories, and essays, Cooper has earned comparisons to LANGSTON HUGHES and ZORA NEALE HURSTON for her incorporation of African-American folklore, her use of dialects, and the underlying moral focus of her writing.

J. California Cooper was born Joan Cooper in Berkeley, California, the daughter of Maxine and Joseph Cooper. A reluctant literary celebrity, Cooper has revealed few biographical details about her personal life. She began writing at an early age, composing plays and stories for her paper dolls, which she continued to play with until the age of 17. Cooper has been married, admitting only that she has had more than one husband, and has a daughter, Paris A. Williams.

Most of Cooper's writings were unknown until she achieved success as a playwright. She has written more than a dozen plays, including *Everytime It Rains, The Unintended,* and *Strangers.* For *Strangers,* which was performed at the San Francisco Palace of Fine Arts, Cooper was named Black Playwright of the Year in 1978. Another play, *Loners,* was anthologized in Eileen Ostrow's *Center Stage* (1981). Like her short stories and novels, Cooper's plays, which have been performed on stage, radio, and public television, focus particularly on the relationships between men and women.

Though critically acclaimed as a playwright, Cooper is best known for her short stories. Cooper published her first collection of short stories, *A Piece of Mine,* in 1984, the first title to be released by novelist ALICE WALKER's Wild Trees Press. "In its strong folk flavor," Walker wrote in her introduction to *A Piece of Mine,* "Cooper's work reminds me of Langston Hughes and Zora Neale Hurston." Cooper's short stories generally feature female narrators who relate the details of their relationships with friends, other women, and the men in their lives, in an easy, conversational style, often employing dialect and almost always containing a moral lesson. Cooper's other short story collections include *Homemade Love* (1986), which

won the American Book Award, *Some Soul to Keep* (1987), *The Matter Is Life* (1991), *Some Love, Some Pain* (1995), and *The Future Has a Past: Stories* (2000).

In addition to plays and short fiction, Cooper has published three novels: *Family* (1991), *In Search of Satisfaction* (1994), and *The Wake of the Wind* (1998). *Family* chronicles the life of a slave named Always during the Civil War era and describes the four generations of her family that followed. *In Search of Satisfaction,* another historical novel, depicts the life of an ex-slave, Josephus Josephus, and his descendants, and spans a period from the American Civil War to the 1920s. Her third novel, *The Wake of the Wind,* is a rich historical tale of two African friends, Kola and Suwaibu, who are brought to America as slaves, and follows the generations of their families, which unite in the marriage of Kola and Suwaibu's great-great-great grandchildren.

J. California Cooper has earned several literary honors, including the Black Playwright of the Year award for 1978, an American Book Award in 1986 for *Homemade Love,* the James Baldwin Writing Award in 1988, and the Literary Lion Award from the American Library Association, also in 1988. She lives in northern California and claims that she writes her stories and novels by hand, only when it rains, as the characters come to her and tell their stories. "This happens during the rainy season," she explained in a 1995 interview with *Emerge.* "With the rain comes these people." Despite her intense concern for personal privacy, Cooper often gives public readings of her works, always wearing a yellow and green floral print muumuu. "All my characters fit in there with me," she says of the dress. "I've worn it for every single reading for every book for the last ten years."

Further Reading

Andrews, William L., Frances Smith Foster, and Trudier Harris, eds. *The Concise Oxford Companion to African American Literature.* New York: Oxford University Press, 2001.

Cooper, J. California. *Family*. New York: Doubleday, 1991.

———. *The Future Has a Past: Stories*. New York: Doubleday, 2000.

———. *Homemade Love*. New York: St. Martin's Press, 1986.

———. *The Wake of the Wind*. New York: Doubleday, 1998.

Corrothers, James
(James David Corrothers, James David Carruthers)
(1869–1917) *poet, journalist*

James Corrothers was one of the most productive and widely published African-American writers of the late 19th and early 20th centuries. His work, both in prose and poetry, appeared in numerous magazines and newspapers, and several poems are still included in anthologies of black literature.

Corrothers was born in Cass County, Michigan, on July 2, 1869, the son of James and Maggie Carruthers. He grew up in the predominantly white community of South Haven, Michigan, where he was raised by his grandfather. A good student when he was able to attend school, Corrothers, who changed the spelling of his last name in grade school, spent most of his youth working to help support himself and his grandfather. When he had the time, he read poetry, including the works of Henry Wadsworth Longfellow, Alfred, Lord Tennyson, and James Whitcomb Riley, among others.

As a teenager, Corrothers moved frequently, living in Muskegon, Michigan, and Springfield, Ohio, and finding work where it was available. While in Springfield, he published his first poem, "The Deserted School House," in a local newspaper. His literary career gained momentum when, at age 18, he moved to Chicago, Illinois. He met the journalist and social reformer Henry Demarest Lloyd while working in a white barbershop. Lloyd helped him publish one of his poems in the *Chicago Tribune* and arranged for his employment at the newspaper as a porter. He was also given

an assignment to write an article on the black community in Chicago.

Also with Lloyd's help, and the assistance of the temperance leader Frances Willard, Corrothers continued his education at a preparatory school operated by Northwestern University and later attended Bennett College in North Carolina. Initially interested in a career in journalism, he was inspired by the success of the poet PAUL LAURENCE DUNBAR and his dialect poetry. After publishing several humorous sketches of urban African-American life, later collected in *The Black Cat Club* (1902), Corrothers published his own dialect poem "Way in de Woods" in the magazine *Century* in 1899, and his reputation as a poet began to grow.

Finding his opportunities in journalism as an African American increasingly limited, Corrothers joined the African Methodist Episcopal Church and became a minister, a career he maintained in several denominations to the end of his life. He continued to write poetry, and his religious faith informed his work by adding an element of hope to his perspective on race relations in America.

With the publication of his poem "The Snapping of the Bow" in 1901, Corrothers began to rely more on Standard English than dialect, and his verse exhibited a quiet but powerful protest of racism. In that poem, he describes a black youth who, Atlas-like, "clutched the stars" and "shook / The pillars of the firmament of God." He also uses the image of the Sphinx to suggest that "The race might rise that built the awful thing / That holds its secret still in Egypt's sands." Corrothers remained hopeful that, given time, social and political conditions would improve for African Americans. He also located the roots of African-American culture in a distant past that was both mysterious and magnificent.

Corrothers devoted most of his final years to his wife, Rosina, whom he married in 1906, his son Henry, and his work in the church, while also producing some of his most acclaimed work, including the poem "At the Closed Gate of Justice," published in 1913. Less hopeful than his early poetry, the poem reflects Corrothers's increasing frustration with racial prejudice and a growing belief that justice, referred to in the poem as "the glorious goal unwon," would remain beyond reach. Prior to his death on February 12, 1917, he also published a number of prose works, including his autobiography, *In Spite of the Handicap* (1916). James David Corrothers died of a stroke on February 12, 1917, in West Chester, Pennsylvania.

Further Reading

Andrews, William L., Frances Smith Foster, and Trudier Harris, eds. *The Concise Oxford Companion to African American Literature.* New York: Oxford University Press, 2001.

Corrothers, James D. *The Black Cat Club: Negro Humor and Folk-Lore.* New York: AMS Press, 2002.

Gates, Henry Louis, Jr., and Nellie Y. McKay, eds. *The Norton Anthology of African American Literature.* New York: W. W. Norton, 1997.

Cortez, Jayne
(1936–) *poet*

Jayne Cortez has earned international acclaim as a literary and performance poet. In her politically charged writing, and in her live performances, where she is often accompanied by jazz and blues musicians, Cortez celebrates the strength of African Americans in the face of social, economic, and racial oppression. "I think that poets have the responsibility to be aware of the meaning of human rights," Cortez explained in a 1996 interview, ". . . to be familiar with history, to point out distortions, and to bring their thinking and their writing to higher levels of illumination."

Born in Fort Huachuca, Arizona, on May 10, 1936, Jayne Cortez was raised in Los Angeles, California. She attended Compton Junior College and initially pursued a career in acting. In 1954 Cortez married jazz musician Ornette Coleman,

with whom she had one son, Denardo Coleman. Jazz music would eventually play a central role in her work as a poet. Cortez and Coleman divorced in 1964. That same year, Cortez cofounded the Watts Repertory Theatre and served as its artistic director until 1970.

Cortez moved to New York City in 1967 and published her first collection of poems, *Pissstained Stairs and the Monkey Man's Wares,* two years later. In poems like the frequently anthologized "How Long Has Trane Been Gone," an elegiac tribute to jazz saxophonist John Coltrane, Cortez demonstrated her keen ability to capture the rhythm and intensity of jazz in her verse. In 1970 Cortez started her own publishing company, Bola Press, through which she published *Festivals and Funerals* (1971), *Scarifications* (1973), *Mouth on Paper* (1977), *Firespitter* (1982), and *Poetic Magnetic* (1991), all of which feature illustrations by sculptor and illustrator Melvin Edwards, whom she married in 1975. Her other poetry collections include *Somewhere in Advance of Nowhere* (1996) and *Jazz Fan Looks Back* (2002).

During her years of involvement with the Watts Repertory Theatre, and later in the coffeehouses and clubs of Manhattan, Cortez honed her skills as a stirring performance poet. Combining vivid, often disturbing images of urban life with lyrical and percussive language, Cortez thrilled listeners with her passionate verse. She released her first CD recording of her poetry, *Celebrations and Solitudes,* in 1975. Later recordings included *Unsubmissive Blues* (1980), *There It Is* (1982), *Maintain Control* (1986), *Everywhere Drums* (1991), and *Taking the Blues Back Home* (1997). On most of her recordings, her band, The Firespitters, featuring her son on drums, accompanies her.

In November 2001 Cortez received the LANGSTON HUGHES Award during the annual Langston Hughes Festival. Commenting on the role of improvisation in her poetry, she described it as "where you came from at the time," saying that poets "should have enough experience and knowledge to have something to improvise about." Much of Cortez's improvisation seems to spring from spontaneous and violent reactions to the physical, racial, and psychological abuse of women, and her perceptions of the lingering presence of racial discrimination in American society and ever-increasing globalization by a corporate-driven country that continues to value commodities over communities and products over people.

An internationally celebrated performance artist and poet, Jayne Cortez has performed and lectured at various organizations, universities, and events throughout the United States and Europe, including the Fourth World Congress of Women in Beijing, China, and the Berlin Jazz Festival. In 1999 she was instrumental in bringing UNESCO's symposium, *Slave Routes: The Long Memory*, to New York University. She has also been the recipient of numerous fellowships and grants, and she won the American Book Award in 1980 for *Mouth on Paper* (1977). The renowned memoirist and poet MAYA ANGELOU has described Cortez as "an explorer, probing the valleys and chasms of human existence." Cortez's poetry embodies much of the political and racial protest themes that grew out of the Black Arts Movement in the 1960s, and her success has helped renew critical interest in this often-neglected era in African-American literature.

Further Reading

Andrews, William L., Frances Scott Smith, and Trudier Harris, eds. *The Concise Oxford Companion to African American Literature*. New York: Oxford University Press, 2001.

Bolden, Tony. "All the Birds Sing Bass: The Revolutionary Blues of Jayne Cortez." *African American Review* 35, no. 1 (spring 2001): 61.

Cortez, Jayne. *Jazz Fan Looks Back*. New York: Hanging Loose Press, 2002.

———. *Somewhere in Advance of Nowhere*. New York: Serpent's Tale Press, 1996.

Cullen, Countee
(Countee Leroy Porter, Countee Porter Cullen)
(1903–1946) *poet, novelist, editor, educator*

Considered by many to be the most promising poet of the Harlem Renaissance, Countee Cullen, perhaps more than any other writer of his generation, embodied the ideals of what the philosopher and patriarch of the Harlem Renaissance, ALAIN LOCKE, called the "New Negro." Praised by white and African-American critics alike for the lyrical beauty of his verse, Cullen also drew criticism from fellow writers for his resistance to writing about predominantly racial themes and his reliance on traditional forms of poetic expression. Though Cullen, like JAMES WELDON JOHNSON before him, was more concerned with being a poet than a black poet, he remained somewhat divided on this point. Some of his most celebrated poetry speaks eloquently to the pain and disillusionment of African-American life in a racially oppressive society.

Countee Leroy Porter was born on May 30, 1903, probably in Louisville, Kentucky, though he would later claim New York City as his birthplace. He moved to New York City at the age of nine, where Elizabeth Porter, thought to be his grandmother, raised him until her death in 1918. The Reverend Frederick Cullen, the pastor of Harlem's Salem Methodist Episcopal Church, took charge of Countee following his grandmother's death. Though the Cullens never formally adopted him, they provided Countee with a loving and stable family. He was equally devoted to them, ultimately choosing their surname as his own.

Cullen attended DeWitt Clinton High School from 1918 to 1921, where he distinguished himself as an outstanding student, orator, and burgeoning poet. He was a member of the school's honor society, Arista, and he served as associate editor of *Magpie*, the school's literary magazine. His first poem, "Song of the Poets," appeared in *Magpie* in 1918, and Cullen later won first prize in a citywide poetry contest with his poem "I Have a

Rendezvous with Life." The vice president of his senior class, Cullen graduated from DeWitt Clinton in 1921 and enrolled in New York University on a State Regents Scholarship.

As an undergraduate, Cullen won second prize in the Walter Bynner Poetry Contest, open to all American undergraduate students, in 1923 and 1924. He also began publishing poems in the *Crisis*, the National Association for the Advancement of Colored People's literary magazine; *Opportunity*, published by the National Urban League and edited by Charles S. Johnson; and the literary journals *Poetry, Bookman, Harper's,* and H. L. Mencken's *American Mercury.* Cullen's conservative and erudite style as a poet, and the remarkable lyricism of his verse, caught the attention of white and African-American critics. In 1925 Cullen won first prize in the Walter Bynner Poetry Contest and graduated from New York University, where he was elected to the academic honor society Phi Beta Kappa.

Cullen began his graduate studies at Harvard University in 1925. That same year, he published his first volume of poetry, *Color,* and won the John Reed Memorial Prize from *Poetry* magazine for his poem "Threnody for a Brown Girl," as well as the Spingarn Medal from *Crisis* for his poem "Two Moods of Love." The publication of *Color* secured Cullen a reputation as the most celebrated African-American poet since PAUL LAURENCE DUNBAR. A collection of 74 poems, *Color* included some of Cullen's most memorable verse, including "Heritage," praised by the poet LANGSTON HUGHES as the most beautiful poem that he knew, and the frequently anthologized "Yet Do I Marvel," in which Cullen muses on a God that would "make a poet black, and bid him sing!"

In 1927 Cullen graduated from Harvard with a master's degree in English and French and returned to New York to work as an assistant editor for *Opportunity.* During the late 1920s Cullen won numerous literary prizes, a Guggenheim Fellowship, and the Harmon Foundation Literary Award for his celebrated anthology of African-American poetry, *Caroling Dusk,* published in

1927. He also released two more volumes of poems, *Copper Sun* and *The Ballad of the Brown Girl.* During the height of his popularity as a poet and literary icon in Harlem, Cullen married Yolande DuBois, the daughter of the eminent sociologist and literary critic W. E. B. DuBOIS, in 1928. Thousands of spectators, including all of the leading social and literary figures of Harlem, attended the wedding, which was performed in Reverend Cullen's church. Two months after his marriage, however, Cullen left New York to study in Europe without his wife, and he concluded divorce proceedings from Paris two years later.

With the publication of *The Black Christ and Other Poems* (1929), Cullen's literary reputation began to suffer. His predominantly romantic themes put him at odds with the work of contem-

Countee Cullen poses in Central Park in New York City. *(Library of Congress)*

poraries like Langston Hughes, Claude McKay, and Zora Neale Hurston. His assertion, in the preface to *Caroling Dusk,* that "Negro poets . . . may have more to gain from the rich background of English and American poetry than from any nebulous atavistic yearnings toward an African inheritance," drew considerable criticism from other black writers and artists.

In 1932 Cullen published the novel *One Way to Heaven,* a parody of Harlem life in the tradition of WALLACE THURMAN's *Infants of the Spring* (1932) and GEORGE SCHUYLER's *Black No More* (1931). Though it provided an insider's perspective on Harlem life during the pivotal period of the Harlem Renaissance, some critics, including the novelist RUDOLPH FISHER, dismissed the novel as uneven, with multiple plots that seemed unrelated. To support himself, Cullen began teaching French at Frederick Douglass Junior High School in 1934. He also continued to write, but his later works never generated the interest of his early poetry. Critics took exception to Cullen's use of romantic themes and conventions.

Cullen's later writings included *The Medea and Some Poems* (1935), a translation of the Greek playwright Euripides' tragedy *Medea; The Lost Zoo* (1940), a collection of children's verse; and *My Lives and How I Lost Them* (1942), a collection of children's stories told from the perspective of a feline narrator, Christopher the Cat. Cullen also collaborated with the novelist ARNA BONTEMPS on a musical adaptation of Bontemps's novel *God Sends Sunday,* which premiered in New York in 1946 under the title *St. Louis Woman.* Cullen also collaborated with poet and playwright OWEN DODSON on the play *The Third Fourth of July,* published in *Theatre Arts* in August 1946.

Countee Porter Cullen died suddenly from uremic poisoning and high blood pressure on January 9, 1946, two months prior to the opening of *St. Louis Woman.* At the time of his death, he had been working on an autobiography, *The Sum of My Days,* another collection of children's stories, and a collected volume of his poetry, published posthumously in 1947 as *On These I Stand.* Though his accomplishments never matched the expectations placed upon him as a young poet, the decline of his literary career late in life had less to do with the beauty and brilliance of his writing than with the aesthetic ideals of the late Harlem Renaissance and the more political and Afrocentric literature of the 1960s. In his poem "To Certain Critics," published in *The Black Christ and Other Poems,* Cullen defended his artistic principles against those who criticized his methods: "Never shall the clan / Confine my singing to its ways / Beyond the ways of man." Cullen produced some of the most remarkable and literate verse of the Harlem Renaissance. He was the first African-American poet to appear regularly in anthologies of American poetry, and many of his works have appeared in recent reprint editions.

Further Reading

Cullen, Countee. *Color.* American Negro: His History and Literature, No. 3. Manchester, N.H.: Ayer Company Publishers, 1993.

Early, Gerald. *My Soul's High Song: The Collected Writings of Countee Cullen, Voice of the Harlem Renaissance.* New York: Doubleday, 1991.

Powers, Peter. "'The Singing Man Who Must Be Reckoned With': Private Desire and Public Responsibility in the Poetry of Countee Cullen." *African American Review* 34 (winter 2000): 661–679.

Danticat, Edwidge

(1969–   ) *novelist, short story writer, editor*

Since the publication of her first novel, *Breath, Eyes, Memory* (1994), when she was 25, the Haitian-born Edwidge Danticat has earned wide critical acclaim as one of the finest young black writers of her generation, and one of only a few writers of Haitian heritage who publish in English. Danticat's novels and short stories highlight the poverty and political injustice of life in Haiti, and the unique challenges that confront émigrés to America.

Edwidge Danticat was born in Port-au-Prince, Haiti, on January 19, 1969. When she was two, her father immigrated to America to establish a home for his family. Danticat's mother joined him two years later, leaving Danticat and her brother in the care of relatives. "My most vivid memories of Haiti," Danticat writes about her early childhood, "involved incidents that represent power failures. At those times, you can't read, or study, or watch TV, so you sit around a candle and listen to stories from the elders in the house." These oral traditions of her childhood would play an important role in shaping Danticat's literary vision as a writer.

When Edwidge was 12, she and her younger brother moved to New York to join their parents. Apart from the difficulty of adjusting to her parents after such a long absence, Danticat also struggled with the language barrier. She was enrolled in a bilingual educational program, which she credits for her later success as a student. However, conflicts often arose among African-American students and Haitian immigrants, and Danticat was often ridiculed for her accented English.

Interested in a career in medicine, Danticat later enrolled at Columbia University's Barnard College, where she received her bachelor's degree in French literature in 1990. Against the wishes of her parents, who disapproved of her desire to write, Danticat entered the graduate writing program at Brown University and graduated in 1993. As an undergraduate at Barnard College, Danticat had begun an essay on her childhood in Haiti. On the advice of a literary agent, she expanded the essay and used it as her thesis at Brown University. This essay eventually became the foundation for her first novel.

Published in 1994, *Breath, Eyes, Memory* became an instant success, winning the Black Caucus of the American Library Association's Fiction Award in 1994, and *Granta* magazine listed Danticat among their Twenty Best Young American Novelists in 1996. Largely autobiographical, *Breath, Eyes, Memory* portrays the life of a young Haitian girl, Sophie, who leaves her emotionally comfortable home among relatives to join her mother in the United States. The novel follows

Edwidge Danticat speaks during an interview in New York City in 1998. *(AP/Wide World Photos)*

explained in a 1995 interview. "They end up in a prison dungeon, where their bodies are covered in scalding tar before they're forced to eat their own waste."

In 1995 Danticat published *Krik? Krak!*, a collection of nine interrelated short stories about life in Haiti. The title derives from Danticat's native Creole language, in which a storyteller announces a folktale with the expression "Krik?," and the listener signifies a desire to hear the tale with the expression "Krak!" Set in Haiti's capital city of Port-au-Prince and the rural Ville Rose, the stories in *Krik? Krak!* examine the hopes and hardships of life in Haiti. "The treasuring of memories and legends," writes Donna Seaman in a 1995 *Booklist* review, "is at the heart of each of Danticat's tales and is often the only legacy anyone can hold on to." Widely acclaimed by critics, *Krik? Krak!* was nominated for the National Book Award in 1995.

In her second novel, *The Farming of Bones* (1998), Danticat uses a historical incident, the slaughter of tens of thousands of Haitian immigrants living in the Dominican Republic ordered by the Dominican dictator Raphael Trujillo in 1937, as a framework for her story. The novel portrays the life of Amabelle Desir, a young woman who lives and works in the Dominican Republic and who ultimately becomes a victim of Trujillo's slaughter. *The Farming of Bones* also traces the lasting effects of the tragic events of 1937 in the methods and language used to recount the events. Danticat received the American Book Award for *The Farming of Bones* in 1999.

Edwidge Danticat has become a celebrated and influential figure among Haitian-American and African-American writers, devoting her life and writing to the expression of voices and stories that have long been overlooked. She has edited several collections of writing by women and children of many ethnic backgrounds. She contributed to *The Magic Orange Tree and Other Haitian Stories* (1997), a collection of Haitian folktales, and *Walking on Fire: Haitian Women's Stories of Survival and Resistance* (2001). She also edited

Sophie through childhood to adulthood, highlighting the difficulties of adjusting to a new cultural environment, and the emotional and psychological difficulties created by her strained relationship with her mother.

On the heels of her overwhelmingly successful debut as a novelist, Danticat returned to Haiti with filmmaker Jonathan Demme, with whom she began working as an associate producer in 1993. There they filmed a documentary, *Courage and Pain*, about the lives of torture survivors under Haiti's oppressive political regime. "In our world, if you are a writer, you are a politician, and we know what happens to politicians," Danticat

The Butterfly's Way: Voices from the Haitian Diaspora in the United States (2000), and *The Beacon Best of 2000: Creative Writing by Women and Men of All Colors* (2000). Her other works include *After the Dance: A Walk through Carnival in Jacmel* (2002), a documentary work about her return to Haiti to attend her first Carnival celebration and the lives of local Haitians that she meets during her travels, and *Behind the Mountain* (2002), her first young adult novel, about a young Haitian girl's coming of age in Haiti and the United States.

Further Reading

Danticat, Edwidge. *After the Dance: A Walk through Carnival in Jacmel.* New York: Crown Publishers, 2002.

———. *Breath, Eyes, Memory.* New York: Soho Press, 1994.

———. *The Farming of Bones.* New York: Soho Press, 1998.

———. *Krik? Krak!* New York: Soho Press, 1995.

Wucker, Michele. "Edwidge Danticat: A Voice for the Voiceless." *Americas* 52 (May/June 2000): 40.

Delany, Samuel R.
(Samuel Ray "Chip" Delany, Jr., K. Leslie Steiner, Richmond Arriey, S. L. Kermit)
(1942–) *novelist, short story writer, essayist, literary critic, educator*

A prolific and critically acclaimed author of science fiction novels and short stories, essays, literary criticism, and literary theory, Samuel R. Delany is one of the few African-American authors to write predominantly in the science fiction genre. His complex and compelling narratives, in which he challenges traditional assumptions about race, gender, and sexual identity, have earned some of science fiction's highest honors, including two Hugo and four Nebula Awards. He was also awarded the Bill Whitehead Award for Lifetime Achievement in Gay and Lesbian Literature.

Samuel Ray Delany, Jr., was born on April 1, 1942, in New York City, the son of a prominent Harlem undertaker, Samuel Ray Delany, Sr., and Margaret Cary Boyd Delany, a licensed funeral director and a clerk in the New York Public Library. Delany was educated at the prestigious Dalton School, a private academy in New York, and the Bronx High School of Science, where he met Marilyn Hacker, a young poet who would later become his wife. Following his graduation in 1960, Delany received a fellowship to attend the Bread Loaf Writers Conference in Vermont, where he met Robert Frost and other celebrated writers.

Delany began writing as a child, at which time he steeped himself in the works of classic science fiction authors such as Jules Verne, Ray Bradbury, and Robert Heinlein. In his personal journal, he wrote several fantasy stories as a child and completed several unpublished novels before his teenage years. In addition to writing, Delany also studied the violin and the guitar, with which he later performed in cafés in Greenwich Village during the 1960s.

In 1961 Delany and Hacker were married in Detroit, Michigan, in order to escape New York's parental consent law. Delany and Hacker separated in 1975 and finally divorced in 1980. They have one child. Delany attended the City College of New York (now City University) intermittently from 1960 to 1965, during which he edited the campus poetry magazine *The Promethean.* In 1962, with the help of his wife, who worked as a science fiction editor at Ace Books, Delany published his first novel, *The Jewels of Aptor.*

After a mental breakdown in 1964 and his final departure from City College in 1965, Delany traveled to Mexico with a friend and worked on a shrimping boat. He also traveled extensively in Europe and Turkey from 1965 to 1966. From 1963 to 1968 Delany published a flurry of novels, including The Fall of the Towers trilogy, comprising *Captives of the Flame* (1963), *The Towers of Toron* (1964), and *City of a Thousand Suns* (1965); *The Ballad of Beta-2* (1965); and *Empire Star* (1966). Delany was influenced by his early interest in mythic quests, particularly those found in Greek mythology, and his early novels have been characterized as space operas, which feature conventional themes and narrative devices of the science fiction genre while also transcending those conventions in the use of complex literary language.

With the publication of *Babel-17* (1966), *The Einstein Intersection* (1967), and *Nova* (1968), Delany began to receive greater attention from the science fiction community. *Babel-17* and *The Einstein Intersection* earned the Science Fiction Writers of America's prestigious Nebula Award. Delany won another Nebula Award in 1967 for his short story "Aye, and Gomorrah." One of his best known short stories, "Time Considered as a Helix of Semi-Precious Stone," won the Nebula Award in 1969 and the World Science Fiction Society's Hugo Award in 1970. Delany's short fiction has been collected in *Driftglass: Ten Tales of Speculative Fiction* (1971), *Distant Stars* (1981), *Driftglass/Starshards* (1994), and *Aye, and Gomorrah: And Other Stories* (2003).

Delany added to his repertoire of artistic accomplishments with two experimental short films, *Tiresias* (1970) and *The Orchid* (1971). He also coedited the journal *Quark* (1970–71) with Hacker. He contributed two scripts for the *Wonder Woman* comics series (1972) and wrote the script for a radio play, *The Star Pit* (1972), which he adapted from his short story of the same title.

The publication of Delany's novels *Dhalgren* (1975) and *Triton* (1976) signaled a shift in his narrative and thematic focus. In 1973 Delany had traveled to London to join his wife, who was pregnant with their only child. He attended classes in philosophy and linguistics at the University of London, and these novels reflect the influence of his studies. Though much more complex and theoretical in narrative structure, these novels still focused thematically on issues of race, sexuality, and mythology.

Delany returned from London in 1974 after the birth of his daughter, Iva Hacker-Delany, and joined the faculty of the State University of New York in Buffalo as the Butler Professor of English.

He also held teaching positions briefly at the University of Wisconsin's Center for Twentieth-Century Studies in Madison in 1977, and at Cornell University's Society for the Humanities in 1987, before a long academic appointment at the University of Massachusetts at Amherst, from 1988 to 1998. In 1999 Delany accepted a position as an adjunct professor at the State University of New York at Buffalo.

During the 1980s Delany began exploring the genre of "sword-and-sorcery" fantasy fiction. He published his first fantasy novel, *Tales of Neveryon*, in 1979, followed by *Neveryona: Or, the Tale of Signs and Cities* (1983), *Flight from Neveryon* (1985), and *The Bridge of Lost Desire* (1987), the latter two of which incorporate discussions about the impact of acquired immunodeficiency syndrome (AIDS). He also wrote his only dramatic text, *Wagner/Artaud: A Play of Nineteenth and Twentieth Century Critical Fictions* (1988), and published a memoir, *The Motion of Light in Water: Sex and Science-Fiction Writing in the East Village, 1957–1965,* (1988), which won a Hugo Award for best nonfiction book in 1989. Delany returned to the science fiction genre with *Stars in My Pocket Like Grains of Sand* (1984) and *They Fly at Çiron* (1993).

In addition to his award-winning science fiction novels, Delany has published a collection of traditional (non–science fiction) short stories, *Atlantis: Three Tales* (1995), and a large body of essays and critical studies. Indeed, one of his most celebrated literary achievements has been the application of traditional and postmodern critical theory to the genre of science fiction. Delany has published his critical essays in several collections, including *The Jewel-Hinged Jaw* (1977), *The American Shore: Meditations on a Tale by Thomas Disch—"Angouleme"* (1978), *Starboard Wine: More Notes on the Language of Science Fiction* (1984), *The Straits of Messina* (1987), *Longer Views* (1996), *Shorter Views: Queer Thoughts and the Politics of the Paraliterary* (2000), and *Times Square Red, Times Square Blue* (2001), a meditation on the once-ubiquitous sex theaters and clubs in Times Square and their eventual removal during the 1990s in an attempt to "clean up" the city.

Perhaps the most controversial of Delany's writings appeared in the 1990s. Beginning with *Equinox* (1994, originally published as *The Tides of Lust* in 1973), Delany began to explore the physical and psychological limits of human sexuality in a series of erotic novels. In *Equinox,* the crew of a ship called the *Scorpion* sail the seas in search of new and extreme sexual adventures. Delany's other erotic novels include *Hogg* (1993), *The Mad Man* (1994), and a comic book–style sexual autobiography, *Bread and Wine: An Erotic Tale of New York* (1998), in which he speaks frankly and graphically about, among other things, his homosexuality. The sometimes violent depictions of sexuality in these novels have disturbed readers and critics, though many have praised Delany for expanding the traditional boundaries of acceptable literature and for discussing sexual issues with unflinching honesty.

Critics have hailed Samuel Delany as one of the finest American authors of the 20th century, which is unusual praise for an author who writes predominantly within the genre of science fiction. One of only a few African Americans to do so (OCTAVIA BUTLER is another), Delany has attained international success with the complexity and depth of his fiction and criticism. In all of his writing, Delany challenges accepted notions of race, gender, identity, and sexuality. He writes of racial, sexual, and ideological outcasts, providing a voice to those who have often been relegated to silence. "The constant and insistent experience I have had," Delany stated in a 1986 interview, "as a black man, as a gay man, as a science fiction writer in racist, sexist, homophobic America, with its carefully maintained tradition of high art and low, colors and contours every sentence I write."

Over the course of a writing career that has spanned more than half a century, Samuel R. Delany has accumulated numerous literary honors. His novels and short fiction have been awarded six of science fiction's most coveted prizes (two Hugo and four Nebula Awards). His fantasy novel *Tales of Neveryon* (1988) earned an American Book Award nomination. He was also the recipient of the Science Fiction Research Association's Pilgrim Award in 1985. In 1993 Delany received the Bill Whitehead Award for Lifetime Achievement in Gay and Lesbian Literature. As a testament to Delany's remarkable popularity as a writer, many of his early novels and several collections of his short fiction and essays remain in print. In 2000 Delany published *1984,* a collection of his personal correspondence that offers a provocative glimpse into his intellectual and literary development.

Further Reading

Delany, Samuel R. *The Einstein Intersection.* New York: Ace Books, 1967. Reprint, Middletown, Conn.: Wesleyan University Press, 1998.

———. *The Motion of Light in Water: Sex and Science-Fiction Writing in the East Village, 1956–1965.* New York: Arbor House, 1988.

———. *Triton.* New York: Bantam Books, 1976. Reprint, Vintage Books, 2002.

Sallis, James, ed. *Ash of Stars: On the Writing of Samuel R. Delany.* Jackson: University Press of Mississippi, 1996.

Demby, William
(William E. Demby, Jr.)
(1922–) *novelist, screen and television writer, educator*

William Demby began his writing career as an American expatriate in Rome, Italy, where he published his first novel and wrote scripts for Italian film and television. A patient, methodical writer, Demby has published only four novels since 1950. His work is characteristically dense and experimental in nature, drawing on the existentialist philosophy of Jean-Paul Sartre, particularly in his later works, to explore issues of race and identity in American society as well as on a global scale.

William E. Demby, Jr., was born on December 25, 1922, in Pittsburgh, Pennsylvania. His parents, William and Gertrude Demby, had aspired to professional careers in architecture and medicine, respectively. Prevented from pursuing their goals because of their race, they settled in Pittsburgh to start a family. Demby and his siblings grew up in a middle-class, ethnically mixed neighborhood of Pittsburgh, where his father's employment at Hopewell Gas Company as a file clerk provided the family with a comfortable existence.

Following his graduation from Langley High School in 1941, Demby and his family moved to the small coal-mining town of Clarksburg, West Virginia, where his father had accepted a job with the Standard Oil Company. The predominantly black town of Clarksburg played an important role in shaping Demby's artistic focus, and would eventually inspire the setting of his first novel. He enrolled at West Virginia State College, where he studied under MARGARET WALKER, but his attention was soon drawn to the world of jazz. He began to perform regularly in clubs and neglected his studies.

In 1942 Demby left school to join the U.S. Army, spending his two-year tour in Italy and North Africa. After his return to the United States in 1944, he enrolled at Fisk University, in Tennessee, and received his bachelor's degree in liberal arts in 1947. After graduation, Demby decided to move back to Italy to pursue his interest in painting. He befriended the Italian filmmaker Roberto Rossellini, with whom he collaborated on two films, and began work on his first novel. He also married Italian poet Lucia Drudia, with whom he has one child, James, a composer.

Demby published his first novel, *Beetlecreek,* in 1950. Set in the fictional West Virginia community of Beetlecreek, reminiscent of Clarksburg, West Virginia, where Demby lived as a teenager, the novel explores individual and racial conflicts among its three primary characters: Johnny John-son, a black teenager whose need for belonging and a sense of purpose leads him to join a gang of black youths called the Nightriders; Bill Trapp, a white former carnival performer, now middle-aged and lonely, who uses alcohol to ease the pain of an unfulfilled life; and David Diggs, Johnny's uncle, a frustrated artist who makes his living as a sign painter. The lives of Demby's three primary characters intersect throughout the novel, first in the development of emotionally renewing friendships, and finally as the catalyst for disaster. The narrative complexity and vivid language of Demby's *Beetlecreek* earned international critical acclaim.

In his second novel, *The Catacombs* (1965), Demby employs a more experimental narrative structure, creating a fictional persona named William Demby, an expatriate novelist who writes a novel about another expatriate, a young black actress employed as a bit actor in a film production of the life of Cleopatra. Though less accessible than his first novel, *The Catacombs* becomes an interesting meditation on the process of writing and character development. It also explores the function of the author within those creative processes, which often blur the distinction between reality and fantasy.

Demby's third novel, *Love Story Black* (1978), is similarly experimental in its depiction of Professor Edwards, an African-American instructor at a New York college and former expatriate novelist, whose research on the life of an elderly female vaudeville performer, the virginal Mona Pariss, for an article in *New Black Woman* magazine leads to unusual events in his personal life. Torn between the love of two women, Edwards makes his choice and leaves for Africa with his lover, only to suffer the humiliation of losing her to a political revolutionary. At the novel's conclusion Edwards returns to New York and makes love to the aged Mona Pariss on her deathbed, in an act of unusual kindness and love.

In addition to his three novels, Demby also published several journalistic essays, including "The Geisha Girls of Pontocho," "They Surely

Can't Stop Us Now," "A Walk in Tuscany," and "Blueblood Cats of Rome," during the 1950s and 1960s; and he has written and translated extensively for Italian television and film. Having made Italy his home since the late 1940s, Demby returns to the United States periodically. In 1969 he accepted a position as an associate professor of English at the City University of New York's College of Staten Island, a post he held until 1989. In the late 1990s Demby was reputed to have been preparing a fourth novel for publication, though it has yet to be published.

Further Reading

Demby, William. *Beetlecreek.* New York: Rinehart, 1950. Reprint, Jackson: University Press of Mississippi, 1998.

———. *The Catacombs.* New York: Pantheon Books, 1965. Reprint, Boston, Mass.: Northeastern University Press, 1991.

———. *Love Story Black.* New York: Dutton, 1978. Reprint, 1986.

Hall, James C. *Mercy, Mercy Me: African American Culture and the American Sixties.* New York: Oxford University Press, 2001.

Jaskoski, Helen. "The Catacombs and the Debate Between the Flesh and the Spirit." *Critique* 35 (spring 1994): 181.

Derricotte, Toi
(Toi Webster)
(1941–   ) *poet, memoirist, educator*

An award-winning poet and distinguished university professor, Toi Derricotte has earned critical comparisons to poets Sylvia Plath and Anne Sexton for the confessional nature and emotional force of her poetry. Derricotte's poems reflect the various transitions in her life, from motherhood to her meditations on death, and the ways that broader racial, political, and cultural forces affect individual development. "For me speaking is a very political act," she explained in a 1991 interview in the journal *Callaloo.* "I think in every book I have tried to claim some part of myself that has been stifled."

Toi Webster was born on April 12, 1941, in Detroit, Michigan, the daughter of a Creole mother, Antonia Baquet, and Kentucky native Benjamin Sweeney Webster. As a child, Webster began a private journal in which she recorded the details of her early life, including the crumbling of her parents' marriage and the devastating loss of her grandmother. Her early childhood was characterized by an emotional distance from her parents and feelings of isolation. Light-skinned, she lived on the margins of white and black culture, a condition that would continue to inform her adult life.

In 1959 she graduated from Girls Catholic Central school in Detroit and enrolled at Wayne State College. During her junior year, she gave birth to her son, Anthony, in a home for unwed mothers. She married Clarence Reese, an artist and the father of her son, in 1962. The couple divorced two years later. In 1965 she graduated from Wayne State College with a bachelor's degree in special education and worked briefly as a teacher for mentally impaired children at the Farland School in Detroit.

Her early poetry, which she began to write as a teenager, revealed a preoccupation with death, or rather the transition from life to death. In her grandparents' home, the basement of which served as a funeral parlor where bodies were prepared for viewing, she often prayed over the bodies there, particularly those of children. The intensely personal nature of her writing contrasted sharply with the literary trends of the 1960s and 1970s, particularly within the Black Arts Movement in New York, where she relocated in 1967.

She married Clarence Bruce Derricotte in 1967. Two years later, she joined the staff of Jefferson School in New Jersey as a teacher of remedial reading and devoted her free time to writing. She published her first poem in the *New York Quarterly* in 1972 and began to develop her creative focus in local community writing workshops and as a master teacher and poet-in-residence for the New Jersey State Council on the Arts from 1974 to 1988.

Derricotte published her first collection of poems, *Empress of the House of Death*, in 1978. The poems in this volume explore the anger and repression that characterized Derricotte's childhood and adolescence, when the discussion of issues related to race and sexuality were strictly forbidden. *Empress of the House of Death* represents in some ways Derricotte's rebellion against this early silence, as she explores her past in frank and often explicit language and imagery.

In *Natural Birth* (1983), Derricotte depicts the shame and humiliation that she experienced during the birth of her son in a maternity home for unwed mothers, and the expansion of her identity in her transition from the role of young woman to that of mother. Widely acclaimed by critics, *Natural Birth* established Derricotte's reputation as a major new voice in contemporary African-American poetry. Her subsequent volumes, *Captivity* (1989) and *Tender* (1997), have added to her considerable critical stature as a poet. In 1997 Derricotte published her memoir, *The Black Notebooks: An Interior Journey*, which collects her personal journal entries over a 20-year period.

In addition to writing poetry, Derricotte has taught at several universities. After completing her master's degree in creative writing at New York University in 1984, she served as an associate professor of creative writing and minority literature at Old Dominion University in Norfolk, Virginia. Her other university appointments include visiting professorships at George Mason University and the University of South Florida. In 1991 Derricotte joined the faculty of the University of Pittsburgh.

Toi Derricotte's considerable talents as a poet have garnered several literary honors, including the Lucille Medwick Memorial Award from the Poetry Society of America (1985), a Pushcart Prize (1989), the Folger Shakespeare Library Poetry Book Award (1990), and the Distinguished Pioneering of the Arts Award from United Black Artists, Inc. (1993). In 1996 Derricotte helped found Cave Canem, which began as a summer retreat and workshop and has since become a major cultural and literary resource for African-American poets and writers. Guest faculty members at Cave Canem have included poet SONIA SANCHEZ and novelist WALTER MOSLEY.

Further Reading

Andrews, William L., Frances Smith Foster, and Trudier Harris, eds. *The Concise Oxford Companion to African American Literature.* New York: Oxford University Press, 2001.

Derricotte, Toi. *The Black Notebooks: An Intimate Journey.* New York: W. W. Norton, 1997.

———. *Captivity.* Pittsburgh, Pa.: University of Pittsburgh Press, 1989.

———. *Natural Birth.* New York: Firebrand Press, 2000.

Lee, Don. "Toi Derricotte, Contributor Spotlight." *Ploughshares* 22 (spring 1996): 208.

Dodson, Owen
(Owen Vincent Dodson)
(1914–1983) *poet, playwright, novelist, educator*

Recognized as a fine poet whose work has often been compared to that of Robert Frost and Carl Sandburg, Owen Dodson is most frequently remembered as a playwright and celebrated drama director. His reliance on classical themes in his poetry and drama, and a lack of political rhetoric, prevented him from garnering the attention that more radical poets and writers received during the social and racial upheavals of the 1970s. His contributions as a writer and instructor, however, came to influence the work of renowned African-American dramatists, poets, and actors, including AMIRI BARAKA and Ossie Davis.

Born on November 28, 1914, in Brooklyn, New York, Owen Dodson was the ninth child of Nathaniel and Sarah Elizabeth Goode Dodson.

Owen's father, a journalist and director of the National Negro Press Association, introduced him at a young age to the works of leading black thinkers and artists, including W. E. B. DuBOIS and JAMES WELDON JOHNSON. Dodson graduated from Brooklyn's Public School 64, and later from Thomas Jefferson High School, where he distinguished himself as an orator. In 1932 he attended Bates College in Lewiston, Maine, where he began writing poetry, wrote and performed in plays, and joined the editorial staff of the *Garnet,* the college's biannual literary magazine. Prior to his graduation in 1936, Dodson had published several sonnets in the *Garnet,* and his poem "Ode to the Class of 1936 Everywhere" appeared in the *New York Herald Tribune.*

Dodson's literary success as an undergraduate earned him an invitation to the graduate program of Yale School of Drama. As a student, he saw two of his verse plays, *Divine Comedy* (1938), inspired by the life and exploits of the charismatic and controversial black spiritualist Father Divine, and *Garden of Time* (1939), a reworking of Euripides' *Medea* set in the postbellum South, successfully produced. He received his master's degree in 1939. Following his graduation, Dodson began a long and distinguished career as a teacher and drama director at Spelman College, in Atlanta; the Hampton Institute, in Virginia; and, most notably, at Howard University, in Washington, D.C., where he began teaching in 1947.

In 1940 Dodson interrupted his teaching career to enlist in the U.S. Navy, where he served at a training facility in Illinois. He established a drama group and wrote morale-building plays about the lives of naval heroes and great African-American leaders. One of these plays, *New World A-Comin: An Original Pageant of Hope,* was successfully staged at Madison Square Garden for a multiracial audience of 25,000 people during the Negro Freedom Rally of 1944.

In addition to his remarkable success as a dramatist, Dodson earned critical acclaim for his poetry. He published his first volume, *Powerful Long Ladder,* in 1946, and was hailed by many as one of the leading African-American poets of his day. Dodson published three more volumes of poetry during his lifetime. *Cages,* a small collection of poems dedicated to a former professor at Bates College, was published in 1953. In 1970 he published *The Confession Stone: Song Cycles,* a collection of religious monologues that focus on the life of Jesus. Dodson's final volume, *The Harlem Book of the Dead,* a collaboration with the celebrated photographer James Van der Zee, appeared in 1981. In 1960 Dodson recorded some of his verse for the Library of Congress and was invited to read there in 1973.

In 1947 Dodson began his distinguished career at Howard University, where he would eventually become chair of the Drama Department. There, he directed more than 100 productions, including Arthur Miller's *All My Sons* in 1948, which drew white theater critics for the first time to a production at Howard University. After seeing a production of Henrik Ibsen's *The Wild Duck,* a Norwegian delegate to the United Nations invited Dodson to tour northwestern Europe with his students, where they performed plays by Ibsen and DuBose Heyward. Dodson and his actors were the first African-American theatrical group to undertake such a tour.

Having earned wide critical acclaim as a poet and dramatist, Dodson added to his prolific literary output with two novels, *Boy at the Window,* published in 1951 and reprinted in 1977 (also appears under the title *When Trees Were Green*), and *Come Home Early, Child,* written in 1952 but not published until 1977. Though the novels as a whole received minor critical attention, individual chapters won several awards. Excerpts from *Boy at the Window* appeared in *The Book of Negro Folklore,* edited by LANGSTON HUGHES and ARNA BONTEMPS in 1958. "Summer Fire," the first chapter of *Come Home Early, Child,* appeared in the book *Best Short Stories from the Paris Review* in 1959.

Dodson retired from the faculty of Howard University in 1969 but continued to direct plays and lecture on campuses and in writing workshops.

He also taught creative writing at the City College of New York. In 1972 two of Dodson's former drama students produced a collage of his drama, poetry, and stories in *Owen's Song,* which paid tribute to his prolific and influential contributions to African-American drama and literature. *Owen's Song* premiered at the Colony Theatre in Washington, D.C., and later played at the Kennedy Center on New Year's Eve in 1974, with Robert Hooks directing. After struggling for years with arthritis and a growing dependence on alcohol, Owen Vincent Dodson died in 1983.

Beloved by his students, and a distinguished artist in three literary genres, Owen Dodson never achieved the celebrity of such contemporaries as Langston Hughes, COUNTEE CULLEN, with whom Dodson collaborated on two plays, and Arna Bontemps. His legacy, however, endured in the theatrical and literary artists who followed him, including writers AUGUST WILSON and Amiri Baraka and actors Ossie Davis and Debbie Allen.

Further Reading

Andrews, William L., Frances Smith Foster, and Trudier Harris, eds. *The Concise Oxford Companion to African American Literature.* New York: Oxford University Press, 2001.

Hatch, James Vernon, and Arnold Rampersad. *Sorrow Is the Only Faithful One: The Life of Owen Dodson.* Urbana-Champaign: University of Illinois Press, 1995.

Peterson, Bernard L., Jr. "The Legendary Owen Dodson of Howard University: His Contributions to the American Theatre." *Crisis* 86 (November 1979): 373–378.

Douglass, Frederick
(Frederick Augustus Washington Bailey)
(1818–1895) *autobiographer, journalist, abolitionist*

As an orator, autobiographer, editor, and journalist, Frederick Douglass argued passionately and eloquently against the institution of slavery. His 1845 autobiography, *The Narrative of the Life of Frederick Douglass, An American Slave, Written by Himself,* became an instant international success and has endured as a document of central importance to the canon of African-American literature. Douglass also distinguished himself as an American statesman and diplomat, serving as an adviser to President Abraham Lincoln and as minister-general to the Republic of Haiti.

Frederick Douglass was born Frederick Augustus Washington Bailey in February 1818 (the exact date is unknown) in Talbot County, Maryland, the son of Harriet Bailey, a field slave. He never knew his father, who he believed was white, and his mother died when he was a child. During his early years as a slave, Bailey suffered more from privations of food and clothing than physical violence, though he often witnessed the brutal conditions under which plantation slaves lived.

At the age of seven or eight, Bailey was sent to Baltimore to serve in the house of Hugh Auld. "Going to live at Baltimore," he would later recall, "laid the foundation, and opened the gateway, to all my subsequent happiness." First under the instruction of Sophia Auld, his master's wife, and later by enlisting the help of white children with whom he became acquainted, Bailey learned to read and write by the age of 12. He purchased a copy of *The Columbian Orator,* a popular reader used in schools, and devoted every spare moment to reading.

Having come into the possession of Thomas Auld in 1832, Bailey was soon shipped off to Edward Covey, a ruthless land-renter and renowned slave-breaker. Suffering routine whippings and unrelenting labor, Bailey soon relinquished his hope of education and freedom. "The dark night of slavery closed in upon me," he would later record in his autobiography, "and behold a man transformed into a brute!"

Bailey's hopes for freedom revived when a violent confrontation with Covey finally ended his brutal treatment and restored to Bailey a sense of dignity and self-respect. His term of service to

Covey expired in 1833, and he was hired out to a small landowner, Mr. Freeland. Bailey convened a small Sabbath school to teach fellow slaves to read and write. He also made his first attempt at escape, but his plan was discovered and Bailey was jailed until his owner, Thomas Auld, retrieved him and returned him to Baltimore.

Bailey remained in Baltimore until 1838, during which time he was trained as a ship's caulker and allowed to hire his time for work wherever he might find it. This situation provided him with unprecedented freedom. On September 3, 1838, Bailey successfully made his escape to New York. "How I did so—what means I adopted—what direction I traveled, and by what conveyance," he wrote in his autobiography, "I must leave unexplained." Following his escape, Bailey adopted the surname of Douglass.

In New York Douglass married Anne Murray, a free black whom he had met in Baltimore. They settled in New Bedford, Massachusetts. He became an agent of the Massachusetts Antislavery Society in 1841 and began to address conventions with his haunting stories of life as a slave. Astonished at his intellectual abilities and his imposing physical stature, Douglass's audiences began to doubt the veracity of his personal history. To address these doubts, and against the advice of fellow abolitionists, Douglass published his *Narrative of the Life of Frederick Douglass, An American Slave, Written by Himself* in 1845.

Douglass's *Narrative* recounted the details of his life under slavery and his eventual escape in vivid and passionate detail, showing that the inhumanity of slavery had a moral and physical impact on all levels of society, from slaves to slaveholders. The book became an instant best-seller, but his use of real names and places put him in danger of recapture. He spent the next two years in Great Britain and continued to lecture against slavery.

Upon his return to the United States in 1847, Douglass remained active within the abolitionist movement. He founded the *North Star*, an antislavery newspaper, and maintained friendships and rivalries with every major social and abolitionist reformer of the mid-19th century. In 1855 Douglass published a second autobiography, *My Bondage and My Freedom*, which contained one of his most famous speeches, "What to the Slave Is the Fourth of July?"

In the wake of the Emancipation Proclamation in 1863, a first step toward the abolition of slavery, Douglass encouraged the participation of black soldiers in the Union army and played a central role in the creation of the renowned 54th Massachusetts Regiment, in which two of his sons served. Throughout the Civil War, and as an adviser to three U.S. presidents, Douglass continued to fight for the full enfranchisement and integration of African Americans in social and political life.

Douglass's final years included several government appointments. In 1877 he became the first U.S. marshal for the District of Columbia. In 1881 he was appointed recorder of deeds. That

An acclaimed abolitionist and orator, Frederick Douglass also became a respected political figure during and subsequent to the Reconstruction era. *(Library of Congress)*

year Douglass also published *The Life and Times of Frederick Douglass*, his third autobiography. Having survived the torments of slavery, Douglass devoted his life to the elimination of all forms of oppression. Following an address to the National Council of Women on February 20, 1895, Frederick Augustus Bailey Douglass suffered a heart attack and died at his home in Washington, D.C.

Frederick Douglass was one of the most influential and celebrated African-American leaders of his time. While his contemporaries in the abolitionist movement, white and black, did not always agree with him, Douglass's eloquent message of freedom and racial equality for African Americans, delivered in his many speeches and in the pages of his autobiographies and editorials, helped solidify support for the end of slavery in America and the recognition of African Americans as legitimate and vital members of American society and culture. *Narrative of the Life of Frederick Douglass*, though not the first slave narrative, was to become a standard by which the genre would be measured.

Further Reading

Douglass, Frederick. *Narrative of the Life of Frederick Douglass, An American Slave, Written by Himself.* Norton Critical Edition. New York: W. W. Norton, 1997.

Foner, Philip S., ed. *Frederick Douglass: Selected Speeches and Writings.* Westport, Conn.: Lawrence Hill, 2000.

Sundquist, Eric J., ed. *Frederick Douglass: New Literary and Historical Essays.* New York: Cambridge University Press, 1990.

Dove, Rita
(Rita Frances Dove)

(1952–) *poet, short story writer, novelist, essayist, playwright, educator*

One of America's most celebrated contemporary poets, Rita Dove has earned numerous literary honors, including the Pulitzer Prize for poetry, the National Humanities Medal, and the Duke Ellington Lifetime Achievement Award. In 1993 Dove

was named the U.S. poet laureate. Critics have praised Dove for her skilled use of language and the universal appeal of her poetry. "Obviously, as a black woman, I am concerned with race," Dove has stated about the focus of her poetry. "But certainly not every poem mentions the fact of being black. They are poems about humanity, and sometimes humanity happens to be black. I cannot run from, I won't run from any kind of truth."

Rita Frances Dove was born on August 28, 1952, in Akron, Ohio. Her father, Ray Dove, was the first African-American chemist to work for Goodyear Tire Company. From her mother, Elvira, Dove received early encouragement as a student and an aspiring writer. She graduated from high school in 1970 and earned an invitation to the White House as a Presidential Scholar, a distinction awarded annually to the nation's 100 outstanding high school seniors.

Dove attended Miami University in Oxford, Ohio, as a National Achievement Scholar and graduated summa cum laude with a bachelor's degree in English in 1973. After studying for two years in West Germany at Tübingen University, Dove returned to the United States and completed her master's degree at the University of Iowa's Writer's Workshop in 1977.

Since 1974 Dove's poetry had appeared in such periodicals as the *Georgia Review* and *Poetry*. She published her first collections of poetry in two chapbooks, *Ten Poems* (1977) and *The Only Dark Spot in the Sky* (1980). Many of these poems later appeared in *The Yellow House on the Corner* (1980), her first major work. Critics quickly noted her disciplined use of language, and her second major collection, *Museum* (1983), drew national attention. In poems such as "Nestor's Bathtub" and "Parsley," Dove renders profound psychological insights in simple and haunting language.

With the publication of *Thomas and Beulah* in 1986, Dove established herself as one of America's leading contemporary poets. The collection loosely depicts the lives of Dove's maternal grandparents, tracing their individual histories through childhood, marriage, children, and old age in two sections, "Mandolin" and "Canary in Bloom." Dove is less concerned with the factual histories of her grandparents' stories than with the substance of their lives together. "I was after the essence of my grandparents' lives and survival," she explained in a 1989 interview in *Iowa Review,* "not necessarily the facts of their survival." For *Thomas and Beulah,* Dove received the Lavin Younger Poet Award from the Academy of American Poets in 1986 and the Pulitzer Prize for poetry in 1987.

Dove's next collection of poems, *Grace Notes* (1989), also draws on autobiographical elements and explores the seemingly small but significant moments in life. In "Pastoral," she describes the euphoria of a mother breast-feeding her child: "I felt then / what a young man must feel / with his first love asleep on his breast: / desire, and the freedom to imagine it."

In 1993 Dove published *Selected Poems,* which collected the poems of three earlier volumes: *The Yellow House on the Corner, Museum,* and *Thomas and Beulah.* Also that year, in recognition of her achievement as a poet, Dove was named U.S. poet laureate, and served from 1993 to 1995. Since the post was renamed in 1986 (ROBERT HAYDEN served as Poetry Consultant to the Library of Congress in 1976), Dove is the first African American to be named to the position. "It is significant," Dove explained about being the first black poet laureate, "in terms of the message it sends about the diversity of our culture and our literature."

Dove's other volumes of poetry include *Mother Love: Poems* (1995), which uses the Greek myth of Demeter and Persephone to explore the bond between mother and daughter, and *On the Bus with Rosa Parks: Poems* (1999), which includes poems that honor the lives of civil rights workers and highlights the causes for which they fought. Though she is known primarily for her award-winning poetry, Dove has also published works in other genres. Her novel *Through the Ivory Gate* (1992) depicts a gifted young African-American woman's return to her hometown in Ohio, where

Rita Dove served as U.S. poet laureate from 1993 to 1995. *(Photograph of Rita Dove © by Fred Viebahn)*

she confronts the memories of her past. She has also published a collection of short stories, *Fifth Sunday* (1985), and a verse drama, *The Darker Face of the Earth* (1994), a reinterpretation of Sophocles' *Oedipus Rex.*

A prolific and critically acclaimed writer, Rita Dove has earned numerous literary honors. In addition to the Pulitzer Prize for poetry and her election to the post of U.S. poet laureate, Dove was also the recipient of a Fulbright Fellowship, a Guggenheim Foundation Fellowship, and grants from the National Endowment for the Arts and the National Endowment for the Humanities. Since 1984 Dove has held teaching positions at Arizona State University and the University of Virginia in Charlottesville, where she was appointed Commonwealth Professor of

English in 1993. Dove lives in Charlottesville with her husband, German novelist Fred Viebahn, whom she married in 1979 and with whom she has one daughter.

Further Reading

Dove, Rita. *Grace Notes.* New York: W. W. Norton, 1989.

———. *Mother Love: Poems.* New York: W. W. Norton, 1995.

———. *Selected Poems.* New York: Pantheon Books, 1993.

Ingersoll, Earl G., ed. *Conversations with Rita Dove.* Jackson: University Press of Mississippi, 2003.

Steffen, Therese. *Crossing Color: Transcultural Space and Place in Rita Dove's Poetry, Fiction, and Drama.* New York: Oxford University Press, 2001.

DuBois, W. E. B.
(William Edward Burghardt DuBois, W. E. B. Du Bois)
(1868–1963) *sociologist, literary and cultural critic, essayist, novelist, poet, playwright, editor, civil rights leader*

Among civil rights activists and African-American cultural leaders of the 20th century, W. E. B. DuBois was one of the most celebrated and controversial. He was instrumental in setting the tone of racial debate at the turn of the 20th century, and, with ALAIN LOCKE, provided a philosophical foundation for the cultural flowering known as the New Negro movement or Harlem Renaissance in the 1920s. Also the author of novels, poetry, plays, essays, and sociological and cultural studies, DuBois is best known for his landmark work, *The Souls of Black Folk* (1903).

William Edward Burghardt DuBois was born on February 23, 1868, in Great Barrington, Massachusetts, to Alfred and Mary Sylvania DuBois. DuBois's father, of French and Haitian ancestry, died during his childhood, and DuBois grew up in the care of his mother and her extended family. He attended Great Barrington High School, where he excelled as a student and edited *The Howler,* the school's newspaper. To help support his family, DuBois worked several odd jobs and contributed articles to the *Springfield Republican* and the *New York Age* (later known as the *New York Globe*) on life in Great Barrington's black community.

In 1885 DuBois graduated high school as class valedictorian and enrolled at Fisk University in Nashville, Tennessee, where he studied Greek, mathematics, philosophy, and science. As a senior he edited the *Fisk Herald,* the university's literary magazine, by which he helped to focus attention on local and national issues affecting young African Americans.

DuBois's studies at Fisk and his participation in a summer teaching program in rural eastern Tennessee provided a new perspective on the culture and traditions of rural African-American communities in the South and the racism they suffered. He graduated with honors from Fisk University in 1888 and earned a scholarship to Harvard, where his academic accomplishments earned the respect of such eminent professors as the renowned sociologist Max Weber and the philosophers William James and George Santayana.

In 1890 DuBois completed a second bachelor's degree at Harvard and earned his master's degree there a year later. After two years of study at the University of Berlin, DuBois returned to Harvard and completed his Ph.D. in history in 1895, the first African American to earn that distinction. His dissertation, published by Harvard as *The Suppression of the African Slave-Trade to the United States of America, 1638–1870* (1896) was the first volume published in the Harvard Historical Series.

Following his graduation from Harvard, DuBois accepted a teaching position at Wilberforce University in Ohio as a professor of Greek and Latin. He married Nina Gomer, a Wilberforce student, in 1896 and the following year accepted a research position at the University of Pennsylvania in Philadelphia, where he conducted extensive research on local black communities. His research, published in *The Philadelphia Negro* (1899), was the first sociological study of an African-American community to be published in the United States and is considered a pioneering work in the field of urban sociology.

In 1897 DuBois was appointed professor of economics and history at Atlanta University and embarked on a prolific period of writing and political involvement. He published essays in journals such as *Dial* and the *Atlantic Monthly*. In 1900 he attended the Pan African Conference in London, where he argued to preserve the independence of Africa's few remaining republics in the face of continued European domination. In 1903 he published *The Souls of Black Folk*, his most acclaimed and enduring work.

In 14 related essays, DuBois traces the social, political, and racial history of African Americans in the United States, focusing particularly on the unfulfilled promises of freedom in the wake of emancipation. His pronouncement in the "Forethought" of *The Souls of Black Folk* that "the problem of the Twentieth Century is the problem of the color line" would prove to be prophetic; and his articulation of what he called the "double consciousness" of blacks in America, "this sense of always looking at one's self through the eyes of others, of measuring one's soul by the tape of a world that looks on in amused contempt and pity," had a profound effect on the progression of African-American intellectual and artistic history throughout the 20th century.

During his tenure at Atlanta University, DuBois published more than a dozen sociological studies on various aspects of African-American life, from economic and educational opportunities in *The Negro in Business* (1899) and *The Negro Common School* (1901) to issues of creativity and spirituality in works such as *The Negro Artisan* (1902) and *The Negro Church* (1903). He also helped found the Niagara Movement, which convened for the first time in Ontario, Canada, in 1905, and which demanded the full and immediate acceptance of African Americans in American society. In 1910 the Niagara Movement was restructured as the National Association for the Advancement of Colored People (NAACP).

DuBois left Atlanta University in 1910 to join the NAACP's executive board in New York. He was appointed director of publications and research and became the founding editor of *Crisis*, the NAACP's literary and political journal. During his 24 years as editor of *Crisis*, DuBois played a vital role in promoting the literary works of virtually every major writer of the Harlem Renaissance. He also used *Crisis* to provide information on national and global events that affected African Americans, from the continued struggle for civil rights in the United States to the heroism of African-American soldiers in France during World War I.

During his years with the NAACP, DuBois published numerous books, including *Dark Water: Voices within the Veil* (1920), a collection of autobiographical essays and poems, and the formidable *Africa: Its Place in Modern History* (1930). He also published two novels: *The Quest of the Silver Fleece* (1911), a novel about the dehumanizing qualities of American labor practices, and *Dark Princess: A Romance* (1928), a love story set against the racism of 1920s America.

DuBois's reputation as a writer, scholar, and leading African-American intellectual brought both fame and controversy. His political activism put him at odds with others in the NAACP, and his emphasis on higher education and greater social and political involvement for African Americans conflicted with other early 20th-century black leaders, particularly BOOKER T. WASHINGTON, whose respected Tuskegee Institute emphasized the economic enfranchisement of blacks with no immediate demand for social or political equity.

Another point of contention among DuBois's critics involved his outspoken advocacy of

Pan-Africanism and his unrelenting criticisms of American racism. He participated in all five Pan-African congresses, held between 1919 and 1945, and argued consistently for the core beliefs of the movement—preserving the independence of free African republics and allowing those under European control more autonomy in governing their people. DuBois believed passionately that Africans and African Americans shared a common political as well as cultural destiny.

DuBois left the NAACP in 1934 to chair the department of sociology at Atlanta University, a position he retained until 1943, after which he returned to the NAACP as the director of special

Widely recognized as one of the most influential African-American intellectuals and critics, W. E. B. DuBois was also a pioneer in the field of sociology. *(Library of Congress)*

research. His politics again created conflicts, and he resigned for the last time in 1948. During the 1950s, DuBois's interest in socialism and his support of the Soviet Union resulted in an indictment for failing to register as an agent of a foreign government. With the assistance of Shirley Graham, whom he had married following the death of his first wife in 1950, DuBois was eventually acquitted in 1951.

In his final years DuBois traveled widely in Europe, the Soviet Union, and China. He also published a trilogy of novels: *The Ordeal of Mansart* (1957), *Mansart Builds a School* (1959), and *Worlds of Color* (1961). In 1960 DuBois joined the Communist Party and was later invited to live in the newly independent West African nation of Ghana by that country's first president, Kwame Nkrumah. Months after receiving his Ghanaian citizenship, William Edward Burghardt DuBois died on August 27, 1963, in Accra, Ghana.

Perhaps the most celebrated intellectual in African-American history, W. E. B. DuBois was also one of the most controversial. The publication of *The Souls of Black Folk* in 1903 galvanized debate on race relations in the early 20th century and has remained a fundamental document in the history of African-American history and literature. Despite a decline in his reputation during the years after his death, due in large part to his membership in the Communist Party, W. E. B. DuBois has remained a focus of critical attention with the publication of numerous studies of his life and work, and the reissue of several of his essay collections and novels.

Further Reading

Hubbard, Dolan. The Souls of Black Folk *One Hundred Years Later.* Columbia: University of Missouri Press, 2002.

Lewis, David Levering. *W. E. B. DuBois: Biography of a Race, 1868–1919.* New York: Henry Holt, 1993.

———. *W. E. B. DuBois: The Fight for Equality and the American Century, 1919–1963.* New York: Henry Holt, 2000.

Dumas, Henry
(Henry Lee Dumas)
(1934–1968) *poet, short story writer, educator*

A promising young poet and fiction writer whose life was tragically cut short, Henry Dumas owes his literary stature largely to the efforts of Eugene Redmond, TONI MORRISON, and QUINCY TROUPE. They saw that Dumas's manuscripts were published posthumously; once published, the works received wide critical acclaim for their innovative techniques and original perspective on African-American life and culture.

Born in Sweet Home, Arkansas, on July 20, 1934, Henry Dumas moved to Harlem at the age of 10. He graduated from Commerce High School in 1953 and enrolled in the City College of New York. In 1954 he left school to join the U.S. Air Force, and was stationed first at Lackland Air Force Base, in San Antonio, Texas, and later in the Middle East, where he developed an interest in Arabic language and culture. He married Loretta Ponton in 1955, while still in the air force. Their first child, David, was born in 1958.

During his service in the military, Dumas began to submit poems and stories to air force periodicals and won several writing awards. Upon his discharge from the military in 1958, Dumas enrolled at Rutgers University, where he studied part time until 1965. His second son, Michael, was born in 1962. Despite his obligations as a college student, family man, and employee at IBM from 1963 to 1964, Dumas became active in the Civil Rights movement, transporting supplies to protestors in Mississippi and Tennessee.

In 1967 Dumas taught briefly at Hiram College in Ohio before joining the Experiment in Higher Education program at Southern Illinois University as a director of language workshops. There, he met Eugene Redmond, a fellow teacher, and the two became close friends and literary collaborators. While living in East St. Louis briefly in 1968, Dumas performed his poetry in clubs and cafés and continued his involvement in civil rights work and the Black Power movement.

While on a visit to New York, Henry Dumas was shot and killed on May 23, 1968, by a New York Transit Authority police officer in what was alleged to be a case of mistaken identity. Dumas left behind a wife, two sons, and several unpublished poems and stories. Eugene Redmond, acting as literary executor, began editing Dumas's writing for publication.

Dumas's first posthumous collection of poems, *Poetry for My People*, appeared in 1970; it was later reprinted in 1974 as *Play Ebony, Play Ivory*. Also in 1970, Redmond edited and published a collection of Dumas's short stories, *Ark of Bones*. Blending natural and supernatural elements in his fiction and poetry, Dumas drew from sources as varied as Christian theology, Middle Eastern mythology, and jazz to create a unique vision of the African-American experience. His writing captured the attention of critics and fellow writers such as JAMES BALDWIN, GWENDOLYN BROOKS, and MAYA ANGELOU; Angelou praised the mythical scope and rhythm of his language.

Redmond published several additional volumes of Dumas's writing, including an unfinished novel, *Jonah and the Green Stone*, in 1976, *Rope of Wind and Other Stories* in 1979, the verse anthology *Goodbye, Sweetwater* in 1988, and *Knees of a Natural Man: The Selected Poetry of Henry Dumas* in 1989. As his writings gained a wider audience, Dumas became recognized as one of the most influential and innovative poets and writers of his generation.

Further Reading
Andrews, William L., Frances Smith Foster, and Trudier Harris, eds. *The Concise Oxford Companion to African American Literature*. New York: Oxford University Press, 2001.

Black Writers. Detroit, Mich.: Gale Research Corp., 1989.

Redmond, Eugene B. "30 Years Later: Remembering Henry Dumas." *Essence*, February 1999, p. 63.

Worley, Demetrice A., and Jesse Perry, Jr., eds. *African-American Literature: An Anthology*. Lincolnwood, Ill.: NTC Publishing Group, 1998.

Dunbar, Paul Laurence

(1872–1906) *poet, novelist, short story writer, essayist*

Known primarily as a poet, Paul Laurence Dunbar also wrote novels, short fiction, essays, and lyrics for theatrical productions. Versatile and erudite, Dunbar was the first African-American writer to receive national recognition. His writing provided a foundation for generations of later authors, particularly those of the Harlem Renaissance, who almost universally recognized him as the standard by which later African-American writers would be measured.

Dunbar's father, Joshua, had escaped slavery in Kentucky prior to the Civil War and fled to Canada. He returned during the war to enlist in the 55th Massachusetts Infantry, one of the first all-black units in the Union army. Following the war, he settled in Dayton, Ohio, and in 1871 married Matilda Murphy, also a former slave from Kentucky. Paul Laurence Dunbar was born a year later, on June 27, 1872.

A quiet and reserved child, Dunbar distinguished himself as a gifted student. He attended public schools in Dayton, and graduated from Central High School, where he had served as the editor of the school newspaper, the president of the literary society, and the senior class poet. His dignified bearing and remarkable oratorical skills earned him the nickname "Deacon Dunbar" among his classmates, who included the future inventor and aviator Orville Wright. Dunbar published his first poem, "Our Martyred Soldiers," as a high school student and wrote the class song for his graduating class. He also edited the *Dayton Tattler*, a short-lived newspaper for African Americans published by Orville Wright. Unable to afford the cost of enrolling in college, he began to look for work to support himself and his widowed mother following his graduation in 1891.

Dunbar sought employment as a writer and reporter with several of Dayton's daily newspapers, in some of which he had published poems as a teenager. His hopes were soon dimmed when he discovered that no professional employment opportunities, indeed very few opportunities of any kind, existed for African-Americans. After several months of unsuccessful searching, he reluctantly accepted a position as an elevator attendant at the Callahan Bank Building in downtown Dayton. He devoted his spare moments to reading and writing, and began to submit poems and short stories to numerous publishers and newspapers. The Kellogg Newspaper Company of Chicago, Illinois, published his first short story, "The Tenderfoot," in 1891, and Dunbar received a check for six dollars, the equivalent of almost two weeks' pay as an elevator operator.

In 1892, a chance meeting with a former teacher led to an invitation to address the annual convention of the Western Association of Writers in Dayton. There he read some of his poetry to the assembled writers and journalists. One of the association's members, Dr. James Matthews, later published some of Dunbar's poems in his syndicated column, bringing Dunbar to the attention of readers across the country, including the celebrated poet James Whitcomb Riley. Inspired by his growing reputation as a poet, Dunbar made plans to publish his first collection of verse.

With the assistance of Charles Whitcomb Riley, who sent him a letter of commendation, and his former classmate Orville Wright, Dunbar convinced United Brethren Publishing in Dayton to publish *Oak and Ivy*, his first book of poetry, in 1893. Consisting of both conventional verse and dialect poems inspired by the everyday language of African Americans, *Oak and Ivy* appealed to black and white audiences alike, and Dunbar's reputation as a poet gained momentum. Later in 1893 he was invited to recite his poetry at the World's Columbian Exhibition in Chicago, Illinois, where he met several leading African-American activists and social leaders, including FREDERICK DOUGLASS, Mary Church Terrell, and Ida B. Wells-Barnett. Despite the critical success of *Oak and Ivy*, the book generated little revenue. Dunbar continued his work as an elevator operator and sold copies of his book to interested passengers.

With the assistance of two prominent Toledo, Ohio, residents, Dr. Henry Tobey, a psychiatrist, and Dr. Charles Thatcher, a lawyer, Dunbar published his second volume of poetry, *Majors and Minors*. Like his previous book, this volume contained standard and dialect verse, with the standard verse grouped under the heading "Majors," and dialect poems under the heading "Minors." Inspired by the works of such classic English poets as William Wordsworth and Samuel Taylor Coleridge, Dunbar's standard verse displayed a remarkable lyricism and thorough knowledge of traditional forms. His dialect poetry, however, earned wider acclaim, particularly among white readers. A favorable review of *Majors and Minors* by the eminent American novelist William Dean Howells contributed to the book's critical and commercial success.

In 1896 the New York publishing firm Dodd, Mead, and Company released *Lyrics of Lowly Life,* which collected poems from Dunbar's first two books and featured an introduction by William Dean Howells. Now a nationally known and respected poet, Dunbar embarked on a six-month reading tour of England. During his trip, he befriended British composer Samuel Coleridge-Taylor, with whom he collaborated on *Dream Lover: An Operatic Romance.* The opera was produced in 1898.

In 1895 Dunbar established a correspondence with Alice Ruth Moore, a young teacher and aspiring writer (see ALICE RUTH MOORE DUNBAR-NELSON). The two met in 1897 prior to Dunbar's departure for England. After his return, he and Moore married in 1898 and settled down in Washington, D.C., where Dunbar had accepted a clerical position at the Library of Congress. In 1898 he published his first collection of short stories, *Folks from Dixie,* and his first novel, *The Uncalled.* Though his short story collection received favorable reviews, critics largely dismissed the novel, citing Dunbar's inability to por-

Paul Laurence Dunbar was the first nationally acclaimed African-American poet. *(Library of Congress)*

tray realistic African-American characters and create a believable plot.

Dunbar's health began to decline in 1899. The onset of tuberculosis compelled him to give up his position at the Library of Congress, but despite his physical suffering and a growing reliance on alcohol, Dunbar continued to write. His fourth volume of poetry, *Lyrics of the Hearthside,* was published in 1899. *The Strength of Gideon, and Other Stories* appeared in 1900. Dunbar's reputation as a novelist continued to suffer with the publication of his next two novels, *The Love of Landry* (1900), and *The Fanatics* (1901). A third novel, *The Sport of the Gods* (1902), received moderate acclaim as a work of social protest.

Dunbar's marriage ended in 1902. His publication of *Lyrics of Love and Laughter* in 1903 reaffirmed his reputation as a poet of incredible sensitivity and skill. In his final years, Dunbar published two collections of short stories, *In Old Plantation Days* (1903) and *The Heart of the Happy Hollow* (1904). He also produced two more volumes of poetry, *Lyrics of Sunshine and Shadow* (1905) and *Howdy, Howdy, Howdy* (1905), which contained poems from previous collections. After a further decline in health, Paul Laurence Dunbar died on February 9, 1906.

Described by the educator BOOKER T. WASHINGTON as the "poet laureate of the Negro race," Paul Laurence Dunbar enjoyed international recognition during his lifetime as the leading African-American poet of his or any other age. Scholars in the years following his death, however, became increasingly critical of his work, particularly his dialect poetry. Recently, though, critics and writers have generated renewed interest in Dunbar's works, particularly his traditional verse. The poet NIKKI GIOVANNI described Dunbar's writing as "a natural resource for our people," adding that "there is no poet, black or nonblack, who measures his achievement."

Further Reading

Gayle, Addison, Jr. *Oak and Ivy: A Biography of Paul Laurence Dunbar.* New York: Doubleday, 1974.

Martin, Herbert Woodward, Ronald Primeau, and Henry Louis Gates, Jr., eds. *In His Own Words: The Dramatic and Other Uncollected Works of Paul Laurence Dunbar.* Athens: University of Ohio Press, 2002.

Martin, Jay, ed. *A Singer in the Dawn: Reinterpretations of Paul Laurence Dunbar.* New York: Dodd, Mead, 1975.

Dunbar-Nelson, Alice Ruth Moore
(1875–1935) *poet, short story writer, diarist*

A gifted writer of short stories and a celebrated orator, Alice Dunbar-Nelson nevertheless was known during the Harlem Renaissance primarily as a poet. In her writing as well as in her dedication to numerous social and political causes, she struggled to promote racial and gender equality.

Her versatile range as a writer, including diaries and newspaper columns, provides valuable insight into the challenges facing African-American women in the late 19th and early 20th centuries.

Alice Dunbar-Nelson was born Alice Ruth Moore in 1875 to a mixed Creole, African-American, and Native American family in New Orleans. Her father, Joseph, was a seaman, and her mother, Patricia, worked as a seamstress. A gifted student, she enrolled in Straight College (now Dillard University) at the age of 15 and received her teaching degree in 1892. She also studied nursing and stenography, and worked as an editor for a black fraternity publication.

In 1895 Moore published her first book, *Violets, and Other Tales,* a collection of poems, stories, and essays whose themes were predominantly romantic in nature. In the story "The Woman," she addressed the controversial subjects of female independence and self-determination, ideas that would engage her throughout her life.

That same year, Moore moved with her family to Massachusetts, where she began a correspondence with the poet PAUL LAURENCE DUNBAR. After two years of courtship through letters, the two met in 1897, prior to Dunbar's departure for a reading tour of England. During his absence, she lived in New York City, where she taught school and helped found the White Rose Mission in Harlem. The two writers were married in 1898.

In 1899 Alice Dunbar published her most acclaimed work, *The Goodness of St. Rocque and Other Stories,* in which she portrayed life among the Creole communities of New Orleans. These 14 stories demonstrated her considerable talents as a regional writer and her ability to portray the lives of New Orleans' Creole population in vivid and authentic detail.

Because of Paul Laurence Dunbar's fragile health and frequent travel, the marriage ended in 1902. Alice Dunbar moved to Wilmington, Delaware, and resumed her teaching career. A second marriage, to a fellow teacher, Henry

Arthur Callis, in 1910, ended a year later. During these personally tumultuous years, she continued to pursue her literary career, publishing stories and poems in various periodicals and editing a volume of African-American oratory, *Masterpieces of Negro Eloquence,* in 1914. In 1916 she married Robert J. Nelson, a journalist, and remained with him for the rest of her life.

During World War I, Dunbar-Nelson became active in numerous relief efforts, including the Circle of Negro War Relief and the Women's Commission on the Council of Defense, through which she organized volunteers in several Southern states. She published a second volume of oratory, *The Dunbar Speaker and Entertainer,* in 1920, then left her teaching career to devote her time to journalism and political activism. She also continued to publish stories and poems, many of which appeared in the journals *Opportunity* and *Crisis,* and contributed columns to the *Pittsburgh Courier* and the *Washington Eagle.*

Dunbar-Nelson cofounded and edited the *Wilmington Weekly* in 1920, but by the end of the decade her literary output had slowed. From 1928 to 1931, she served as executive secretary of the American Friends Inter-Racial Peace Committee and spent much of her time speaking on behalf of the organization. Alice Dunbar-Nelson died on September 18, 1935.

Praised for her erudition and her mastery of a wide range of literary expression, Alice Dunbar-Nelson was one of the most accomplished and articulate female African-American writers of the early 20th century and a champion of women's rights and racial equality. Her diary, published in 1984 under the title *Give Us Each Day: The Diary of Alice Dunbar-Nelson,* provides valuable insights into the challenges she faced as an activist and as a writer.

Further Reading

Andrews, William L., Frances Smith Foster, and Trudier Harris, eds. *The Concise Oxford Companion to African American Literature.* New York: Oxford University Press, 2001.

Brooks, Kristina. "Alice Dunbar-Nelson's Local Colors of Ethnicity, Class, and Place." *MELUS* 23, no. 2 (summer 1998): 3.

Gates, Henry Louis, Jr., and Nellie Y. McKay, eds. *The Norton Anthology of African American Literature.* New York: W. W. Norton, 1997.

Hull, Gloria T., ed. *The Works of Alice Dunbar Nelson.* New York: Oxford University Press, 1988.

Ellison, Ralph
(Ralph Waldo Ellison)
(1914–1994) *novelist, short story writer, essayist, literary critic, educator*

An author, literary critic, and educator, Ralph Ellison achieved international acclaim as a writer with the publication of his first novel, *Invisible Man*, in 1952. The range of his writing included short stories, essays, reviews, and numerous pieces on jazz. His works demonstrated a mastery of the literary traditions of his African-American and European literary predecessors; among the latter Ellison cited T. S. Eliot, James Joyce, and Fyodor Dostoevski as particularly influential. A meticulous and demanding writer, Ellison spent seven years completing *Invisible Man*. This lone work, which has been translated into 14 languages and is considered a classic of modern American and African-American literature, secured Ellison's reputation as one of the most influential writers of the 20th century.

Ralph Waldo Ellison was born on March 1, 1914, in Oklahoma City, Oklahoma, where his parents, Ida and Lewis Alfred Ellison, had relocated from South Carolina in order to find a less oppressive environment in which to raise their two sons. Ellison excelled as a student at Frederick Douglass High School, where he studied music theory and learned to play several instruments, including the trumpet. In 1933 he earned a scholarship to Tuskegee Institute, in Alabama, where he studied music composition and literature. When financial difficulties compelled him to leave school, Ellison moved to New York in 1936 and befriended RICHARD WRIGHT, who encouraged him to explore a career as a writer.

In 1938 Ellison joined the Federal Writers' Project of the Works Progress Administration as a compiler of African-American folklore. He also published essays and stories in several small periodicals and served briefly as managing editor of *Negro Quarterly* in 1942. After a two-year tour in the U.S. Merchant Marine from 1943 to 1945, Ellison returned to New York and received a Rosenwald Fellowship that enabled him to begin work on his first novel. He married Fanny McConnell in 1946 and for the next six years he published reviews and short stories, and worked as a photographer to support himself while writing his first novel.

Ellison published *Invisible Man* in 1952. Generally regarded as one of the finest works of 20th-century American fiction, *Invisible Man* depicts the personal travails of its unnamed narrator, an African-American male whose struggle against racial prejudice mirrors the broader history of black oppression. "I am an invisible man," the narrator explains in the novel's prologue. "I am invisible, understand, simply because people refuse to see me." In the prologue, the narrator describes his "hibernation" in the basement of an exclusively white apartment building.

Through the course of the novel, the narrator explains how he has come to take refuge in his basement hideaway and has suffered repeated humiliation as he struggles to understand his own identity. In his various roles as promising college student, factory worker, and associate of Ras the Destroyer, an influential leader of a Black Nationalist movement, the narrator attempts to identify with various social and cultural groups. Inevitably, though, these efforts lead to alienation and the threat of physical harm.

In the novel's epilogue, the narrator explains his resolve to abandon hibernation and return to society, having determined that his former preconceptions about the world were false: "Now I know men are different and that all life is divided and that only in division is there true health." It is the diversity of life, and a resistance to any kind of conformity, that provides some sense of peace to the narrator. "America is woven of many strands," he concludes. "I would recognize them and so let it remain."

Though *Invisible Man* contained elements of the classic protest novel, embodied in works such as Richard Wright's *Native Son* (1940) and ANN PETRY's *The Street* (1946), some critics condemned it for what they considered a distortion of black experience. Despite such criticisms, the novel became an instant success and earned the National Book Award in 1953.

Following the overwhelming popular and critical success of *Invisible Man*, Ellison lectured in the United States and Europe and held academic appointments at several institutions, including Bard College, in upstate New York; New York University; Rutgers University, in New Jersey; the University of Chicago; and Yale University. He also began work on a second novel and published numerous essays, several of which were included in his renowned collection *Shadow and Act* (1964), which Ellison described as being "con-

cerned with three general themes: with literature and folklore, with Negro musical expression—especially jazz and blues—and with the complex relationship between the Negro American subculture and North American culture as a whole."

For the next 30 years, Ellison taught, lectured in the United States and Europe, and worked methodically on his second novel, a large portion of which he rewrote after a house fire in 1967 destroyed most of the manuscript. He also published a second collection of essays, *Going to the Territory* (1986). Ralph Ellison died of cancer on April 16, 1994, in New York City.

After two posthumous publications, *The Collected Essays of Ralph Ellison* (1995) and *Flying Home and Other Stories* (1996), Ellison's second novel, *Juneteenth*, was published in 1999. Unfinished at the time of his death, the novel's depiction of the personal and political evolution of its protagonist, Bliss, from a potentially influential cultural leader in the black community to an

Ralph Ellison earned international acclaim for *Invisible Man*, his first novel, and the only one to be published during his lifetime. *(National Archives)*

oppressive and racist politician, earned mixed critical reviews, but left Ellison's literary reputation undiminished.

Critical evaluations of Ralph Ellison's contributions to the African-American literary tradition were varied throughout his life. During the 1960s, African-American nationalist movements decried Ellison for his strident condemnation of cultural separatism and an aesthetic framework that they considered too European. Later generations, however, confirmed the complex artistry of his writing and the depth of his literary vision. Ellison continues to be regarded as one of the most influential African-American, and American, authors of the 20th century. On May 2, 2003, the City of New York unveiled a monument to Ralph Ellison on Riverside Drive in West Harlem, where Ellison lived for many years. The monument depicts a human figure cut out of a 15-foot-high bronze panel, a symbolic representation of Ellison's protagonist in his classic 1952 novel *Invisible Man*.

Further Reading

Butler, Robert J., ed. *Critical Responses to Ralph Ellison.* Westport, Conn.: Greenwood Publishing Group, 2000.

Ellison, Ralph. *Invisible Man.* New York: Random House, 1952.

———. *Shadow and Act.* New York: Random House, 1964.

Jackson, Lawrence. *Ralph Ellison: Emergence of Genius.* New York: John Wiley and Sons, 2002.

Equiano, Olaudah
(Gustavus Vassa)
(1745–1797) *autobiographer, abolitionist*

With the publication of *The Interesting Narrative of the Life of Olaudah Equiano, or Gustavus Vassa the African, written by himself* in 1789, Olaudah Equiano founded the slave narrative tradition in African-American literature. An active abolitionist who bore witness to the atrocities of the transatlantic slave trade, Equiano helped bring an end to the slave trade in England and also became the most influential African-American writer of the 18th century.

The son of an Ibo leader in the Benin Province of Africa, now known as Nigeria, Olaudah Equiano was born in 1745. At the age of 11, he was kidnapped by African traders and sold to British slavers in 1756. He was sent to Barbados, in the West Indies, and then to Virginia, where Lt. Michael Henry Pascal of England's Royal Navy purchased him.

Given the name Gustavus Vassa, Equiano worked as a seaman aboard Pascal's ship and saw military action at the siege of Louisburg and the capture of Belle Island in Canada during the Seven Years' War. In 1757 he traveled to England, where he mastered the English language and converted to Christianity. After nearly 10 years of faithful service, Equiano expected to earn his freedom. Instead, he was sold to an American, Robert King, in 1763.

By then an experienced seaman, Equiano gained the respect of his new master. He worked as a clerk and captain's assistant aboard trading ships that, among other things, brought slaves to the English colonies in America. Equiano was allowed to trade on his own account, and by 1766 had earned enough to purchase his freedom. Choosing to resume his life at sea, he worked as a trader, a valet in the Mediterranean, and a surgeon's assistant during a voyage to the Arctic. He also lived for a time among the Moskito Indians in Nicaragua.

In 1777 Equiano returned to England, where he became active in the abolitionist movement. He brought to the attention of white abolitionist lawyer Granville Sharpe the massacre aboard the slave ship *Zong*, in which 132 slaves were thrown overboard alive and later claimed as an insurance loss. The account of the massacre increased support in the English Parliament for the abolition of the slave trade. In 1787 Equiano was appointed to serve as a steward for an expedition to repatriate Africans in London to Sierra Leone. In a letter published in London prior to his departure,

Equiano described the corruption of the officials in charge of the project and their mistreatment of the Africans in their charge. He was subsequently dismissed from his post.

Equiano remained in London, where he began his autobiography, *The Interesting Narrative of the Life of Olaudah Equiano, or Gustavus Vassa, the African, written by himself*, which was published in 1789. The first authentic example of the slave narrative, Equiano's book provided a firsthand account of the slave trade. Equiano also described his childhood in Africa prior to his capture, and he argued eloquently against slavery on humanistic and economic grounds. His argument for the legitimate trade of English goods in Africa instead of the trade in humans gained wide support for abolition in England and abroad. Equiano's autobiography went through nine editions in England, was also published in America, and was translated into Dutch, German, and Russian.

Equiano married an Englishwoman, Susanna Cullen, in 1792, and fathered two children. He continued to lecture and write in support of abolition until the end of his life. Olaudah Equiano died in London on April 31, 1797. The influence of his autobiography can hardly be overestimated. Its structure and content provided a crucial example for the numerous slave narratives that appeared in America in the 19th century, most notably FREDERICK DOUGLASS's *The Life and Times of Frederick Douglass*, published in 1845.

Further Reading

Andrews, William L., Frances Smith Foster, and Trudier Harris, eds. *The Concise Oxford Companion to African American Literature*. New York: Oxford University Press, 2001.

Appiah, Kwame Anthony, and Henry Louis Gates, Jr., eds. *Africana: The Encyclopedia of the African and African American Experience*. New York: Basic Civitas Books, 1999.

Gates, Henry Louis, Jr., and Nellie Y. McKay, eds. *The Norton Anthology of African American Literature*. New York: Norton, 1997.

Sabino, Robin, and Jennifer Hall. "The Path Not Taken: Cultural Identity in the Interesting Life of Olaudah Equiano." *MELUS* 24, no. 1 (spring 1999): 5.

Evans, Mari
(E. Reed, Mari E. Evans)
(1923–   ) *poet, children's fiction writer, short story writer, essayist, playwright, editor, educator*

In her influential anthology *Black Women Writers 1950–1980, A Critical Evaluation*, published in 1984, Mari Evans credited LANGSTON HUGHES and his book of poems *Weary Blues* (1926) with introducing her to the world of African-American literature. Known primarily as a poet, Evans has also distinguished herself as a dramatist, children's and short fiction writer, essayist, and television writer/producer.

Born on July 16, 1923, in Toledo, Ohio, Mari Evans published her first writing in a grade school newspaper. Though attracted to literature and writing from an early age, an interest that her father strongly encouraged, Evans studied fashion design at the University of Toledo. She eventually left the university without taking a degree to pursue a career as a writer. She worked for three years as an assistant editor in a manufacturing plant, where she honed her writing skills under the guidance of a meticulous and demanding professional writer.

Evans's first published poems appeared in the periodical *Negro Digest* and in Abraham Chapman's influential literary anthology *Black Voices* (1968). Evans identified with the poetry of the Black Arts Movement, particularly the works of AMIRI BARAKA (then known as LeRoi Jones), and HAKI MADHUBUTI (then writing under the name Don L. Lee). Her first collection of poetry, *Where Is All the Music?* (1968), reflects an increasingly Afrocentric approach that would be more fully realized in later collections. Also, from 1967 to 1973, Evans produced, directed, and wrote for the popular Indianapolis, Indiana, television program *The Black Experience.*

In 1970 Evans published her second collection of poetry, *I Am a Black Woman.* Her tone in these poems is defiant, as she confronts the political and social forces that threaten to stifle African-American culture. In the title poem, Evans creates a sense of community among African Americans, as well as the oppressed of all nations, with the image of the universal female or mother figure that is "tall as a cypress" and challenges those who suffer to "look on me and be renewed." *I Am a Black Woman* earned Evans an award from Indiana University's Writers' Conference as well as the first annual prize for poetry from the Black Academy of Arts and Letters, in 1971. Evans's other volumes of poetry include the critically acclaimed *Nightstar: 1973–1978,* published in 1980, *A Dark and Splendid Mass* (1992), and *How We Speak* (2002).

In her poetry, Evans celebrates the courage of civil rights leaders such as Malcolm X and Martin Luther King, Jr., the creativity of legendary jazz musicians, and the endurance of an ancestral heritage steeped in tradition and suffering, whose "bony symbols of indomitable will" (in her poem "The Elders") testify to the strength and self-sufficiency of black culture. Evans's poetry also confronts the injustice of racism with defiance and power. "i / Have Arrived," she writes in "Status Symbol." "i / am the / New Negro."

In addition to her numerous volumes of poetry, Evans has published several children's books that feature African-American characters and use black idioms. *I Look at Me,* published in 1974, examines issues of African-American identity and affirms the beauty of black culture in a way that is accessible to young children. *Rap Stories* (1974) and *Singing Black* (1976) use music and poetry to teach positive family and cultural values. Evans's other children's books include *J. D.* (1973), a collection of juvenile stories; *Jim Flying High* (1979); and *Dear Corrine, Tell Somebody! Love, Annie: A Book about Secrets* (1999), which addresses the issue of child abuse.

Like her poetry and children's fiction, Evans's theatrical works reflect her desire to reinforce the strength of African-American values and culture in the face of adversity. *River of My Song,* first produced in 1977, was a meticulously orchestrated theatrical production that included actors, dancers, and musicians. Evans used a split stage in her 1979 production of *Portrait of a Man* to show the past and present experiences of an African-American man, with events from his young adulthood on one side, and those of his old age on the other. Also in 1979, Evans staged her one-woman monologue, *Boochie.* The play portrays an old woman preparing a meal for her son, during which she meditates on the social and political forces that shaped the experiences of her family and the values that sustained them through various hardships. Evans's other plays include *Eyes* (1979), an adaptation of ZORA NEALE HURSTON's 1937 work *Their Eyes Were Watching God; New World* (1984), a children's musical; and two unproduced plays, *The Way They Made Beriani* and the musical *Glide and Sons.*

One of the most acclaimed and versatile African-American poets of the late 20th century, Mari Evans has achieved international recognition as a writer whose works celebrate the vitality and beauty of African and African-American culture and explore the social and political challenges confronting black women. Her writing has been translated into numerous languages, including French, German, and Dutch. In 1997 Evans was honored by the African nation of Uganda, which issued a postage stamp in recognition of her accomplishments. Apart from her international success as a poet and fiction writer, Evans has held teaching and writing positions at numerous universities, including Indiana University, Purdue, Northwestern, Spelman College, and Cornell. Her groundbreaking literary anthology, *Black Women Writers 1950–1980: A Critical Evaluation* (1984), helped focus critical attention on the works of numerous female authors, including MAYA ANGELOU and TONI MORRISON. It remains an important resource in the study of African-American literature.

Further Reading

Evans, Mari. *Black Women Writers 1950–1980: A Critical Evaluation.* New York: Doubleday, 1984.

———. *A Dark and Splendid Mass.* New York: Harlem River Press, 1992.

———. *How We Speak.* Chicago, Ill.: Third World Press, 2002.

Gates, Henry Louis, Jr., and Nellie Y. McKay, eds. *The Norton Anthology of African American Literature.* New York: Norton, 1997.

Everett, Percival
(Percival Everett Leonard)

(1956–   ) *novelist, short story writer, poet, children's fiction writer, educator*

A prolific and imaginative author of novels, short stories, and children's fiction, Percival Everett has earned wide critical acclaim for his complex narratives and compelling, often surreal characters. His writing, which some critics have called avant-garde, tends to defy easy classification. Everett resists the use of labels that limit the nature and scope of his writing. "I think readers, black and white, are sophisticated enough to be engaged by a range of black experience," Everett explained in a 2001 interview, "just as one accepts a range of so-called white experience."

Percival Everett was born to Percival Leonard Everett and Dorothy Stinson Everett on December 22, 1956, at Fort Gordon, a military base near Augusta, Georgia, where his father served as a sergeant in the U.S. Army. Shortly after Everett's birth, his family moved to Columbia, South Carolina, where he spent his childhood. Everett graduated from A. C. Flora High School and earned a bachelor's degree in philosophy from the University of Miami in 1977. He later attended graduate school at the University of Oregon and Brown University, from which he graduated in 1982 with a master's degree in creative writing.

Everett published his first novel, the acclaimed *Suder,* in 1983. The protagonist, a black professional baseball player named Craig Suder, sets out on a journey of self-discovery when his career and marriage begin to fail. With only a saxophone, a phonograph, and a recording of Charlie Parker's *Ornithology,* Suder meets an unusual cast of characters, including a young runaway and an elephant named Renoir, on his way to fulfilling a long-neglected childhood dream.

Everett continued to explore new and unconventional material in later novels such as *Zulus* (1989), a postapocalyptic story of the last surviving fertile woman on Earth; *Watershed* (1996), in which a black hydrologist becomes involved in a land dispute between Native Americans and the federal government; *Frenzy* (1997), Everett's unusual take on Dionysus, the half man/half god figure from Greek mythology; and *Glyph* (1999), which parodies the intellectual elitism of academia in its depiction of a child genius and the adults who try to take advantage of his knowledge.

In 2001 Everett published *Erasure,* one of his most acclaimed and ambitious novels. The protagonist, Thelonious "Monk" Ellison, author of several erudite but generally overlooked books, decides to write a parody of so-called ghetto prose called *My Pafology,* under the pseudonym Stagg R. Leigh. To his surprise, Ellison's literary joke becomes a runaway best-seller, and he must confront the advantages and disadvantages of his newfound wealth and popularity. Everett's other novels include *Walk Me to the Distance* (1985), *Cutting Lisa* (1986), *For Her Dark Skin* (1989), *God's Country* (1994), *The Body of Martin Aguilera* (1994), and *Grand Canyon, Inc.* (2002).

In addition to novels, Everett has published two collections of short stories, *The Weather and Women Treat Me Fair* (1989) and *Big Picture: Stories* (1996), and a children's book, *The One That Got Away* (1992), which uses mathematical concepts as the framework for its characters and plot. Everett's short fiction has appeared in several literary journals, including *Callaloo* and *Black American Literature Forum.* He has also published poetry in Cyclops Press's *One Eye Review.*

Percival Everett has earned wide critical acclaim for the imaginative range and intellectual depth of his writing. He was the recipient of the PEN/Oakland–Josephine Miles Award for Excellence in Literature in 1996 for *Big Picture.* He also received the New American Writing Award in 1990 for *Zulus.* Everett has held academic appointments at the University of Kentucky in Lexington, the University of Notre Dame in Indiana, and the University of California at Riverside. Since 1999 he has been a professor of English at the University of Southern California.

Further Reading

Everett, Percival. *Erasure.* Hanover, N.H.: University Press of New England, 2001.

———. *Glyph.* St. Paul, Minn.: Graywolf Press, 1999.

———. *Grand Canyon, Inc.* San Francisco, Calif.: Versus Press, 2001.

Fauset, Jessie Redmon
(Jessie Fauset)
(1882–1961) *novelist, poet, essayist, educator*

A novelist, editor, and pivotal figure in the Harlem Renaissance, Jessie Redmon Fauset was described by novelist LANGSTON HUGHES as someone who "midwifed the so-called New Negro literature into being." Fauset's literary parties provided a forum for authors to meet and discuss their work; and during her career as an editor, she influenced the literary careers of such key Harlem Renaissance writers as Langston Hughes, JEAN TOOMER, CLAUDE MCKAY, and COUNTEE CULLEN. An important author in her own right, Fauset was the most prolific novelist of the Harlem Renaissance.

Jessie Redmon Fauset was born on April 27, 1882, in Fredericksville, New Jersey, to Redmon Fauset, an African Methodist Episcopal minister, and Annie Seamon Fauset, who died shortly after her birth. Fauset moved to Philadelphia with her father, who remarried and encouraged his daughter to pursue a career in teaching. Fauset attended Philadelphia High School for Girls, where she excelled, despite being the only African-American student in her class. After being denied admission to Bryn Mawr College because of her race, she earned a scholarship to Cornell University, where she studied classical languages and became the first African-American woman admitted to Phi Beta Kappa, an academic honor society.

After graduating from Cornell in 1905, she was refused a teaching position in Philadelphia's public schools but accepted a position at Douglas High School in Baltimore, Maryland. A year later, she moved to Washington, D.C., and taught French and Latin at the M Street High School (later renamed Dunbar High School), where she remained for 14 years. During this period, Fauset also earned her master's degree in French from the University of Pennsylvania and began writing a column, "Looking Glass," for the *Crisis* magazine.

Persuaded by W. E. B. DuBOIS, the eminent African-American sociologist and civil rights leader, to move to New York and join the staff of the *Crisis,* Fauset accepted a position as literary editor in 1919. In this role, she increased the circulation of the magazine and furthered the careers of numerous "New Negro" writers. She also began publishing her own stories, essays, reviews, and translations, including the essay "The Gift of Laughter," a seminal work on the limited and stereotypical roles available to African-American actors. ALAIN LOCKE published the essay in his book *The New Negro* in 1925.

In 1920 Fauset collaborated with Augustus Granville Dill, a sociologist and business manager at the *Crisis,* on DuBois's periodical for children,

The Brownies' Book: A Monthly Magazine for the Children of the Sun, which featured stories and biographies intended to "teach Universal Love and Brotherhood for all little folks—black and brown and yellow and white." The following year, Fauset took part in DuBois's second Pan-African Congress in Paris, a gathering of international representatives devoted to the equality of all races and democratic reforms in largely colonial Africa.

In 1924 Fauset returned to Europe to study at the Sorbonne and the Alliance Française. She also published her first novel, *There Is Confusion*, in which she explored the limited roles available for African-American women in a white society. The novel was written in part as a response to T. S. Stribling, a white author whose novel *Birthright* (1922) portrayed the lives of African-Americans, in Fauset's view, in an unrealistic and prejudiced way. Fauset also addressed the issue of "passing," whereby a light-skinned African American passes for white. This issue would remain a key element of her next three novels.

In 1927 Fauset left the *Crisis* and began teaching French at DeWitt Clinton High School in New York. She also embarked on the most prolific phase of her writing career. Considered by many scholars to be her most accomplished work, *Plum Bun: A Novel without a Moral* was published in 1929. Using the familiar nursery rhyme "To Market, To Market" as a framework, Fauset portrays the lives of two sisters, Angela and Virginia Murray, who leave their middle-class home in Philadelphia to pursue a more meaningful life in New York. The light-skinned Angela, an aspiring painter, decides to pass for white to further her artistic career. Virginia takes a different path by moving to Harlem and becoming an activist for racial equality. The novel addresses an important issue of the Harlem Renaissance, namely the link between racial and artistic identity.

Also in 1929, Fauset married Herbert Harris, a World War I veteran and insurance broker. She published two more novels, *The Chinaberry Tree* in 1931 and *Comedy, American Style* in 1933, both

of which dramatize the challenges faced by women of illegitimate and interracial relationships. These works also suggest that "becoming" white, in the context of passing, does not remove the physical and emotional barriers of a racially polarized society.

Fauset remained at DeWitt Clinton High School until 1944, when she and her husband moved to Montclair, New Jersey. She documented her travels in Europe and Africa during 1934 in essays published in the *Crisis*. In her later life she wrote poetry, taught briefly at the Hampton Institute in 1949, and published very little. Following the death of her husband in 1958, Fauset's health began to decline. She returned to Philadelphia to live with her brother-in-law, where she died of heart disease on April 30, 1961.

Though generally well received by critics, Fauset's novels and poetry were also criticized for what was perceived as an unrealistic portrayal of African-American life. The genteel middle-class status of many of her characters seemed at odds with the experience of many African-Americans living in grim urban conditions. Recent scholarship, however, has focused on her sensitive portrayal of women who confront racial and gender biases and who challenge the racial stereotypes of white society. In her efforts as an editor to create opportunities for other African-American authors, particularly women, and her prolific contribution to African-American literature, Fauset has been recognized as one of the most significant and influential authors to come out of the Harlem Renaissance.

Further Reading

Fauset, Jessie Redmon. *Plum Bun: A Novel without a Moral.* Boston: Beacon Press, 1999.

Miller, Nina. "Femininity, Publicity, and the Class Division of Cultural Labor: Jessie Redmon Fauset's *There Is Confusion.*" *African American Review* 30, no. 2 (summer 1996): 205.

Sylvander, Carolyn Wedin. *Jessie Redmon Fauset, Black American Writer.* Troy, N.Y.: Whitston Publishing Co., 1981.

Wall, Cheryl A. *Women of the Harlem Renaissance.* Bloomington: Indiana University Press, 1995.

Fisher, Rudolph
(Rudolph John Chauncey Fisher)
(1897–1934) *short story writer, novelist*

Described by LANGSTON HUGHES as "the wittiest of these new Negroes of Harlem," Rudolph Fisher became one of the best known writers of the Harlem Renaissance during the 1920s. His stories and novels provided compelling portraits of the social and artistic forces that shaped one of the most fertile periods in African-American cultural and literary history. Apart from his success as a writer, Fisher maintained a distinguished career as a physician, becoming a pioneer in the field of roentgenology in the early years of X-ray technology.

Rudolph John Chauncey Fisher was born on May 9, 1897, in Washington, D.C., to Glendora Fisher and the Reverend John Wesley Fisher, and grew up in Providence, Rhode Island. He graduated with honors from Classical High School in Providence in 1915 and received his bachelor's degree in 1919 from Brown University, where he won several prizes in oratory as well as memberships in the academic honor society Phi Beta Kappa and the fraternities Delta Sigma Rho and Sigma Xi. After earning a master's degree from Brown University in 1920, he studied medicine at Howard University Medical School and graduated with highest honors in 1924. Later that year, he began his residency at Freedmen's Hospital in Washington, D.C., and married Jane Ryder, a grade-school teacher.

In 1925 Fisher published his first short story, "The City of Refuge," in the prestigious *Atlantic Monthly.* The protagonist, King Solomon Gillis, flees North Carolina after killing a white man, and arrives in New York. Having been led to believe that Harlem offered a welcome change from the corruption and racial prejudice of the South, Gillis discovers that the same prejudices exist within the African-American communities in Harlem. "The City of Refuge," one of Fisher's best-known stories, was included in editor Edward J. O'Brien's *The Best Short Stories of 1925,* and secured Fisher a reputation as a sharp-tongued iconoclast and a brilliant storyteller.

Fisher published three more stories in 1925, including "The South Lingers On," "Ringtail," and "High Yaller," for which he was awarded the Spingarn Prize from the *Crisis* magazine. "High Yaller" drew its title from a slang term used for African Americans of light complexion and describes the intraracial prejudices that existed among African-American communities in Harlem.

Following his residency at Freedmen's Hospital, Fisher moved to New York to study medicine at Columbia University. He trained in the new field of roentgenology, and worked in several New York City hospitals.

In 1927 Fisher opened his own practice and became chair of the Department of Roentgenology at Manhattan's International Hospital. He also published four more stories: "The Promised Land" and "Blades of Steel" in the *Atlantic Monthly,* and "The Backsliders" and "Fire by Night" in *McClure's.* His essay "The Caucasian Storms Harlem," published that same year in H. L. Mencken's *American Mercury,* lamented the growing presence of white patrons in Harlem's cabarets and nightclubs. Fisher published six more short stories during his writing career. His last, "Miss Cinthie" (1933), received wide critical praise for its sensitive exploration of moral and generational conflicts within an African-American family. The story, considered one of his most mature works of fiction, was later anthologized in *Best Short Stories of 1934.*

Hailed during his lifetime as one of the most accomplished writers of short fiction during the Harlem Renaissance, Fisher received mixed reviews as a novelist. *The Walls of Jericho,* published in 1928, elicited a negative review from W. E. B. DuBOIS, the eminent African-American literary critic and sociologist, for its criticism of middle- and upper-class African Americans, while others praised Fisher's uncompromising condemnation of class prejudices within African-American urban communities. Fisher's second novel, *The Conjure-Man Dies: A Mystery Tale of Dark Harlem,* was published in 1932.

One of the earliest examples of African-American detective fiction, *The Conjure-Man Dies* reintroduces two characters from Fisher's first novel, Jinx Jenkins and Bubber Brown. The mystery revolves around the murder of N'Gana, a Harvard-educated African prince and "conjure man," a practitioner of African folk religion. Bubber Brown enlists the help of black detective Perry Dart and his associate Dr. John Archer to exonerate Jenkins, who is suspected of being the murderer. The novel was well received critically for its blend of humor and intrigue. Fisher later adapted it for the stage, and the play was produced under the title *Conjur' Man Dies* at the Lafayette Theatre in Harlem in 1936.

From 1931 to 1934, Fisher served as a first lieutenant in the New York National Guard's 369th Medical Corps, while also working as a superintendent at the International Hospital and as an X-ray technician at the New York City Health Department. He also coauthored and published two scientific papers in the *Proceedings of the Society of Experimental Biology* and the *Journal of Infectious Diseases.* After three operations to correct a stomach ailment, Rudoph John Chauncey Fisher died on December 26, 1934, at Edgecomb Sanitarium in New York City.

ARNA BONTEMPS praised Fisher's writing for its "intermingling of kindly satire and bittersweet tensions," as well as its depiction of "the ordinary workaday black who was largely neglected by other [Harlem] Renaissance writers." Fisher had completed several undated stories at the time of his death, among which only one, "John Archer's Nose," appeared posthumously, in 1935. Though Fisher's reputation as a writer diminished in the years following his death, renewed interest in his life and work in recent years has spurred the publication of several collected volumes of his short stories as well as reprint editions of his novels. *The Conjure-Man Dies* has also appeared twice in French translation.

Further Reading

Fisher, Rudolph. *The Conjure-Man Dies: A Tale of Dark Harlem.* Ann Arbor: University of Michigan Press, 1992.

———. *The Walls of Jericho.* Ann Arbor: University of Michigan Press, 1994.

Gates, Henry Louis, Jr., and Nellie Y. McKay, eds. *The Norton Anthology of African American Literature.* New York: W. W. Norton, 1997.

Forrest, Leon
(Leon Richard Forrest)
(1937–1997) *novelist, poet, essayist, editor, educator*

Despite the considerable acclaim that Leon Forrest has received in African-American literary circles, his works are not as widely known as those of many contemporaries. Forrest drew his inspiration from many sources, including family folklore, jazz, religion, and the works of such authors as RALPH ELLISON, James Joyce, and William Faulkner.

Leon Richard Forrest was born on January 8, 1937, in Chicago, Illinois, the son of a Creole Catholic mother and a Mississippi Protestant father. He attended Wendell Phillips School and later became one of the few black students to attend Hyde Park High School, graduating in 1955. Between 1955 and 1960, he took classes at Wilson Junior College, Roosevelt University, and the University of Chicago before serving in the U.S. Army in Germany. Upon his return, he worked part-time in a bar and liquor store managed by his mother and stepfather, and resumed his studies at the University of Chicago.

With a view to becoming a writer, Forrest worked as an editor for the *Woodlawn Observer* and became an associate editor of *Muhammad Speaks,* a newspaper published by the Nation of Islam, in 1969. He was promoted to managing editor three years later. In 1974 Random House published his first novel, *There Is a Tree More Ancient than Eden.* The novel was edited by TONI MORRISON and had a preface by Ralph Ellison. Forrest was praised as a major new talent. Forrest later joined the faculty of Northwestern University as professor and eventually chair of African-American studies.

The fictional Forest County, introduced in *There Is a Tree More Ancient than Eden,* would remain the focus of his next three novels. Using a stream-of-consciousness narration, letters, sermons, and dialogue, Forrest portrays the life of Nathaniel Witherspoon, a young man caught between his white and African-American roots. When his mother dies, Nathaniel begins a search for personal and cultural identity. With a large cast of characters, including such historical figures as Harriet Tubman and Louis Armstrong, Forrest created a compelling and, at times, surreal landscape.

Forrest's next two novels, *The Bloodworth Orphans,* published in 1977, and *Two Wings to Veil My Face,* published in 1984, find Nathaniel Witherspoon in the role of family chronicler as he hears and records tales of hardship and triumph surrounding the interconnected Bloodworth and Witherspoon families. Forrest uses the recurring image of the orphan to explore issues of race and identity in the lives of his characters and, more broadly, in American society.

Divine Days, Forrest's epic fourth novel, diverges in theme and focus from his previous work and depicts a week in the life of Joubert Antoine Jones, an aspiring writer. Also set in Forest County, the novel relies heavily on jazzlike improvisation as the characters present their various histories.

Forrest became an associate professor of literature and African-American studies at Northwestern University shortly after the publication of his first novel, and eventually became chair of African-American studies. He published two volumes of essays, *The Furious Voice for Freedom* in 1992 and *Relocations of the Spirit* in 1994. He also wrote two operatic libretti, *Re-Creation* (produced in 1978) and *Soldier Boy, Soldier* (produced in 1982). After 24 years as a distinguished professor and increasing recognition as one of the most innovative novelists of the late 20th century, Leon Forrest died on November 6, 1997.

Further Reading

Andrews, William L., Frances Smith Foster, and Trudier Harris, eds. *The Concise Oxford Companion to African American Literature.* New York: Oxford University Press, 2001.

Forrest, Leon. *Meteor in the Madhouse.* Chicago: Northwestern University Press, 2000.

———. *The Bloodsworth Orphans.* Chicago: University of Chicago Press, 2001.

———. *There Is a Tree More Ancient Than Eden.* Chicago: University of Chicago Press, 2001.

Forten, Sarah Louise
(Ada, Magawisca, Sarah Forten Purvis)
(1814–ca. 1898) *poet, abolitionist, social activist*

A daughter of one of Philadelphia's most prominent free African-American families, Sarah Forten began publishing her antislavery poems and essays in abolitionist journals such as *The Liberator* and *The Abolitionist* at the age of 17. Particularly concerned with the issue of women's rights, Forten helped found the Philadelphia Female Anti-Slavery Society in 1833, through which she worked to secure racial and gender equality for African-American women.

Sarah Louise Forten was born in 1814 in Philadelphia, Pennsylvania, the youngest of James Forten and Charlotte Vandine Forten's three daughters. Forten's father had served as a powder boy during the American Revolution and grew up to become one of New England's most prominent and wealthy African-American businessmen. James Forten was committed to abolition and women's rights, and his home became a meeting place for many of the early 19th century's most prominent reformers, including William Lloyd Garrison and John Greenleaf Whittier.

Having grown up in an environment that was steeped in the rhetoric of reform, and an early reader of Garrison's influential antislavery journal *The Liberator,* Sarah Forten began to contribute her own words to the abolitionist movement in essays and poems that she published as a teenager in *The Liberator* and *The Abolitionist.* Her early poems appeared under single-name pseudonyms, including Ada and Magawisca. "The grave to the weary is welcome and blest; / And death, to the captive, is freedom and rest," Forten wrote in "The Grave of the Slave," published in 1831.

Forten highlighted the hypocrisy of a nation that sanctioned slavery but claimed to be based on the principle of freedom for all. In her essay "The Abuse of Liberty," published in *The Liberator* in 1831 under the pseudonym Magawisca, Forten argued that the hour was coming when freedom, traditionally the exclusive province of white males, would be more justly distributed. "He will wipe the tears from Ethiopia's eye; He will shake the tree of liberty, and its blossoms shall spread over the earth."

Forten was also an early advocate of women's rights and an important voice for African-American women. With her sisters Harriet and Margaret, Forten established the Philadelphia Female Anti-Slavery Society in 1833. In one of her best-known poems, "An Appeal to Woman" (1834), Forten challenged her white contemporaries within the women's movement to address the needs of all women, not simply white women: "Our skins may differ, but from thee we claim / A sister's privilege, in a sister's name."

Forten's active involvement in the antislavery movement ended with her marriage to Joseph Purvis in 1838. She left Philadelphia and devoted her time to raising eight children and managing her husband's farm. Following the death of her husband in 1857, Sarah Forten Purvis returned to her childhood home in Philadelphia, where she is thought to have died in about 1898.

Sarah Forten distinguished herself as one of the leading abolitionists and women's rights activists of her day. With her mother and sisters, Forten helped establish the first interracial antislavery organization, the Female Anti-Slavery Society, whose white membership included Lucretia Mott, Maria Davis, and Anna Hopper. Forten's literary achievements would serve as an example to her niece, CHARLOTTE FORTEN GRIMKÉ, whose personal journals would provide important insight on the lives of African Americans during the antebellum era.

Further Reading

Gates, Henry Louis, Jr., and Nellie Y. McKay, eds. *The Norton Anthology of African American Literature.* New York: W. W. Norton, 1997.

"Sarah Forten Purvis." *Notable Black American Women.* Book 1. Detroit, Mich.: Gale Research, 1992.

Winch, Julie. *A Gentleman of Color: The Life of James Forten.* New York: Oxford University Press, 2002.

Fuller, Charles
(Charles Henry Fuller, Jr.)
(1939–) *playwright, screenwriter, educator*

The winner of two Obie awards for off-Broadway achievement and a Pulitzer Prize for drama, Charles Fuller is one of the most respected and successful contemporary playwrights in the American theater. His work also includes an Oscar-nominated film adaptation of his Pulitzer Prize–winning *A Soldier's Play,* and *Love Songs,* a television trilogy that aired on the cable channel Showtime in 1999, and numerous other television and film writing credits.

Charles Henry Fuller, Jr., was born on March 5, 1939, in Philadelphia, Pennsylvania, one of three children born to Charles Henry Fuller, Sr., and Lillian Anderson Fuller. Because his father was a commercial printer, young Fuller grew up among books, even helping his father by proofreading some of his work. Following his graduation from high school, Fuller attended Villanova University from 1956 to 1958. As an English major and aspiring writer, he was frustrated by professors who discouraged him from pursuing a writing career, and by racially biased editors who refused to publish his stories in the university's literary magazine.

After leaving Villanova without a degree, he joined the U.S. Army in 1959, using his free time during assignments in the United States and Asia to develop his skills as a writer. After his discharge, he took evening classes at La Salle College in Philadelphia and supported himself with a variety of part-time jobs, including student counselor at Temple University and housing inspector. He married Miriam Nesbitt, a nurse and teacher, in 1962 and fathered two sons, Charles III and David.

Fuller's interest in drama began as a teenager when he attended his first play, performed in Yiddish at the Walnut Street Theatre in Philadelphia. Though his interest in writing focused initially on poetry, short stories, and essays, Fuller became increasingly interested in dialogue, which led him to explore drama as a medium for the stories he hoped to tell. In 1967, with the help of several friends, Fuller cofounded the Afro-American Theatre of Philadelphia and began composing short plays. In 1968 Fuller wrote *The Village: A Party* for the McCarter Theater in Princeton, New Jersey. The play later moved to New York and debuted off-Broadway as *The Perfect Party* in 1969. He also published his play *The Rise in New Plays from the Black Theatre* (1969), edited by ED BULLINS.

The Village is set in a utopian community inhabited by racially mixed couples, whose peaceful existence is shattered when the village's black leader falls in love with a black woman and is later killed by angry villagers. The play received generally positive reviews for its unconventional approach to the question of integration, which in Fuller's view can sometimes magnify racial tensions within a community. It also launched Fuller's career as a dramatist. He and his family relocated to New York City, where he wrote two more plays, *The Candidate* and *In the Deepest Part of Sleep,* both produced by the Negro Ensemble Company in 1974.

In 1976 Fuller drew on his military experience in *The Brownsville Raid,* also produced by the Negro Ensemble Company. Based on actual events, *The Brownsville Raid* portrays the events surrounding the unprecedented dismissal of an entire regiment of African-American soldiers in 1906 after they were falsely accused of fomenting a riot in Brownsville, Texas. The play enjoyed more than 100 performances off-Broadway at the Theater de Lys. Fuller's next play, *Zooman and the Sign,* earned him national critical acclaim and two Obie Awards for its compelling and ambitious story of a young girl's murder at the hands of Zooman, a black teenager trying to cope with his own rage and a racist and apathetic society that seems to encourage his self-destruction.

In 1982 Fuller became only the second African American to win a Pulitzer Prize for drama when he received the award for *A Soldier's Play,* dedicated to the memory of LARRY NEAL, a lifelong friend and fellow playwright. Set on an army base in Louisiana during World War II, the play depicts the psychological effects of racism on the soldiers in an all-black company and highlights the increasingly strained relationships among black and white soldiers and their superiors following the murder of a black sergeant. Fuller adapted *A Soldier's Play* for the screen in 1984, and the film earned two Academy Award nominations for best picture and best screenplay.

During the late 1980s, Fuller began work on a proposed cycle of five plays set during Reconstruction. *Sally* and *Prince* were produced collectively as *We* in 1989 by the Negro Ensemble Theater. Fuller portrays the struggles of African Americans in the aftermath of the Civil War and amid the turbulence of Reconstruction. *Jonquil and Burner's Frolic* appeared in 1990. In general, Fuller's historical plays have not earned the critical attention that his earlier dramas *Zooman* and *A Soldier's Play* have received.

Apart from his work as a dramatist, Fuller has written several scripts for television, including *Roots, Resistance, and Renaissance* (1967); *The Sky Is Gray*, adapted for television from a short story by ERNEST J. GAINES (1980); an adaptation of Gaines's novel *A Gathering of Old Men* (1987); and an adaptation of *Zooman and the Sign* for television in 1995. He also wrote a segment of Showtime's 1998 Vietnam War drama *The Wall* and served as writer and producer of the 1999 Showtime production of *Love Songs*. Throughout the 1990s, Fuller focused his attention on television and film and received a writing credit for director Spike Lee's 1994 film *Malcolm X*. In a 1999 interview in *American Theatre*, he explained this shift away from theater: "I am very much committed to the theatre. But right now I am concerned with reaching as many people as I can, and motion pictures allow me to do this."

Charles Fuller's distinguished career as a playwright has included numerous prestigious fellowships, two Obie Awards, and a Pulitzer Prize for drama. As a writer, Fuller is concerned with combating the perpetuation of distorted images of African Americans. "What I wanted most to do when I became a writer," Fuller explained in a 1999 profile, "was to change how black men were perceived. Later I set out to change clichés we carry about ourselves." Fuller has also published short stories and essays in journals such as *Liberator* and *Negro Digest*, and he was a professor of African-American studies at Temple University from 1988 to 1993.

Further Reading

Anadolu-Okur, Nilgun. *Contemporary African American Theater: Afrocentricity in the Works of Larry Neal, Amiri Baraka, and Charles Fuller*. New York: Garland, 1997.

Andrews, William L., Frances Smith Foster, and Trudier Harris, eds. *The Concise Oxford Companion to African American Literature*. New York: Oxford University Press, 2001.

Fuller, Hoyt
(Hoyt William Fuller, William Barrow)
(1923–1981) *essayist, short story writer, literary critic, editor, educator*

One of the principal forces behind the Black Arts Movement, Hoyt Fuller played a considerable role in shaping African-American literary and cultural discourse in the 1960s and 1970s. His essays have appeared in seminal anthologies of African-American thought, including *The Black Aesthetic* and *Black Expression*, both edited by ADDISON GAYLE, JR., and Fuller was published frequently in such periodicals as *The New Yorker*, *The New Republic*, and *North American Review*.

Hoyt William Fuller was born on September 10, 1923, in Atlanta, Georgia, one of three sons of Thomas and Lillie Fuller. During his high school years, Fuller moved with his family to Detroit, Michigan. After high school, he served in the army during World War II, and later enrolled in Wayne State College (now University), where he received his bachelor's degree in English and journalism in 1950. For the next seven years, he worked for several publications, including the *Michigan Chronicle*, the *Detroit Tribune*, and *Collier's Encyclopedia*.

Fuller left the United States in 1957 to escape its increasing racial intolerance, living in France, Spain, and Africa. In 1960 he returned to America and accepted a position as editor of the revived periodical *Negro Digest* (renamed *Black World* in 1970 to better reflect its emphasis on issues related to African as well as African-American life and thought). Under his leadership, *Negro Digest* became one of the leading forums for artists and critics of the Black Arts Movement. In addition to his work as an editor,

Fuller also participated in the creation of the Organization of Black American Culture (OBAC), a writers' collective that featured such notable African-American literary figures as HAKI R. MADHUBUTI (then known as Don L. Lee), CAROLYN M. RODGERS, and NIKKI GIOVANNI.

Though he published numerous essays and columns in *Negro Digest* and elsewhere, Fuller published only one book-length work, *Return to Africa* (1971), which contains essays describing his life in Africa in the late 1950s and his search for his African roots. His essays and short stories also appeared in numerous anthologies of African-American writing, including John Henrik Clarke's *American Negro Short Stories* (1966), *Beyond the Angry Black* (1966), edited by JOHN A. WILLIAMS, and two landmark anthologies of the Black Arts Movement, *Black Expression: Essays in the Creative Arts by and about Black Americans* (1969) and *The Black Aesthetic* (1971), both edited by Addison Gayle, Jr.

Fuller played an active role in promoting international cultural exchanges among African and African-American communities. He attended the First World Festival of Negro Arts and Culture in Senegal in 1966, and the Colloquium on Negritude in Dakar in 1971. In addition to his work as an editor, writer, and activist, Fuller taught creative writing and African-American literature at several colleges and universities, among them Columbia College in Chicago, Northwestern University, and Cornell University. In 1976 the publishers of *Black World* terminated the periodical. Fuller returned to Atlanta, where he founded a new publication, *First World*, which he produced from 1977 until 1981. Hoyt William Fuller died of a heart attack on May 11, 1981.

Addison Gayle, Jr., called Hoyt Fuller "the voice of young black writers across the country who dared to differ . . . with . . . the mainstream of American literature." At a time when African-American artists and writers were struggling to find their voices, Fuller argued convincingly for the rejection of traditional literary standards imposed by white writers and editors; instead he urged the creation of an authentic black literature, an appropriate critical framework, and a black aesthetic, for understanding and interpreting the art and expression of African Americans.

Further Reading

Fuller, Hoyt. *Journey to Africa.* Chicago: Third World Press, 1991.

Gates, Henry Louis, Jr., and Nellie Y. McKay, eds. *The Norton Anthology of African American Literature.* New York: W. W. Norton, 1997.

Gayle, Addison, Jr., ed. *The Black Aesthetic.* New York: Doubleday, 1972.

Gaines, Ernest J.
(Ernest James Gaines)

(1933–) *novelist, short story writer, educator*

Ernest J. Gaines is one of the most successful and most widely read African-American writers of the late 20th century. His writing recreates the characters and culture of his childhood home in rural Louisiana, a region that he fictionalizes in his novels and short stories as "Bayonne." Gaines uses the fictional Bayonne to address issues of race, community, and personal identity on a regional level, while also exploring the broader applications of these issues in contemporary American society.

Ernest James Gaines was born on January 15, 1933, on River Lake Plantation in Pointe Coupée Parish, Louisiana, to Manuel Gaines, a laborer, and Adrienne J. Gaines. As he explained in a *New York Times Book Review* article, Gaines spent his early childhood "working in the fields, going fishing in the swamps with the older people, and, especially, listening to the people who came to my aunt's house, the aunt who raised me." Gaines's aunt, Augusteen Jefferson, had a profound influence on his life and writing. "Anytime someone asks who had the greatest influence on me as an artist or a man," he explained in a 1993 interview, "I say she had."

At age 15, Gaines moved to Vallejo, California, to live with his mother and stepfather, who had moved to California during World War II. There he immersed himself in reading at the local library, which, unlike libraries in Louisiana, allowed black patrons. His early literary influences included John Steinbeck, Willa Cather, and Ivan Turgenev. Gaines completed his first novel at age 17, typing it single-spaced on both sides of the paper and sending it to a New York publisher. Though the novel was rejected, Gaines continued to work on it for the next several years. He also served in the U.S. Army from 1953 to 1955. After his discharge, Gaines enrolled at San Francisco State College (now University) and received his bachelor's degree in 1957.

In 1956, while a student at San Francisco State, Gaines published his first work, a short story, in the school literary magazine. He was accepted to Stanford University in 1958 on a Wallace Stegner creative writing fellowship, and turned his attention away from short fiction to the novel he had begun as a teenager. The novel, *Catherine Carmier*, was finally published in 1964. The story of a young man who returns to his native Louisiana and falls in love with a local woman, *Catherine Carmier* generated little interest among critics and sold poorly; but its setting, a fictional plantation region in Louisiana called Bayonne, became the geographical focus of his later novels.

Gaines published a second novel, *Of Love and Dust,* in 1967, and followed it with *Bloodlines,* a collection of short stories, the following year. One story in the collection, "A Long Day in November," was published separately as a children's book in 1971, and another, "The Sky Is Gray," appears in many literary anthologies. The publication of *The Autobiography of Miss Jane Pittman* in 1971 secured Gaines's reputation as a popular and critically acclaimed novelist. Set in Bayonne, the novel explores issues of race and personal identity in a multiethnic environment that included whites, blacks, Cajuns, and Creoles.

Of particular importance for Gaines's male characters in the novel is the definition of what it means to be a man. "You must understand," Gaines explained in a *New York Times Book Review* interview in 1978, "that the blacks who were brought here as slaves were prevented from becoming the men that they could be." The characters in *The Autobiography of Miss Jane Pittman,* whose individual stories form the substance of the novel, describe the struggles they experience in their personal development and their efforts to remain connected to their community. Successfully adapted as a television movie in 1974, *The Autobiography of Miss Jane Pittman* remains one of Gaines's best-known works.

Gaines continued to explore the world of Bayonne, Louisiana, in his subsequent novels: *A Gathering of Old Men* (1983), in which a group of elderly black men decides to take a stand against the generations-old racism of the white and Cajun communities in Bayonne; and *A Lesson before Dying* (1993), a compelling tale of a young man's courage and personal growth in the face of racial injustice during the 1940s, and the elderly schoolteacher who mentors him. Winner of a National Book Critics Circle Award for Fiction in 1993, *A Lesson Before Dying* was adapted for television in 1999.

In addition to a distinguished career as a novelist, Gaines served as writer-in-residence at Denison University (1971), Stanford University (1981), and Whittier College (1986). Since 1983 he has

Ernest J. Gaines has earned comparisons to celebrated southern novelist William Faulkner. *(© Jerry Bauer)*

maintained a visiting professorship in English and creative writing at the University of Southwestern Louisiana in Lafayette, where he also serves as writer-in-residence. In addition to prestigious fellowships from the Guggenheim and MacArthur foundations, Gaines has been awarded France's Chevalier de L'Ordre des Artes et des Lettres (1996), elected to the American Academy of Arts and Letters (1998), and presented the Louisiana Governor's Award for Lifetime Achievement (2000).

Since he first gained wide critical acclaim with *The Autobiography of Miss Jane Pittman,* Ernest J. Gaines has become one of the most respected American and African-American novelists of the late 20th century. Often compared to the works of William Faulkner—whose fictional

Yoknapatawpha County in Mississippi is similar in function to Bayonne, Louisiana—Gaines's novels evoke the rural roots of African-American culture and the struggles against the racism associated with the rural South. "So many of our novels deal only with the great city ghettos," Gaines explained in a 1974 interview. "We've only been living in these ghettos for 75 years or so, but the other 300 years—I think this is worth writing about."

Further Reading

Clark, Keith. *Black Manhood in James Baldwin, Ernest J. Gaines, and August Wilson.* Urbana: University of Illinois Press, 2002.

Doyle, Mary Ellen. *Voices from the Quarters: The Fiction of Ernest J. Gaines.* Baton Rouge: Louisiana State University Press, 2002.

Gaines, Ernest J. *The Autobiography of Miss Jane Pittman.* New York: Dial, 1971.

———. *Bloodlines.* New York: Dial, 1968. Reprint, New York: Vintage Contemporaries, 1997.

———. *A Lesson before Dying.* New York: Knopf, 1993.

Lowe, John, ed. *Conversations with Ernest Gaines.* Jackson: University of Mississippi Press, 1995.

Gates, Henry Louis, Jr.
(Henry Louis "Skip" Gates, Jr.)
(1950–   ) *literary and cultural critic, editor, educator*

One of the most influential figures in contemporary African and African-American studies, Henry Louis Gates, Jr., is a prolific author and editor, and director of Harvard University's prestigious W. E. B. DuBois Institute for Afro-American Research. Gates has been instrumental in the preservation and popularization of neglected literary texts by early African-American writers, including works by HARRIET E. WILSON and Hannah Crafts.

Henry Louis "Skip" Gates, Jr., was born on September 16, 1950, in Keyser, West Virginia, the son of Paulina Augusta Gates and Henry Gates, Sr., a loader at Keyser's Westvaco Paper Mill who

also worked nights as a janitor at the local telephone company. Gates excelled as a student, graduating from high school in 1968 as class valedictorian. That fall, he enrolled at Potomac State College and planned for a career in medicine. However, a professor at the college encouraged Gates to take courses in literature and later convinced him to apply to Ivy League schools to complete his education.

Gates graduated summa cum laude from Yale University in 1973 with a bachelor's degree in history. He earned a fellowship to study at Cambridge University's Clare College in England and completed his master's degree in 1974 and his Ph.D. in 1979. That year, he also married Sharon Lynn Adams, with whom he has two children. After academic appointments at Yale University,

Henry Louis Gates, Jr., has made significant contributions to the canon of African-American literature with several discoveries of early 19th-century texts. *(Harvard University)*

Cornell University, and Duke University, Gates joined the faculty of Harvard University in 1991, serving as the chair of the Afro-American Studies Department and the director of the W. E. B. DuBois Institute for Afro-American Studies.

During his graduate studies in England, Gates met Wole Soyinka, an acclaimed African author and future recipient of the Nobel Prize for literature (1986). Soyinka served as a mentor to Gates and introduced him to the culture and literature of Africa, areas that would form the foundation of Gates's career as an educator and author.

Gates quickly established a reputation as a brilliant, though sometimes controversial, literary critic. His early criticism appeared in works such as *Figures in Black: Works, Signs, and the Racial Self* (1987); *The Signifying Monkey: A Theory of Afro-American Literary Criticism* (1988), which received an American Book Award in 1989; and *Loose Cannons: Notes on the Culture Wars* (1992). Gates argued that texts by African-American authors should be understood and interpreted outside of European frames of reference.

A tireless literary historian, Gates has also edited and reissued numerous historical texts by early African-American authors who have generally been overlooked, forgotten, or were previously unknown. In 1983 Gates edited *Our Nig; or Sketches from the Life of a Free Black* (1854), which he discovered in a used bookshop. Virtually forgotten for more than a century, the novel, written by Harriet E. Wilson, was the first to be published in the United States by an African-American woman. Gates's exhaustive research into early African-American texts culminated in a landmark 30-volume work, the *Oxford-Schomburg Library of Nineteenth-Century Black Women Writers*. Gates's most recent literary excavation, Hannah Craft's *The Bondwoman's Narrative* (published in 2002), has further reshaped African-American literary history as the earliest known novel by an African-American woman and the first to be written by a fugitive slave.

One of the most visible African-American public intellectuals, Gates has contributed signif-icantly to the study of African-American cultural history. In works such as *Colored People: A Memoir* (1994), *The Future of the Race* (1996, with CORNEL WEST), *Thirteen Ways of Looking at a Black Man* (1997), *The African American Century: How Black Americans Have Shaped Our Country* (2000, with Cornel West), and in numerous essays pub-lished in such periodicals as the *New Yorker, Time,* and the *New Republic,* Gates has helped to shape public discourse on social and political issues that affect African Americans.

Henry Louis Gates, Jr., has received numer-ous honors for his contributions to American and African-American culture. He has lectured in Europe and at universities throughout the United States. He is also coeditor of two essential anthologies for the study of African-American lit-erature and culture: the *Norton Anthology of African American Literature* (1997, with Nellie Y. McKay) and the formidable *Africana: The Ency-clopedia of the African and African American Expe-rience* (1999, with Kwame Anthony Appiah).

Further Reading

Craft, Hannah. *The Bondwoman's Narrative: A Novel.* Edited by Henry Louis Gates, Jr. New York: Warner Books, 2002.

Gates, Henry Louis, Jr. *The Signifying Monkey: A Theory of Afro-American Literary Criticism.* New York: Oxford University Press, 1988.

———. *Colored People: A Memoir.* New York: Knopf, 1994.

Gayle, Addison, Jr.
(1932–1991) *literary critic, editor, essayist, biographer, educator*

A respected and influential literary theorist and educator, and the author of essays, personal mem-oirs, and biographies of celebrated African-American writers, Addison Gayle, Jr., is best known as the editor of *The Black Aesthetic* (1971). "The question for the black critic today," Gayle wrote in the introduction, "is not how beautiful is a melody, a play, a poem, or a novel, but how much more beautiful has the poem, melody, play, or novel made the life of a single black man?" Drawing from the Black Nationalist and Black Arts Movements of the 1960s, Gayle and other black aesthetic theorists maintained that African-American artists should address exclusively the social and political needs of the black community.

Addison Gayle, Jr., was born on June 2, 1932, in Newport News, Virginia, to Addison and Carrie Gayle. During a childhood characterized by poverty and the extreme racial prejudice of the Jim Crow South, Gayle turned to books and writing as a possible means of escape. He graduated from high school in 1950 and joined the U.S. Air Force. In 1960 he enrolled in the City University of New York, where he received his B.A. degree in 1965 and where he met his wife, Rosalie Norwood, a lecturer at the university. Gayle received his M.A. degree in literature from the University of California at Los Angeles in 1966. He then returned to New York and accepted a teaching position at the City University of New York, where he remained as a professor of English until his death.

Gayle's early works include *Black Expression: Essays by and about Black Americans in the Creative Arts* (1969), in which he edited critical works on various aspects of African-American literature and folklore; *The Black Situation* (1970), a collection of personal essays that describe the evolution of his literary and political thought; and his highly influential *The Black Aesthetic* (1971), which became the seminal text of the Black Arts Movement. Gayle also published essays in numerous periodicals, including HOYT FULLER's *Black World*.

Comprising essays by prominent African-American authors and theorists, and arranged under four headings (Theory, Music, Drama, and Fiction), *The Black Aesthetic* maintained that African-American literature and art could not legitimately be evaluated according to traditional aesthetics. An American aesthetic, if one even existed, would reflect the biases and prejudicial politics of an essentially racist society. Gayle's anthology became an important compendium of Black Arts theory during the 1970s, influencing the work of numerous contemporary artists, including poets JUNE JORDAN and NIKKI GIOVANNI and novelists TONI MORRISON and ISHMAEL REED.

Gayle further explored the implications of black aesthetic theory in *Way of a New World* (1975), an examination of the historical development of the African-American novel. He also published three biographies: *Oak and Ivory: A Biography of Paul Laurence Dunbar* (1971), *Claude McKay: The Black Poet of War* (1972), and *Richard Wright: Ordeal of a Native Son* (1980). In his autobiography, *Wayward Child: A Personal Odyssey* (1977), Gayle describes a lifetime of struggles: against his own self-hatred as a child; in his growth as a political and literary scholar; and amid the controversies created by his commitment to black aesthetic principles.

As passionate and devoted in the classroom as he was in his writing, Gayle became a distinguished professor of English at the City University of New York in 1980. He also participated in the Search for Education, Elevation, and Knowledge (SEEK) program by promoting greater educational opportunities among ethnic minorities. Addison Gayle, Jr., died on October 3, 1991, from complications of pneumonia.

Further Reading

Andrews, William L., Frances Smith Foster, and Trudier Harris, eds. *The Concise Oxford Companion to African American Literature*. New York: Oxford University Press, 2001.

Gates, Henry Louis, Jr., and Nellie Y. McKay, eds. *The Norton Anthology of African American Literature*. New York: W. W. Norton, 1997.

Gayle, Addison, Jr. *The Black Aesthetic*. New York: Doubleday, 1971.

———. *Wayward Child: A Personal Odyssey*. New York: Doubleday, 1977.

Giovanni, Nikki
(Yolanda Cornelia Giovanni, Yolande Cornelia Giovanni, Jr., Yolande Cornelia Giovanni)
(1943–   ) *poet, essayist, editor, autobiographer, educator*

Nikki Giovanni first gained national prominence as a poet during the late 1960s, becoming one of the most outspoken and influential voices to emerge from the Black Power and Black Arts Movements. Since that time, Giovanni has continued to address issues of race and gender discrimination with passionate intensity. "My work is not that different now than when I was starting out," Giovanni explained in a 2000 interview. "You keep trying to say what you're learning and keep sharing it with your audience." Giovanni's numerous literary and academic honors include a National Book Award nomination, the Langston Hughes Award, and several fellowships and grants.

Nikki Giovanni was born Yolande Cornelia Giovanni on June 7, 1943, in Knoxville, Tennessee, to Gus Giovanni, a probation officer, and Yolande Giovanni, a social worker. Though she grew up primarily in Cincinnati, Ohio, Giovanni retained a connection with her roots in the South, particularly through the influence of her maternal grandparents, Emma Louvenia Watson and John Brown Watson. Giovanni often spent her summer vacations in Knoxville with her grandparents and lived with them while attending Austen High School, from which she graduated in 1960.

At 17, Giovanni enrolled at Fisk University in Nashville, Tennessee, but was dismissed after her first semester because, as she would later recall in her 1971 autobiography, *Gemini,* her "attitudes did not fit those of a Fisk woman." Giovanni returned to Ohio and attended the University of Cincinnati briefly before being readmitted to Fisk in 1974. While there she resurrected the Fisk chapter of the Student Nonviolent Coordinating Committee (SNCC) and participated in the Fisk Writing Workshops directed by JOHN OLIVER KIL-

LENS. Giovanni graduated magna cum laude from Fisk in 1967 with a bachelor's degree in history.

Giovanni made a deep impression on black culture during the late 1960s with the publication of her first two collections of poetry, *Black Feeling* (1967) and *Black Judgment* (1968). Revolutionary in tone and theme, these volumes addressed racial oppression with unbridled rage, extolling the use of any means, violent or otherwise, to combat racism. Published during the height of the Black Power movement, Giovanni's poems found a receptive audience among young black activists, and she became one of the most celebrated African-American poets of her generation.

Although explicitly militant in nature, Giovanni's early poetry also captured the joy of family life and the strong love within black communities. "I really hope no white person ever has cause to write about me," she wrote in "Nikki-Rosa," one of her best known poems from *Black Judgment,* "because they never understand Black love is Black wealth and / they'll / probably talk about my hard childhood and never understand that / all the while I was quite happy." The theme of remembrance, of personal and familial history, informs much of Giovanni's writing, particularly her autobiographical and nonfiction works. In *Gemini: An Extended Autobiographical Statement on My First Twenty-Five Years as a Black Poet* (1971), Giovanni addressed her personal and artistic development in autobiographical poems and essays. She further explored her private and public personas in two later volumes of essays, *Sacred Cows . . . And Other Edibles* (1988) and *Racism 101* (1994).

Though her affirmation of black culture has remained consistent in all her writing, Giovanni adopted a less militant tone in future collections of poetry, perhaps reflecting the changes in her personal life. In 1969 Giovanni became a single mother with the birth of her only child, Thomas Watson Giovanni. In *Re: Creations* (1970) and her widely celebrated *My House* (1972), Giovanni's creative focus became more introspective as she charted her personal growth as a poet, a woman, and a mother.

Addressing issues of feminism, family, and love, Giovanni's later collections of poetry include *The Women and the Men* (1975), *Those Who Ride the Night Winds* (1983), *Love Poems* (1997), *Blues: For All the Changes: New Poems* (1999), and *Quilting the Black-Eyed Pea: Poems and Not Quite Poems* (2002).

Giovanni received wide critical acclaim for her spoken word performances, in which musicians and singers often accompanied her. During the early 1970s, she released several spoken word recordings that included *Truth Is on Its Way* (1971), *Like a Ripple on a Pond* (1973), and *The Way I Feel* (1975). She also toured the United States and performed her poetry in clubs and on college campuses worldwide. During this period, Giovanni participated in two important literary exchanges published in *A Dialogue: James Baldwin and Nikki Giovanni* (1972) and *A Poetic Equation: Conversations Between Nikki Giovanni and Margaret Walker* (1974).

In addition to her works for adults, Giovanni published several volumes of children's verse. One of her most successful, *Ego Tripping and Other Verse for Young Adults* (1973), challenges African-American youths to take pride in their African ancestry, an ancestry that offers a rich and varied assortment of cultural heroes. Her other works for children include *Spin a Soft Black Song: Poems for Children* (1971) and *Vacation Time: Poems for Children* (1980).

Apart from her work as a poet and essayist, Giovanni maintains a distinguished career as a college professor and lecturer. She has held academic appointments at Rutgers University, in New Jersey, and Ohio State University in Columbus, Ohio. In 1987 she joined the faculty of Virginia Tech in Blacksburg, Virginia, serving as a professor of English and the Gloria D. Smith Professor of Black Studies.

An internationally acclaimed poet, essayist, and lecturer, Nikki Giovanni has earned numerous honors for her contributions to African-American literature. In 1989 the National Association for the Advancement of Colored People (NAACP) named her Woman of the Year.

She also received the Jeanine Rae Award for the Advancement of Women's Culture in 1995 and the prestigious Langston Hughes Award in 1996. While contemporary critics have focused more on her early, militant poems, Giovanni has maintained a wide readership, and she remains one of the most successful and respected modern American poets.

Further Reading

Bashir, Samiya. "Giovanni's World." *Black Issues Book Review* 4 (November–December 2002): 32.

Giovanni, Nikki. *Gemini: An Extended Autobiographical Statement on My First Twenty-Five Years of Being a Black Poet*. Indianapolis, Ind.: Bobbs-Merrill, 1971.

———. *Quilting the Black-Eyed Pea: Poems and Not Quite Poems*. New York: William Morrow and Co., 2002.

———. *The Selected Poems of Nikki Giovanni: 1968–1995*. New York: William Morrow and Co., 1996.

Griggs, Sutton
(Sutton Elbert Griggs)
(1872–ca. 1933) *novelist, essayist, biographer*

Best known for two early novels, *Imperium in Imperio* (1899) and *The Hindered Hand; or, The Reign of the Repressionist* (1905), Sutton Griggs was one of the most prolific and enterprising authors of the early 20th century, publishing more than 33 works in all.

Sutton Elbert Griggs was born on June 19, 1872, in Chatfield, Texas, the son of Allan R. Griggs, a Baptist minister. He attended public schools in Dallas, and studied at Bishop College in Marshall, Texas, and Richmond Theological Seminary (now Virginia Union University), from which he graduated in 1893. Ordained as a Baptist minister, Griggs received his first pastorate at the First Baptist Church in Beckley, Virginia, where he served until 1895. In 1897 he married Emma Williams, a schoolteacher.

Over the next three decades, Griggs led Baptist congregations in East Nashville and Memphis, Tennessee, and in Denison, Texas, as the pastor of Hopewell Baptist Church, his father's former congregation. A supporter of W. E. B. DuBOIS's Niagara Movement and the National Association for the Advancement of Colored People (NAACP), Griggs devoted his life to the spiritual and social welfare of African Americans. He became a leader in the National Baptist Convention and served as president of the American Baptist Theological Seminary from 1925 to 1926.

Griggs began his prolific writing career in 1899 with the publication of *Imperium in Imperio,* his first and best-known novel. Prefiguring the Black Nationalist and Black Power movements, Griggs's novel depicts a nationalist group called Imperium in Imperio, meaning "nation within a nation" in Latin, which sought to annex the state of Texas as an all-black nation separate from the United States.

Griggs published four additional novels: *Overshadowed* (1901), *Unfettered* (1902), *The Hindered Hand; or, The Reign of the Repressionist* (1905), and *Pointing the Way* (1909). Of these, *The Hindered Hand,* written as a response to what he felt was the racist propaganda of Thomas Dixon's novel *The Leopard's Spots* (1902), was the most successful. Griggs published his five novels privately and marketed them in black communities, even selling them door to door.

Apart from novels, Griggs published numerous social and political works addressing issues of race and religion. In 1914 he established the National Public Welfare League, through which he issued his later writings, including *The Story of My Struggles* (1914), *The Reconstruction of a Race* (1917), *The Guide to Racial Greatness* (1923), and *Paths of Progress; or, Co-operation between the Races* (1925). In his novels and nonfiction, Griggs articulated pride in his African-American heritage and tried to combat the growing intolerance and oppression against blacks in the South at the turn of the 20th century and in the decades that followed.

Though he enjoyed modest commercial success with his novels, Griggs's later writings drew little interest, and his final years were characterized by increasing poverty. He left Memphis, Tennessee, in 1930 and returned to Texas to assume the pastorate of Hopewell Baptist Church. He later resigned his position and moved to Houston, where he intended to start a Baptist organization devoted to religious and political affairs. Sutton Elbert Griggs died on January 2, 1933.

In recent years, Sutton Griggs has drawn only slight critical attention, and his literary reputation rests almost exclusively on his five novels. Often militant in tone, with plots that were at times melodramatic and farfetched, Griggs's novels foreshadowed themes that would find greater expression and popularity in the works of later writers such as JOHN A. WILLIAMS, GEORGE SCHUYLER, and CHESTER HIMES.

Further Reading

Campbell, Jane. *Mythic Black Fiction: The Transformation of History.* Nashville: University of Tennessee, 1986.

Gates, Henry Louis, Jr., and Nellie Y. McKay, eds. *The Norton Anthology of African American Literature.* New York: W. W. Norton, 1997.

Tal, Kali. "That Just Kills Me." *Social Text* 20 (summer 2002): 65.

Grimké, Angelina Weld
(Angelina Weld Emily Grimké)
(1880–1958) *poet, playwright, short story writer*

Though not as celebrated as many of her contemporaries during the Harlem Renaissance, Angelina Weld Grimké published poetry in many of the leading anthologies and periodicals of the time. She also authored one of the first American plays written by and for African Americans.

Angelina Emily Weld Grimké was born on February 27, 1880, in Boston, Massachusetts. Her father, Archibald Grimké, was the son of a slave, Nancy Weston, and her master, Henry Grimké, and the nephew of white abolitionists Sarah and Angelina Grimké. Sarah Stanley Grimké, Angelina's mother, was the white daughter of a prominent Boston clergyman. Sarah left her husband in 1883 and took custody of Angelina until 1887, when she returned her to her father. Angelina never saw her mother again.

Grimké received her early education at the prestigious Cushing Academy in Massachusetts and the Carleton Academy in Northfield, Minnesota, before graduating from the Boston Normal School of Gymnastics in 1902 with a degree in physical education. She later moved to Washington, D.C., and taught at the Armstrong Manual Training School until 1916. She later transferred to M Street High School (later renamed Dunbar High School), where she taught English.

Grimké's poetry, essays, and reviews appeared in numerous periodicals such as the *Colored American Magazine,* the *Boston Transcript,* and *Opportunity.* Despite her privileged and sheltered upbringing, Grimké used her writing as a vehicle for addressing racial oppression. She employed subtle and stylized imagery to portray her longing for racial equality, the fulfillment of love, and a growing despair over the plight of African Americans. Her poem, "The Black Finger," published in 1925, compares a lone cypress tree to a black finger pointing skyward. "Tenebris," published in 1927, depicts a shadow at night, like a black hand "With Fingers long and black / All through the dark / Against the white man's house."

In her play, *Rachel,* produced in Washington, D.C., in 1916, Grimké depicts the damage inflicted on a middle-class black family by racism and the constant threat of lynching. *Rachel* was published in book form in 1920 to mixed reviews, but many critics praised it as the first drama written by an African American and intended for a black audience. A second, unpublished play, *Mara,* also portrays a middle-class black family destroyed by racial violence.

Grimké also wrote short fiction, publishing her most acclaimed story, "The Closing Door," in 1919 in *The Birth Control Review.* The story echoes the fear of racial violence and lynching in her portrayal of an African-American woman who kills her newborn son to prevent him from dying at the hands of a lynch mob. The corrupting influence of an oppressive white society remained a common theme in Grimké's poetry and prose.

Many scholars have noted the presence of homoerotic themes in Grimké's poetry, particularly in the recurrent theme of unrequited love in such poems as "El Beso," published in 1909 in the *Boston Transcript.* In works published after her death, numerous poems address her lesbianism more explicitly, and several love letters attest to affairs with women. Other themes in her work include the impending threat of violence by African Americans in response to continued racial oppression, expressed in the poem "Beware When He Awakens," published in the periodical *Pilot* in 1902, and in the story "Goldie," published in 1920.

Having published several poems in leading periodicals and anthologies such as ALAIN LOCKE's *The New Negro* in 1925 and COUNTEE CULLEN's *Caroling Dusk: An Anthology of Verse by Black Poets* in 1927, and having earned the respect of her contemporaries for her poetry and drama, Grimké fell into relative obscurity in the 1930s. Frustrated by the racial and sexual restrictions of an intolerant and repressive society, she stopped trying to publish. Angelina Weld Grimké died on June 10, 1958.

A passionate writer whose poetry, drama, and prose captured an intense longing for racial equality and self-fulfillment, Angelina Weld Grimké struggled throughout her life with the social and racial constraints placed upon her as an African American and a lesbian. Her sense of inner isolation found its greatest expression in the subtle and poignant imagery of her poetry.

Further Reading

Cullen, Countee, ed. *Caroling Dusk: An Anthology of Verse by Black Poets.* New York: Carol Publishing Group, 1993.

Herron, Carolivia, ed. *The Selected Works of Angelina Weld Grimké.* New York: Oxford University Press, 1991.

Hull, Gloria T. *Color, Sex, and Poetry: Three Women Writers of the Harlem Renaissance.* Bloomington: Indiana University Press, 1987.

Grimké, Charlotte Forten
(Charlotte Lottie Forten)
(1838–1914) *diarist, essayist, educator*

Known primarily for her *Journal,* a personal diary kept primarily between 1854 and 1864, Charlotte Forten Grimké documented a critical era in the abolitionist movement prior to and during the Civil War. She records in moving detail the brutality of slavery and its effects on those in bondage as well as on those who are free. She also describes the efforts of leading abolitionist leaders such as John Greenleaf Whittier, Wendell Phillips, and William Lloyd Garrison, with all of whom she interacted.

Charlotte Forten Grimké was born on August 17, 1838, to a prosperous family in Philadelphia, Pennsylvania, that had a long heritage of support for the abolitionist cause. Her grandfather, James Forten, Sr., had been a powder boy during the American Revolution and earned a large fortune in later life from a patented sailing device. He also studied with Anthony Benezet, the famous Quaker abolitionist. Her father, James Forten, Jr., was an abolitionist lecturer who insisted that Charlotte receive her education from private tutors instead of the segregated schools in Philadelphia.

Grimké's mother died during her childhood, and she moved to Byberry, just outside Philadelphia, to live with her uncle Robert Purvis, a wealthy abolitionist leader. Later, she lived with Charles and Sarah Redmond, also wealthy abolitionists, in Salem, Massachusetts. There she entered public school and graduated from the integrated Higginson Grammar School in 1855, and became the first African American to teach in Salem schools when she accepted a position at Epes Grammar School. She had begun keeping a journal, in which she documented her reflections on the abolitionist move-

ment and the leaders with whom she had practically grown up, the year before. At this time, she also began publishing occasional poems and essays.

Early entries in her journal reveal Grimké's considerable intellect and a youthful arrogance about her sympathies with abolition. She records her eyewitness accounts of the sufferings of captured runaway slaves and describes the debilitating effect of discrimination on her worldview. "I wonder that every colored person," Grimké writes, "is not a misanthrope. Surely we have everything to make us hate mankind." She also records her efforts to improve her education, which included the study of French, German, and Latin.

In 1862 Grimké traveled to Hilton Island, part of the Sea Islands off the coast of South Carolina, where in 1861 the Union army had captured the Confederate stronghold of Fort Walker. There she participated in what came to be called the Port Royal Experiment, a program initiated to provide for the education of contraband slaves, or slaves who had been captured by the Union army and were considered to be "contraband of war." While in South Carolina, Grimké also nursed wounded Union soldiers.

In Beaufort, South Carolina, she met Harriet Tubman, who described in harrowing detail her efforts to assist runaway slaves. "My own eyes," Grimké writes, "were full as I listened to her." During this period Grimké wrote one of her best-known essays, "Life in the Sea Islands," published in the *Atlantic Monthly* in 1864. The essay describes her experiences among the people of the Sea Islands off the coast of South Carolina, and her fascination with the language and music of its former slaves.

Grimké spent much of 1863 among the soldiers of the all-black Fifty-fourth regiment. She witnessed the reading of Abraham Lincoln's Emancipation Proclamation, and recorded her grief over the decimation of the regiment at Fort Wagner. In 1864, she returned to Philadelphia, where she continued to teach and write poetry. In 1876 she married Francis James Grimké, a former slave and graduate of Princeton Theological Seminary, and settled in Washington, D.C. Their home became a cultural and literary hub for writers and activists who continued the struggle against racial oppression.

Having resumed her journal entries in 1885 after nearly 21 years of silence, Grimké describes a meeting with FREDERICK DOUGLASS and her support of BOOKER T. WASHINGTON's Normal School. She also recalls the age that her daughter, Theodora, who died in infancy, would have been. Grimké's journal ends in 1892. For the next 14 years she lived in Florida, Washington, D.C., and finally in Massachusetts, where she died of a cerebral embolism on July 23, 1914.

An accomplished poet and essayist, Charlotte Forten Grimké also translated Emilie Erckmann and Alexander Chatrain's novel *Madame Therese: or, The Volunteers of '92*, published in 1869. Her literary legacy, however, stems primarily from her journal, published first in 1954, in which her vivid accounts of the abuses of slavery and her portraits of abolitionist leaders and activities provide crucial insight into the life of free blacks in the early years of emancipation and an important record of the Civil War era.

Further Reading

Andrews, William L., Frances Smith Foster, and Trudier Harris, eds. *The Concise Oxford Companion to African American Literature*. New York: Oxford University Press, 2001.

Appiah, Kwame Anthony and Henry Louis Gates, Jr., eds. *Africana: The Encyclopedia of the African and African American Experience*. New York: Basic Civitas Books, 1999.

Gates, Henry Louis, Jr. and Nellie Y. McKay, eds. *The Norton Anthology of African American Literature*. New York: W. W. Norton, 1997.

Guy, Rosa Cuthbert

(1925–) *novelist, young adult fiction writer, essayist, playwright*

An award-winning author of children's and young-adult fiction, novels, essays, and plays, Rosa Guy is best known for depicting the challenges that face young people growing up in modern urban environments. Critics have praised the rich detail and genuine characters in her novels. "I write about people," Guy explained in a 1984 address given at the *Boston Globe* Book Fair. "I want my readers to know people, to laugh with people, to be angry with people, to despair of people, and to have hope . . ." A cofounder with JOHN OLIVER KILLENS of the Harlem Writer's Guild in the 1940s, Guy has earned numerous literary honors, including the Coretta Scott King Award and the *New York Times* Outstanding Book of the Year citation.

Rosa Cuthbert Guy was born Rosa Cuthbert on September 1, 1925, in Diego Martin, Trinidad, the daughter of Henry and Audrey Cuthbert. In 1927 her parents immigrated to the United States, leaving her and her sister, Ameze, with relatives in Trinidad. The two children joined their parents in Harlem in 1932, but their reunion was brief. In 1933 Audrey Cuthbert became ill and the children moved to the home of a cousin in Brooklyn. After her mother's death in 1934, Rosa returned to Harlem to live with her father until his death in 1937.

For the next four years, Rosa and her sister lived in a series of foster homes and orphanages. Rosa dropped out of school and took a job in a garment factory to support herself and her sister. In 1941 she married Warner Guy and gave birth to a son, Warner Guy, Jr., a year later. While her husband served overseas during World War II, Guy struggled to support her son as a factory worker. She developed an interest in writing and theater and attended writing classes at New York University. She also studied acting at the American Negro Theater.

Following her husband's return from the war, Guy moved with her family to Connecticut, where she lived until her marriage failed in 1950. Back in New York, Guy resumed her work at the factory while continuing to seek opportunities for creative expression. She joined the Committee for the Negro in the Arts, an organization created to combat racial stereotypes in the arts.

In 1951 Guy joined a group of other writers, including John O. Killens, John Henrik Clarke, and Walter Christmas, in establishing a writing workshop. Later named the Harlem Writers Guild, the workshop became a renowned proving ground for such notable black authors as PAULE MARSHALL, AUDRE LORDE, MAYA ANGELOU, and WALTER MOSLEY.

In 1954 Guy wrote and acted in her first play, *Venetian Blinds,* a one-act drama produced off-Broadway by the Committee for the Negro in the Arts. When her interest in theater and acting began to wane, Guy turned her attention to fiction. Her first published works, the short stories "Magnify" and "Carnival," appeared in 1960 in a Trinidadian newspaper.

Guy published her first novel, *Bird at My Window,* in 1966, four years after the murder of her ex-husband. Wade Williams, the novel's protagonist, possesses exceptional intellectual talents. His life, however, begins to unravel as he confronts racial and economic barriers to his success. In a 1988 interview, Guy characterized *Bird at My Window* as a sociological novel that explores the shift toward violence when creative and intellectual outlets are stifled by a racially oppressive society.

Though Guy published other novels for adults, including *A Measure of Time* (1983), *My Love, My Love; or, The Peasant Girl* (1985), and *The Sun, The Sea, a Touch of the Wind* (1995), she has received the greatest critical attention for her numerous works for young adult readers. In the wake of the assassinations of Martin Luther King, Jr., and Malcolm X, Guy traveled across the United States to discover the effects of violence on young people. She published her findings in a collection of essays, *Children of Longing* (1970), and began to explore the lives of young adults in her fiction.

Guy's trilogy of young adult novels—*The Friends* (1973), *Ruby* (1976), and *Edith Jackson* (1978)—is based on the author's childhood as a West Indian immigrant in New York. Set in New York and Trinidad, the novels examine the divisions of race, class, and economy as they relate to the lives of young people. Critics praised the realism of Guy's characters and their struggles to overcome the grim reality of modern urban environments. Each book in the trilogy earned the American Library Association's Best Book for Young Adults citation, and *The Friends* was selected by the *New York Times* as Outstanding Book of the Year for 1973.

Among Guy's other works for young adults, *The Disappearance* (1979), *Mirror of Her Own* (1981), *New Guys around the Block* (1983), *Paris, Pee Wee, and Big Dog* (1984), *And I Heard a Bird Sing* (1987), *The Ups and Downs of Carl Davis III* (1989), *Billy the Great* (1992), *The Music of Summer* (1992), and *The Sun, the Sea, a Touch of Wind* (1995) received wide critical acclaim. Her novel *My Love, My Love; or, The Peasant Girl* (1985), a reworking of Hans Christian Anderson's "The Little Mermaid," was adapted to the stage as the musical *Once on This Island.* Guy has also translated and adapted an African fable, *Mother Crocodile: An Uncle Amadou Tale from Senegal* (1981).

The works of Rosa Cuthbert Guy have been translated into numerous languages, including Japanese, Danish, French, German, and Italian. She has also published articles in periodicals such as *Cosmopolitan,* the *New York Times Magazine,* and *Redbook.*

Further Reading

Andrews, William L., Frances Smith Foster, and Trudier Harris, eds. *The Concise Oxford Companion to African American Literature.* New York: Oxford University Press, 2001.

Guy, Rosa. *Bird at My Window.* Philadelphia, Pa.: Lippincott Co., 1966.

———. *The Friends.* New York: Holt, Rinehart, and Winston, 1973.

Norris, Jerrie. *Presenting Rosa Guy.* New York: Twayne Publishers, 1988.

H

Haley, Alex
(Alexander Palmer Haley, Alexander Murray Palmer Haley)
(1921–1992) *novelist, biographer, journalist*

Though Alex Haley's literary output comprised only four published volumes, his writing has had a lasting effect on African-American literature and culture in the United States. *The Autobiography of Malcolm X* (1965), on which he collaborated with Malcolm X, remains one of the most influential works of African-American autobiography in the 21st century. His second and perhaps better-known work, *Roots: The Saga of an American Family* (1976), became an international best-seller and spawned a television miniseries that broke all viewing records. During his writing career, Haley earned numerous literary honors, including special citations from the Pulitzer Prize advisory committee and the National Book Award, and the prestigious Spingarn Medal of the National Association for the Advancement of Colored People (NAACP).

Alexander Murray Palmer Haley was born on August 11, 1921, in Ithaca, New York, and grew up in Henning, Tennessee. He was the first of three sons born to Simon Henry Haley, a professor of agriculture, and Bertha George Palmer Haley, a schoolteacher. After enrolling at Hawthorne College in Mississippi in 1937, he transferred to Elizabeth City State Teachers College in North Carolina, where he spent the next two years. In 1939 he enlisted in the U.S. Coast Guard and began a 20-year nautical career during which time he began to compose sketches and stories.

Haley retired from the Coast Guard in 1959 to pursue a career as a freelance writer. He began to publish regularly in periodicals such as *Coronet, Reader's Digest,* and the *Atlantic Monthly.* He also published a series of interviews in *Playboy* magazine. Haley's interview with Malcolm X in 1963 eventually led to his collaboration on a proposed autobiography, for which Malcolm X provided the information and Haley shaped the material into a cohesive narrative.

Though he would not live to see his autobiography published, Malcolm X read and approved Haley's manuscript prior to his assassination on February 21, 1965. The autobiography, which reads like a novel, chronicles Malcolm X's transformation from career criminal to a charismatic civil rights leader. Haley's depiction of Malcolm X provided a more complete and compelling portrait of the man and the social leader than anything previously available.

Haley's next book would consume nearly 12 years of research, during which Haley traveled by ship from Africa to America in an effort to recreate the conditions of the Middle Passage, the route by which most slave ships traveled. Haley's research began with the stories he heard as a child

Alex Haley, shown here in 1988, revitalized the study of African-American ancestry with his 1976 publication of *Roots*. *(AP/Wide World Photos)*

about "The African," his earliest known family member, who was kidnapped from West Africa and brought to America as a slave. *Roots: The Saga of an American Family* was published in 1976. Blending historical fact and elements of fiction, Haley traced his family's history through stories passed down orally through the generations.

Roots became an international best-seller and Haley received special Pulitzer Prize and National Book Award citations in 1977, as well as the Spingarn Medal. Haley also adapted *Roots* for television in 1977. The miniseries broke all previous viewing records and was nominated for 37 Emmy Awards. The publication of *Roots* addressed crucial misrepresentations, particularly the myth that Africa had no meaningful political and cultural life before colonization by white Europeans. Haley's research also highlighted the historical

roots of African-American literature in the oral traditions of African culture.

Haley's overwhelming popular success with the publication of *Roots* and the production of the television miniseries was soon mixed with controversy. Two lawsuits, filed separately by Harold Courlander and MARGARET WALKER, alleged that Haley had plagiarized significant portions of *Roots*. Walker claimed that Haley had plagiarized elements of her 1963 novel *Jubilee*. Her case was ultimately dismissed. Courlander argued that the character of Kunta Kinte was based on the protagonist of his own 1967 novel *The African*. Haley claimed that the error was the result of improper citation by researchers and settled the case out of court.

Haley's later writings never surpassed the critical and popular success of his earlier books. He served as a script consultant for *Roots: The Next Generation*, a sequel to the original series, in 1979. In 1980 Haley collaborated with television producer Norman Lear on a series about race relations in the rural South during the 1930s called *Palmerstown, U.S.A.*, which aired until 1981. In 1988 Haley published *A Different Kind of Christmas*, which depicted the life of an antebellum slaveholder who becomes a member of the Underground Railroad and assists the flight of escaped slaves to the North.

Alexander Murray Palmer Haley died unexpectedly on February 10, 1992, in Seattle, Washington. Two additional books were published posthumously: *Alex Haley's Queen: The Story of an American Family* (1993, with David Stevens), which chronicles the lives of Haley's paternal ancestors, and *Mama Flora's Family* (1998, with David Stevens), which depicts a mother's struggle to raise her family in the hostile racial climate of the post–World War II South. Both books were adapted for television in 1993 and 1998, respectively.

Alex Haley's best-known books, *The Autobiography of Malcolm X* (1965) and *Roots: The Saga of an American Family* (1976), have become classics of African-American literature by focusing critical and popular attention on the historical foundations of African-American culture and the misconceptions promulgated over many centuries about the roots of black culture and history. Though debate continues over the historical accuracy of *Roots* and the veracity of its author, none can dispute the enduring impact that Haley's landmark work has made on people of all cultures. In 2002 construction was completed on the Kunta Kinte–Alex Haley Memorial in Annapolis, Maryland, located where Haley's celebrated ancestor Kunta Kinte is thought to have arrived in America.

Further Reading

Andrews, William L., Frances Smith Foster, and Trudier Harris, eds. *The Concise Oxford Companion to African American Literature.* New York: Oxford University Press, 2001.

Haley, Alex, ed. *The Autobiography of Malcolm X.* New York: Grove Press, 1965.

———. *Roots: The Saga of an American Family.* Garden City, N.Y.: Doubleday, 1976.

Hamilton, Virginia
(Virginia Esther Perry Hamilton)

(1936–2002) *children's and young adult novelist, short story writer*

A prolific and internationally renowned author of children's and young adult fiction, Virginia Hamilton has written in a variety of genres, including historical fiction, the slave narrative, African folklore and mythology, science fiction, fantasy, and mystery. She has also been the recipient of a remarkable number of literary honors, including the National Book Award, the Newbery Medal, and the Hans Christian Andersen Medal.

Virginia Esther Perry Hamilton was born in Yellow Springs, Ohio, on March 12, 1936. The youngest of five children born to Kenneth James and Etta Belle Hamilton, she developed an early

fascination for storytelling and books. Her parents often recounted the history of ancestors who escaped slavery in Virginia to settle in Ohio. These stories, which included accounts of her family's involvement in the Underground Railroad and the assistance received by local Native Americans, provided a rich source of material for her later writings.

In 1952 Hamilton received a full scholarship to Antioch College, where she studied writing for three years before transferring to Ohio State University and eventually to the New School for Social Research, in New York City. In 1960 she married Arnold Adoff, a poet and anthologist, with whom she had two children, a daughter, Leigh, and a son, Jaime. While working several odd jobs to support her family, she devoted her spare time to writing. Her first published book, *Zeely* (1967), was inspired by her travels in northern Africa with her husband and depicts a young girl's fascination with an older woman named Zeely, whom she believes to be a Watusi queen. *Zeely* was awarded the Nancy Block Memorial Award, the first of Hamilton's many literary honors.

With her husband and children, Hamilton returned to her ancestral home in Ohio in 1967, where she built a house on land originally owned by her grandparents. Hamilton's connection with this land provided an ideal writing environment. "Here on the land," she says of her Yellow Springs home, "is the best place for me to write. I have a long kinship with so many people here, with the landscape and the Ohio sky." Averaging a book a year, Hamilton continued to enjoy critical and popular success with the publication of *The House of Dies Drear* (1968), *The Time-Ago Tales of Jahdu* (1969), *The Planet of Junior Brown* (1971), and the acclaimed *M. C. Higgins, the Great* (1974), which became the first book to receive both the National Book Award and the National Library Association's Newbery Medal.

Hamilton's focus in her young adult fiction on unconventional and complex themes contributed to her international success, and she created young protagonists with whom African-American children could readily identify. *The Magical Adventures of Pretty Pearl* (1983) and *In the Beginning: Creation Stories from around the World* (1986), presented young readers with accessible stories of early African mythology and folklore. In *The White Romance* (1987), Hamilton examines the issue of interracial dating from a young adult's perspective.

During her long and distinguished literary career, Hamilton earned numerous national and international literary awards. She was the first author of children's and young adult fiction to receive the MacArthur Fellowship (also called the genius grant), the first African American to win the coveted Newbery Medal, and the first American to be awarded the Hans Christian Andersen Medal (sometimes referred to as the Little Nobel Prize), in 1992, by the International Board on Books for Young People in Switzerland in recognition of Hamilton's lifetime contributions to children's literature.

Hamilton's books, written primarily about, and for, African Americans, are noted for the universality of their themes, their imaginative narratives, and the author's obvious love of stories. "I write books," explained Hamilton, "because I love chasing after a good story and seeing fantastic shapes rise out of the mist of my imaginings. It is my way of exploring the known, the remembered, and the imagined, the literary triad of which all stories are made." Virginia Esther Perry Hamilton died of breast cancer on February 12, 2002.

Further Reading

Andrews, William L., Frances Smith Foster, and Trudier Harris, eds. *The Concise Oxford Companion to African American Literature.* New York: Oxford University Press, 2001.

Hamilton, Virginia. *The All Jahdu Storybook.* New York: Harcourt, 1991.

Mikkelsen, Nina. *Virginia Hamilton.* New York: Twayne Publishers, 1994.

Trites, Roberta Seelinger. "'I double never ever never lie to my chil'rn': Inside People in Virginia Hamilton's Narratives." *African American Review* 32 (spring 1998): 146–156.

Hammon, Jupiter
(1711–ca. 1806) *poet*

Credited with publishing the first poem by an African-American writer in the United States, Jupiter Hammon was a poet of profound spiritual faith. He wrote fewer than a dozen known works in his lifetime, but his poetry and sermons stand as the foundation of a formal African-American literary tradition. Born in Oyster Bay, New York, in 1711, Hammon spent his entire life in bondage, first as a trusted slave of Henry Lloyd, a wealthy businessman and slave trader, and later in the service of Henry's son Joseph and grandson John. Hammon's master gave him advantages that most slaves never enjoyed, including access to the Lloyds' extensive library and admittance to schoolhouses on the Lloyd estate.

His duties on the Lloyd estate are not well known, though the family acknowledged him for his manual skills and gave him some responsibility for the family's bookkeeping. Among the Lloyd family ledgers, there is also a notation that marks the purchase by Hammon of a Bible from Henry Lloyd in 1733 for seven shillings and sixpence, which indicates that he may have received monetary compensation for his service to the family.

Hammon published his first work, a broadside poem entitled "An Evening Thought: Salvation by Christ, with Penitential Cries," in 1760. In it, he exhorts his readers to seek salvation through Christ, whom he calls "thy captive slave," and assures that "your souls are fit for heaven." He uses the word *nation* to describe himself and his audience and emphasizes that redemption is for everyone. His use of inclusive terms and phrases carried an unmistakable meaning to his predominantly black audience.

Critics have often disparaged Hammon's writing for its limited range as well as its perceived accomodationist attitude toward his white masters. While his writing certainly lacks overt attacks on slavery, and though he urges slaves to be obedient to their masters because the Bible demands it, he conveys a clear sense of the injustice of slavery. In "An Address to the Negroes in the State of New York," he uses the Revolutionary War, only recently ended, as a way of addressing liberty for African Americans. "How much money has been spent, and how many lives have been lost, to defend liberty. I must say that I have hoped that God would open their eyes, when they were so engaged for liberty, to think of the state of the poor blacks, and to pity us." His address, made on September 24, 1786, before the African Society of the City of New York, was reprinted in Philadelphia by the Pennsylvania Society for Promoting the Abolition of Slavery, and a third edition was printed following Hammon's death.

Hammon exhorted his fellow slaves, whom he calls "a poor despised nation" in his first sermon, "A Winter Piece," published in 1782, to improve themselves spiritually and to remain united as a community of believers and Africans, a term he uses frequently. Some scholars have noted that, rather than accomodationist, Hammon's approach is nationalist, a prelude to later 19th-century black nationalists such as DAVID WALKER.

Hammon remained a slave until his death in about 1806. Aside from four poems, including an homage to his fellow poet PHILLIS WHEATLEY in 1778, and three sermon essays, he published several other works that are no longer extant, including a celebratory poem marking the visit of Prince William Henry to Oyster Bay and a sermon that was advertised in the Connecticut *Courant* in 1779. In his small body of work, Jupiter Hammon established an African-American literary presence during the pivotal years of a new nation struggling for liberty.

Further Reading

Andrews, William L., Frances Smith Foster, and Trudier Harris, eds. *The Concise Oxford Companion to African American Literature.* New York: Oxford University Press, 2001.

O'Neale, Sondra A. *Jupiter Hammon and the Biblical Beginnings of African-American Literature.* Lanham, Md.: Scarecrow Press, 1993.

Richards, Philip M. "Nationalist Themes in the Preaching of Jupiter Hammon." *Early American Literature* 25, no. 2 (1990): 123.

Hansberry, Lorraine
(Lorraine Vivian Hansberry)
(1930–1965) *playwright, essayist, editor*

At the age of 28, Lorraine Hansberry achieved instant and enduring success with *A Raisin in the Sun,* her first play and the first by an African-American woman to be produced on Broadway. The play also earned Hansberry the New York Drama Critics Circle Award for best play in 1959, the first such distinction for an African-American playwright. Also the author of essays published in periodicals such as *Negro Digest* and the *Village Voice,* Hansberry emphasized the dignity of African-American life and culture in her writing and in her active involvement in the Civil Rights movement.

Lorraine Vivian Hansberry was born on May 19, 1930, in Chicago, Illinois, to Carl Augustus and Nannie Perry Hansberry. The youngest of four children, Lorraine grew up in a middle-class black neighborhood on Chicago's South Side. She described her parents as "strong-minded, civic-minded, exceptionally race-minded people who made enormous sacrifices on behalf of the struggle for civil rights." Leading African-American cultural figures and activists such as Paul Robeson, LANGSTON HUGHES, and W. E. B. DuBOIS were frequent visitors to the Hansberry home during Lorraine's childhood, and she learned at an early age the courage required to stand against racial injustice.

In 1938 Hansberry's father challenged a Chicago statute that prohibited African Americans from living in white neighborhoods. When the family moved to their new home, an angry mob surrounded the house, threw bricks, and threatened further violence. An Illinois court ordered the Hansberrys to leave, but Carl fought the order until 1940, when he won a landmark U.S. Supreme Court decision in *Hansberry v. Lee,* which overturned the state court decision.

Hansberry attended Betsy Ross Elementary School and Englewood High School in Chicago. Unlike her siblings, who chose to attend black colleges, she enrolled at the predominantly white University of Wisconsin to study journalism. As a student, Hansberry integrated an all-white dormitory and joined the Young Progressive Association, a leftist student organization, for which she served as president during her sophomore year. She also resolved to become a writer. Having developed an interest in theater as a high school student, Hansberry was further inspired by the works of playwright Sean O'Casey, particularly a university performance of *Juno and the Paycock.*

In 1950 Hansberry moved to New York; accepted a position on the staff of the monthly newspaper *Freedom,* founded by Paul Robeson; and began contributing articles to various magazines, including *Freedom, New Challenge,* and the *Village Voice.* In 1952 Hansberry attended an international peace conference in Montevideo, Uruguay, in the place of Robeson, whose passport had been revoked by the U.S. State Department. During a protest against discrimination at New York University in 1953, Hansberry met Robert Nemeroff, a white graduate student at New York University and an aspiring writer, and the two were married later that year. They settled in Greenwich Village, where Hansberry held an assortment of odd jobs before her husband's success as a songwriter allowed her to write full time.

Borrowing her title from a line in "Harlem," a poem by Langston Hughes, Hansberry finished her first play, *A Raisin in the Sun,* in 1958. Set in a working-class neighborhood on Chicago's South Side, the play depicts an African-American family's dream of moving from their crumbling inner-city neighborhood and their overcrowded apartment to a better life in the predominantly white Chicago suburbs. The forces that stand in the way of the Younger family's hopes for a better future also threaten to break the family apart.

A Raisin in the Sun was initially rejected by Broadway producers. It debuted in smaller venues in New Haven, Connecticut, and Philadelphia, Pennsylvania. On March 11, 1959, the play made its Broadway opening at the Ethel Barrymore Theatre in New York City and became an instant popular and critical success. The first play by an African-American woman to be produced on Broadway, *A Raisin in the Sun* ran for 530 performances and was awarded the New York Drama Critics Circle Award for best play in 1959, also a first for an African-American woman. Hansberry later wrote a screenplay for the 1961 film version and won a special award from the Cannes Film Festival.

Hailed by many critics as the most promising young playwright of her generation following the success of *A Raisin in the Sun,* Hansberry divided her time during the early 1960s between writing and civil rights activism. She was diagnosed with pancreatic cancer in 1963, but she remained active creatively and politically. She lectured and raised funds for the Student Nonviolent Coordinating Committee (SNCC) and met with Robert Kennedy to discuss race relations. She also published a pictorial study of the Civil Rights movement, *The Movement: Documentary of a Struggle for Equality,* in 1964. Her second play, *The Sign in Sidney Brustein's Window,* opened on Broadway in 1964 to mixed reviews. With financial support from friends and admirers, the play, which depicts the life of a Jewish newspaper editor and his circle of Greenwich Village intellectuals during the 1960s, ran for 103 performances. Her marriage to Robert Nemeroff ended in 1964, in part because of Hansberry's growing awareness of her homosexuality; but the two remained close friends. Lorraine Vivian Hansberry died on January 12, 1965, the day that her second play closed on Broadway.

At the time of her death, Hansberry had been working on several projects. Robert Nemeroff spent the remainder of his life editing and producing many of these works. He adapted selections from Hansberry's personal journals, essays, and letters into a successful off-Broadway play *To Be Young, Gifted, and Black*, produced in 1969. *Les Blancs*, a two-act play about civil rights movements, was produced on Broadway in 1970. Two other plays, *The Drinking Gourd*, a television drama commissioned by NBC but never produced, and *Where Are All the Flowers?*, a play about the aftermath of a nuclear holocaust, were collected with *Les Blancs* and published by Random House in 1972. Other works included a commentary on Simone de Beauvoir's *The Second Sex*, a stage adaptation of the novel *The Marrow of Tradition*, by CHARLES W. CHESNUTT, and a musical adaptation of Oliver LaFarge's *Laughing Boy*.

Poet and playwright AMIRI BARAKA described Hansberry's *A Raisin in the Sun* as the "quintessential civil rights drama" and noted its influence on the black theater movement of the 1960s, which produced such distinguished playwrights as Baraka, LARRY NEAL, and ED BULLINS. Hansberry's depiction of an African-American family's pursuit of the American dream in the face of overwhelming racial discrimination resonated with audiences and highlighted social and economic issues central to the Civil Rights movement. A classic of American theater, *A Raisin in the Sun* has been produced and published in more than 30 countries, and it continues to be staged in university and community productions across the United States.

Further Reading

Andrews, William L., Frances Scott Smith, and Trudier Harris, eds. *The Concise Oxford Companion to African American Literature*. New York: Oxford University Press, 2001.

Gates, Henry Louis, Jr., and Nellie Y. McKay, eds. *The Norton Anthology of African American Literature*. New York: W. W. Norton, 1997.

In 1959 Lorraine Hansberry became the first African-American woman to have a play produced on Broadway. *(Library of Congress)*

Hansberry, Lorraine. *Les Blancs: The Collected Last Plays*. New York: Vintage Books, 1994.

———. *A Raisin in the Sun and The Sign in Sidney Brustein's Window*. Edited by Robert Nemeroff. New York: Vintage Books, 1995.

———. *To Be Young, Gifted, and Black: Lorraine Hansberry in Her Own Words*. Adapted by Robert Nemeroff. New York: Vintage Books, 1995.

Harper, Frances Ellen Watkins (Effie Afton, Frances Ellen Watkins)
(1825–1911) *poet, novelist, essayist, short story writer, abolitionist*

One of the 19th century's best-known African-American poets, Frances Harper devoted her life and writing to the cause of racial and gender equality. In poetry, novels, essays, and short stories, Harper became the voice of African-American women and men in the struggle to abolish slavery and, during the Reconstruction era, to claim their rightful place in American society.

Harper was born Frances Ellen Watkins to free parents on September 24, 1825, in Baltimore, Maryland. Following the death of her parents when she was still a child, she was raised by an aunt and uncle and educated in her uncle's William Watson Academy for Negro Youth, where she distinguished herself as a gifted student. Following the passage of the Fugitive Slave Act of 1850, whereby fugitive slaves (and often free blacks) could be captured and returned to slavery, she moved to Columbus, Ohio. There, she became the first female professor at Union Seminary (later Wilberforce University).

In 1853 she moved to Philadelphia, Pennsylvania, and became active in the Underground Railway. That year, her home state of Maryland enacted laws permitting any free black living or traveling in the state to be sold into slavery. In a highly publicized case, a free African-American man was captured by slavers in Maryland and shipped south. After trying to escape, he was recaptured, tortured, and killed. "Upon that grave," she wrote, recalling the incident in a letter, "I pledged myself to the Anti-Slavery cause." Harper joined the Maine Antislavery Society and electrified audiences throughout New England, Canada, and the Midwest with the passion of her message and the vivid imagery of her poetry, which she often incorporated into her speeches.

Watkins is believed to have published her first collection of poetry, *Fallen Leaves*, in 1845, though no surviving copies have been discovered. *Poems on Miscellaneous Subjects,* published in 1854 and featuring an introduction by the renowned white abolitionist William Lloyd Garrison, sold thousands of copies and went through 20 editions by 1871. The most popular and frequently anthologized poem, "Bury Me in a Free Land," became an anthem of the abolitionist movement. Other poems in the volume addressed her concern for women's rights, African-American history, and the temperance movement. Also in 1854, she published *Eventide,* a collection of poems under the pseudonym Effie Afton.

In the years leading up to the Civil War, Watkins contributed essays to numerous abolitionist journals, including Garrison's *Liberator* and the *National Anti-Slavery Standard.* She also joined such esteemed abolitionists and writers as FREDERICK DOUGLASS, Martin R. Delany, and WILLIAM COOPER NELL as an editor and contributor to the *Anglo-African Magazine,* one of the earliest African-American literary journals. In 1859 the *Anglo-African Magazine* published her story "The Two Offers," which is widely considered to be the first published short story by an African American.

Following her marriage to Fenton Harper in 1860, Frances Harper withdrew from public life and settled in Ohio to raise a family. She soon returned, however, after the death of her husband in 1864. From 1865 to 1870 Harper traveled widely in the South, lecturing to white and black audiences and publishing letters in northern newspapers to enlist support for the social and educational needs of freed slaves. Her experiences in the South became the subject of several literary works. In 1868 she published *Moses, A Story of the Nile,* a collection of poems in which she adapted the biblical story of Moses to symbolize the plight of African Americans during Reconstruction. *Sketches of Southern Life,* a collection of poems that used regional dialect and featured the meditations of a matriarchal figure, Aunt Chloe Fleet, was published in 1870.

Though her literary reputation rests primarily on her poetry, Harper also published several novels. In 1867 *Sowing and Reaping: A Temperance Story* was serialized in the *Christian Recorder,* and *Trial and Triumph* was published in 1888. Her best-known novel, *Iola Leroy: Or, Shadows Uplifted,* was published in 1892 and portrays the struggles of a young mulatto girl in her search for her family during the close of the Civil War. Considered a classic of African-American literature, *Iola Leroy* was praised by contemporary critics for its balanced portrayal of the racial, gender, and class struggles of African Americans during the Reconstruction era. Harper also continued to publish poetry, releasing three additional volumes, *Atlanta Offering, Martyr of Alabama and Other Poems*, and *Poems*, all in 1895.

Harper provided valuable support for numerous educational and women's organizations during the late 19th century. In the 1860s, she joined several celebrated social and racial activists, including Frederick Douglass, Sojourner Truth, Susan B. Anthony, and Elizabeth Cady Stanton, in the American Equal Rights Association, providing a critical voice for African-American women. She also helped found the National Association of Colored Women, for which she served as vice president, and became director of the American Association of Education of Colored Youth in 1894. Harper attended the American Women Suffrage Association conferences in 1875 and 1887, and she was a featured speaker at the meetings of the International Council of Women in 1888, the National Council of Women in 1891, and the World Congress of Representative Women at the Columbian Exposition in Chicago in 1893. Following a lengthy period of ill health beginning in 1900, Frances Harper died on February 20, 1911.

As a lecturer and writer, Frances Ellen Watkins Harper became a powerful and persuasive advocate for the social and political enfranchisement of African Americans and women. Praised by contemporaries such as the celebrated critic and sociologist W. E. B. DuBois for her contributions to African-American literature and culture, Harper has become the subject of renewed critical interest for her role as a pioneering feminist and author. Her poetry continues to appear in anthologies of African-American and American literature, and several of her early serial novels have been reprinted in modern editions.

Further Reading

Boyd, Melba Joyce. *Discarded Legacy: Politics and Poetics in the Life of Frances E. W. Harper*. Detroit, Mich.: Wayne State University Press, 1994.

Gates, Henry Louis, Jr., and Nellie Y. McKay, eds. *The Norton Anthology of African American Literature*. New York: W. W. Norton, 1997.

Harper, Frances Ellen Watkins. *Minnie's Sacrifice, Sowing and Reaping, Trial and Triumph: Three Rediscovered Novels*. Boston: Beacon Press, 1994.

Harper, Michael S.
(Michael Steven Harper)
(1938–   ) *poet, editor, educator*

Considered by many critics to be one of America's premier contemporary poets, Michael S. Harper has earned international acclaim for the range and complexity of his literary themes. His poetry has earned two National Book Award nominations and awards from the Black Academy of Arts and Letters and the National Institute of Arts and Letters. In 1988 Harper was named Rhode Island's first poet laureate. As a poet, educator, and editor, Harper has demonstrated with passion and vigor the immense contributions of African Americans to the legacy of American history and culture.

Michael Steven Harper was born on March 18, 1938, in Brooklyn, New York, the son of Walter Warren Harper, a postal supervisor, and Katherine Johnson Harper, a medical stenographer. In 1951 Harper moved with his family to a recently integrated white neighborhood in west Los Angeles where racial violence was an imminent threat. Expected by his parents to pursue a career in medicine, Harper attended Dorsey High School and enrolled at Los Angeles State College (now California State University) as a premed student, though his interest soon turned to literature. He received his bachelor's degree in 1961.

Inspired by RALPH ELLISON's *Invisible Man* (1952) and the works of the English romantic poet John Keats, Harper decided to study writing at the University of Iowa's renowned Iowa Writers Workshop, where he completed his master's degree in creative writing in 1963. Harper's first poems appeared in such periodicals as the *Quarterly Review of Literature,* the *Southern Review,* and *Negro Digest* in the 1960s, and during this time he also taught English and creative writing at colleges in California and Oregon.

In 1970 Harper published *Dear John, Dear Coltrane,* his first collection of poems. Inspired by the legendary jazz saxophonist John Coltrane, *Dear John, Dear Coltrane* uses the life and music of Coltrane and other jazz musicians such as Charlie Parker and Miles Davis to address broader issues of race, culture, aesthetics, and love. In the collection's title poem, the physical and spiritual torments in the life of John Coltrane become a metaphor for the human condition of suffering that ultimately gives rise to creative expression rooted in "a love supreme," a frequent refrain in the poem and the name of one of Coltrane's most cherished jazz compositions. *Dear John, Dear Coltrane* earned a National Book Award nomination in 1970.

Harper continued to develop his unique aesthetic perspective in later collections of poetry, including *History Is Your Own Heartbeat* (1971); *Photographs: Negatives: History as Apple Tree* (1972); *Song: I Want a Witness* (1972); *Debridement* (1973); and *Nightmare Begins Responsibility* (1975). In these collections, Harper uses a variety of compelling images to address the historical divisions of race and culture in America. *Debridement* takes its title from the medical term that refers to the removal of dead flesh in a wound to prevent further infection. In the book Harper uses the lives of John Brown, a militant white abolitionist, the novelist RICHARD WRIGHT, and the fictional John Henry Louis to suggest that American history must be salvaged from the stereotypes and misinformation that have created the rotting wounds of racial oppression.

In 1977 Harper earned a second National Book Award nomination for *Images of Kinship.* In poems such as "Goin' to the Territory," "The Pen," and "The Militance of a Photograph in the Passbook of a Bantu under Detention," Harper identifies with his African-American, Native American, and black South African kin, bound together by suffering as well as hope. The concept of kinship serves an important function in much of Harper's poetry by showing that historical and cultural corruptions have divided humanity of all colors and traditions and led to a potent mythology of racial stereotypes that converge in violence and oppression.

Harper's other works of poetry include *Rhode Island: Eight Poems* (1981), *Healing Song for the Inner Ear* (1985), *Honorable Amendments: Poems* (1995), and *Songlines in Michaeltree: New and Collected Poems* (2000). In 1979 Harper coedited *Chant of Saints: A Gathering of Afro-American Literature, Art, and Scholarship,* which became one of the 20th century's most influential anthologies of African-American literature. He also compiled and edited *The Collected Poems of Sterling A. Brown* (1980), coedited *Every Shut Eye Ain't Asleep: An Anthology of Poetry by African Americans Since 1945* (1994), and *The Vintage Book of African American Poetry* (2000).

In 1971 Harper began a lengthy and distinguished career as a professor of English and creative writing at Brown University, in Providence, Rhode Island. In 1983 the university named him the Israel J. Kaplan Professor of English. Harper was selected to participate in the bicentennial exchange between the United States and Great Britain in 1976 and the International Conference of Africanists' tour of Africa in 1977, sponsored by the U.S. State Department. In 1988 he was named Rhode Island's first poet laureate, a post he held until 1993.

As a poet, editor, and educator, Michael Steven Harper has emphasized the connections between African-American and American history and culture in compelling, though often controversial ways. Some critics have condemned his identification with nonblack cultural and literary sources and his insistence on being considered, like STERLING BROWN, an American poet rather than a black poet. Yet Harper's poetry has consistently sought to preserve the unity and diversity that exists between different cultures and to identify the connections that, through ignorance, ambivalence, and hatred, have been neglected or forgotten.

Further Reading

Antonucci, Michael. "The Map and the Territory: An Interview with Michael S. Harper. *African American Review* 34 (fall 2000): 501.

Brown, Joseph A. "Their Long Scars Touch Ours: A Reflection on the Poetry of Michael Harper." *Callaloo* 9 (1986): 209.

Harper, Michael S. *Songlines in Michaeltree: New and Collected Poems.* Urbana: University of Illinois Press, 2000.

Loudon, Michael. "Michael S. Harper." *Critical Survey of Poetry.* Hackensack, N.J.: Salem Press, 2003.

Hayden, Robert
(Robert Earl Hayden, Asa Bundy Sheffey)
(1913–1980) *poet, essayist, educator*

Hailed by many critics as one of America's most technically skilled poets, Robert Hayden achieved international acclaim for his erudite and stylistically complex poetry. Hayden drew the criticism of more militant African-American scholars and peers during the 1960s for his perceived ambivalence toward black culture and politics. Yet many of his most celebrated poems reveal an abiding interest in African-American history and his concern for racial equality.

Robert Hayden was born Asa Bundy Sheffey on August 4, 1913, in Detroit, Michigan. His parents, Ruth and Asa Sheffey, separated prior to his birth, and Hayden grew up in the home of William and Sue Ellen Hayden, friends and neighbors of Hayden's parents. Coming of age in the dangerous inner-city neighborhood of Paradise Valley in Detroit, Hayden lived a childhood characterized by poverty, physical abuse, and divided loyalties between his mother, who lived for a time in the Hayden household, and his foster parents.

Severely nearsighted as a child, Hayden suffered the disappointment of his foster father for his inability to participate in athletics and his increasing interest in academics. Hayden took consolation in literature and spent much of his youth reading. In high school, he read the fiction of George Eliot and the poetry of Nathaniel Hawthorne, T. S. Eliot, and George Edward Bulwer-Lytton. "I loved those books," he explained in an interview, "partly because they took me completely out of the environment I lived in, and they appealed to my imagination."

Following his graduation from high school in 1930, and lacking the financial means to attend college, Hayden read widely in American and European literature. He discovered the works of Harlem Renaissance authors in ALAIN LOCKE's landmark anthology *The New Negro* (1925) and developed an avid interest in the poetry of COUNTEE CULLEN. Hayden also drew inspiration from the English romantic poet John Keats and modern American poets such as Carl Sandburg and Edna St. Vincent Millay, as well as the playwright Eugene O'Neill.

Hayden received a scholarship to attend Detroit City College (now Wayne State University) in 1932, and he pursued a degree in Spanish with a minor in English. He also participated in the college's drama department. Hayden performed in a play by LANGSTON HUGHES and met the author, who had come to view the production. Hughes agreed to read some of Hayden's poetry and encouraged the young poet to develop his own unique style and voice.

From 1936 to 1938 Hayden worked in the Detroit branch of the Federal Writers' Project as a research assistant in local African-American history and folklore. He also wrote theater and music reviews for the *Michigan Chronicle,* a local black newspaper. In 1938 Hayden enrolled in graduate courses at the University of Michigan in Ann Arbor and completed his first collection of poems, *Heart-Shape in Dust,* which received the university's Hopwood Prize for student poetry. The collection was published in 1940. Highly derivative in theme and style, these early poems revealed an enormous debt to Harlem Renaissance poets such as Countee Cullen and CLAUDE McKAY.

Hayden married Erma Morris in 1941, and the couple moved to New York so that Erma could attend the Juilliard School of Music. In New York Hayden received further literary encouragement from Countee Cullen, whom he met through one of his wife's relatives. Hayden returned with his wife to Detroit that year and continued his graduate studies at the University of Michigan, where he studied with the renowned poet W. H. Auden, who inspired Hayden with "the range of his learning, and the breadth of his knowledge," as he later explained in a 1973 interview.

Robert Hayden, shown here in 1975, became the first African American to serve as consultant in poetry to the Library of Congress, a position that would come to be known as the U.S. poet laureate. *(Library of Congress)*

In 1944 Hayden completed his graduate studies and became a teaching assistant at the University of Michigan. Two years later he joined the faculty of Fisk University, in Nashville, Tennessee, where he would remain until 1969. During his 23 years at Fisk, Hayden balanced the demands of his teaching career and the maintenance of his wife and daughter, Maia, with the exigency of his writing.

Hayden's next two volumes of poetry, *The Lion and the Archer* (1948, a limited edition collaboration with poet Myron O'Higgins) and *Figure of Time: Poems* (1955), revealed his increasing independence as an artist and the development of a complex poetic vision. The publication of *A Ballad of Remembrance* in 1962, however, secured a national audience for his poetry. In poems such as "Frederick Douglass," "Runagate, Runagate," and "Middle Passage," Hayden experimented with language and narrative structure.

"Middle Passage," one of Hayden's best-known poems, employs multiple shifts in perspective in its masterful telling of the harrowing journey suffered by enslaved Africans on their passage to America. Shifting between multiple voices, from the entry in a slave ship's log and the reminiscences of a slave trader, to the refrains of spirituals and Protestant hymns, the poem becomes a montage of images, held together by the recurring words, "Voyage through death / to life upon these shores," with which the poem concludes.

Ballad of Remembrance was awarded the Grand Prize for Poetry at the First World Festival of Negro Arts in Dakar, Senegal. Hayden's later collections of poetry, including *Selected Poems* (1966), *Words in the Mourning Time* (1970), which received a National Book Award nomination, *The Night-Blooming Cereus* (1972), *Angle of Ascent: New and Selected Poems* (1975), and *American Journal* (1978), also a nominee for the National Book Award, continued to extend his reputation as one of America's most respected poets.

In 1969 Hayden returned to the University of Michigan as a professor of English, where he remained until his death. In 1976 Hayden was named consultant in poetry to the Library of Congress, a post that later became known as U.S. poet laureate, and the first such honor for an African American. Hayden's other literary honors included the Russell Loines Award from the National Institute of Arts and Letters in 1970, and a fellowship from the American Academy of Poets in 1977. Robert Earl Hayden died on February 25, 1980, in Ann Arbor, Michigan.

Robert Hayden was often criticized during his lifetime for a range of influences and interests that extended beyond the African-American community. The scope of his writing was influenced in large part by his conversion to the Baha'i faith in 1942, a belief system that emphasized the unity of all people and religions. Nevertheless, Hayden remained committed to an artistic vision that honored his racial heritage and sought to locate African-American history and culture within a broader nexus of global interests.

Further Reading

Conniff, Brian. "Answering 'The Waste Land': Robert Hayden and the Rise of the African American Poetic Sequence." *African American Review* 33 (fall 1999): 487.

Goldstein, Laurence, and Robert Chrisman, eds. *Robert Hayden: Essays on the Poetry.* Ann Arbor: University of Michigan Press, 2001.

Hatcher, John. *From the Auroral Darkness: The Life and Poetry of Robert Hayden.* Abingdon, England: George Ronald Publishers Ltd., 1984.

Williams, Pontheolla Taylor. *Robert Hayden: A Critical Analysis of His Poetry.* Urbana: University of Illinois Press, 1987.

Hemphill, Essex

(ca. 1957–1995) *poet, essayist, editor*

One of few outspoken African-American gay authors and activists, Essex Hemphill became an important leader in the development of an African-American perspective in gay literature. He published two poetry chapbooks and a collection of poetry and prose. His poems also appeared in numerous periodicals, including *Obsidian, Black Scholar, Callaloo,* and *Essence,* and in several anthologies, including *In the Life* (1986) and *Tongues Untied* (1987), both landmark collections of poetry by African-American gay men. Concerned with the relative invisibility of African-American gay and lesbian men and women in society and literature, Hemphill sought to address the double minority status of African-American gays, who are confronted with intolerance and oppression for their racial as well as sexual identities.

Essex Hemphill was born on April 16, 1957, in Chicago, Illinois, the oldest of five siblings. He lived briefly as a child in Anderson, Indiana, and Columbia, South Carolina, but grew up primarily in Washington, D.C. He graduated from Ballou High School in 1975 and studied English and journalism at the University of Maryland and the University of the District of Columbia. Hemphill acknowledged his homosexuality during a poetry reading at Howard University in 1980. Much of his poetry explores the impact that his identity as a gay man had on his family. "I am the invisible son. / In the family photos / nothing appears out of character. / I smile as I serve my duty," he wrote in a frequently anthologized poem, "Commitments."

Hemphill published his first two collections of poems, the chapbooks *Earth Life* (1985) and *Conditions* (1986), privately, under the imprint Be Bop Books. In language both explicit and lyrical, Hemphill celebrated romantic love between men as a kind of covenant that held the promise of a future free of racial and sexual prejudice. "They don't know," he wrote in a poem from *Conditions,* "we are becoming powerful. / Everytime we kiss / we confirm the new world coming." Rather than being simply an apologist for gay love, Hemphill addresses the nature and practice of love in all its manifestations, emphasizing the dignity and respect that love should imply. "But we so called men, / we so called brothers / wonder why it's so hard / to love *our* women / when we're about loving them / the way america / loves us."

In 1986 Hemphill contributed poems to a groundbreaking anthology of black gay literature, *In the Life,* edited by Joseph Beam. A companion volume to *In the Life* titled *Brother to Brother* was left unfinished after Joseph Beam's death from AIDS in 1988. Hemphill took over the project, with the help of Beam's mother, and published *Brother to Brother* in 1991. Containing poems, essays, and stories, *Brother to Brother* received mixed critical reviews. In a review in the *New Republic,* David Van Leer called it "a ringing political indictment of the homophobia of the black community and the racism of the gay community." Other critics dismissed the anthology on the basis of what they saw as the questionable literary merit of some of its contributors.

Hemphill published his last volume of poetry, *Ceremonies: Prose and Poetry,* in 1992. This collection included poems from his chapbooks *Earth Life* and *Conditions,* as well as new poems and essays, in which he addressed issues ranging from the photographs of Robert Mapplethorpe and AIDS within the African-American community to racism among the white gay community. *Ceremonies* was well received critically, winning the American Library Association's Gay, Lesbian, and Bisexual Book Award in 1993.

In addition to his work as a poet and editor, Hemphill also contributed to two film documentaries: Marlon Riggs's *Tongues Untied* (1991), a film companion to the 1987 literary anthology, to which Hemphill also contributed poetry; and Isaac Julien's controversial *Looking for Langston* (1989), which characterized the renowned Harlem Renaissance poet LANGSTON HUGHES as a homosexual. Hemphill also narrated the 1990 documentary *Out of the Shadows,* which examined the challenges faced by African-Americans from a variety of backgrounds in publicly acknowledging their homosexuality.

Though he rarely addressed the matter publicly, Essex Hemphill lived for several years with the knowledge that he suffered from AIDS. "It's just one more thing that you have to contend with," he explained in an interview with the *Advocate,* "and if you believe in yourself fiercely enough, you'll find a way to deal with it." Essex Hemphill died on November 4, 1995, of complications from AIDS.

A critically acclaimed author of poetry and essays, whose writing has been featured in numerous periodicals and anthologies, Essex Hemphill was a provocative and influential voice among African-American gay authors. The recipient of fellowships from the National Endowment for the Arts and the District of Columbia Commission for the Arts, Hemphill also served as a visiting scholar at the Getty Center for the History of Art and the Humanities, and he taught a course on black gay identity at the Institute for Policy Studies in Washington, D.C.

Further Reading

Gates, Henry Louis, Jr., and Nellie Y. McKay, eds. *The Norton Anthology of African American Literature.* New York: W. W. Norton, 1997.

Hemphill, Essex, ed. *Brother to Brother: New Writings by Black Gay Men.* Los Angeles, Calif.: Alyson Publications, 1991.

———. *Ceremonies: Poetry and Prose.* San Francisco, Calif.: Cleis Press, 2000.

Himes, Chester
(Chester Bomar Himes)
(1909–1984) *novelist, short story writer, autobiographer*

A prolific author of novels, short stories, and a two-volume autobiography, Chester Himes first gained success as a writer in Europe, where, like JAMES BALDWIN and RICHARD WRIGHT, he lived for several years as an expatriate and developed a large following with his hard-boiled detective novels. His books captured in grim detail the violent and oppressive nature of modern urban life for many African Americans, who faced intolerance and prejudice from whites as well as others in the African-American community. Though often overlooked by critics, Himes's books have remained popular in America and across Europe, particularly the novels that feature the detectives Coffin Ed Johnson and Grave Digger Jones, two of his best-known and most compelling characters.

Chester Bomar Himes was born on July 29, 1909, in Jefferson City, Missouri, the youngest of Joseph Sandy Himes and Estelle Bomar Himes's three sons. Himes grew up in several cities in the South. His father moved frequently between jobs as a teacher of industrial arts at black institutions in Alabama, Mississippi, and Arkansas. In 1925 Himes settled with his family in Cleveland, Ohio, and graduated from Glenville High School. He enrolled at Ohio State University in 1926, but poor grades and an active social life compelled him to leave after a year.

Having returned to Cleveland, Himes became increasingly involved in criminal activity. After receiving a suspended sentence for writing bad checks, Himes was charged with armed robbery in 1928 and began serving his 20- to 25-year sentence in the Ohio State Penitentiary. During his incarceration, Himes began to write short stories about his experiences in prison. His first published story, "His Last Day," appeared in *Abbott's Monthly* in 1932. Other stories, such as "Crazy in the Stir," "To What Red Hell," and "The Night's for Crying," appeared in periodicals such as *Coronet* and *Esquire.*

Himes was paroled in 1936 and married Jean Lucinda Johnson the following year. They later divorced in 1951. The successful publication of his prison stories convinced Himes to embark on his first novel, tentatively called *Black Sheep.* To earn a living, however, Himes joined the Works Progress Administration, initially as a laborer, but later as a research assistant for the Cleveland Public Library.

Critics generally draw a distinction between Himes's early novels, written in the naturalist style

Chester Himes, shown here in 1946, was one of the first African-American authors to explore the genres of mystery and detective fiction. *(Library of Congress)*

of RICHARD WRIGHT and JAMES BALDWIN, and his later detective fiction. Himes's early novels include *If He Hollers Let Him Go* (1945), *Lonely Crusade* (1947), *Cast the First Stone* (1952, reprinted as *Yesterday Will Make You Cry,* 1998), *The Third Generation* (1954), and *The Primitive* (1955, reprinted as *The End of the Primitive,* 1997). Reviews of these early works were mixed, with some criticizing Himes's use of excessive violence and his bleak portrait of urban African-American life. Others praised the accuracy of his depictions of American racism.

Himes moved to Europe in 1953, where, with the exception of brief visits to the United States, he would remain for the rest of his life. Encouraged by French publisher Marcel Duhamel to produce a novel for his *Série Noir* series of popular crime thrillers, Himes wrote *For Love of Imabelle* (1957, revised as *A Rage in Harlem,* 1965) in a matter of weeks. Immensely successful in France, the novel was awarded the Grand Prix Policier in 1958 and initiated a series of novels that became known as the Harlem Domestics.

These fast-paced and violent crime thrillers were set in Harlem and introduced Himes's most recognized characters, the black detectives Grave Digger Jones and Coffin Ed Johnson. Himes's often absurdist depictions of Harlem's violent urban environment and the racial oppression indicative of American society resonated with readers in Europe, and the novels soon found an avid readership in America. Other titles in the Harlem Domestic series include *The Real Cool Killers* (1959), *The Crazy Kill* (1959), *The Big Gold Dream* (1960), *All Shot Up* (1960), *The Heat's On* (1966), *Cotton Comes to Harlem* (1965), and *Blind Man with a Pistol* (1969).

Himes also published several noir novels outside of the Harlem Domestics series, including *Pinktoes* (1961), a satirical examination of interracial relationships, *Run Man, Run* (1966), which focuses on police brutality, and *A Case of Rape* (1963). *Plan B: A Novel* was published posthumously in 1993. Far more successful upon their publication than his early protest novels, Himes's potboiler crime novels have since received closer scrutiny by critics for their depiction of violence as a logical response to racial oppression, particularly in the figures of detectives Grave Digger and Coffin Ed.

As an expatriate, Himes traveled widely in Europe and eventually settled in Alicante, Spain, with his second wife, Leslie Packard. In the final years of his life, Himes produced a two-volume autobiography: *The Quality of Hurt* (1972) and *My Life of Absurdity* (1977); and *Black on Black: Baby Sister and Selected Writings* (1973), a collection of his prose and dramatic writings. Chester Bomar Himes died on November 12, 1984, in Moreira, Spain.

Originally dismissed by contemporaries and critics (at least in the United States) for the violent nature of his novels and stories, Himes has since become the focus of renewed attention. Contemporary critics generally regard his early novels as classics of African-American protest fic-

tion, and several of his crime thrillers have remained in print. In 1970 *Cotton Comes to Harlem* was adapted to film. A second novel, *The Heat's On*, was adapted to film in 1973 under the title *Come Back Charleston Blue*. Though not the first African-American author to write detective fiction, Himes popularized the genre as a useful form in which to address America's enduring racial inequities, setting an example for later writers such as WALTER MOSLEY.

Further Reading

Cochran, David. "So Much Nonsense Must Make Sense: The Black Vision of Chester Himes." *The Midwest Quarterly* 38 (autumn 1996): 11.

Himes, Chester. *My Life of Absurdity: The Autobiography of Chester Himes, Volume 2.* New York: Doubleday, 1977.

———. *The Quality of Hurt: The Autobiography of Chester Himes, Volume 1.* New York: Doubleday, 1972.

Sallis, James. *Chester Himes: A Life.* New York: Walker and Co., 2001.

hooks, bell
(Gloria Jean Watkins)
(1952–   ) *cultural and literary critic, poet, educator*

An internationally respected intellectual, cultural critic, and feminist theorist, bell hooks has published nearly two dozen books, including essays, poetry, and memoirs. Education is a vital element of hooks's intellectual and literary life; she is also a distinguished professor of literature and women's and black studies. "Fundamentally the purpose of my knowing," hooks has stated, "was so that I could serve those who did not know, so that I could learn and teach my own—education as the practice of freedom." In her writing on subjects as varied as art criticism, feminism, postmodernism, and the nature of love, hooks challenges the assumptions of race, gender, and culture that divide individuals from themselves and others.

bell hooks was born Gloria Jean Watkins on September 25, 1952, in the segregated rural Kentucky town of Hopkinsville, one of seven children born to Veodis Watkins, a custodian for the local post office, and Rosa Bell Watkins, a homemaker. She grew up among strong female role models and benefited particularly from the influence of her mother. "Politically, our young mother, Rosa Bell," hooks wrote, "did not allow the white supremacist culture of domination to completely shape and control her psyche and her familial relationships."

Since 1995, hooks has served as a distinguished professor of English at the City College of New York. She adopted the pseudonym bell hooks, the name of her grandmother, in part to honor the memory of her grandmother's habit of speaking her mind. "I claimed this legacy of defiance . . . affirming my link to female ancestors who were bold and daring in their speech," she explained in *Talking Back* (1989). hooks chose to use all lowercase letters in her name in order to distance her personal identity from the message of her literary works.

Educated primarily in Hopkinsville's segregated public schools, she received a scholarship to attend Stanford University, in Palo Alto, California, where she completed her bachelor's degree in 1973. Three years later, she received her master's degree at the University of Wisconsin in Madison and accepted a teaching position at the University of Southern California, where she remained until 1979. In the early 1980s hooks taught at the University of California at Santa Cruz and completed her Ph.D. there in 1983.

In 1981 hooks published *Ain't I a Woman: Black Women and Feminism*, a study that she started writing as a student at Stanford, and that grew out of her belief that black women were virtually invisible in the emerging discourses on black liberation and feminism in the 1960s and 1970s. *Ain't I a Woman* became the first of many works that articulated the concerns of black women within the feminist movement. *Feminist*

Theory: From Margin to Center (1984), *Talking Back: Thinking Feminist, Thinking Black* (1989), *Feminism Is for Everybody: Passionate Politics* (2000), further established the cultural and political foundations of hooks's feminist perspective.

During the 1990s hooks turned her attention to the depictions of African Americans, particularly women, in popular culture, the media, and the arts. In works such as *Yearning: Race, Gender, and Cultural Politics* (1990), which won an American Book Award in 1991, *Black Looks: Race and Representation* (1992), *Outlaw Culture: Resisting Representations* (1994), *Art on My Mind: Visual Politics* (1995), *Killing Rage: Ending Racism* (1995), *Reel to Real: Race, Sex, and Class at the Movies* (1996), and *Rock My Soul: Black People and Self Esteem* (2002), hooks addresses the continued presence of racist stereotypes within American culture and their effects on the African-American community.

hooks has taught English, women's studies, and African-American studies at several universities, including Yale University, Oberlin College, and since 1993, the City College of New York. As a teacher and an author, hooks seeks to empower black women and to show that the liberation of one marginalized group works toward the liberation of all people from oppressive stereotypes and power structures.

In addition to her cultural and feminist studies, hooks has published books on educational methods (*Teaching to Transgress: Education as the Practice of Freedom*, 1994), one volume of poetry (*A Woman's Mourning Song*, 1993), three books of children's verse (*Happy to Be Nappy*, 1999, *Homemade Love*, 2001, and *Be Boy Buzz*, 2002), autobiographical works (*Bone Black: Memories of Girlhood*, 1997), studies on writing (*Wounds of Passion: A Writing Life*, and *Remembered Rapture: The Writer at Work*, 1999), and a trilogy on the nature of love (*All About Love: New Visions*, 2000; *Salvation: Black People and Love*, 2001; and *Communion: The Female Search for Love*, 2002).

A prolific and influential author, and one of America's leading intellectuals and cultural critics, bell hooks has devoted her career as a writer and educator to the elimination of racial, sexual, and gender bias, in a voice that is at turns fierce, didactic, and always determined.

Further Reading

hooks, bell. *Ain't I a Woman: Black Women and Feminism.* Cambridge, Mass.: South End Press, 1981.

———. *Bone Black: Memories of Childhood.* New York: Henry Holt and Co., 1996.

———. *Yearning: Race, Gender, and Cultural Politics.* Boston, Mass.: South End Press, 1990.

Posey, Carl. "Sister Knowledge." *Essence,* May 1995, 187.

Hopkins, Pauline Elizabeth
(Sarah A. Allen)
(1859–1930) editor, novelist, short fiction writer, essayist, playwright, journalist

An important voice in the early development of the African-American novel, Pauline Hopkins also wrote poetry, short fiction, biography, and one of the earliest dramas created by an African-American woman. Hopkins also worked as an editor for the *Colored American Magazine,* in which she published three of her novels in serialized form and contributed editorials that helped promote racial and political dialogue at the turn of the 20th century.

Pauline Elizabeth Hopkins was born in 1859 in Portland, Maine, the daughter of William A. Hopkins, a Civil War veteran, and Sarah Allen Hopkins. During her infancy, Hopkins moved with her family to Boston, Massachusetts. She graduated from Boston's prestigious Girls' High School and found work as a stenographer, a profession that she would maintain periodically throughout her life to support her literary efforts.

Hopkins began writing at an early age. In 1874, at the age of 15, she won a literary contest sponsored by the Congregational Publishing Society of Boston for her essay "The Evils of Intemperance and Their Remedy." In 1880 her musical drama *Slaves' Escape; or, The Underground Railroad* (also

known as *Peculiar Sam; or, The Underground Railroad*) was produced, featuring Hopkins and other members of her family in the cast. Hopkins also toured with family members in a musical revue, the Hopkins Colored Troubadors, during the 1880s.

In 1900 Hopkins published her short story "The Mystery within Us" in the *Colored American Magazine,* one of the earliest periodicals to target a predominantly African-American audience, and began a prolific and influential association with the periodical. Her first novel, *Contending Forces: A Romance Illustrative of Negro Life North and South,* was published by the Colored Co-operative Publishing Company in 1900.

An early example of protest fiction, though written in the popular format of a historical romance, *Contending Forces* depicted a black family's journey from slavery to freedom. Hopkins characterized her novel as a record of the progress of African-American culture at the turn of the 20th century. "We must ourselves develop the men and women who will faithfully portray the feelings of the Negro," she wrote in the novel, "with all the fire and romance which lies dormant in our history, and, as yet, unrecognized by writers of the Anglo-Saxon race."

Hopkins remained associated with the *Colored American* until 1904. During that period she published numerous stories and essays, and three of her novels appeared in serialized form: *Hagar's Daughter: A Story of Southern Caste Prejudice* (1901–02, published under the name of Sarah A. Allen), *Winona: A Tale of Negro Life in the South and Southwest* (1902), and *Of One Blood, or The Hidden Self* (1902–03). Hopkins also served as an editor for *Colored American* from 1902 to 1904, during which she exerted considerable influence on the editorial content of the magazine and argued for the social and political enfranchisement of blacks in American society.

Following a disagreement with the new owner of the *Colored American* in 1904, Hopkins left the magazine to start her own publishing company, P. E. Hopkins and Co., in 1905, which that year released

A Primer of Facts Pertaining to the Early Greatness of the African Race. In 1915 Hopkins made a last effort at publishing with the creation of the periodical *New Era.* Surviving only two issues, *New Era* published Hopkins's novella *Topsy Templeton* in 1916. In the final years of her life, Pauline Elizabeth Hopkins lived in seclusion, supporting herself by working as a stenographer at the Massachusetts Institute of Technology. She died on August 13, 1930, from burns she received as a result of a house fire.

Largely ignored by mainstream critics during her lifetime, Pauline Hopkins was also dismissed by later scholars and writers such as GWENDOLYN BROOKS, many of whom criticized her perceived assimilationist political views. The republication of many of her early novels in the late 20th century, however, inspired contemporary critics to reevaluate her place in the tradition of African-American literature. In an era dominated by male authors and editors, Hopkins's use of journalism and fiction for social and political justice provided a foundation for later generations of African-American female authors, and her works provided valuable information on the conditions of life in the United States for middle-class African Americans in the late 19th and early 20th centuries.

Further Reading

Allen, Carol. *Black Women Intellectuals: Strategies of Nation, Family, and Neighborhood in the Works of Pauline Hopkins, Jessie Fauset, and Marita Bonner.* New York: Garland Publishing, 1998.

Gruesser, John Cullen, ed. *The Unruly Voice: Rediscovering Pauline Elizabeth Hopkins.* Urbana-Champaign: University of Illinois Press, 1996.

Hopkins, Pauline. *The Magazine Novels of Pauline Hopkins.* New York: Oxford University Press, 1988.

Horton, George Moses
(ca. 1797–ca. 1883) *poet*

Known as the Black Bard of North Carolina, George Moses Horton had a career as a poet that was marked by a number of singularities. He was the first African-American writer to publish a book in the South and the only slave to earn a substantial income from writing. He was also the first slave to protest his bondage in published verse.

Horton was born on a tobacco farm in Northampton County, North Carolina, in about 1797 but moved shortly thereafter with his master William Horton to Chatham. As a teenager, he tended livestock and worked as a farm laborer. He taught himself to read and composed poems and hymns in his head because he did not know how to write. He also began taking weekly walks to the University of North Carolina in Chapel Hill, eight miles away, to sell fruit.

Horton soon became a favorite with the students, entertaining them by composing love poems, which the students transcribed and Horton sold, earning as much as 75 cents a poem. Some students traded books for poems, giving Horton access to the works of Homer, Shakespeare, and John Milton, as well as books on history and geography.

During one of his visits to the campus in Chapel Hill, he drew the attention of Caroline Lee Hentz, a novelist and professor's wife. She taught Horton how to write and helped him transcribe his poetry, and she sent two of his antislavery poems to the Lancaster, Massachusetts, *Gazette,* her hometown newspaper. Sponsored by Hentz and others, including the governor of North Carolina, Horton published his first volume of poetry, *The Hope of Liberty,* in 1829. It was hoped that enough money could be raised to buy his freedom, but the attempt failed. Horton reached an agreement with his master to allow him to spend more time on the Chapel Hill campus. He was allowed to move to Chapel Hill, and he used part of the money he earned from selling his poems to pay his master one dollar a day for the privilege. He married a slave and fathered a son, Free, and a daughter, Rhody, and he worked for Joseph Calwell, the president of the University of North Carolina.

For more than 30 years, Horton spent his days on campus, writing poetry and tirelessly striving for a way to earn his freedom. He wrote letters to William Lloyd Garrison and Horace Greeley, begging their assistance in freeing him. He published poems in numerous antislavery periodicals, including the *Liberator,* the *North Star,* and the *National Anti-Slavery Standard.* His second collection of poetry, *The Poetical Works of George Moses Horton, the Colored Bard of North Carolina,* was published by Dennis Heartt of the Hillsborough (North Carolina) *Recorder* in 1845.

Horton's first two collections of poetry dealt mostly with such traditional subjects as love, religion, and death. He did, however, include a few poems that addressed his feelings about his enslavement and its effect on his writing. "On Hearing of the Intention of a Gentleman to Purchase the Poet's Freedom," published in *The Hope of Liberty,* expresses his intense longing for freedom fueled by the proposed purchase. Perhaps his most poignant and powerful condemnation of the dehumanizing effects of slavery appeared in the poem "Division of an Estate," published in *The Poetical Works,* in which he compares slaves on the auction block to cattle. "Ye cattle, low! Ye sheep, astonish'd, bleat! / Ye bristling swine, trudge squealing through the glades, / Void of an owner to impart your food!"

When Union troops overran Raleigh in 1865, Horton befriended William H. S. Banks, a Union army captain with whom he traveled throughout North Carolina. He wrote poems about the officers and infantrymen and several others on the more familiar subjects of slavery, love, and religion. Captain Banks, acting as something of a literary patron, selected 90 of these new poems and published them with several older ones in 1865 as *Naked Genius,* Horton's final volume of poetry.

Most notable in this collection is "George Moses Horton, Myself." Written when Horton was approaching 70 years of age, the poem captures the contradictory combination of hope and despair in the heart of an enslaved poet who sings of liberty: "My genius from a boy, / Has fluttered like a bird within my heart; / But could not thus confined her powers employ, / Impatient to depart." With his freedom secured by the end of the Civil War, Horton was finally free, and his "restless bird" had leave to "dart from world to world."

George Horton settled in Philadelphia, Pennsylvania, where he is believed to have died in about 1883. He published no poetry after 1865, but his reputation as a poet of remarkable depth and erudition has endured. In 1997 Chatham County declared Horton "Historic Poet Laureate," and a national organization, the George Moses Horton Society for the Study of African American Poetry, was established.

Further Reading

Andrews, William L., Frances Smith Foster, and Trudier Harris, eds. *The Concise Oxford Companion to African American Literature.* New York: Oxford University Press, 2001.

Gates, Henry Louis, Jr., and Nellie Y. McKay, eds. *The Norton Anthology of African American Literature.* New York: W. W. Norton, 1997.

Sherman, Joan. *The Black Bard of North Carolina: George Moses Horton and His Poetry.* Chapel Hill: University of North Carolina Press, 1997.

Hughes, Langston
(James Langston Hughes, James Langston Mercer Hughes)
(1902–1967) *poet, novelist, short story writer, playwright, lyricist, essayist, journalist*

Arguably one of the most influential and acclaimed authors in African-American literature, Langston Hughes had a profound impact on the creative focus of artists during and after the Harlem Renaissance. Hughes distinguished himself in a variety of genres as a prolific author of poetry, novels, short fiction, essays, and drama, and as an editor who helped popularize the work of other black artists. Honored during his lifetime with numerous literary awards, Hughes has remained a central figure in the history and development of African-American literature and a standard by which future generations of writers have been measured.

James Langston Mercer Hughes was born on February 1, 1902, in Joplin, Missouri, the son of James Nathaniel Hughes and Carrie Langston Hughes. During Hughes's infancy, his parents separated, and his father moved to Mexico, where he became a successful businessman. Hughes's childhood was characterized by isolation and poverty, and he spent much of his early youth in Lawrence, Kansas, at the home of his grandmother, Mary Langston, a widow of one of the men involved in John Brown's 1859 raid on Harpers Ferry.

Hughes moved with his mother and stepfather to Lincoln, Illinois, and later to Cleveland, Ohio, where he attended Central High School. There he distinguished himself as an athlete and as a burgeoning writer. His poetry and short stories appeared regularly in the school's literary magazine, and he was named class poet during his senior year. Following his graduation in 1920, Hughes visited his father in Mexico. Hoping that Hughes would join him in a business career, Hughes's father tried to discourage him from writing, though he later reluctantly funded Hughes's move to New York to attend Columbia University.

Though Hughes did attend Columbia until 1922, his interests soon turned to the literary and cultural developments taking place in New York during the Harlem Renaissance. Hughes found eager publishers for his poetry in the literary magazines the *Crisis* and *Opportunity*. In 1922 Hughes left Columbia and worked a series of odd jobs before joining the crew of a freighter bound for West Africa. He also spent six months in Paris before returning to the United States in 1924.

Hughes secured his reputation as one of Harlem's most celebrated young poets with the publication of *The Weary Blues*, his first collection of verse, in 1926. Taking its title from a poem published three years earlier, *The Weary Blues* revealed Hughes's considerable knowledge of blues and jazz,

which would continue to inform the rhythms and imagery of his verse. A second collection of poetry, *Fine Clothes for the Jew*, followed in 1927, initiating a prolific writing career that would span the next four decades and encompass multiple genres.

Hughes traveled extensively during his lifetime in the United States, Mexico, Europe, Africa, central and Southeast Asia, Cuba, the Azores, and the Canary Islands. His familiarity with various cultures, and specifically his interest in African and African-American culture, had a profound impact on his writing and shaped his sensitivity to the working classes.

In 1929 Hughes completed his bachelor's degree at Lincoln University in Pennsylvania and published his first novel, *Not Without Laughter* (1930), a semiautobiographical depiction of his childhood in Kansas. Shortly after the publication of the novel, Hughes ended his association with Charlotte Mason, a wealthy white patron to several African-American writers, including ZORA NEALE HURSTON, with whom Hughes would collaborate on the play *Mule Bone: A Negro Comedy* (1931), and ALAIN LOCKE. Though indebted to Mason, Hughes would have greater freedom as an artist without her patronage.

Hughes traveled to the Soviet Union in 1932 as part of a film crew to make a movie about race relations in America. His visit inspired an interest in communism that, while never strong enough to induce his membership in the Communist Party, nevertheless remained an important influence on his writing. Also during the 1930s Hughes toured the South and performed several successful readings of his poetry. His publications during this period included his first children's book, *Popo and Fifina: Children of Haiti* (1932, with ARNA BONTEMPS); *The Ways of White Folks* (1934), his acclaimed first collection of short stories; and several volumes of poetry: *The Negro Mother and Other Dramatic Recitations* (1931), *Dear Lovely Death* (1931), *The Dreamkeeper and Other Poems* (1932), and *Scottsboro Limited: Four Poems and a Play* (1932).

While Hughes's reputation as an author and poet flourished, he was often criticized for his use of African-American dialect and his incorporation of jazz and blues musical idioms in his poetry. Critics such as the eminent scholar and sociologist W. E. B. DuBOIS considered such elements to be beneath the dignity of true black literature. Hughes's writing, however, continued to reflect his celebration of all aspects of black culture, particularly the southern folk traditions.

During World War II Hughes published a column in the *Chicago Defender* to encourage support for the United States among African-American communities. In these columns, Hughes introduced one of his most popular and enduring characters, Jesse B. Semple, later known as Simple. The fictional Semple provided a uniquely humorous perspective on black culture and became immensely

Celebrated poet Langston Hughes, shown here in 1942, was often referred to as "the Negro poet laureate." *(Library of Congress)*

popular for the barstool wisdom he dispensed. Hughes's first collection of Simple stories, *Simple Speaks His Mind* (1950), was followed by *Simple Takes a Wife* (1953), *Simple Stakes a Claim* (1957), *Simple's Uncle Sam* (1965), and the posthumous *The Return of Simple* (1994).

In addition to poetry and short fiction, Hughes was deeply committed to African-American theater. The author of numerous plays and musical dramas, including *Little Ham* (1935), *Mulatto* (1935), *Front Porch* (1937), and *Tambourines to Glory* (1963), which he adapted from his 1958 novel of the same title, Hughes also helped create and support community theaters in New York, Chicago, and Cleveland, among other cities. In 1940 Hughes published his autobiography *The Big Sea*, considered by many to include the most compelling and accurate depictions of the literary figures and social climate of the Harlem Renaissance.

During the 1950s and 1960s, perhaps the most prolific periods of his writing career, Hughes produced a voluminous body of work. In addition to several biographical and historical works for young readers, Hughes also published several collections of short stories (*Laughing to Keep from Crying*, 1952, *Something in Common and Other Stories*, 1963); a second volume of autobiography (*I Wonder as I Wander: An Autobiographical Journey*, 1956); several volumes of poetry, including *Montage of a Dream Deferred* (1951), a landmark work that incorporated elements of the emerging bebop jazz form; and his acclaimed *Ask Your Mama: Twelve Moods for Jazz* (1961), an epic study of the African-American tradition of verbal combat known as "the dirty dozens."

During the 1960s, as African-American literature turned toward more militant and revolutionary themes, Hughes's works declined in popularity. He attended the First World Festival of Negro Arts in Dakar, Senegal, in 1966, where he was hailed as a historic figure among African-American writers; however, his writing no longer appealed to many of the young writers of the Black Arts and Black Power movements. James

Langston Mercer Hughes died of congestive heart failure on May 22, 1967, in New York.

Perhaps more than any other writer of his day, Langston Hughes embodied the spirit of the Harlem Renaissance in his unflagging belief in the richness and beauty of African-American culture. He was acclaimed by many as the poet laureate of the negro race. In 2002 the University of Missouri published the most comprehensive collection of Hughes's published and formerly unpublished writings in the formidable 17-volume series *The Collected Works of Langston Hughes,* a fitting testament to one of the most prolific and influential African-American authors of the 20th century.

Further Reading

Hughes, Langston. *The Big Sea: An Autobiography.* New York: Knopf, 1940.

Ostrom, Hans L. *A Langston Hughes Encyclopedia.* Westport, Conn.: Greenwood Publishing Group, 2002.

Rampersad, Arnold, ed. *The Collected Poems of Langston Hughes.* New York: Knopf, 1994.

———. *The Life of Langston Hughes, Volume 1, 1902–1941: I, Too, Sing America.* New York: Oxford University Press, 1986.

———. *The Life of Langston Hughes, Volume 2, 1941–1967: I Dream a World.* New York: Oxford University Press, 1988.

Hurston, Zora Neale

(ca. 1891–1960) *novelist, folklorist, short story writer, essayist, anthropologist, autobiographer*

Best known for her novel *Their Eyes Were Watching God* (1937), Zora Neale Hurston was one of the most prolific authors of the Harlem Renaissance era. In addition to novels, Hurston published more than 50 short stories and essays, two books on African-American folklore, and an autobiography. Yet at the time of her death, she was all but forgotten by critics and peers. All of Hurston's writing was informed by her roots in the rural American South and by a love of African-American folk culture. The novelist ALICE WALKER, one of many African-American writers and scholars who helped refocus critical attention on Hurston's life, praised Hurston's writing for exhibiting the quality of "racial health—a sense of black people as complete, complex, undiminished human beings."

Though she often gave conflicting reports about the place and date of her birth, Zora Neale Hurston is thought to have been born on January 7, 1891, in Notasulga, Alabama, a poor plantation town where her parents, John and Lucy Anne Hurston, worked as sharecroppers. The family soon relocated to Eatonville, in central Florida, the first town in the United States to be incorporated by African Americans. Hurston's father became the pastor of Zion Hope Baptist Church in nearby Sanford and later served three terms as Eatonville's mayor.

In Eatonville, Hurston grew up listening to the folktales, or "lies," as she called them, related by family members on the porch of their eight-bedroom home, which her father had built. Hurston displayed a wildness of spirit and a native curiosity that earned the encouragement of her mother, a schoolteacher, to whom Hurston was very close as a child. Hurston attended the Hungerford School in Eatonville until the death of her mother in 1904, after which she enrolled at the Florida Baptist Academy, a boarding school in Jacksonville.

Though Hurston's relationship with her father had often been strained during her childhood, she grew further apart from him when he remarried in 1905. Hurston quarreled incessantly with her stepmother and spent the next few years at the homes of several relatives in Florida and Tennessee, when she was not attending school in Jacksonville. In 1916 Hurston joined a traveling troupe that performed operettas by Gilbert and Sullivan, working as a personal maid to one of the actresses. After several months she departed the troupe in Baltimore, Maryland, and found work as a domestic to support her studies at Morgan Academy (now Morgan State University).

Novelist Zora Neale Hurston also made important contributions to the study of African-American folk culture. *(Library of Congress)*

Hurston completed her high school diploma in 1918 and enrolled at Howard University, in Washington, D.C. After completing her associate's degree in 1920, Hurston remained in Washington, D.C., and she soon found encouragement for her growing interest in writing. ALAIN LOCKE, a professor at Howard University, and poet GEORGIA DOUGLAS JOHNSON introduced Hurston to many of the leading literary figures in what would become known as the Harlem Renaissance, including W. E. B. DuBOIS, JEAN TOOMER, MARITA ODETTE BONNER, and JESSIE REDMON FAUSET.

Hurston's formal entry into the literary world of Harlem came in 1924 when Locke convinced

her to submit her writing to Charles S. Johnson, the editor of the National Urban League's literary magazine *Opportunity*. Hurston moved to New York in 1925 and soon became a popular and influential figure in Harlem's literary circles. Her short stories began to appear regularly in *Opportunity*, and she published her first play, *Color Struck,* in the first and only issue of *Fire!!,* a literary magazine she helped to found with WALLACE THURMAN, LANGSTON HUGHES, and GWENDOLYN BENNETT.

In 1927, while a student at Barnard College, Hurston left New York for the South, beginning a long period of travel during which she compiled research on African-American folk traditions. Her findings would form the basis of most of her literary work and provided a foundation for future research with the eminent American anthropologist Franz Boas, a professor at Columbia University in New York.

Hurston completed many of her most acclaimed works during the 1930s. She collaborated with Langston Hughes on the play *Mule Bone: A Negro Comedy* (1931), an ambitious though controversial drama drawn from her life in Eatonville. A series of misunderstandings between Hurston and Hughes over the authorship of the play eventually led to the end of their friendship. *Mule Bone* was later produced in 1991 to mixed reviews. Its use of authentic southern dialects was considered offensive by many African-American critics.

In 1934 Hurston published her first novel, *Jonah's Gourd Vine,* an autobiographical novel about the life of her father. Hurston's first volume of folklore, *Mules and Men,* appeared in 1935 and contained much of the research gathered during her travels in the South. In 1937 Hurston published her best-known work, *Their Eyes Were Watching God.* Set in her childhood home of Eatonville, the novel depicts the life of Janie Crawford, a woman of unquenchable idealism and strength who seeks the fulfillment of her personal and romantic dreams.

Upon its publication, *Their Eyes Were Watching God* received harsh criticism from novelist RICHARD

WRIGHT for its lack of overt protest against racial injustice in the South. Much of the criticism leveled at Hurston during her lifetime stemmed, more often than not, from her often difficult relationships with fellow authors. Since its original publication, however, the novel has become a classic of African-American literature and an influential work for more recent female authors such as Alice Walker and TONI CADE BAMBARA.

In the final decades of her life, Hurston published two additional novels, *Moses, Man of the Mountain* (1939) and *Seraph of the Sewanee* (1948). She also published a second collection of folktales, *Tell My Horse* (1938), and her autobiography, *Dust Tracks on the Road* (1942), which sold well and earned the Ainsfield-Wolf Award, though the book presented several misleading facts about her life.

Hurston's final years were marked by increasing health problems and poverty. She left New York in 1948 after being falsely accused on a morals charge by a former landlord. During the 1950s Hurston lived in Florida and continued to write, producing two novels that were ultimately rejected by her publisher. She also embarked on a detailed biography of Herod the Great, which she continued to revise until her death. In 1959 Zora Neale Hurston entered St. Lucia Welfare Home in Fort Pierce, Florida, where she died on January 28, 1960.

Upon her arrival in New York during the 1920s, Hurston flourished among the leading figures of the Harlem Renaissance. Her natural exuberance and formidable abilities as a storyteller initially earned the respect and admiration of her peers. In some respects, however, she was ill suited to the growing climate of racial protest that characterized the works of her contemporaries. "I do not belong to that sobbing school of Negrohood who hold that nature somehow has given them a lowdown dirty deal," she wrote in her 1928 essay "How It Feels to Be Colored Me." The publication of collected volumes of Hurston's short fiction and essays during the 1970s and 1980s led to a revival of critical and popular interest in her life and work, and she now stands as one of the most important authors to emerge from the Harlem Renaissance.

Further Reading

Boyd, Valerie. *Wrapped in Rainbows: The Life of Zora Neale Hurston.* New York: Scribner, 2002.

Carter-Sigglow, Janet. *Making Her Way with Thunder: A Reappraisal of Zora Neale Hurston's Narrative Art.* New York: Peter Lang, 1994.

Hurston, Zora Neale. *Every Tongue Got to Confess: Negro Folktales from the Gulf States.* New York: HarperCollins, 2001.

Kaplan, Carla. *Zora Neale Hurston: A Life in Letters.* New York: Doubleday, 2002.

J

Jacobs, Harriet Ann
(Linda Brent)
(ca. 1813–1897) *autobiographer*

Under the pen name Linda Brent, Harriet Ann Jacobs wrote one of the most compelling and detailed accounts of slave life ever written by an African-American woman. Her *Incidents in the Life of a Slave Girl, Written by Herself,* published in 1861, transformed the slave narrative tradition by addressing the sufferings of African-American women under slavery, particularly the taboo subject of sexual abuse.

Harriet Ann Jacobs was born into slavery, probably in 1813, in Edenton, North Carolina. Her mother, Delilah, was owned by a tavern keeper, and her father was likely a skilled house carpenter named Elijah. She enjoyed a happy early childhood, during which she lived with her parents and brother, and, as she wrote in *Incidents,* "never dreamed I was a piece of merchandise." When Jacobs was six, her mother died, and she was taken into the home of her mother's owner, Margaret Horniblow, where she learned to read and sew.

In 1825 Mrs. Horniblow died, and Jacobs was bequeathed to Mary Norcom, the three-year-old daughter of Dr. James Norcom, who became her master. Characterized in *Incidents* as the lecherous Dr. Flint, Norcom subjected the adolescent Jacobs to unrelenting sexual harassment. To avoid his advances, she became the mistress of a young white neighbor, the future congressman Samuel Sawyer, with whom she had two children, Louisa and Joseph. Despite her liaison with Sawyer, Norcom continued to harass her, and she feared that he would make her children plantation slaves if she continued to resist his advances.

To punish Jacobs for her behavior, Norcom sent her to work on his nearby plantation. There, she witnessed the brutal treatment of plantation slaves. When she discovered that Norcom wished to work her children as slaves on the plantation, Jacobs fled in 1835. She hoped that her absence would induce him to sell her children to their father. For the next seven years, she evaded capture, first by hiding with friends, and later by hiding in a small alcove in her grandmother's attic. Since her mother's death, Jacobs had only her grandmother Molly, a freed slave who lived in a house nearby, to provide some semblance of a nurturing family environment.

At her grandmother's house, Jacobs was in close proximity to her children, though they did not know of her presence in the attic. They had been purchased by their father, Samuel Sawyer, and entrusted to Molly's care. In her hiding space in the attic, Jacobs suffered through stifling summers and cold winters for nearly five years, occupying her time in reading, sewing, and writing. In

1842 she resolved to flee to New York to find her daughter, Louisa, who had been sent to live with a family in the North two years earlier. Jacobs's son, Joseph, joined her in New York shortly after her arrival.

Jacobs soon found work as a nurse for Imogen Willis, the daughter of Nathaniel Willis, an editor and magazine writer, and his wife Mary. Following Mary's death, Jacobs was engaged to accompany Imogen on a trip to England for 10 months. "During all that time," she wrote in *Incidents,* "I never saw the slightest symptom of prejudice against color." Upon her return to America, Jacobs and her daughter lived in Boston for two years, where Jacobs worked as a dressmaker. With the assistance of Jacobs's brother, John, an escaped slave who had come North several years earlier, Louisa enrolled in the Young Ladies Domestic Seminary in Clinton, New York.

Meanwhile, Norcom and his family never abandoned their search for Jacobs and her children. Sawyer, the father of Jacobs's children, never followed through on his promise to emancipate them. The passage of the Fugitive Slave Act in 1850, which made harboring escaped slaves in free states a federal crime, further endangered Jacobs's freedom. With the help of the Willis family, to whom she had returned as a nurse for the daughter of Mr. Willis's second wife, Cornelia, Jacobs fled New York for New England. Jacobs's brother, John, went to California with her son Joseph. When Norcom died at the end of 1850, Jacobs and her children became the property of his daughter, Mary, to whom they had been bequeathed in 1825, and who continued to search for them. In 1852, having tried unsuccessfully to find Jacobs for two years, Mary and her husband agreed to sell Jacobs and her two children to Mr. and Mrs. Willis for $300. After almost 17 years as fugitives, Jacobs and her family were free.

Amy Post, a Quaker abolitionist with whom Jacobs maintained a lengthy correspondence after meeting her in Rochester, New York, as a fugitive slave, urged her to publish her autobiography.

Jacobs had originally intended to enlist the support of white novelist Harriet Beecher Stowe, to whom she gave several sketches of her story. When Stowe sent the materials to Mrs. Willis for verification, thereby revealing personal details of Jacobs's life that she preferred to keep hidden, Jacobs was outraged. She decided to write the book herself, working secretly in the evenings while employed by the Willis family.

Jacobs published several anonymous sketches of her story in various newspapers, the first appearing as "Letter from a Fugitive Slave" in Horace Greeley's *New York Tribune.* Getting her book published, however, proved difficult. With letters of introduction from abolitionist leaders in Boston, Jacobs visited England in order to generate interest in her book. In 1860 the African-American author and historian WILLIAM COOPER NELL introduced her to Lydia Marie Child, a respected white abolitionist, who acted as editor of Jacobs's manuscript and secured its publication in 1861. A second edition, published in England under the title *The Deeper Wrong,* appeared in 1862.

Published under the pseudonym Linda Brent and written as a first-person narrative, *Incidents* decried the horrific treatment of slaves in general, and the particularly savage abuses heaped upon female slaves. In her preface to the book, Jacobs expressed a "desire to arouse the women of the North to a realizing sense of the condition of two millions of women at the South, still in bondage, suffering what I suffered, and most of them far worse." Five chapters document the sexual abuse suffered by slaves under the system of concubinage, whereby masters were entitled to take their slaves as mistresses. Jacobs also depicts the plight of mothers routinely separated from their children.

When Jacobs's authorship of the book became known after its publication, she used the resulting celebrity to further the cause of abolition. She and her daughter, Louisa, joined the abolitionist and feminist preacher Sojourner Truth in assisting fugitive slaves caught behind Union lines during the Civil War. Jacobs and Louisa provided emergency relief for refugees and established the Jacobs Free School in Alexandria, Virginia. They also wrote about their activities in regular articles published in northern newspapers. Jacobs and Louisa eventually traveled to England after the war to raise money for the African-American community in Savannah, Georgia. Eventually settling in Washington, D.C., in 1877, Jacobs helped organize early meetings of the National Association of Colored Women. Harriet Ann Jacobs died in Washington, D.C., on March 7, 1897.

In the years following Jacobs's death, her autobiography fell into obscurity, many believing that it was a work of fiction written by Lydia Maria Child. In 1987 Jean Fagan Yellin edited a new edition of *Incidents,* in which she drew on newly released letters from the collected papers of Harriet Jacobs at the University of Rochester, in New York. Having established definitively that *Incidents* was indeed written by Jacobs, Yellin also identified the historical sources for Jacobs's pseudonymous characters. Yellin's book refocused critical attention on a seminal work of African-American literature by an author whose struggle for freedom during the antebellum and postbellum periods inspired later female writers such as the novelist and poet FRANCES ELLEN WATKINS HARPER, whose novel *Iola Leroy* used locations and character names from Jacobs's narrative.

Further Reading

Johnson, Yvonne. *The Voices of African American Women: The Use of Narrative and Authorial Voice in the Works of Harriet Jacobs, Zora Neale Hurston, and Alice Walker.* New York: Peter Lang, 1995.

Randle, Gloria T. "Between the Rock and the Hard Place: Mediating Spaces in Harriet Jacobs's *Incidents in the Life of a Slave Girl.*" *African American Review* 33, no. 1 (spring 1999): 43.

Yellin, Jean Fagan, ed. *Incidents in the Life of a Slave Girl, Written by Herself.* Cambridge, Mass.: Harvard University Press, 1987.

Johnson, Charles
(Charles Richard Johnson)
(1948–) *novelist, short story writer, essayist, screenwriter, cartoonist*

A distinguished author of novels, short stories, and essays, Charles R. Johnson became only the second African-American author to receive the National Book Award, given in 1990 for his novel *Middle Passage.* Initially motivated by the radical spirit of the Black Arts Movement of the 1960s and the writings of AMIRI BARAKA (then known as LeRoi Jones), Johnson later adopted a more philosophical approach to matters of race, culture, and the moral dimensions of African-American life.

Charles Richard Johnson was born on April 23, 1948, in Evanston, Illinois, to working-class parents, Benjamin Lee Johnson and Ruby Elizabeth Johnson. In his childhood, Johnson benefited from the influence of his mother and soon developed an interest in literature and art, deciding early in his youth to pursue a career as an artist. In light of his father's objections, however, Johnson decided to study journalism and enrolled at Southern Illinois University, from which he received his bachelor's degree in 1971 and a master's degree two years later.

Johnson's first published books, two collections of political cartoons entitled *Black Humor* (1970) and *Half-Past Nation Time* (1972), reflected his lingering interest in visual arts and his support of the creative and political objectives of the Black Arts Movement. Johnson later rejected the Black Arts agenda. "I began to see that the intellectual questions I wanted to pursue," he explained, "some of them were foreclosed on by some of the principal spokesmen of the black arts movement." In the works of such authors as JEAN TOOMER, RALPH ELLISON, and RICHARD WRIGHT, Johnson discovered the kind of broad philosophical foundation on which he hoped to build his own literary career.

Johnson's shift in perspective was also due in part to his relationship with John Gardner, a distinguished novelist and professor at Southern Illinois University, with whom Johnson studied as a graduate student in philosophy. "I tried to maintain that most insecure of positions demanded by philosophy: namely, a perpetual openness to thoughts and feelings wherever I found them," he wrote in a 1988 essay. "And a tremendous source of help for this was my 11-year association with John Gardner."

After several unsuccessful attempts at publishing a novel, Johnson finally succeeded in 1974 with the release of *Faith and the Good Thing,* the story of a young African-American woman's quest for physical and spiritual liberation. The novel received wide acclaim for its complex blend of naturalism and metaphysical inquiry, as well as its uniquely philosophical perspective, a quality that would increasingly characterize his later novels.

Johnson blended elements of the traditional slave narrative, parables, and conventional literary forms to explore the philosophical dimensions of his characters in *Oxherding Tale* (1982). Eight years in the making, the novel's early drafts ran to more than 2,000 pages. Johnson nearly abandoned *Oxherding Tale* and writing in general. Inspired by "The Ten Oxherding Pictures," a series of allegorical prints by Zen Buddhist artist Kakuan-Shien, *Oxherding Tale* depicts the efforts of its biracial protagonist, Andrew Hawkins, to discover his true self and his place in the universe. The novel also revealed Johnson's growing personal commitment to Buddhist philosophy.

With the publication of his next novel, *Middle Passage,* in 1990, Johnson achieved one of his greatest successes as a novelist. Winner of the National Book Award for fiction, the first such award won by an African-American author since Ralph Ellison received it for *Invisible Man* in 1953, *Middle Passage,* like Johnson's previous novels, depicts the spiritual evolution of its first-person narrator, Rutherford Calhoun, who stows away on a slave ship to escape an unwanted marriage and his debts to a New Orleans crime boss. His expe-

Charles R. Johnson holds his National Book Award during ceremonies at the Plaza Hotel in New York City in 1990. *(AP/Wide World Photos)*

riences aboard the *Juno* bring Calhoun to a greater awareness of his own life and purpose.

In addition to his novels, Johnson has also published several award-winning short stories. His collection *The Sorcerer's Apprentice* (1986) contained two stories, "Popper's Disease" and "China," that were awarded the *Callaloo* Writing Award (1983) and the Pushcart Prize Outstanding Writer citation (1984), respectively. Johnson published his second collection of stories, *Soulcatcher and Other Stories: Twelve Powerful Tales About Slavery,* in 2001.

Johnson's other literary achievements include his acclaimed collection of essays, *Being and Race: Black Writing Since 1970* (1988), winner of the Washington State Governor's Writers Award in 1988; the literary anthology *Black Men Speaking* (1997, with John McClusky, Jr.); and his fourth novel, *Dreamer,* published in 1998. Johnson has also written several screenplays, including *Charlie Smith and the Fritter Tree* (1978); *Me, Myself, Maybe* (1982); and *Booker* (1984, with John Allmann). A distinguished university professor and international lecturer, Johnson has served as the director of the creative writing program at the University of Washington and currently holds an endowed chair at the University of Washington, the Pollack Professorship for Excellence in English.

Charles Johnson's complex philosophical approach to fiction writing has garnered international acclaim. In 1996 the *African American Review* devoted an entire edition to Johnson's life and work. The publication of several book-length studies of his writing reveals the abiding interest of critics and readers in Johnson's unique perspective on race and identity, and the significance of his contributions to 20th-century African-American literature.

Further Reading

Byrd, Rudolph P., ed. *I Call Myself an Artist: Writings By and About Charles Johnson.* Bloomington: Indiana University Press, 1999.

Johnson, Charles R. *Middle Passage.* New York: Athenaeum, 1990.

Little, Jonathan. *Charles Johnson's Spiritual Imagination.* Columbia: University of Missouri Press, 1997.

Johnson, Fenton

(1888–1958) *poet, short story writer, essayist, playwright*

Though his poetry and fiction lacked the innovations in theme and style that would characterize the literature of the Harlem Renaissance, Fenton Johnson made important contributions to African-American literature in the early 20th century. He experimented with free verse forms and was among the first poets to incorporate the rhythms and imagery of folk spirituals in his literary work.

Fenton Johnson was born on May 7, 1888, in Chicago, Illinois, the only son of Elijah and Jessie Johnson. Coming from a prosperous middle-class family, Fenton indulged his interest in poetry and drama from an early age. He began writing at the age of nine, and at 19, he saw the production of some of his plays at the Pekin Theater in Chicago. He was educated in Chicago's public schools and later attended the University of Chicago, Northwestern University, and the journalism school at Columbia University. After teaching briefly at State University, a private Baptist school in Louisville, Kentucky, and following his marriage to Cecilia Rhone, he spent his years as a writer in Chicago and New York City.

Johnson's first, self-published volume of poetry, *A Little Dreaming,* appeared in 1913. Composed primarily of sentimental verse on the traditional themes of love, birth, and death, the volume also contains poems that celebrate African-American life and culture. One poem, "The Plaint of the Factory Child," addresses the hardships and indignities of African-American urban life, a theme that would become a central focus in African-American literature during and after the Harlem Renaissance. He published two additional volumes, *Visions of the Dark* in 1915, and *Songs of the Soil* in 1916, in both of which he employed dialect and free verse forms that were influenced by traditional folk spirituals.

In addition to his poetry, Johnson also published a collection of short stories, *Tales of Darkest America,* and a collection of essays, *For the Highest Good,* both in 1920. Though largely ignored by critics, Johnson's stories reflect his growing despair over racial oppression and economic hardship in American urban environments.

The story "A Woman of Good Cheer" contrasts the simple life of rural southern African Americans with the urban experiences of those who migrated to the North.

Johnson's later poems, written during the late 1920s and early 1930s, received greater critical attention than his early work. He was published in numerous anthologies of African-American verse, including *The Book of American Negro Poetry*, edited by JAMES WELDON JOHNSON in 1922, and *Caroling Dusk: An Anthology of Verse by Black Poets*, edited by COUNTEE CULLEN in 1927. Johnson also worked as an editor and founded two literary magazines, the most notable being *Favorite Magazine*, published from 1918 to 1920.

During the 1930s, Johnson worked for the Federal Writers' Project, part of President Franklin D. Roosevelt's Works Progress Administration (WPA), in Chicago. He wrote several poems that were later collected by the WPA, but unpublished, in two volumes, *African Nights* and *The Daily Grind*. For the remaining years of his life, Johnson had little connection with the growing literary circles of African-American writers in Chicago and New York, though he maintained a correspondence with ARNA BONTEMPS for several years. Fenton Johnson died on September 17, 1958.

In his poetry and stories, Fenton Johnson captured the hope and despair that marked his experiences of African-American life during a period of intense racial strife. In his poem "The New Day," he celebrated the contributions of African-American soldiers during World War I and pointed out the irony of their fight for liberty under the flag of a country that denied them freedom. Johnson's poetry remains compelling for its expression of a poignant despair of racial injustice and a deep respect for African-American heritage.

Further Reading

Andrews, William L., Frances Smith Foster, and Trudier Harris, eds. *The Concise Oxford Companion to African American Literature.* New York: Oxford University Press, 2001.

Cullen, Countee, ed. *Caroling Dusk: An Anthology of Verse by Black Poets.* New York: Carol Publishing Group, 1993.

Johnson, James Weldon, ed. *The Book of American Negro Poetry.* New York: Harvest Books, 1983.

Johnson, Georgia Douglas (Georgia Blanche Douglas Camp, John Temple, Mary Strong, Paul Tremaine)
(1880–1966) *poet, educator*

Like so many African-American writers before her, Georgia Douglas Johnson contended with racial prejudice and family obligations in the pursuit of her literary career. Despite her struggles, she became one of the best-known African-American poets of the early 20th century, and her home in Washington, D.C., was the site of one of the greatest literary salons of the Harlem Renaissance era.

Georgia Douglas Johnson was born Georgia Blanche Douglas Camp in Atlanta, Georgia, on September 10, 1880, to George and Laura Jackson Camp. Georgia's racial heritage included African-American, Native American, and English ancestors. Though raised primarily in Rome, Georgia, she attended grade school in Atlanta and graduated from Atlanta University in 1896, where she met her future husband, a law student named Henry Lincoln Johnson. They married in 1903. She also studied music at Howard University in Washington, D.C., and Oberlin College in Ohio.

After college, Johnson returned to Atlanta and worked briefly as a schoolteacher. In 1910 she and Henry moved to Washington, D.C., so that her husband could accept a position as recorder of deeds under U.S. President William Howard Taft. Though she excelled as a musician and songwriter, Johnson found few opportunities for a career in music. She began writing stories and plays, and she published her first poetry in the *Crisis*, published by the National Association for the Advancement of Colored People (NAACP), in 1916.

Johnson's early years in Washington, D.C., were devoted almost exclusively to the maintenance of her household and the upbringing of her children, Henry Lincoln, Jr., and Peter Douglas Johnson. Discouraged by her husband from pursuing a literary career, she received encouragement from the celebrated poet WILLIAM BRAITHWAITE and Kelly Miller, dean of Howard University. With little time to write, Johnson nonetheless published her first volume of poetry, *The Heart of a Woman*, in 1918. With the help of fellow poet JESSIE FAUSET, Johnson collected 62 lyrical poems in which she explored female aspirations and emotions, portraying both the joy and heartbreak that characterize the lives of women in general and African-American women in particular.

Bronze: A Book of Verse, Johnson's second volume of poetry, was published in 1922, and featured an introduction by W. E. B. DuBOIS. With this volume, Johnson began to explore issues of race in greater depth. Still concerned with the emotional lives of women, she focuses on the unique characteristics of African-American life and the search for identity common to individuals of mixed racial heritage. The poems in this collection display a broad range of forms, including sonnets, quatrains, and free verse. A third volume of poetry, *An Autumn Love Cycle,* was published in 1928.

Recognized nationally for her accomplishments as a poet, Johnson also wrote several plays during the 1920s, though few remain extant. These dramas protest racial oppression more directly than Johnson's poetry. In her one-act play, *A Bill to Be Passed,* written sometime in the early 1920s, she supported the passage of the Dyer Anti-Lynching Bill, which was eventually defeated in 1922. Another one-act play, *A Sunday Morning in the South* (circa 1925), depicts the lynching of a black man and the devastation that his death engenders among his surviving family members.

Johnson first received public acclaim as a dramatist for her play *Blue Blood,* which received honorable mention in a 1926 competition spon-sored by the journal *Opportunity.* Produced in New York by the Krigwa Players, an all-black theatrical group started by W. E. B. DuBois in 1924, the play was published in 1927. *Blue Blood* examines the sexual abuse of black women by whites in the years following the Civil War and depicts the tragic consequences as they affect the future generations of one family. A second play, *Plumes,* won first prize from *Opportunity* in 1927 and was produced in New York, Boston, Washington, D.C., and Chicago.

After the death of her husband in 1925, Johnson was forced to devote more time to making a living. She worked for several years in the U.S. Department of Labor, in a post to which she was appointed by President Calvin Coolidge. Long hours kept her from devoting much time to her literary interests. However, she began to hold literary gatherings in her home at 1941 S Street in Washington, D.C. Her S Street salon, which she called her Half-Way House, became the most famous gathering place in Washington for intellectuals and artists during the Harlem Renaissance. Writers such as LANGSTON HUGHES, COUNTEE CULLEN, JAMES WELDON JOHNSON, and ZORA NEALE HURSTON, to name only a few, met frequently to discuss literature and read from their works. Many writers, including Hurston, found a safe haven from economic hardship in her home.

In her later years Johnson became active as a lecturer and reader throughout the United States and worked tirelessly for numerous social and political groups. Experiencing financial difficulties in the 1940s, Johnson found work where she could, in numerous odd jobs and temporary clerical pools. She also tried to get financial support for her writing by applying for fellowships. Despite her own personal difficulties, Johnson remained a solicitous patron of other artists in need until the end of her life. Georgia Douglas Johnson died on May 14, 1966, in her home of 50 years, on S Street.

Recognized nationally as the most significant female African-American poet to come out of the Harlem Renaissance era, Georgia Douglas Johnson enjoyed wide critical acclaim from critics and scholars. In addition, she earned the enduring love of her fellow writers and artists for her generous friendship and patronage, no less than for her remarkable talent. Douglas's poetry appears frequently in literary anthologies, and her poem *Tomorrow's World* was read on the senate floor and recorded in the *Congressional Record.* In 1999 two typed manuscripts of previously lost plays, *And Yet They Paused* and *A Bill to Be Passed,* were discovered among a batch of NAACP papers at the Library of Congress.

Further Reading

Andrews, William L., Frances Scott Smith, and Trudier Harris, eds. *The Concise Oxford Companion to African American Literature.* New York: Oxford University Press, 2001.

Cullen, Countee, ed. *Caroling Dusk: An Anthology of Verse by Black Poets.* New York: Carol Publishing Group, 1993.

Gates, Henry Louis, Jr., and Nellie Y. McKay, eds. *The Norton Anthology of African American Literature.* New York: W. W. Norton, 1997.

Hull, Gloria T. *Color, Sex, and Poetry: Three Women Writers of the Harlem Renaissance.* Bloomington: Indiana University Press, 1987.

Stevens, Judith. "'And Yet They Paused' and 'A Bill to Be Passed': Newly Recovered Lynching Dramas by Georgia Douglas Johnson." *African American Review* 33, no. 3 (fall 1999): 519.

Johnson, Helene
(Helen Johnson, Helene Johnson Hubbell)
(1907–1995) *poet*

Considered to be an exciting and promising new voice among Harlem Renaissance writers when she began to publish her poetry in the 1920s and 1930s in New York, Helene Johnson never achieved the celebrity of her contemporaries. More than two dozen of her poems appeared in numerous African-American and mainstream lit-

erary journals of the period, including the *Crisis, Opportunity,* and *Vanity Fair.* As her writing career began to gain momentum, Johnson withdrew from literary circles and stopped publishing, choosing instead to raise a family. Nonetheless, her small body of work remains an important element of African-American literary history, and her poems continue to appear regularly in anthologies of African-American literature.

Helene Johnson was born Helen Johnson on July 7, 1907, in Boston, Massachusetts, the only child of William and Ellie Johnson. Her father abandoned the family in her infancy, and Johnson never knew him. Raised in Boston by her mother and several aunts, where she lived with her cousin DOROTHY WEST, Johnson attended Lafayette School and Girl's Latin School (now the Boston Latin Academy). A bright student, Johnson aspired to a writing career from an early age. In 1925, at the age of 19, she gained the attention of critics with her poem "Trees at Night," which won an honorable mention in a literary contest sponsored by the National Urban League's *Opportunity* magazine. Another poem, "The Road," was selected for publication in the landmark anthology *The New Negro* (1925), edited by ALAIN LOCKE.

In 1926 Johnson was invited to New York to attend an awards banquet sponsored by *Opportunity,* where she received an award for her poem "Fulfillment." A year later, she left Boston University and moved to New York, where she enrolled briefly at Columbia University. During her early years in New York, Johnson befriended anthropologist and author ZORA NEALE HURSTON, who became a mentor to the young poet. Johnson was also a close friend of WALLACE THURMAN, whose short-lived literary journal *Fire!!* published Johnson's poem "Southern Road." Thurman also used Johnson as the model for the character of Hazel Jamison in his iconoclastic novel *Infants of the Spring* (1932).

Critics and contemporaries praised Johnson's poetry for its lyrical and stylistic qualities. Employing various poetic forms, from the sonnet to free verse and black vernacular, Johnson depicted the beauty and complexity of African-American life, the joys of youth and love, and the mystery of the natural world. Poems such as "Sonnet to a Negro in Harlem" (1927) celebrated the physical beauty and the proud spirit of African Americans. "You are disdainful and magnificent—, / Your perfect body and your pompous gait, / Your dark eyes flashing solemnly with hate."

Johnson enjoyed an exalted place among her contemporaries in Harlem during the 1920s. Countee Cullen included eight of her poems in his influential anthology *Caroling Dusk* in 1927. That year, Johnson's poem "Bottled" was published in *Vanity Fair*, increasing her popularity considerably in Harlem. The renowned poet JAMES WELDON JOHNSON selected six of Johnson's poems for his celebrated *Book of American Negro Poetry* (1931).

In the 1930s Johnson withdrew from the literary society of Harlem. She married William Hubbell in 1934, and her only child, Abigail, was born in 1940. Johnson's last published poem appeared in 1935. Although she continued to write, she focused the remaining years of her life on her marriage and her daughter. Helene Johnson died on July 6, 1995, in New York.

During the 1920s and 1930s in Harlem, Johnson was considered one of the most gifted and promising young poets of the Harlem Renaissances. Her virtual disappearance from public and literary life in the decades that followed led many critics to overlook the significance of her contributions to early 20th-century African-American literature. However, the publication of *This Waiting for Love* in 2000, which collects all of her published poems and many unpublished poems and letters from the 1960s and 1970s, has renewed critical and public interest in her life and writing.

Further Reading

Hill, Patricia Loggins, ed. *Call and Response: The Riverside Anthology of the African American Literary Tradition*. New York: Houghton Mifflin Co., 1998.

Lewis, David Levering, ed. *The Portable Harlem Renaissance Reader*. New York: Penguin Books, 1994.

Mitchell, Verner D., ed. *This Waiting for Love: Helene Johnson, Poet of the Harlem Renaissance*. Amherst: University of Massachusetts Press, 2000.

Johnson, James Weldon
(James William Johnson)
(1871–1938) *poet, novelist, essayist, editor, lyricist, literary critic, civil rights leader*

A civil rights leader, lawyer, diplomat, and respected author of poetry, novels, essays, and song lyrics, James Weldon Johnson devoted his life to the advancement of social and political reforms for African Americans in a wide variety of creative and professional endeavors. Like his contemporary W. E. B. DuBOIS, Johnson served as a mentor and patriarch for many young authors during the Harlem Renaissance.

James Weldon Johnson was born on June 17, 1871, in Jacksonville, Florida, the eldest son of James Johnson, a headwaiter at Jacksonville's luxurious St. James Hotel, and Helen Louise Johnson, a schoolteacher. Johnson enjoyed a comfortable middle-class upbringing, and he distinguished himself early in childhood as a bright and eager student. Because Jacksonville had no high schools for African Americans at the time, Johnson attended Atlanta University in Georgia for his secondary and collegiate education.

During his undergraduate years at Atlanta University, Johnson spent a summer teaching in rural Georgia, where he saw firsthand the poverty and racism that characterized the lives of African Americans in the antebellum South. Determined to contribute to the improvement of life for blacks in the United States, Johnson returned to Jacksonville after his graduation in 1894 and became the principal of Stanton School, where he successfully implemented a secondary education program.

In addition to his duties as principal of Stanton School, Johnson founded a short-lived daily newspaper, *The Daily American,* in 1895, and studied law. In 1897 he was admitted to the Florida State Bar. He maintained a private law practice from 1898 to 1901, and also began writing poetry. In 1900 Johnson and his brother, John Rosamond Johnson, collaborated on the song "Lift Every Voice and Sing," for which Johnson wrote the lyrics. Intended for a Stanton School commemoration of Abraham Lincoln's birthday, the song soon gained wider popularity. It was eventually adopted by the National Association for the Advancement of Colored People (NAACP) and became known unofficially as the Negro national anthem.

Johnson left Jacksonville for New York City in 1901, where he continued to write music with his brother and with songwriter Robert Cole. Johnson also attended graduate school at Columbia University and studied literature with the renowned author and educator Brander Matthews. Influenced by the works of Walt Whitman and PAUL LAURENCE DUNBAR, whom he met in New York, Johnson began to lose interest in traditional poetic forms, preferring instead to explore the use of African-American dialect.

Johnson's career as a writer coincided with his increasing involvement in politics during the early 1900s. In 1906 he accepted a position as U.S. consul in Porta Cabello, Venezuela. He transferred in 1909 to Corinto, Nicaragua. Johnson married Grace Nail in 1910 and completed his only novel, *The Autobiography of an Ex-Coloured Man,* published anonymously in 1912. Set in the United States and Europe, the novel depicts the struggle of its unnamed narrator to understand and accept his racial heritage. Initially motivated by a desire to validate African-American culture, the narrator ultimately repudiates his heritage and attempts to live as a white man.

Johnson returned to New York in 1914 and, at the suggestion of W. E. B. DuBois, became field secretary for the NAACP. By 1917, he rose to the position of executive secretary and helped expand the organization to more than 300 branch offices. Johnson also embarked on his most prolific period as an author. Between 1914 and 1930, when he resigned from the NAACP, Johnson published two volumes of poetry, *Fifty Years and Other Poems* (1917) and *God's Trombones: Seven Negro Sermons in Verse* (1927); a survey of life in Harlem during the 1920s, *Black Manhattan* (1930); and he also edited three influential literary anthologies: *The Book of American Negro Poetry* (1922), *The Book of American Negro Spirituals* (1925), and *The Second Book of Negro Spirituals* (1927).

God's Trombones, one of Johnson's best-known works of poetry, was inspired by a sermon he heard in 1917. Drawing upon seven sermons on topics from the Old and New Testaments of the Bible, Johnson incorporates the language and

A celebrated novelist and poet, James Weldon Johnson also wrote the song "Lift Every Voice and Sing," which came to be known as the Negro National Anthem. *(Library of Congress)*

rhythms of African and African-American folk culture and the traditional rhetorical devices of 19th-century preachers. Johnson uses the trombone as a metaphor for the preacher's voice because, as he states in his preface to the collection, that instrument "possesses above all others the power to express the wide and varied range of emotions encompassed by the human voice—and with greater amplitude." Johnson's portrait of the preacher validates the depth and dignity of his character, and it highlights the rich rhetorical artistry of African-American folk spirituals and religious traditions.

Following his resignation from the NAACP in 1930, Johnson accepted a teaching position at Fisk University, in Nashville, Tennessee, as a professor of literature and creative writing. He also lectured widely at such colleges and universities as Northwestern University, Oberlin College, and Yale University. Johnson also published several additional works: *Along This Way: The Autobiography of James Weldon Johnson* (1933); *Negro Americans, What Now?* (1934), a book-length argument for racial integration and cooperation; and a final volume of poems, *St. Peter Relates an Incident: Selected Poems* (1935). James Weldon Johnson died after an automobile accident on June 26, 1938, in Wiscasset, Maine.

A beloved social, political, and literary figure, James Weldon Johnson was buried in Brooklyn's Green-Wood Cemetery in a ceremony that drew more than 2,000 participants. In his various roles as an author, civil rights leader, and statesman, James Weldon Johnson was a tireless advocate for social and political equality for African Americans during an era of intense and open racial hostility. In particular, Johnson's writing empowered African Americans to honor their racial identity. "I will not allow one prejudiced person or one million or one hundred million to blight my life," Johnson wrote in an NAACP pamphlet about his personal focus as a black American. "My inner life is mine, and I shall defend and maintain its integrity against all the powers of hell."

Further Reading

Johnson, James Weldon. *Along This Way: The Autobiography of James Weldon Johnson.* New York: Viking Press, 1933.

———. *Complete Poems.* New York: Penguin, 2000.

Oliver, Lawrence, and Kenneth M. Price, eds. *Critical Essays on James Weldon Johnson.* New York: G. K. Hall and Co., 1997.

Wilson, Sondra K., ed. *The Selected Writings of James Weldon Johnson: Social, Political, and Literary Essays.* New York: Oxford University Press, 1995.

Jones, Gayl
(1949–   ) *novelist, poet, short fiction writer, literary critic, educator*

A widely acclaimed author of novels, poetry, short fiction, and literary criticism, Gayl Jones has impressed critics and readers alike with her intense and often brutal explorations of the legacy of violence in African-American communities. In particular, Jones confronts the sexual and psychological abuse of women, while also focusing on the social and cultural forces that contribute to that violence. Highly acclaimed as a novelist, Jones was a finalist for the National Book Award in 1998.

Gayl Jones was born on November 23, 1949, in Lexington, Kentucky, to Franklin and Lucille Jones. Jones began writing short stories in grade school and soon impressed her family and teachers with her natural ability. She received a scholarship to attend Connecticut College and completed her bachelor's degree in 1971. As a student, Jones received several undergraduate writing awards, including the Frances Steloff Award for her short story "The Roundhouse" (1970).

Jones was accepted to the graduate writing program at Brown University, and she completed her master's degree in 1973 and her Ph.D. in 1975. During this time she wrote her first play, *Chile Woman*, which won the award for best original production at the New England Regional American College Theatre Festival in 1973. As a graduate student, Jones studied with poet MICHAEL S. HARPER, who took an interest in the manuscript of her first novel. He submitted the manuscript to TONI MORRISON, then an editor at Random House, and *Corregidora* was published in 1975.

The novel portrays the life of a blues singer, Ursa Corregidora, who confronts the legacy of exploitation in her family's past and the manifestations of abuse in her personal life. Jones's frank depictions of the psychological dimensions of racial and sexual violence earned high praise from such notable critics as novelist John Updike. "One of the book's merits," wrote Updike, "is the ease with which it assumes the writer's right to sexual specifics, and its willingness to explore exactly how our sexual and emotional behavior is warped within the matrix of family and race."

Jones continued to explore the dynamics of violence between men and women in her next novel, *Eva's Man* (1976). A grim tale of murder and sexual brutality, the novel describes the painful experiences of its narrator, Eva Medina Canada, whose life has been characterized by physical and sexual abuse, and who relates her personal history after being incarcerated in an insane asylum for the sexual mutilation and murder of her lover.

In 1975 Jones joined the faculty of the University of Michigan in Ann Arbor, where she taught courses in creative writing and African-American literature. She also published a collection of short fiction, *White Rat* (1977), and two volumes of poetry: *Song for Anninho* (1981) and *The Hermit-Woman* (1983). Jones left her tenured teaching position at the University of Michigan in 1983 and moved to Europe with her husband, Robert Higgins. While in Europe, Jones published a third volume of poetry, *Xarque and Other Poems* (1985), and a novel in German, *Die Vogelfängerin* (1986).

Jones returned with her husband to the United States in 1988 and settled in Lexington, Kentucky. In 1991 Jones published a collection of literary criticism, *Liberating Voices: Oral Tradition in African American Literature,* in which she discusses the nature of oral traditions in African-American literature as well as the storytelling techniques of classic and contemporary European and American literature.

After several years of silence, Jones returned to the literary spotlight with her fourth novel, *The Healing,* in 1998. Different in style and tone from her earlier novels, *The Healing* relies on a narrative structure that more closely resembles oral storytelling in its depiction of the transformation of Harlan Jane Eagleton from a beautician and manager of a popular rock star to a faith healer. *The Healing* received wide critical acclaim and earned Jones a National Book Award nomination.

Jones suffered a tragedy in 1998 when her husband committed suicide after a confrontation with police. After a short residence in a psychiatric hospital, where she was placed on suicide watch, Jones returned to Lexington and published her fifth novel, *Mosquito*, in 1999. Like *The Healer, Mosquito* marked a further departure from the themes of Jones's earlier work in its depiction of the fiercely independent and opinionated Sojourner Jane Nadine Johnson, nicknamed Mosquito, who uses her south Texas trucking company to help immigrants cross the border from Mexico.

In Claudia Tate's *Black Women Writers at Work* (1983), Gayl Jones described her interest in African-American and other oral storytelling traditions, "in which there is always the consciousness and importance of the hearer, even in the interior monologues where the storyteller becomes her own hearer." Jones's ability to tell the stories of her characters in vivid and even disturbing detail, particularly in her early novels, has earned considerable critical acclaim and invited comparisons to the works of such notable contemporary authors as Toni Morrison and ALICE WALKER.

Further Reading

Coser, Stelamaris. *Bridging the Americas: The Literature of Paule Marshall, Toni Morrison, and Gayl Jones.* Philadelphia, Pa.: Temple University Press, 1994.

Jones, Gayl. *Corregidora.* New York: Random House, 1975.

―――. *The Healing.* Boston: Beacon Press, 1998.

―――. *Mosquito.* Boston: Beacon Press, 1999.

Tate, Claudia, ed. *Black Women Writers at Work.* New York: Continuum Publishing Company, 1983.

Jordan, June
(June Meyer)

(1936–2002) *poet, novelist, essayist, playwright, children's fiction writer, biographer, lyricist, educator*

One of the most prolific contemporary African-American writers, June Jordan published numerous books, including volumes of poetry, children's novels, essays, and plays. She was a professor at several universities, including Yale University, Sarah Lawrence College, the City University of New York, and the University of California at Berkeley, where she taught African-American studies. Jordan pioneered the use of Black English in print in her 1971 young adult novel *His Own Where,* which was nominated for a National Book Award, and she has remained a formidable proponent of its aesthetic and linguistic merits.

Born on July 9, 1936, in the Harlem section of New York City to working-class immigrants from Jamaica, Granville Ivanhoe Jordan and Mildred Maude Jordan, June Jordan was raised in Brooklyn from the age of five. Her father worked the night shift as a postal worker, and her mother was a nurse. In a 2000 interview, Jordan characterized her father as a "complicated human being" who was "very violent and brutal where I was concerned," but also a man whose "inordinate ambitions for me have everything to do with most of the really happy, productive aspects of my life." Starting in Jordan's girlhood, her father fostered her growing interest in literature, giving her books by Shakespeare, PAUL LAURENCE DUNBAR, and westerns by Zane Grey, which were among her favorites as a child.

Jordan spent one year at Midwood High School in Brooklyn, where she was the only black student, before her parents sent her to the Northfield School for Girls in Massachusetts. Following her graduation in 1953, Jordan enrolled in Barnard College. She met Michael Meyer, a white student at Columbia University, and the two were married in 1955. Jordan interrupted her studies at Barnard to attend the University of Chicago from 1955 to 1956, where her husband was completing a graduate degree in anthropology. She returned to Barnard in 1956 and graduated a year later.

In 1958 Jordan gave birth to a son, Christopher David Meyer. A meeting with Malcolm X in 1964 convinced Jordan to become more actively involved in the Civil Rights movement. Her dedication to the cause of civil rights, and Michael's increasingly distant participation in the raising of their son, strained their marriage. They divorced in 1965. Struggling to raise her son as a single parent and suffering the devastating loss of her mother, who committed suicide in 1966, Jordan began her teaching career at the City University of New York in 1966. As a literature instructor at Connecticut College from 1968 to 1974, she directed the Search for Education, Elevation, and Knowledge (SEEK) program. By 1982 she had received full tenure at the State University of New York in Stony Brook.

Jordan published several poems and stories during the early 1960s under the name June Meyer in periodicals such as *Esquire,* the *Nation,* the *Village Voice,* and the *New York Times.* In 1969 she published her first volume of poetry, *Who Look at Me.* Her second published book, the young adult novel *His Own Where,* was nominated for the 1971 National Book Award. *His Own Where* describes the attempts of 16-year-old Buddy Rivers to find his place in a world that offers few options for African Americans. Jordan wrote her novel using Black English, which attempts to convey the natural rhythms and vocabulary of spoken English in African-American communities, and which Jordan has elsewhere referred to as "an endangered species" and "a perishing, irreplaceable system of community intelligence." Among her other works for young adults are *Dry Victories* (1972), the biography *Fannie Lou Hamer* (1972), *New Life: New Room* (1975), and *Kimako's Story* (1981).

Jordan's numerous collections of poetry include *Some Changes* (1971), *New Days: Poems of Exile and Return* (1974), *Things That I Do in the Dark: Selected Poetry* (1977, edited by novelist TONI MORRISON), *Passion: New Poems, 1977–1980* (1980), *Naming Our Destiny: New and Selected Poems* (1989), *The Haruko: Love Poems* (1994), and *Kissing God Goodbye: New Poems* (1997). In a 2000 interview in *Essence,* Jordan described her approach to poetry: "The first function of poetry is to tell the truth . . . to find out what you really feel and what you really think. To tell the truth is to become beautiful, to begin to love yourself, value yourself. And that's political, in its most profound way."

Throughout her distinguished career as a writer and educator, Jordan emphasized the transformational qualities of poetry. In 1970 Jordan edited *Soulscript: Afro-American Poetry,* which brought together original poems written by children and young adults, as well as the works of celebrated African-American poets. With a similar aim, she initiated *Poetry for the People,* a program at the University of California at Berkeley, in 1991. Designed as an outreach program to bring the study of poetry to educationally disadvantaged youth, *Poetry for the People* trains selected students to become poetry teachers in the community. The program received the Chancellor's Recognition for Community Partnership in 2000 for its efforts to engage local high schools, universities, churches, and correctional facilities. Jordan also received the Barnes & Noble 2001 Writers for Writers Award in recognition of her achievements as founder and director of the program.

Known primarily for her compelling and confrontational poetry, Jordan was also a prolific essayist. Her numerous collections include *Civil Wars: Selected Essays, 1963–1980* (1981), *Technical Difficulties: African-American Notes on the State of the Union* (1994), and *Affirmative Acts: New Political Essays* (1998). Jordan's essays range in subject matter from the aggressively political to the intensely personal. She wrote with equal ease and openness about African-American rights, the Palestinian struggle for nationhood, and her own battle with breast cancer. Central to all of Jordan's work, and her essays in particular, is a radical opposition to racism, sexism, and prejudice of all kinds. Emphasizing the power of community, she also championed the strength of individual creativity, honest discourse, and language to effect political change and social renewal.

In addition to fiction, poetry, and essays, Jordan also wrote drama, including *In the Spirit of Sojourner Truth,* produced in 1979; *For the Arrow that Flies by Day,* a staged reading produced in 1981; and the lyrics and libretti for two operas, *Bang Bang Ueber Alles* (1985) and *I Was Looking at the Ceiling and Then I Saw the Sky,* which premiered in Berkeley, California, in 1995. Though critics were decidedly less enthusiastic about Jordan's theatrical works, her plays further testify to the remarkable diversity of her literary achievements. In 2000 Jordan published her 26th book, the memoir *Soldier: A Poet's Childhood,* which chronicles her childhood struggles with a demanding and sometimes violent father, a preoccupied and powerless mother, and the social forces that shaped her personal and artistic vision. Written in a mixture of prose, poetic, and anecdotal styles, *Soldier* exhibits Jordan's brilliance and eclecticism as a storyteller. After a decade-long battle with breast cancer, June Jordan died on June 14, 2002.

A professor of African-American studies at the University of California at Berkeley for nearly a decade, Jordan performed her poetry on college campuses and in classrooms throughout the country, at the United Nations, the U.S. Congress, and the Library of Congress. Described by Nobel laureate Toni Morrison as "our premier Black woman essayist," Jordan was the recipient of numerous literary, community, and teaching honors. She was also awarded the Prix de Rome for environmental design in 1970–71 for her collaboration with R. Buckminster Fuller on a plan to revitalize Harlem's East Side.

Further Reading

Bashir, Samiya A. "June Jordan's True Grit." *Black Issues Book Review* 2, no. 5 (September/October 2000): 32.

Gates, Henry Louis, Jr., and Nellie Y. McKay, eds. *The Norton Anthology of African American Literature.* New York: Norton, 1997.

Jordan June. *Affirmative Acts: Political Essays.* New York: Doubleday, 1998.

———. *Kissing God Goodbye: Poems, 1991–1997.* New York: Doubleday, 1997.

———. *Soldier: A Poet's Childhood.* New York: Basic Books, 2000.

Kaufman, Bob
(Robert Garnell Kaufman, Bomkauf)
(1925–1986) *poet*

A legendary figure among the Beat poets of the 1950s and 1960s, Bob Kaufman is credited by some with coining the term *Beat*. He was inspired by the improvisational nature of bebop and jazz, and his poetry emphasizes the creative possibilities of spoken verse and the inherent musicality of language. A self-educated and well-read wanderer and merchant marine, Kaufman performed his poetry on street corners, in diners and coffeehouses, or wherever he happened to be. While much of his verse appeared in broadsides and books, Kaufman preferred a more spontaneous outlet for his art. Much of his published poetry was based on transcriptions of public performances.

Robert Garnell Kaufman was born on April 18, 1925, in New Orleans, Louisiana, one of 13 children born to an African-American Jewish father and a Roman Catholic mother of African descent. Kaufman grew up among intersecting faiths, and his search for a spiritual identity would play a significant role in his later poetry. After attending grade school in New Orleans, Kaufman ran away from his family and joined the U.S. Merchant Marine. For the next 20 years, he traveled the world and developed a taste for literature. He read widely, favoring the works of Walt Whitman, Herman Melville, and Albert Camus, among many others.

In the 1950s Kaufman settled in San Francisco, California, with his wife, Eileen, and soon made a name for himself among the emerging Beat writers and poets of the North Beach district, who included Lawrence Ferlinghetti, Jack Kerouac, and Allen Ginsberg. Kaufman's first published poems appeared in three broadsides: *Does the Secret Mind Whisper, Second April,* and *Abomunist Manifesto,* all published by City Lights in 1959. These early works, particularly *Abomunist Manifesto,* displayed Kaufman's revolutionary political views in his criticism of contemporary social norms and the insufficiency of any programmatic system of belief.

In 1959 Kaufman cofounded the magazine *Beatitude* with Allen Ginsberg, John Kelley, and William Margolis. The magazine helped popularize the work of unknown poets and fiction writers. The following year, Kaufman was nominated for Great Britain's prestigious Guiness Poetry Award. He was also invited to read his poetry at Harvard University. Kaufman settled in New York City with his wife and son, Parker, for the next few years. Drug abuse and increasing poverty plagued him during this period. Following an arrest in 1963, Kaufman was admitted to Bellevue Hospital, where he underwent shock treatments for alleged behavioral problems. Later that year, he and his family returned to San Francisco. Following the assassination of President John Kennedy in November 1963, Kaufman is said to have taken a Buddhist vow of silence that he maintained until the end of the Vietnam War in 1973.

In 1965 New Directions published *Solitudes Crowded with Loneliness,* which included Kaufman's three broadsides from 1959. In poems like "Walking Parker Home" and "Bagel Shop Jazz," Kaufman tried to capture the rhythm and movement of bebop and jazz in his words. Kaufman's next book of poetry, *Golden Sardine,* was published in 1967 with the help of a friend, Mary Beach, who gathered selections from Kaufman's various manuscripts. These poems, and others that followed in *Watch My Tracks* (1971) and *The Ancient Rain: Poems 1956–1978* (1981), were more experimental in nature, emphasizing the sounds of words more than their literal meanings.

In 1978 Kaufman withdrew again into silence, ceasing to write or publish, and desiring, as friends of that period have recalled, public and artistic anonymity. Robert Garnell Kaufman died of emphysema in San Francisco on January 12, 1986. Critics have noted Kaufman's influence on many celebrated writers of the Beat era, though several of these writers have been slow to recognize their debt. Despite his limited popularity in the United States, Kaufman became an important influence on the spread of Beat poetry in Europe. A 1996 collection of his poetry, *Cranial Guitar,* has brought Kaufman's writing to the attention of a new generation of readers, while also refocusing critical attention on Kaufman's legacy to other contemporary African-American performance poets, such as WANDA COLEMAN and MARI EVANS.

Further Reading

Gates, Henry Louis, Jr., and Nellie Y. McKay, eds. *The Norton Anthology of African American Literature.* New York: W. W. Norton, 1997.

Harper, Michael S., and Anthony Walton, eds. *The Vintage Book of African American Poetry.* New York: Vintage, 2000.

Kaufman, Bob. *Cranial Guitar.* Minneapolis, Minn.: Coffee House Press, 1996.

Kelley, William Melvin

(1937–) *novelist, short story writer, essayist*

Known primarily for four novels and one collection of short stories, all published between 1962 and 1970, William Kelley earned critical acclaim for his frank, satiric, and sometimes surreal depictions of race relations in America during the volatile 1960s and 1970s. Kelley was inspired by and helped shape the cultural and political objectives of the Black Arts Movement, though some critics have objected to his emphasis on character and story over ideological agendas.

William Melvin Kelley was born on November 1, 1937, in the Bronx borough of New York, to William Kelley, an editor, and Narcissa Garcia Kelley. Raised in a predominantly Italian neighborhood, Kelley attended the private Fieldston School, where most of his classmates were white. His early exposure to racial divisions in America played an important role in shaping the focus of his later writing. In 1957 Kelley enrolled at Harvard University and intended to study the law. He later decided to pursue a career as a writer, due in large part to the influence of two professors, novelist John Hawkes and poet Archibald MacLeish. In 1960 Kelley won the Dana Reed prize, awarded to the best undergraduate writing published in an undergraduate journal. He graduated from Harvard in 1961, and the following year he married Karen Isabella Gibson, with whom he has two children.

Kelley's first novel, *A Different Drummer* (1962), won the Richard and Hilda Rosenthal Award from the National Institute of Arts and Letters. Using multiple points of view and blending several narrative styles, including stream-of-consciousness, *A Different Drummer* depicts Tucker Caliban's renunciation of his family's past as former slaves. After purchasing part of the plantation on which his predecessors labored as slaves, Caliban proceeds to destroy the land and burn the house, leading other African Americans in the fictional southern town of Sutton to make similar demonstrations of liberation from the past.

William Melvin Kelley, shown here in 1963, achieved his greatest success as a writer during the tumultuous 1960s and 1970s. *(Library of Congress)*

Throughout the 1960s, Kelley continued to explore themes of personal and racial identity in his short story collection *Dancers on the Shore* (1964), which incorporated some of the characters from *A Different Drummer,* and in his novels *A Drop of Patience* (1965), a poignant tale of a blind jazz musician, and *dem* (1968), a satiric portrait of a white couple with twin sons—one white and one black. In his experimental novel *Dunsford Travels Everywhere* (1970), inspired by James Joyce's *Finnegans Wake* (1939), Kelley combined African dialects, Harlem slang, and numerous African-American idioms to create a unique language spoken by his protagonists Chig Dunford and Carlyle Bedlow.

After 1970 Kelley stopped writing fiction and turned to other creative and educational endeavors. He has taught literature and creative writing at several universities, including the New School for Social Research (now New School University), the State University of New York at Geneseo, the University of Paris at Nanterre, France, and Sarah Lawrence College. In 1988 Kelley produced *Excavating Harlem,* a video documentary. His stories and essays have appeared in numerous literary anthologies and journals, including *Negro Digest, Partisan Review,* and the *New York Times Magazine.*

In his preface to the short story collection *Dancers on the Shore,* William Melvin Kelley explained that his primary concern as a storyteller was to "depict people, not symbols or ideas disguised as people." The complexity of much of Kelley's fiction, the increasingly esoteric and surreal qualities of his later novels, and perhaps the absence of any novels since 1970, have led many critics to overlook Kelley's contributions to African-American literature. However, modern reprint editions of many of his early works have brought his unique perspective on race relations to a new generation of readers.

Further Reading

Hill, Patricia Liggins, ed. *Call and Response: The Riverside Anthology of the African American Literary Tradition.* Boston: Houghton Mifflin Company, 1998.

Kelley, William Melvin. *Dancers on the Shore.* New York: Doubleday, 1964.

———. *dem.* New York: Doubleday, 1967.

———. *Dunsford Travels Everywhere.* New York: Doubleday, 1970.

Kennedy, Adrienne
(Adrienne Lita Hawkins)

(1931–   ) *playwright, short fiction writer, essayist*

During her prolific and distinguished career as a dramatist, Adrienne Kennedy has expanded the scope of American and African-American theater with unique characterizations, experimental language, and a dramatic focus on the roots of African-American identity and culture. Her plays have garnered three Obie Awards, numerous grants and fellowships, and international critical acclaim.

Adrienne Kennedy was born Adrienne Lita Hawkins on September 13, 1931, in Pittsburgh, Pennsylvania. Her father, Cornell Wallace Hawkins, worked as a social worker and served as the executive secretary of the local YMCA. Her mother, Etta Haugabook Hawkins, was a schoolteacher. At the age of four, Hawkins moved with her family to Cleveland, Ohio. A precocious child, she learned to read at a young age, and she began keeping a diary in which she recorded her thoughts and impressions of family members.

Hawkins enjoyed a comfortable, middle-class upbringing. Her white maternal grandparents, wealthy peach growers, helped shape the direction of her later writing by making the girl aware of the African and European sides of her family heritage. She attended integrated and ethnically diverse public schools in Cleveland and later enrolled at Ohio State University in Columbus. She experienced racial intolerance as an undergraduate that resembled nothing she had witnessed during her childhood in northern Ohio, and her suffering would have a lasting impact on her later writing.

In 1953 Hawkins graduated from Ohio State University with a degree in elementary education. She married Joseph Kennedy two weeks later. When he was sent overseas to serve in the Korean War shortly after their marriage, she returned home to live with her parents in Cleveland. There she gave birth to her first child, Joseph, Jr., and began to write in earnest. Kennedy's husband returned from the war in 1955 and the family moved to New York. While her husband pursued a graduate degree, Kennedy began to develop her literary talents by attending creative writing classes at Columbia University and the American Theatre Wing.

Though she had begun writing during her senior year in college, Kennedy could generate no interest in her manuscripts. She had completed several short stories and her first play, *Pale Blue Flowers*, which remains unpublished and unproduced. In 1960 her husband, then a professor at Hunter College, received a grant from the Africa Research Foundation. The couple traveled to Europe and Africa, during which Kennedy continued to write. She completed a new story, "Because of the King of France," at that time. When she arrived in Ghana with her husband, she decided to submit the story for publication in the literary periodical *Black Orpheus*, which accepted it.

Kennedy's experiences in Africa, including the shocking murder of the African liberation leader Patrice Lumumba, helped shape her dramatic vision. "Just when I had discovered the place of my ancestors, just when I had discovered this African hero," she explained in her autobiography *People Who Led to My Plays* (1987), "he had been murdered." Also influenced by the exotic and exaggerated features of African masks, Kennedy resolved to create her characters with similarly exaggerated dimensions.

Kennedy earned her first dramatic success with *Funnyhouse of the Negro* (1964), a one-act play in which she depicts a young girl's emotional turmoil over her mixed racial heritage. Though some critics dismissed the play for its unconventional imagery and characterization, *Funnyhouse of the Negro* won an Obie Award for best new off-Broadway play in 1964. Kennedy followed this success with several acclaimed one-act productions, including *The Owl Answers* (1963), *The Rat Mass* (1966), *The Lennon Play: In His Own Write* (1967, with John Lennon and Victor Spinetti), *A Lesson in Dead Language* (1968), *Sun: A Poem for Malcolm X Inspired by His Murder* (1968), and *A Beast's Story* (1969).

In 1971 Kennedy cofounded the Women's Theatre Council, through which she helped to create greater opportunities for other female playwrights, directors, and actors. She also began a distinguished teaching career, which included positions at Yale University (1972–74), Princeton University (1977), Brown University (1979–80), the University of California at Berkeley (1980, 1986), and Harvard University (1990–91).

Though the decade of the 1960s was her most prolific and acclaimed period as a playwright, Kennedy continued to generate critical interest in her writing. Over the next three decades, she published several plays, including *An Evening with Dead Essex* (1973); *A Movie Star Has to Star in Black and White* (1976); *Orestes and Electra* (1980); *Diary of Lights* (1987); *The Alexander Plays* (1992), a cycle of four interrelated plays that includes *She Talks to Beethoven, The Ohio State Murders, The Film Club,* and *The Dramatic Circle; June and Jean in Concert* (1995); and *Sleep Deprivation Chamber* (1996, with her son Adam Patrice Kennedy).

Known principally as a dramatist, Kennedy has also experimented with fiction in her novel *Deadly Triplets: A Theatre Mystery and Journal* (1990), and with children's theater in *A Lancashire Lad* (1980), based on the early life of Charlie Chaplin. In 1987 she published an autobiography, *People Who Led to My Plays,* a highly personal account of the influences and motivations behind her writing.

For more than four decades, Adrienne Kennedy has helped shape the direction of American and African-American theater. Her early plays brought increased attention to the innovative works of off-Broadway playwrights and the artists of the emerging Black Arts Movement during the 1960s. "I see my writing as a growth of images," Kennedy wrote in a 1977 essay published in *Drama Review.* "I think all my plays come out of dreams I had two or three years before." Kennedy's emphasis on the interior lives of her characters, often manifested in a montage of surreal imagery, as in her acclaimed *Funnyhouse of the Negro,* has had a profound impact on contemporary African-American drama, particularly in the works of Pulitzer Prize–winning playwright and novelist SUZAN-LORI PARKS.

Further Reading

Brown, E. Barnsley. "Passed Over: The Tragic Mulatta and (Dis)Integration of Identity in Adrienne Kennedy's Plays." *African American Review* 35 (summer 2001): 281.

Kennedy, Adrienne. *The Adrienne Kennedy Reader.* Minneapolis: University of Minnesota Press, 2001.

Overbeck, Lois More, and Paul K. Bryant-Jackson, eds. *Intersecting Boundaries: The Theatre of Adrienne Kennedy.* New York: Theatre Communications Group, 1992.

Killens, John Oliver
(John O. Killens)

(1916–1987) *novelist, playwright, screenwriter, young adult fiction writer, biographer, essayist, educator*

A respected and versatile writer of politically charged novels, plays, screenplays, and essays, John O. Killens was twice nominated for the Pulitzer Prize for fiction. During the 1950s he became the principal founder of the Harlem Writers Guild, which produced such esteemed authors as ROSA CUTHBERT GUY, MAYA ANGELOU, and PAULE MARSHALL. A close friend of several leading civil rights activists, including Martin Luther King, Jr., and Malcolm X, Killens devoted his life and writing to the cause of racial equality and social justice for African Americans.

John Oliver Killens was born on January 14, 1916, in Macon, Georgia. His parents, Charles Myles Killens and Willie Lee Killens, encouraged his early interest in African-American literature by supplying Killens with works by PAUL LAURENCE DUNBAR and LANGSTON HUGHES. However, Killens credits the stories told to him by his paternal great-grandmother with inspiring him to become a writer. "She seemed to encompass within herself all the wisdom of the ages," Killens later wrote of the influence of her storytelling.

Despite his early interest in literature, Killens initially pursued a career in the law. From 1936 to

1942 he worked for the National Labor Relations Board and studied at Edward Waters College, Morris Brown College, Atlanta University, Howard University, Columbia University, and New York University. After serving three years in the U.S. Army during World War II, Killens returned to New York and soon emerged as a compelling new voice in the post–Harlem Renaissance era.

In 1952 Killens gathered with a group of fellow authors, including Rosa Guy, John Henrik Clarke, and Walter Christmas, in a Harlem storefront to develop the manuscript of his first novel. The group would later become known as the Harlem Writers Guild, and the manuscript of Killens's novel, *Youngblood,* would be published in 1954. Set in the fictional town of Crossroads, Georgia, the novel chronicles one family's struggle for survival in the oppressive atmosphere of the American South during the early 20th century.

Killens was nominated for a Pulitzer Prize for his second novel, *And Then We Heard Thunder* (1962), in which he depicts a young black soldier's confrontation with racism during World War II. *'Sippi,* published in 1967, also addressed racism, this time in Mississippi during the voting rights movement of the 1960s. More militant in tone than his previous works, *'Sippi* captures in vivid detail the violence committed against African Americans in their struggle for greater political representation.

In *The Cotillion; or One Good Bull Is Half the Herd,* published in 1971, Killens addressed social and cultural divisions within the African-American community during the 1970s in his satirical look at an exclusive Brooklyn women's club. Against the group of older black women who have embraced the values and conventions of Eurocentric white society, Killens sets the characters of Lumumba, a young man who rejects such values as foreign to his African heritage, and Yoruba, a young woman caught between the passionate separatism of Lumumba, her boyfriend, and the values of her elders. *The Cotillion* was nominated for a Pulitzer Prize in 1971.

Killens's other literary works include a critically acclaimed volume of essays, *Black Man's Burden* (1965), in which he argued for the use of violence to resist racial oppression; two biographies for young readers, *Great Gittin' Up Morning: A Biography of Denmark Vesey* (1972) and *A Man Ain't Nothin' but a Man: The Adventures of John Henry* (1975); and two plays, *Ballad of the Winter Soldier* (1964, with Loften Mitchell) and *Lower Than the Angels* (1965). Killens also collaborated on two screenplays: *Odds against Tomorrow* (1959, with Nelson Gidding) and *Slaves* (1969, with Herbert Biberman and Alida Sherman).

At the time of his death, Killens had completed several additional manuscripts. *The Great Black Russian: A Novel on the Life and Times of Alexander Pushkin,* the product of more than 10 years of research, was published posthumously in 1989. Killens also authored a comic novel, *The Minister Primarily,* and *Write On!: Notes from a Writer's Workshop.* John Oliver Killens died of cancer on October 27, 1987, in Brooklyn, New York, and was survived by his wife, Grace Killens, and their two children.

John Oliver Killens achieved international acclaim as an author and activist, and his works have been translated into more than a dozen languages. In addition to serving as a vice president of the Black Academy of Arts and Letters and a board member of the National Center for Afro-American Artists, Killens also maintained a distinguished teaching career at universities such as Medgar Evers College, where he founded the Black Writers Conference in 1986, the New School for Social Research (now New School University), Cornell University, Rutgers University, and the University of California at Los Angeles.

Further Reading

Andrews, William L., Frances Smith Foster, and Trudier Harris, eds. *The Concise Oxford Companion to African American Literature.* New York: Oxford University Press, 2001.

Gilyard, Keith. *Liberation Memories: The Rhetoric and Poetics of John Oliver Killens.* Detroit: Wayne State University Press, 2003.

Killens, John Oliver. *Black Man's Burden.* New York: Trident Press, 1965.

———. *The Cotillion; or One Good Bull Is Half the Herd.* New York: Trident Press, 1971.

Kincaid, Jamaica
(Elaine Potter Richardson)
(1949–   ) *short fiction writer, novelist, essayist, memoirist, editor, educator*

From her humble origins on the West Indian island of Antigua, Jamaica Kincaid has become an internationally acclaimed author of short fiction, novels, essays, and memoirs. Her intimate depictions of family relationships, particularly the complex bond between mothers and daughters, and her exploration of the legacy of slavery and colonialism in her native Antigua have earned her a large and devoted readership. Kincaid's works have been nominated for the National Book Critics Circle Award, the PEN/Faulkner Award, and the National Book Award.

Jamaica Kincaid was born Elaine Potter Richardson on May 25, 1949, in St. John's, Antigua, in the British West Indies. Her childhood was characterized by extreme poverty and a growing awareness of the cultural alienation imposed by the colonial rule of her homeland. "I was always being told I should be something," she wrote in a 1990 essay, "and then my whole upbringing was something I was not: it was English." A gifted student, Richardson earned a scholarship to the Princess Margaret School.

However, a growing enmity with her mother and a strong desire to escape the stifling atmosphere of colonial Antigua led Richardson to depart for New York at age 17. She found work as an au pair in Scarsdale, New York, and later in New York City. During her three years in the service of writer Michael Arlen, whose four children

she cared for, Kincaid attended community college to complete her high school diploma and to study photography. She gave up her position as an au pair in 1970 and accepted a scholarship to Franconia College in New Hampshire, though she returned to New York after her first year. She adopted the name Jamaica Kincaid and made her first foray into the world of publishing.

In 1973 Kincaid published her first professional writing, an interview with feminist Gloria Steinem for the teen magazine *Ingenue.* After publishing articles in the *Village Voice* and *Partisan Review,* Kincaid was invited by an acquaintance to submit an article for the "Talk of the Town" section of the *New Yorker* and remained a staff writer for the publication until 1995. In 1978 the *New Yorker* published her first short story, *Girl,* and Kincaid turned her attention to fiction. The following year, Kincaid married composer Allen Shawn, with whom she has two children.

In her short stories and novels, Kincaid recreates the physical and emotional landscape of her youth in Antigua, capturing in poignant detail her painful relationship with her mother, a woman by whom Kincaid was both inspired and enraged. *At the Bottom of the River* (1983), Kincaid's first collection of short stories, comprised 10 interrelated tales of a young Antiguan girl's struggle for self-awareness and her relationship with an emotionally distant mother. Critics praised the collection for its vibrant language and the psychological depth of Kincaid's characters. "Kincaid's particular skill," wrote reviewer David Leavitt in the *Village Voice,* "lies in her ability to articulate the internal workings of a potent imagination without sacrificing the rich details of the external world on which that imagination thrives." *At the Bottom of the River* was awarded the Morten Dauwen Zabel Award from the American Academy and Institute of Arts and Letters in 1983.

Kincaid continued to explore her Antiguan roots in her first novel, *Annie John* (1985), about a young woman's transition from childhood to maturity. Kincaid's other fictional works include the novel *Lucy* (1990), about a young woman who leaves her home and family in Antigua to work as an au pair in the United States; *The Autobiography of My Mother* (1996), a moving tale of a woman's search for identity in the harsh cultural climate of the Caribbean island of Dominica; and *Mr. Potter* (2002), a fictional portrait of Kincaid's father, which depicts the life of an Antiguan chauffeur who struggles with the financial and emotional support of his family.

The legacy of colonialism and slavery in the West Indies informs Kincaid's fiction and nonfiction. Kincaid returned to Antigua in the 1980s and recorded her profoundly bitter impressions in the essay collection *A Small Place* (1988), in which she describes a small island nation "settled by human rubbish from Europe" and ravaged by years of colonial rule. Kincaid's other nonfiction works include a memoir, *My Brother* (1997), in which she reflects on the death of her brother from AIDS, and *My Garden* (1999), a collection of essays that illustrate her passion for gardening. *Talk Stories*

Born on the Caribbean island of Antigua, Jamaica Kincaid is a passionate critic of the colonial history of her homeland. *(Sigrid Estrada)*

(2001) collects Kincaid's contributions to the "Talk of the Town" section of the *New Yorker*.

Jamaica Kincaid has earned wide critical acclaim as an author. Her works have drawn attention to Caribbean-American literature in general, illuminating an area that has, until recently, been frequently overlooked by mainstream critics and readers. Kincaid's literary honors include nominations for the National Book Critics Circle Award and the PEN/Faulkner Award, both for *The Autobiography of My Mother*, and a National Book Award nomination for *My Brother*. She has also served as a visiting professor at Harvard University in Cambridge, Massachusetts. In 2002 California's Monterey Symphony Orchestra presented a commissioned symphonic work by Allen Shawn, Kincaid's husband, in honor of the centennial anniversary of novelist John Steinbeck's birth. *And in the air these sounds . . .*, subtitled "a monodrama for baritone and orchestra," featured original text by Kincaid.

Further Reading

Bloom, Harold. *Jamaica Kincaid*. Boston: Chelsea House Publishers, 1998.

Kincaid, Jamaica. *Autobiography of My Mother*. New York: Farrar, Straus and Giroux, 1996.

———. *A Small Place*. New York: Farrar, Straus and Giroux, 1988.

Paravisini-Gebert, Lizabeth. *Jamaica Kincaid: A Critical Companion*. Westport, Conn.: Greenwood Publishing Group, 1999.

Knight, Etheridge
(1931–1991) *poet, essayist*

Etheridge Knight emerged during the late 1960s and early 1970s as a leading voice in the Black Arts Movement. His imprisonment on robbery charges in 1960 led Knight to write poetry as an emotional and creative outlet. With the encouragement of such respected authors as GWENDOLYN BROOKS, Dudley Randall, and SONIA SANCHEZ, Knight found a receptive audience for his poetry. His works garnered an American Book Award and nominations for the Pulitzer Prize and the National Book Award.

Etheridge Knight was born on April 19, 1931, in Corinth, Mississippi, to Etheridge and Belzora Cozart Knight. One of seven children, Knight grew up with the knowledge that his opportunities in the South were extremely limited. He dropped out of high school at the age of 16 and enlisted in the army. While on active duty in Korea during the war, Knight suffered a shrapnel wound that resulted in his discharge in 1951. To alleviate the lasting pain of his injuries, Knight turned to drugs and alcohol; eventually, he resorted to criminal activity to support his addictions. After his arrest on robbery charges in 1960, Knight received a 10-to-25-year sentence at Indiana State Prison.

Prior to his conviction, Knight had excelled in a form of oral poetry known as toasting, in which the speaker recounted physical, sexual, and even criminal exploits in rhyming verse, usually with an emphasis on humor. His natural facility for language led him to explore poetry as a means of countering his growing resentment of what he considered an unjust and racially motivated prison sentence. The theme of imprisonment, literal and metaphorical, would provide the framework for many of his best-known poems.

While in prison, Knight enjoyed the support of several celebrated literary figures, including poets Gwendolyn Brooks, Sonia Sanchez, and Dudley Randall, whose Broadside Press would publish much of Knight's early poetry. In his first collection, *Poems from Prison* (1968), published shortly before his parole, Knight depicted the hopelessness and isolation that characterized prison life. "The Idea of Ancestry," one of his most frequently anthologized poems, expresses the poet's longing for freedom and the pain of separation from his community and family.

Knight married Sonia Sanchez in 1969, but his continuing battle with drug addiction led to their divorce a year later. Knight would marry and divorce two more times. Despite the turmoil in Knight's personal life, his poetry resonated with the young poets and political activists of the Black Arts Movement. Like his contemporaries AMIRI BARAKA and HAKI R. MADHUBUTI, Knight believed passionately in a community-based, Afrocentric context for his poetry.

Expanding his critical and popular reputation with the publication of *Black Voices from Prison* (1970), an anthology that included works by Knight's fellow inmates, and *A Poem for Brother/Man (After His Recovery from an O.D.)* (1972), Knight achieved his greatest critical success with *Belly Song and Other Poems* (1973), considered by many to be one of the defining works of the Black Arts Movement. *Belly Song* was nominated for the Pulitzer Prize and the National Book Award.

In his final collections of poetry, *Born of a Woman: New and Selected Poems* (1980), and *The Essential Etheridge Knight* (1986), which won an American Book Award in 1987, Knight demonstrated the range of his linguistic skills. Blending elements of traditional blues ballads, black vernacular, and street slang, Knight explores his personal history in the American South and his identity as an African-American.

During his distinguished career as a poet, Knight served as poet-in-residence at the University of Pittsburgh (1968–69), the University of Hartford (1969–70), and Lincoln University (1972). A frequent lecturer throughout the United States, Knight drew large crowds for his poetry readings, in which he presented his poems from memory. Knight also published poems and essays in numerous periodicals, including *Black Digest, Essence,* and *American Poetry.* Etheridge Knight died of lung cancer on March 10, 1991, in Indianapolis, Indiana.

"I died in Korea from a shrapnel wound and narcotics resurrected me," Knight wrote in the frequently quoted preface to *The Essential Etheridge Knight.* "I died in 1960 from a prison sentence and poetry brought me back to life." His words provide a fitting explanation of the scope of his poetry. Both redemptive and political, Knight's poetry revealed the losses suffered by the inmates of physical or socially constructed prisons, while not neglecting the things that captivity could not destroy.

Further Reading

Hill, Patricia Liggins, ed. *Call and Response: The Riverside Anthology of the African American Literary Tradition.* Boston: Houghton Mifflin Co., 1998.

Knight, Etheridge. *Belly Song and Other Poems.* Detroit, Mich.: Broadside Press, 1973.

———. *The Essential Etheridge Knight.* Pittsburgh: University of Pittsburgh Press, 1986.

Komunyakaa, Yusef
(James Willie Brown, Jr.)
(1947–) *poet, essayist, editor, educator*

A prolific poet whose work has appeared frequently in literary periodicals and anthologies, Yusef Komunyakaa is also the recipient of a Pulitzer Prize for poetry, awarded in 1994 for *Neon Vernacular: New and Selected Poems* (1993). Komunyakaa's poetry draws on his family roots in the West Indies and the rural Louisiana of his childhood, as well as his experiences during the Vietnam War. Often employing sparse language and surrealistic imagery in his poems, Komunyakaa also incorporates the cadences of blues and jazz. In *Blue Notes: Essays, Interviews, and Commentaries* (2000), Komunyakaa described poetry as "a kind of insinuation. It's a way of talking around an idea or a question. Sometimes, more actually gets said through such a technique than a full frontal assault."

Yusef Komunyakaa was born James Willie Brown, Jr., on April 29, 1947, in Bogalusa, Louisiana, the oldest of five children. He would later give up his father's name, taking instead the name of his grandfather, an immigrant from Trinidad. The Bogalusa of Brown's childhood was a small, segregated mill town. His father worked as a carpenter and tried to instill in his son the virtue of hard work in order to achieve success in America. "He worked twelve to fourteen hours a day," Komunyakaa explained in a 1994 interview, "and saw others who were hard workers yet weren't paid that much. I questioned those contradictions from early on." Relations with his father were strained throughout his childhood and would later become the subject of his poetry.

As a child, Brown was drawn to the world of books. His earliest reading consisted of the Bible and a set of encyclopedias purchased by his mother. Having read many of the classics of English literature as a schoolboy, he later discovered a copy of *Nobody Knows My Name* (1961), by JAMES BALDWIN, in a church library (blacks were not yet admitted to the town's public library), and was inspired to become a writer. He graduated from Bogalusa's all-black Central High School in 1965, and he enlisted four years later in the army. He was sent to Vietnam, where he served as a correspondent on the front lines and edited *The Southern Cross*, a military newspaper. Komunyakaa received a Bronze Star for his service in Vietnam, and his experiences there would play an important role in defining the thematic focus of much of his later poetry.

After his discharge from the army, Komunyakaa completed his bachelor's degree at the University of Colorado in 1975 and master's degrees at Colorado State University and the University of California at Irvine, in 1979 and 1980 respectively. Komunyakaa taught English for a year at the University of New Orleans. There he met Mandy Sayer, whom he married in 1985. In 1986 Komunyakaa joined the faculty of Indiana University in Bloomington.

Komunyakaa's earliest collections of poetry, such as the chapbooks *Dedication and the Other Darkhorses* (1977) and *Lost in the Bonewheel* (1979), employ biblical allusions and macabre imagery to discuss racial and social injustice, particularly in the South. With the publication of *Copacetic* (1984) and *I Apologize for the Eyes in My Head* (1986), Komunyakaa began to receive greater critical attention. Both volumes introduced themes and styles that would remain central to his later writing: a reliance on jazz and blues rhythms, memories of his childhood in the South, and his wartime experiences.

In *Toys in the Field* (1986) and *Dien Cai Dau* (1988), which means "crazy" in Vietnamese, Komunyakaa further explored the pain and disillusionment occasioned by his service in Vietnam. In "We Never Know," he compares the disparate images of dancing with a woman to the death of an enemy soldier, whose corpse he tenderly examines. "Tu Du Street" offers an unusual meditation on race as black and white soldiers, divided by racism even in Vietnam, transcend such barriers with regard to the women with whom they seek consolation.

In *Magic City* (1990), Komunyakaa explores his family roots in the West Indies and the American South, highlighting the joy and the suffering of family members of various generations and their struggle against poverty and racism. The publication of *Neon Vernacular: New and Selected Poems* in 1993, however, solidified Komunyakaa's reputation as one of the finest poets of his generation.

Many of the new poems in this collection explore the nature of memory. "Songs of My Father" presents a series of poignant meditations on Komunyakaa's turbulent relationship with his father. Highly acclaimed by critics, *Neon Vernacular* was awarded the Pulitzer Prize for poetry and the Kingsley Tufts Poetry Award, both in 1994. Komunyakaa explained his approach in *Neon Vernacular* in a 1994 interview. "Each poem relates to a place—the internal terrain as well as the external terrain—to try to make sense out of the world at large, which is often chaotic."

Komunyakaa continued to explore new methods of expression in his later collections of poetry, including *Thieves of Paradise* (1998), *Talking Dirty to the Gods* (2000), which was nominated for the National Book Critics Circle Award, and *Pleasure Dome: New and Collected Poems* (2001). In addition to his poetry, Komunyakaa has published *Blue Notes: Essays, Interviews, and Commentaries* (1999), and he coedited *The Jazz Poetry Anthology* (1991)

Pulitzer Prize–winning poet Yusef Komunyakaa speaks to reporters at the University of Indiana in 1996. *(AP/Wide World Photos)*

and *The Second Set: The Jazz Poetry Anthology, Volume Two* (1995), both with Sascha Feinstein.

Yusef Komunyakaa has earned international acclaim as a poet for the intensely personal but accessible nature of his imagery and language. Bruce Weber, a columnist for the *New York Times*, has described Yusef Komunyakaa as "the dreamy intellectual, a Wordsworthian type whose worldly, philosophic mind might be stirred by something as homely and personal as a walk in a field of daffodils." Also a distinguished professor of English and creative writing, Komunyakaa has held teaching positions at Indiana University, the University of California at Berkeley, and Princeton University, where he taught in the Council of Humanities and Creative Writing. In 1999 Komunyakaa was named a chancellor of the American Academy of Poets.

Further Reading

Baer, William. "Still Negotiating with the Images: An Interview with Yusef Komunyakaa." *Kenyon Review* 20 (summer/fall 1998): 16.

Citino, David, ed. *The Eye of the Poet: Six Views of the Art and Craft of Poetry.* New York: Oxford University Press, 2001.

Komunyakaa, Yusef. *Blue Notes: Essays, Interviews, and Commentaries.* Ann Arbor: University of Michigan Press, 1999.

———. *Neon Vernacular: New and Selected Poems.* Middletown, Conn.: Wesleyan University Press, 1993.

L

Larsen, Nella
(Nellie Marian Walker, Nellie Marian
Larsen, Allen Semi)
(1891–1964) *novelist, short story writer*

Nella Larsen was one of Harlem's leading writers during the era of the "New Negro"—the Harlem Renaissance of the 1920s and 1930s in New York City. Though she published only two novels and a handful of short stories during her brief literary career, Larsen earned the respect of distinguished contemporaries, including the venerated African-American critic and scholar W. E. B. DuBOIS, and became the first female African-American recipient of the prestigious Guggenheim Fellowship.

Larsen was born Nellie Marian Walker in Chicago, Illinois, on April 13, 1891, to Peter Walker, a West Indian, and Marie Hanson Walker, a Dutch immigrant. According to Larsen, her father died when she was three, and her mother later married Peter Larsen, a white Chicago railroad worker. Some biographers have speculated that Peter Walker and Peter Larsen were in fact the same man, arguing that Walker decided to pass for white in order to get employment with the railroad. This and other speculations about Larsen's family and early childhood remain inconclusive.

In 1907 Larsen enrolled in Fisk University's Normal School in Nashville, Tennessee, but left without a diploma the following year. She studied at the University of Copenhagen from 1910 to 1912 and began training as a nurse at the Lincoln School for Nurses in New York, completing the program in 1915. After spending a year at the Tuskegee Institute, in Alabama, as the head nurse at John A. Andrew Hospital and Nurse Training School, Larsen returned to New York in 1916 to work at Lincoln Hospital and later the New York Department of Health.

Larsen married a distinguished physicist, Elmer Imes, in 1919, and left the nursing profession two years later to work at the 135th Street Branch (later renamed the Countee Cullen Branch) of the New York Public Library in Harlem. She also studied library science at Columbia University, receiving her certification in 1923. Her first published works, two essays for children, appeared in *The Brownies' Book: A Monthly Magazine for the Children of the Sun,* founded by W. E. B. DuBois and edited by JESSIE REDMON FAUSET.

Larsen's acquaintance with Fauset and the white literary critic and author Carl Van Vechten brought her into contact with many promising authors of the early Harlem Renaissance period. By 1925 Larsen had begun devoting more of her time to writing. She published her first novel, the semi-autobiographical *Quicksand,* in 1928, and became an instant literary success. Acclaimed by DuBois as "the best piece of fiction that Negro America has produced since the heyday of Chesnutt,"

Quicksand explores the social, psychological, and sexual frustrations of Helga Crane, a young woman of mixed racial descent who feels equally out of place in white and black society.

In 1929 Larsen published her second novel, *Passing,* in which she further examines the social, racial, and sexual displacement of middle-class African-American women forced to choose between the convenience of passing for white and the hardships involved with remaining true to their cultural heritage. Though not as widely acclaimed as her first novel, *Passing* received generally positive reviews for its compelling depiction of the physical and psychological consequences associated with the issue of passing.

Nella Larsen, shown here circa 1930, was among a coterie of celebrated authors during the Harlem Renaissance. *(Library of Congress)*

The recipient of the Harmon Foundation's bronze medal in 1928 for *Quicksand,* Larsen became the first African-American woman to receive a Guggenheim Fellowship, awarded to her in 1930 on the basis of her two published novels. Larsen made arrangements to leave New York for Europe in 1930 to work on another novel. Prior to her departure, she published a short story, "Sanctuary" (1930), in *Forum* magazine. Citing similarities between Larsen's "Sanctuary" and a story by Shelia Kaye-Smith, "Mrs. Adis," published in *Century* magazine in 1922, readers accused Larsen of plagiarism. Larsen defended herself against the charge and was later exonerated by her editors, but the experience effectively marked the end of her literary career.

Though she continued to write, Larsen published nothing after 1930. Her publisher rejected the novel she had worked on during her trip to Europe. In 1933 Larsen divorced her husband and dropped out of Harlem's literary society. After the death of her ex-husband in 1941, whose alimony had allowed her to remain unemployed, Larsen returned to nursing and spent the final years of her life in seclusion. Nella Larsen is believed to have died during the last week of March in 1964. Her body was discovered in her home on March 30, after she failed to appear for work for a week.

Nella Larsen enjoyed popular and critical success as a novelist during her lifetime. Not until several years after her death, however, did she become widely recognized as one of the most important writers of the Harlem Renaissance. Larsen's focus on the restricted roles available to African-American women, and the resulting crisis of identity experienced by women in a society dominated by racial and gender biases, initiated themes that have continued to inform modern African-American literature.

Further Reading

Davis, Thadious M. *Nella Larsen, Novelist of the Harlem Renaissance: A Woman's Life Unveiled.* Baton Rouge: Louisiana State University Press, 1994.

Gates, Henry Louis, Jr., and Nellie Y. McKay, eds. *The Norton Anthology of African American Literature*. New York: W. W. Norton, 1997.

Larsen, Nella. *The Complete Fiction of Nella Larsen*. New York: Anchor Books, 2001.

Sullivan, Nell. "Nella Larsen's *Passing* and the Fading Subject." *African American Review* 32, no. 3 (fall 1998): 373.

Locke, Alain
(Alain LeRoy Locke)
(1886–1954) *essayist, editor, literary critic, biographer, educator*

In 1925 Alain Locke published what would effectively become the foundational text of the Harlem Renaissance. *The New Negro: An Interpretation* featured articles, poetry, and fiction by Locke and other African-American scholars and writers of the time, including W. E. B. DuBOIS, JAMES WELDON JOHNSON, LANGSTON HUGHES, and ANNE SPENCER. As an editor and educator, Locke fostered a sense of community among black artists and writers and emphasized the importance of honoring their cultural history. In the process, he helped usher in one of the most fertile and influential eras in African-American art and literature.

Alain Locke was born Alain LeRoy Locke on September 13, 1886, the only son of Pliny and Mary Locke, both upper-class Philadelphia schoolteachers. Locke attended Central High School and later the Philadelphia School of Pedagogy, where his father taught. In 1907 Locke graduated magna cum laude from Harvard University and became the first African American to be awarded a Rhodes scholarship. He earned a degree in literature from Oxford University in 1910 and studied philosophy for a year at the University of Berlin before returning to the United States in 1912. He joined the faculty of Howard University, in Washington, D.C., as a professor of English, philosophy, and education. After completing his doctorate in philosophy at Harvard University in 1917, Locke became the chair of the philosophy department at Howard.

In March 1925 Locke was selected by Phil Kellogg, editor of the social science periodical *Survey Graphic*, to prepare a special edition devoted to issues of race in New York. The edition, subtitled *Harlem: Mecca of the New Negro*, highlighted the creative developments taking place within Harlem's large community of artists and writers. Later that year, Locke edited and published *The New Negro: An Interpretation*, in which he argued that "the more intelligent and representative elements of the two race groups have at so many points got quite out of vital touch with one another." By showcasing the talents of African-American writers and intellectuals, Locke hoped to bridge this gap.

Though the period known as the Harlem Renaissance did not begin with Locke's *The New Negro*, the movement gained momentum under his influence. Locke provided direction for such young writers as Langston Hughes, CLAUDE McKAY, and ZORA NEALE HURSTON, and he helped find patrons and publishers for their writing. Locke edited several works on African-American art and culture, including *Plays of Negro Life* (1927, with Montgomery Gregory), *Four Negro Poets* (1927), *The Negro in Art: A Pictorial Record of the Negro Artist and of the Negro Theme in Art* (1940), and *When Peoples Meet: A Study in Race and Culture Contacts* (1942, with Bernhard J. Stern). His influence as a writer and critic was eclipsed, however, by his greater significance as a mentor and advocate of young writers.

As an editor and distinguished professor at Howard University, Locke devoted the greater part of his life to instilling a sense of cultural identity and racial pride in a new and vital generation of African-American writers and thinkers. In the process, he brought the accomplishments of black artists to the attention of a wider audience of white editors and readers. It was his belief that such cultural contacts would create greater understanding and equality among the races. Locke continued to teach at Howard University until 1953. He was also a visiting professor and lecturer at several other universities in the United States, Europe, Haiti, and Africa. Alain LeRoy Locke died on June 9, 1954, in New York City.

Locke ranks as one of the most influential African-American intellectuals of the 20th century. As an educator, he helped make Howard University an internationally known center of African-American education. His influence as an editor extended to nearly every major writer of the Harlem Renaissance. Due in large part to his efforts, African-American writers and artists of the early 20th century began to view themselves as part of a larger social and cultural movement, the results of which continue to inform and enrich the modern African-American literary tradition.

Further Reading

Butcher, Margaret J. *The Negro in American Culture: Based on Materials Left by Alain Locke.* New York: Knopf, 1956.

Gates, Henry Louis, Jr., and Nellie Y. McKay, eds. *The Norton Anthology of African American Literature.* New York: W. W. Norton, 1997.

Locke, Alain, ed. *The New Negro: Voices of the Harlem Renaissance.* New York: Scribner, 1997.

Washington, Johnny. *A Journey into the Philosophy of Alain Locke.* Westport, Conn.: Greenwood Press, 1994.

Lorde, Audre
(Audrey Geraldine Lorde, Rey Domini, Gamba Adisa)
(1934–1992) *poet, essayist, autobiographer*

A self-described "Black lesbian, mother, warrior, poet," Audre Lorde challenged the traditional boundaries of race and sexuality in her poetry, essays, and autobiographical writings. Her fierce individualism as a person and an artist had a profound impact on American and African-American literature, feminist theory, and gender studies. In designating Audre Lorde the poet laureate of New

York in 1991, a post she held until her death, Governor Mario Cuomo called her "the voice of the eloquent outsider who speaks in a language that can reach and touch people everywhere."

Born on February 18, 1934, in New York City, Audrey Geraldine Lorde (she later shortened her name to Audre) was the daughter of West Indian immigrants Frederic Byron Lorde, a real estate broker, and Linda Gertrude Lorde. As a child, Lorde had difficulty learning to speak. "I didn't speak until I was five . . . not really until I started reading and writing poetry," she explained in Claudia Tate's *Black Women Writers at Work.* At the age of 15, Lorde published her first poem, in the magazine *Seventeen,* a love poem that had been refused by her high school newspaper.

Following her graduation from Hunter High School in 1951, Lorde spent the next few years working in New York and traveling in the United States and Mexico. "In Mexico I learned to walk upright," Lorde explained, "to say the things I felt." After returning to New York, she earned her bachelor's degree from Hunter College, now a part of the City University of New York, and a master's degree in library science from Columbia University in 1961. The following year, she married Edwin Rollins, a white attorney, with whom she had two children. Lorde and her husband divorced eight years later.

Lorde began publishing her poetry in the late 1960s and soon became an inspiring voice in the Black Arts Movement. Her early collections—including *The First Cities* (1968); *Cables to Rage* (1970); *From a Land Where Other People Live* (1973), which earned a National Book Award nomination; and *Between Our Selves* (1976)—established Lorde as a formidable and passionate critic of racial and political injustice.

The publication of *Coal* (1976) and *The Black Unicorn* (1978), one of her most respected works, further extended Lorde's reputation as a poet. In these collections, she addressed more personal themes, such as her relationships with friends and family members and, in *The Black Unicorn,* her identification with the empowering myths and culture of Africa.

Lorde published her first prose work, *The Cancer Journals*, in 1980, in which she chronicled her early struggle with the disease that would ultimately take her life. An unflinchingly honest and groundbreaking examination of the physical and psychological implications of cancer, *The Cancer Journals* won the American Library Association's Gay Caucus Book of the Year Award in 1981. Lorde's other prose and fictional works include *Zami: A New Spelling of My Name* (1982), a semi-autobiographical novel in which Lorde depicts her emerging sexuality, and two collections of essays and speeches: *Sister Outsider* (1984) and *A Burst of Light* (1988), which won the American Book Award.

The final years of Lorde's life were among her most productive. In works such as *A Comrade Is as Precious as a Rice Seedling* (1984), *Our Dead behind Us* (1986), *Need: A Chorale for Black Woman Voices* (1990), and *The Marvelous Arithmetic of Distance: Poems, 1987–1992*, published posthumously in 1993, Lorde's tone is contemplative but forceful as she meditates on her life and art. In 1991 Lorde received her highest honor, the Walt Whitman Citation of Merit, which included the designation of poet laureate of New York.

In addition to her work as a poet and author, Lorde maintained an eminent teaching career, holding positions at the City University of New York, John Jay College of Criminal Justice, and Hunter College, where she was named the Thomas Hunter Distinguished Professor in 1987. An outspoken feminist and lesbian, Lorde was also a founding member of Sisters in Support of Sisters in Africa (SISA) and a cofounder of Kitchen Table: Women of Color Press. Adopting the African name Gamba Adisa, which means "warrior: she who makes her meaning clear," Lorde spent the last years of her life in the Virgin Islands with her companion, Gloria I. Joseph. After a 14-year battle, Audre Lorde finally suc-

Poet and essayist Audre Lorde was a committed and passionate advocate for feminism and gay and lesbian rights. *(Ingmar Schullz, courtesy of W. W. Norton and Company)*

cumbed to liver cancer on November 17, 1992, in Christiansted, St. Croix, Virgin Islands.

In the poem "There Are No Honest Poems About Dead Women," collected in *Our Dead behind Us*, Audre Lorde wrote: "I am a Black woman stripped down / and praying / my whole life has been an altar / worth its ending." As an author and educator, Lorde affirmed the power of poetry to transform the lives of individuals and societies by challenging entrenched assumptions about race, gender, and sexuality. In 1994 the Audre Lorde Project was established in Brooklyn, New York, to honor Lorde's achievements as an internationally acclaimed poet and activist, and to provide a community-based, politically oriented organization and support group for "lesbian, gay, bisexual, two-spirit, and transgender people of color."

Further Reading

Keating, Analouise. *Women Reading Women Writing: Self-Invention in Paula Gunn Allen, Gloria Anzaldúa, and Audre Lorde.* Philadelphia: Temple University Press, 1996.

Lorde, Audre. *The Cancer Journals.* San Francisco, Calif.: Spinsters Ink, 1980.

———. *The Collected Poems of Audre Lorde.* New York: W. W. Norton, 1997.

———. *Sister Outsider: Essays and Speeches.* Trumansburg, N.Y.: Crossing Press, 1984.

M

Mackey, Nathaniel
(Nathaniel Ernest Mackey)
(1947–) *poet, novelist, essayist, editor, educator*

Influenced by the literature of the Black Arts Movement of the 1960s, particularly the poetry of AMIRI BARAKA, as well as the experimental and free-form nature of jazz, Nathaniel Mackey has published novels, poetry, and literary criticism that emphasize the fluid and rhythmic nature of language. He also incorporates African and Middle Eastern folklore and religious imagery to create compelling stories that stretch the boundaries of traditional fiction and verse.

Nathaniel Ernest Mackey was born on October 25, 1947, in Miami, Florida. His parents, Sadie Jane Wilcox and Alexander Obadiah Mackey, separated when he was four, and he moved with his mother to California. As a high school student, Mackey became interested in music, particularly free jazz. He also began reading the poetry of William Carlos Williams and Amiri Baraka, who would become the subject of his senior thesis as a Princeton undergraduate. Other early influences on Mackey's writing included the avant-garde, projectivist poets Charles Olson and Robert Duncan. Mackey graduated magna cum laude from Princeton University in 1969 and received his doctorate in English and American literature from Stanford University in 1975. In 1976 he became the director of black studies at the University of Southern California and an assistant professor of English and ethnic studies. Since 1979 he has been a professor of American literature at the University of California at Santa Cruz.

Mackey's first published poetry, *Four for Trane* and *Septet for the End of Time,* appeared in chapbooks in 1978 and 1983, respectively. His first volume of poetry, *Eroding Witness,* was published in 1986 and included the poems from his chapbooks. Considered a postmodern poet, Mackey alluded in his early poems to a variety of literary, musical, and cultural referents. Also in 1986, he published *Bedouin Hornbook,* the first volume in a serialized work titled *From a Broken Bottle Traces of Perfume Still Emanate.*

Written as an epistolary novel, *Bedouin Hornbook* introduces the character of N., a poet-musician who writes letters to the Angel of Dust that document the substance and progress of his jazz ensemble, the Mystic Horn Society. In *Djbot Baghostus's Run* (1993) and *Atet A.D.* (2001), Mackey continues N.'s correspondence with the Angel of Dust. In a unique and imaginative fashion, Mackey infuses each volume of *From a Broken Bottle Traces of Perfume Still Emanate* with social and philosophical commentary that attempts to subvert or eliminate the boundary between music and language.

Apart from his *From a Broken Bottle* series, and several collections of poetry, which include the volumes *Outlantish* (1992), *School of Udhra* (1993), *Song of the Andoumboulou* (1994), which he continues to expand in installments, and *Whatsaid Serif* (1998), Mackay has also written a collection of literary criticism, *Discrepant Engagement: Dissonance, Cross-Culturality, and Experimental Writing,* published by Cambridge University Press in 1993, that contains essays on a wide range of African-American, Caribbean, and avant-garde authors and poets addressing commonalities among writers of disparate ethnic and stylistic backgrounds. In 1995 Mackey released a compact disc of selected poems from *Song of the Andoumboulou* titled *Strik,* on which jazz musicians Royal Hartigan and Hafez Modirzadeh provide accompaniment. Mackey is also coeditor of *Moment's Notice: Jazz in Poetry and Prose* (1993) and editor of the literary journal *Hambone.*

Further Reading

Gates, Henry Louis, Jr., and Nellie McKay, eds. *The Norton Anthology of African American Literature.* New York: W. W. Norton, 1997.

Mackey, Nathaniel. *Atet A.D.* San Francisco: City Lights Books, 2001.

———. *Discrepant Engagement: Dissonance, Cross-Culturality, and Experimental Writing.* New York: Cambridge University Press, 1993.

O'Leary, Peter. "An Interview with Nathaniel Mackey." *Chicago Review* 43 (1997): 30–46.

Madhubuti, Haki R.
(Donald Luther Lee, Don L. Lee)
(1942–   ) *poet, essayist, editor, educator*

A principal voice among the poets of the Black Arts Movement in the 1960s and 1970s, Haki R. Madhubuti has remained one of the most militant proponents of black cultural nationalism in America. "I use my writing as a weapon," Madhubuti wrote in a 1978 essay, "offensively and defensively, to help raise the consciousness of myself and my people." A prolific poet, essayist, and editor, Madhubuti also founded the successful Third World Press, through which he has promoted the works of black authors for more than three decades.

Haki R. Madhubuti was born Donald Luther Lee in Little Rock, Arkansas, on February 23, 1942, to Jimmy and Maxine Lee, but he and his sister grew up principally in Detroit. When his father abandoned the family, Madhubuti found work at the age of 10 to help support his family. From his mother, Madhubuti acquired a love of literature and music; her death, when he was 16, left a deep void. "At her death," he recalled, "it was almost too hard to cry." Madhubuti moved to Chicago to live with an aunt. There, he attended Dunbar Vocational High School, Wilson Junior College, and Roosevelt University prior to his enlistment in the army at the age of 18.

During his time in the army, Madhubuti read avidly and developed an interest in writing. After his discharge, he returned to Chicago and supported himself with a succession of odd jobs. In 1967 he wrote his first collection of poems, *Think Black!,* and privately printed 1,000 copies. After selling more than 600 copies at elevated railway stations throughout Chicago, Madhubuti decided to pursue writing full time.

At a poetry workshop in 1967, Madhubuti met poet GWENDOLYN BROOKS, who remained an important source of inspiration for him until her death in 2000, and Dudley Randall, a poet and publisher whose Broadside Press released Madhubuti's next four volumes of poetry: *Black Pride* (1968), *Don't Cry, Scream* (1969), *We Walk the Way of the New World* (1970), and *Directionscore: New and Selected Poems* (1971). Madhubuti's early poetry captured the emotions and language of the disenfranchised among African-American urban communities, and typically exhibited unconventional structures and syntax. Until 1973 Madhubuti published under his birth name, Don L. Lee. Reflecting his increasing commitment to the Black Arts Movement, he adopted the name Haki R. Madhubuti, a Swahili name of several meanings, including "justice," "awakening," and "precision."

Madhubuti cofounded the Third World Press in 1967 with poet CAROLYN M. RODGERS and Johari Amini, both of whom he had met in Gwendolyn Brooks's poetry workshop. A first step toward what Madhubuti called "institution building" for black Americans, the press provided an alternative for black authors whose works were routinely rejected by mainstream, white-owned presses. Madhubuti published *Book of Life* in 1973, his first work of poetry published by Third World Press, and the first under his newly adopted name. In later works such as *Earthquakes and Sunrise Missions: Poetry and Essays of Black Renewal, 1973–1983* (1984); *Killing Memory, Seeking Ancestors* (1987); *Groundwork: New and Selected Poems by Don L. Lee/Haki R. Madhubuti, 1966–1996* (1996); and *Heartlove: Wedding and Love Poems* (1998), Madhubuti displayed an increasingly versatile range of themes as a poet, informed by a keen political sense and an innovative structural approach.

Madhubuti extended the scope of his institution building to the area of education with the founding of the Institute of Positive Education in 1969 and the New Concept Development Center in 1972, both of which sought to create a new cultural framework for African-American education. As his writing career gained momentum in the late 1960s and 1970s, Madhubuti began to devote himself to political and Pan-African causes. He participated in the First Pan-African Festival in Algiers (1969) and the Sixth Pan-African Congress in Dar es Saalam, Tanzania (1974). At the invitation of the Senegalese government in 1976, Madhubuti participated in Encounter: African World Alternatives. In collaboration with poet LARRY NEAL, one of the early architects of the Black Arts Movement, Madhubuti founded the *Black Books Review* (BBR) in 1971. Published for eight years, *BBR* was one of the earliest reviews devoted exclusively to the works of black authors.

Known particularly for his unconventional and emotionally charged poetry, Madhubuti has also published numerous collections of essays, including *Dynamite Voices: Black Poets of the 1960s* (1971); *From Plan to Planet, Life Studies: The Need for Afrikan Minds and Institutions* (1973); and the influential *Enemies: The Clash of Races* (1978). Like his poetry, Madhubuti's essays affirmed the strength and beauty of African-American life and culture, and they exhorted the African-American community to support independent black institutions of education, business, and creative expression. *Black Men: Obsolete, Single, and Dangerous?* (1990), a groundbreaking work that combined nonfiction, poetry, and statistical data, won the American Book Award in 1991. Madhubuti's other nonfiction works include *Claiming Earth: Race, Rage, Rape, Redemption; Blacks Seeking a Culture of Enlightened Empowerment* (1994) and *Tough Notes: Letters to Young Black Men* (2002).

Madhubuti received a master's degree from the Iowa Writers Workshop at the University of Iowa in 1984 and joined the faculty of Chicago State University (CSU) as a professor of English. He was later appointed director of CSU's Gwendolyn Brooks Center. Madhubuti has also lectured widely in the United States, Europe, South America, and Africa. In addition to his prolific career as a poet and essayist, Madhubuti has edited numerous anthologies of poetry and essays, including *Say That the River Turns: The Impact of Gwendolyn Brooks* (1987), *Why L.A. Happened: Implications of the 1992 Los Angeles Rebellion* (1993), and *Million Man March/Day of Absence: A Commemorative Anthology* (1996).

Haki R. Madhubuti has described his artistic vision as an extension of his political self and as a means of empowering African Americans to resist the social, political, and artistic limitations created by racial prejudice. "Black artists are cultural stabilizers," Madhubuti wrote in his introduction to *Think Black*, "bringing back old values, and introducing new ones." With such poets as AMIRI BARAKA and SONIA SANCHEZ, Madhubuti was an influential figure in the Black Arts Movement; and in the decades that followed, he has remained committed to the preservation of a uniquely black aesthetic in contemporary African-American literature.

Further Reading

Hill, Patricia Liggins, ed. *Call and Response: The Riverside Anthology of the African American Literary Tradition.* Boston: Houghton Mifflin Co., 1998.

Louden, Michael. "Haki R. Madhubuti." *Critical Survey of Poetry.* Hackensack, N.J.: Salem Press, 2002, pp. 2439–2448.

Madhubuti, Haki R. *Groundwork: New and Selected Poems by Don L. Lee/Haki R. Madhubuti, 1966–1996.* Detroit, Mich.: Third World Press, 1996.

Major, Clarence (Clarence Lee Major)

(1936–   ) *poet, novelist, essayist, short story writer, editor, educator*

Often described as a postmodern author in the tradition of Donald Barthelme and Thomas Pynchon, Clarence Major is best known for the ambiguous narrative structures and fragmented imagery of his novels, poetry, and short fiction. His stories and essays have appeared in more than 100 literary journals and anthologies in the United States, Europe, South America, and Africa. The recipient of numerous literary awards, Major received a Pushcart Prize for short fiction in 1989 and a nomination for the National Book Award for poetry in 1999.

Clarence Lee Major was born on December 31, 1936, in Atlanta, Georgia, to Clarence and Inez Major. Though he retained a deep connection to the South, Major grew up in Chicago, Illinois, where he moved with his mother following the divorce of his parents. An avid reader during childhood, Major read widely among African-American, American, and European authors; but his first creative interest was painting. "Before my first clear memories, I was drawing and painting," he wrote in a 1989 essay, "while the writing started at a time within memory."

Major's discovery of modern art at the Art Institute of Chicago, where he studied briefly as a teenager, had a profound impact on his creative development as a visual and literary artist. In the works of Paul Cézanne, Edvard Munch, and Vincent Van Gogh, all of whom transcended the artistic norms of their day, Major found models for his burgeoning creative vision.

Major's career as a writer began inauspiciously with the publication of *The Fires That Burn in Heaven* (1954), a 12-page pamphlet of what he later described as "very, very bad poetry." He served two years in the U.S. Air Force from 1955 to 1957, during which he continued to hone his skills as a poet. Following his discharge, Major returned to Chicago and married Joyce Sparrow. In 1958 Major edited and published the *Coercion Review,* a forum that allowed him to further develop his poetic style and brought him into contact with such experimental poets as William Carlos Williams, Allen Ginsberg, and Robert Creeley.

After his marriage ended in 1964, Major moved to Omaha, Nebraska, and published two mimeographed collections of poetry, *Love Poems of a Black Man* (1965) and *Human Juices* (1966), with the small Coercion Press. Major moved to New York City's Lower East Side in 1966 and worked as a writing instructor at the New Lincoln School and Macomb Junior High School. After completing his bachelor's degree at the State University of New York in Albany, Major held successive teaching posts at Brooklyn College, Sarah Lawrence College, Howard University, and the University of Colorado in Boulder. Though he never envisioned a career as an academic, Major completed his Ph.D. at Union Graduate School in Ohio in 1978 and joined the faculty of the University of California at Davis as a professor of English in 1981, where he later served as the chair of the creative writing department.

Major achieved his earliest critical success as a writer with the publication of his first novel, *All Night Visitors* (1969), which also created controversy over Major's use of explicit sexual themes and situations. The novel depicts the life of an African-American Vietnam War veteran, Eli Bolton, whose struggle for greater self-awareness is defined by his insatiable need for sexual gratification. The search for personal meaning and identity in a chaotic and fragmented universe featured prominently in Major's subsequent novels: *No* (1973), *Reflex and Bone Structure* (1975), *Emergency Exit* (1979), *My Amputations* (1986), *Such Was the Season* (1987), *Painted Turtle: Woman with Guitar* (1988), and *Dirty Bird Blues* (1996).

With the publication of *Swallow the River* (1970), a collection of poems that included several previously published works, Major established himself as an influential and innovative figure in the Black Arts Movement. His celebrated literary anthology, *The New Black Poetry* (1969), collected works by such renowned Black Arts poets as AMIRI BARAKA, SONIA SANCHEZ, and NIKKI GIOVANNI.

Major increased his visibility as a poet with the publication of *Private Line* (1971), *Symptoms and Madness* (1971), *The Cotton Club: New Poems* (1972), and *The Syncopated Cakewalk* (1974). Though his literary reputation rests primarily on his novels, Major earned a Pushcart Prize for his 1976 poem "Funeral" and a National Book Award nomination for *Configurations: New and Selected Poems, 1958–1998* (1999). *Waiting for Sweet Betty*, published in 2002, also earned wide acclaim for its compelling visual imagery and its subtle explorations of race and identity.

Major's poetry and fiction, particularly his novels, explore the limits of written language. By incorporating elements of visual art and experimenting with traditional narrative and plot devices, Major creates a unique fictional universe. "Most of Major's fiction," one critic has noted, "unfolds as a bewildering array of discrete bits of visual imagery, fragments of contradictory plot elements, different voices, and reflexive ruminations about fiction."

Major has also published two collections of essays, *The Dark and Feeling: Black American Writers and Their Work* (1974) and *Necessary Distance: Essays and Criticism* (2001); a collection of short stories, *Fun and Games* (1990); a lexicon, *Dictionary of Afro-American Slang* (1970), later revised and expanded as *Juba to Jive: A Dictionary of African-American Slang* (1994); and a biography of his mother, *Come by Here: My Mother's Life* (2002).

A prolific author and one of the most respected figures in contemporary African-American literature, Clarence Major has consistently challenged the cultural and artistic limitations placed on African Americans by a society whose prejudices contribute to a flawed and fragmented social reality. Major has also expressed his unique perspective on American and African-American life in his extensive catalog of original paintings, which have appeared in traveling exhibits throughout the United States.

Further Reading

Bell, Bernard W., ed. *Clarence Major and His Art: Portraits of an African American Postmodernist.* Chapel Hill: University of North Carolina Press, 2001.

Bunge, Nancy, ed. *Conversations with Clarence Major.* Jackson: University Press of Mississippi, 2002.

Major, Clarence. *Configurations: New and Selected Poems, 1958–1998.* Port Townsend, Wash.: Copper Canyon Press, 1998.

Marshall, Paule
(Valenza Pauline Burke)
(1929–) *novelist, short story writer, journalist, essayist, educator*

The daughter of West Indian immigrants, Paule Marshall has earned wide acclaim for her depictions of African-Caribbean life and communities in the United States and the unique social and racial challenges confronted by individuals throughout the African diaspora. Marshall's numerous literary honors include an American Book Award, the Rosenthal Award from the National Institute of Arts and Letters, and grants from the Guggenheim Foundation and the National Endowment for the Arts.

Paule Marshall was born Valenza Pauline Burke on April 9, 1929, in Brooklyn, New York, the daughter of West Indian immigrants Samuel and Ada Burke. Marshall read voraciously as a child among black and white authors; but as she matured, she perceived a lack of authentic female voices in American and African-American literature, the kind of voices she heard around her kitchen table as her mother entertained other West Indian women from her neighborhood. "They taught me my first lessons in narrative art," Marshall wrote of her early motivation toward writing. "This is why the best of my work must be attributed to them; it stands as a testimony to the rich legacy of language and culture they so freely passed on to me in the wordshop of the kitchen."

Marshall graduated Phi Beta Kappa from Brooklyn College in 1953 and found work as a staff writer for *Our World,* which occasioned extensive travel in the West Indies and Brazil. She also began work on her first novel. She married Kenneth Marshall in 1957, with whom she had a son, Eran-Keith, and *Brown Girl, Brownstones,* her best-known novel, was published two years later. The novel depicts the life of a young Afro-Caribbean woman, Selina Boyce, whose personal search for identity and acceptance as a black woman and a West Indian immigrant is further complicated by family discord.

In *Soul Clap Hands and Sing* (1961), her first collection of short fiction, Marshall explores the lives of four black men in four different settings (Barbados, Brooklyn, Guyana, and Brazil), none of whom have fulfilled their life's potential and who feel cut off from their cultural heritage. *Soul Clap Hands and Sing* earned Marshall the Rosenthal Award from the National Institute of Arts and Letters in 1962. *The Chosen Place, the Timeless People* (1969), Marshall's second novel, is a complex study of race and identity set on a fictional island in the West Indies.

Marshall's first marriage ended in 1963. In 1970 Marshall married Nourry Menard, a Haitian businessman, and divided her time between New York and Haiti. In addition to writing, Marshall held teaching positions at several universities throughout the United States. A lecturer at the University of Massachusetts in Boston, Columbia University, and Yale University during the 1970s, Marshall also taught at the University of Iowa's Writers' Workshop in 1983 and served as Regents Professor at the University of California at Berkeley in 1984 and professor of English and creative writing at Virginia Commonwealth University from 1987 until the mid–1990s. A growing force in the burgeoning feminist movement of the 1970s, Marshall was the keynote speaker at numerous conferences and events.

After a long hiatus, during which she traveled extensively in the African nations of Nigeria, Kenya, and Uganda, Marshall published one of her most critically acclaimed works, *Praisesong for the Widow* (1983), in which a middle-aged African-American widow, Avey Johnson, rediscovers her cultural heritage during a cruise in the Caribbean. The reclaiming of one's cultural past, notably in the face of lingering colonial mentalities and the racially oppressive atmosphere of surrogate homelands, is a dominant theme in all of Marshall's fiction. Her other works include *Reena and Other Stories* (1983), reprinted in 1985 as *Merle: A Novella and Other Stories* (1985); and two novels, *Daughters* (1991) and *The Fisher King* (2000).

Throughout her career as an author and educator, Paule Marshall has used her considerable talents as a storyteller and cultural critic to illuminate the lives of African-American and African-Caribbean women. Many scholars have been slow to recognize the significance of her contributions to the African-American literary tradition; Marshall's celebrated first novel, *Brown Girl, Brownstones,* now considered a classic of African-American and feminist literature, was largely overlooked until more than a decade after its initial publication. Fellow authors such as TONI MORRISON and ALICE WALKER, however, have acknowledged their debt to Marshall's influence as an author.

Further Reading

Coser, Stelamaris. *Bridging the Americas: The Literature of Paule Marshall, Toni Morrison, and Gayl Jones.* Philadelphia: Temple University Press, 1995.

Denniston, Dorothy Hamer. *The Fiction of Paule Marshall: Reconstructions of History, Culture, and Gender.* Knoxville: University of Tennessee Press, 1995.

Marshall, Paule. *Brown Girl, Brownstones.* New York: Random House, 1959.

———. *Praisesong for the Widow.* New York: Putnam, 1983.

Matthews, Victoria Earle
(Victoria Earle)
(1861–1907) *journalist, short story writer, social activist*

A journalist, writer, and social activist, Victoria Earle Matthews devoted most of her life to the cause of racial and gender equality for African-American women. She distinguished herself as an accomplished journalist, orator, and social leader for the growing community of African Americans who fled the South at the end of the 19th century to search for a better life in New York.

Born Victoria Earle in Fort Valley, Georgia, in 1861 to a slave named Caroline Smith, she spent the early years of her life without her mother. Caroline fled Georgia for New York City to escape the abuse of her master, who is thought to have been Victoria's father. Caroline returned eight years later and gained custody of her two children, returning with them to New York in 1873.

Victoria showed early promise as a student, but she soon left school to work as a domestic. In that capacity, she gained access to the libraries of her employers and began to educate herself. At the age of 18, having married William Matthews and given birth to a son, Lamartine, she began her long and celebrated career in journalism as a junior reporter for the *New York Times*, the *Herald*, and the *Sunday Mercury*. She also served as a correspondent for several African-American newspapers, including the *Boston Advocate* and the *New York Globe*.

In addition to her newspaper articles, Matthews also wrote children's stories and the short story "Aunt Lindy," published in 1893. Aunt Lindy, an ex-slave, discovers that an injured stranger in her care is in fact her former master. Consumed briefly with a murderous rage, she overcomes her temptation to harm the man who had caused her so many years of suffering and who separated her from her children.

Following the death of her son, Lamartine, at the age of 16, Matthews devoted her time increasingly to social causes. In 1892 she founded the Women's Loyal Union, and three years later, she helped found the National Federation of Afro-American Women. She also continued to write, publishing an essay, "The Value of Race Literature," wherein she details the need for black authors to correct negative portraits of African Americans in white literature. She describes the woman's role in this process as "the most important part . . . It is for her to receive impressions and transmit them." Many African-American authors, from ZORA NEALE HURSTON to TONI MORRISON, have recognized and written about the role of women as the keepers of family history and folklore.

In 1897 Matthews established the White Rose Industrial Association, which trained young African-American women newly arrived in New York City for domestic service and taught them about their cultural roots. Prior to founding the White Rose, Matthews had written investigative articles about fraudulent employment agencies that preyed on young women new to the city, luring them into urban prostitution rings. She used the White Rose to combat these crimes and to teach women self-sufficiency by giving them practical job skills in much the same way that BOOKER T. WASHINGTON was doing on a larger scale at the Tuskegee Institute. His influence on her thought was considerable, and she even edited a collection of his speeches, published in *Black Belt Diamonds* in 1898.

Victoria Earle Matthews died on March 10, 1907, having devoted almost 30 years to public service as a journalist, author, and activist. She encouraged African-American women to find their voice and release their "suppressed inner lives" in print, as she wrote in "The Value of Race Literature." She advocated a literature that addressed the needs and experiences of African Americans, an idea that would gain greater momentum during the Harlem Renaissance in the decades following her death.

Further Reading

Matthews, Victoria Earle. "The Awakening of the Afro-American Woman." In *With Pen and Voice: A Critical Anthology of Nineteenth-Century African-American Women,* edited by Shirley Wilson Logan. Carbondale: Southern Illinois University Press, 1995, pp. 1–4.

———. "The Value of Race Literature: An Address." *The Massachusetts Review* 27, no. 2 (1986): 169–191.

Andrews, William L., Frances Smith Foster, and Trudier Harris, eds. *The Concise Oxford Companion to African American Literature.* New York: Oxford University Press, 2001.

McElroy, Colleen
(Colleen Johnson)
(1935–   ) *poet, short fiction writer, autobiographer*

Educated as a linguist and speech therapist, Colleen McElroy began writing poetry in her mid-30s. Critics have praised her ability to capture in vivid and evocative detail the people and places that populate her poetry, short fiction, and memoirs. McElroy has been awarded numerous literary prizes and fellowships, including an American Book Award, a Pushcart Prize, and fellowships from the National Endowment for the Arts and the Rockefeller Foundation.

Colleen McElroy was born Colleen Johnson on October 30, 1935, in St. Louis, Missouri, to Purcia and Ruth Rawls. Johnson's parents divorced when she was three, and she and her mother spent the next five years living with her maternal grandmother. In 1943 her mother married Jesse Dalton Johnson, an army sergeant, and the family lived for the next several years in Missouri, Wyoming, and Munich, Germany. Johnson attended the University of Maryland and Harris Teachers College before receiving her bachelor's (1958) and master's (1963) degrees from Kansas State University, where she studied neurological and language learning patterns.

In 1968 Johnson married David F. McElroy, a writer, with whom she had two children. After the two were divorced, McElroy relocated to the Pacific Northwest, accepting a position as director of Speech and Hearing Services at Western Washington University in 1970. She completed her education at the University of Washington with a Ph.D. in 1973 and joined the faculty as a professor of English and creative writing. At this time, with the encouragement of poets Richard Hugo and Denise Levertov, McElroy began to publish poetry.

McElroy's early poems appeared in the chapbook *The Mules Done Long Since Gone* (1973) and *Music from Home: Selected Poems* (1976). Influenced by the works of other celebrated black authors, including LANGSTON HUGHES, GWENDOLYN BROOKS, and MARGARET WALKER, McElroy explored the inner struggles and aspirations of African Americans as well as the physical landscape of her beloved Pacific Northwest. *Winter without Snow* (1979), an intensely personal portrait of her life, documented her painful divorce from David McElroy.

In *Looking for a Country under Its Original Name* (1985) and *Queen of the Ebony Isles* (1985), McElroy continued to explore the personal and artistic dimensions of her life and documented her extensive travels in Latin America during the early 1980s. *Queen of the Ebony Isles* earned an American Book Award in 1985. McElroy expanded the creative scope of her poetry in her later collections, which include *Blue Flames* (1989), *What Madness Brought Me Here: New and*

Selected Poems, 1968–1988 (1990), and *Travelling Music* (1998).

Perhaps best known for her poetry, McElroy has also published two collections of short fiction: *Jesus and Fat Tuesday and Other Short Stories* (1987) and *Driving under Cardboard Pines* (1990). She also collaborated with ISHMAEL REED on the choreopoem *The Wild Gardens of the Loup Garou* (1982), a dramatic piece that incorporates music and dance, and a children's drama, *Follow the Drinking Gourd* (1987), about the life of Harriet Tubman. In 1997 McElroy published a poetic memoir, *A Long Way from St. Louie,* a personal and compelling portrait of her experiences during a lifetime of travel in the United States, Europe, Australia, and Africa. *Over the Lip of the World: Among the Storytellers of Madagascar* (1999) highlights McElroy's graduate training as a linguist in her documentation of the oral traditions and cultural history of Madagascar, an island off the southeastern coast of Africa.

In her poetry, short fiction, memoirs, and drama, Colleen McElroy has forged a unique combination of personal history, cultural investigation, and a powerful sense of place. Like her travels among the different cultures of the world, McElroy's writing also exhibits a sense of creative exploration. "Each piece of writing is a new port of call," she has explained, "full of surprises and disappointments, pleasures and intrigue." McElroy's poetry, fiction, and essays have appeared in dozens of literary anthologies and periodicals, including the *Pushcart Prize: Best of the Small Presses* (1975).

Further Reading

Gates, Henry Louis, Jr., and Nellie Y. McKay, eds. *The Norton Anthology of African American Literature.* New York: W. W. Norton, 1997.

McElroy, Colleen. *Over the Lip of the World: Among the Storytellers of Madagascar.* Seattle: University of Washington Press, 1999.

———. *What Madness Brought Me Here: New and Selected Poems, 1968–1988.* Hanover, N.H.: University Press of New England, 1990.

McKay, Claude
(Festus Claudius McKay, Eli Edwards)
(1889–1948) poet, novelist, short story writer, autobiographer, essayist, editor

A celebrated and controversial poet and novelist during the Harlem Renaissance, Claude McKay distinguished himself from many of his contemporaries with his focus on social and political militancy and his lyrical depictions of lower- and working-class Harlem society. McKay's passionate resistance to the social and cultural domination of African-American society and the overtly political nature of his writing influenced many leading Harlem Renaissance authors, including LANGSTON HUGHES and RICHARD WRIGHT, and McKay has been hailed as a precursor to the Negritude and Black Nationalist movements that flourished during the civil rights era.

Claude McKay was born Festus Claudius McKay to peasant farmers Thomas and Anne McKay in Sunny Ville, Clarendon Parish, Jamaica, in 1889. As a child, McKay lived with and was educated by his brother, Uriah Theodore McKay, a schoolteacher. McKay studied classical and British literature and philosophy, and his brother encouraged him to write poetry. In 1907 McKay met a British expatriate, Walter Jekyll, who convinced him to explore Jamaica's rich folk traditions and experiment with dialect poetry.

McKay left school to work as a constable in Kingston and to write. With the assistance of Walter Jekyll, McKay published his first two collections of poetry, *Songs of Jamaica* and *Constab Ballads,* both in 1912. Later that year, McKay immigrated to the United States to study agriculture. He attended Tuskegee Institute and Kansas State College before discontinuing his studies in 1914 to pursue a literary career. In 1917 he published two poems in the literary journal *Seven Arts* under the pseudonym Eli Edwards. After discovering McKay's identity, Frank Hattis, a literary critic, solicited additional poems for publication in *Pearson's Magazine.* Notable among these was the poem "To the White Fiends," a defiant condemnation of racism in which McKay challenges the bigotry and racial violence of white society. "Be not deceived, for every deed you do / I could match—out-match: am I not Afric's son / Black of that black land where black deeds are done."

In 1919 McKay met Max Eastman, a communist sympathizer and editor of the *Liberator*, a left-wing political and literary journal. Eastman published several of McKay's poems, including one of his most famous, "If We Must Die." Written in the wake of increasing racial violence in Chicago in the summer of 1919, the poem exhorts its readers to withstand their oppressors. "Like men we'll face the murderous, cowardly pack /

Jamaican-born Claude McKay, shown here in the 1930s, was one of the most prominent and militant voices for racial equality in the early years of the Harlem Renaissance. *(Library of Congress)*

Pressed to the wall, dying, but fighting back!" Though written to incite African Americans to stand nobly against racial oppression and violence, the poem has come to speak for oppressed people of all races in their opposition to political and racial tyranny.

With his reputation as a poet on the rise, McKay traveled to England in 1919, where he met several leading British writers, including George Bernard Shaw. Several of McKay's poems were published in the summer issue of *Cambridge Magazine*, edited by C. K. Ogden, in 1920, and the renowned literary critic I. A. Richards contributed the introduction to McKay's third volume of poetry, *Spring in New Hampshire*, published in London in 1920. McKay returned to New York in 1921 and continued to publish his poetry in numerous journals, including Marcus Garvey's *Negro World*. In 1922 McKay published his most acclaimed volume of poetry, *Harlem Shadows*.

Comprising 74 poems, many of which had appeared previously in various literary journals, *Harlem Shadows* explores the bleak landscape of urban life and the particular challenges of poverty and racism that confronted African Americans. In "The Lynching," McKay contrasts the horror of a young black man's death with the exuberance exhibited by his young, white murderers. In "Enslaved" and "Outcast," he focuses on African Americans as displaced and disinherited people. "For I was born," he writes in "Outcast," "far from my native clime / Under the white man's menace, out of time." McKay's exceptional command of the traditional sonnet form, and his contrasting imagery of the harmony of the natural world and the disharmony of a racially biased society, secured his reputation as one of the most accomplished African-American poets since PAUL LAURENCE DUNBAR.

Following the enormous critical and commercial success of *Harlem Shadows*, McKay traveled to Russia in 1922 to attend the Fourth Congress of the Communist International. He enjoyed wide popular support among his Russian hosts, and his poem "Petrograd: May Day, 1923," was published in translation in *Pravda*. Soon growing disenchanted with the limitations on artistic freedom imposed by the Communist Party, McKay moved on to Paris, where he lived for several years, and later visited Spain and northern Africa.

Having established himself as an innovative and successful poet, McKay turned his attention to fiction. His first novel, *Home to Harlem* (1928) became the first book by an African American to become a best-seller, going through five editions in two months. Critics praised its realistic portrait of Harlem and its inhabitants, though some commented on the absence of a well-defined plot. The novel depicts the experiences of its two protagonists, Jake, an army deserter, and Ray, a Haitian immigrant, whose adventures take them into Harlem's gambling houses, cabarets, and brothels. McKay's second novel, *Banjo: A Story without a Plot* (1929), continues the narrative of *Home to Harlem*, with Ray now in Marseilles, France, and in the company of another pleasure-seeker, Banjo. *Banjo* received little critical attention and sold poorly.

In 1932 McKay published *Gingertown*, a collection of 12 short stories set in Harlem, Africa, and Jamaica. Like his previous novel, *Gingertown* inspired little interest. McKay published his third novel, *Banana Bottom*, in 1933. Considered by many critics to be his most mature work of fiction, *Banana Bottom* was praised for its sensitive portrayal of a young Jamaican girl's sexual exploitation and her eventual triumph over adversity. Despite its favorable critical reception, *Banana Bottom* never generated much public interest.

McKay returned to the United States in 1934 and published two more books: an autobiography, *A Long Way from Home* (1937), and *Harlem: Negro Metropolis* (1940), a collection of essays. Suffering from increasingly poor health and feeling the financial pinch of declining book sales, McKay became involved with the Friendship House, a Catholic community center in Harlem. After converting to Catholicism in 1944, he moved to Chicago, Illinois, where he spent the remainder of his life teaching for the Catholic Youth Organization. He also completed a second autobiography, *My Green Hills of Jamaica* (1979) and compiled a collection of poetry, *Selected Poems of Claude McKay* (1953), both published posthumously. Claude McKay died of heart failure on May 22, 1948.

Claude McKay is widely considered to be a major contributor to the artistic and political ideals of the Harlem Renaissance era in African-American literature. Though he lived abroad during the critical years of the movement, his fierce artistic and political independence earned him the respect of young writers, among them Langston Hughes, whose works came to embody the spirit of the New Negro aesthetic. The influential poet and critic WILLIAM BRAITHWAITE considered McKay a potential "keystone of the new movement in racial poetic achievement." McKay was honored posthumously by the Jamaican government, which named him the national poet and awarded him the Order of Jamaica in 1977.

Further Reading

McKay, Claude. *Banana Bottom*. New York: Harvest Books, 1974.
———. *A Fierce Hatred of Injustice: Claude McKay's Jamaican Poetry of Rebellion*. New York: Verso Books, 2001.
———. *Home to Harlem*. Boston: Northeastern University Press, 1987.
Tillery, Tyrone. *Claude McKay: A Black Poet's Struggle for Identity*. Amherst: University of Massachusetts Press, 1994.

McMillan, Terry
(Terry L. McMillan)
(1951–   ) *novelist, screenwriter*

The author of three *New York Times* best-selling novels, Terry McMillan has achieved widespread commercial success for her moving tales of friendship, love, family, and loss among African-

American middle-class women. Her writing, while focused particularly on the lives of African-American women and men, has a broad appeal across racial and gender lines, and three of her novels have been successfully adapted to film.

Terry L. McMillan was born on October 18, 1951, in Port Huron, Michigan, one of five daughters of Edward Louis and Madeline Washington McMillan. Her father's abusive behavior and alcoholism eventually divided the family, and McMillan's parents divorced when she was 13. McMillan and her sisters lived with their mother, who worked as a domestic and an autoworker to provide for her family. In 1979 McMillan graduated from the University of California at Berkeley with a degree in journalism and later moved to New York to study film at Columbia University.

In her youth McMillan showed little interest in literature until she began working in a library at the age of 16. There, she discovered the works of James Baldwin, the Brontë sisters, and Louisa May Alcott. Her first work of fiction, the short story "The End," was published while she was an undergraduate at Berkeley. While studying at Columbia University, she joined a writing workshop at the Harlem Writers Guild and began to consider pursuing a career as a writer.

During the early 1980s, McMillan divided her time between caring for her son, Solomon, born in 1983, whom she raised as a single parent, and writing. Her first novel, *Mama,* was published in 1987, and McMillan engaged in an aggressive campaign to promote the book in the face of what she saw as relative indifference on the part of her publisher. She sent letters to black organizations, schools, and bookstores, and received numerous offers for public readings. Drawing on her own memories as a child, McMillan recreated the turbulence of her early family life in *Mama,* which depicts the life of Mildred Peacock, a fiercely independent woman who divorces her abusive alcoholic husband and struggles alone to rear her five children. McMillan received the American Book Award for *Mama* in 1987.

With the publication of her second novel, *Disappearing Acts* (1989), McMillan established herself as a bankable literary star. A compelling exploration of the joys and pitfalls of modern relationships, the novel presents two alternating perspectives on a star-crossed romance between Zora Banks, an educated and ambitious professional woman, and Franklin Swift, an uneducated construction worker with a fear of commitment. A critical and commercial success, *Disappearing Acts* was optioned by Home Box Office (HBO) and produced in 2001.

McMillan continued to examine the professional and romantic aspirations of middle-class, professional black women in *Waiting to Exhale* (1992) and *How Stella Got Her Groove Back* (1996), both of which became best-sellers as well as commercially successful film adaptations. *Waiting to Exhale* documented the lives and loves of four African-American women, whose strong bond of friendship allows each to overcome personal tragedy and heartbreak. *How Stella Got Her Groove Back* depicted a wealthy African-American professional woman's search for personal and romantic fulfillment with a Jamaican man who is 22 years her junior. *Waiting to Exhale* was adapted by McMillan and Ronald Bass for Home Box Office in 2001. In 1998 McMillan collaborated again with Ronald Bass on the screenplay for *How Stella Got Her Groove Back,* which starred Angela Bassett, Taye Diggs, and Whoopi Goldberg.

A testament to her growing success as an author, McMillan's fifth novel, *A Day Late and a Dollar Short* (2001), topped the *New York Times* best-seller list after only two weeks. A multigenerational tale of the extended family of Viola and Cecil Price, the novel features a complex narrative from the perspective of multiple family members about the challenges of marriage, family, and parenting.

McMillan edited *Breaking Ice: An Anthology of Contemporary African-American Fiction* (1990) and contributed to *Five for Five: The Films of Spike Lee* (1991). She has also held teaching positions at the University of Wyoming (1987–90) and the University of Arizona (1990–92). In 1998 McMillan married Jonathan Plummer, a younger man whom she had met during a Jamaican vacation, and settled in northern California.

The enormous commercial success of Terry McMillan's novels and film adaptations have led some to speculate that her triumph with *Waiting to Exhale* in 1992, which sold 700,000 copies in hardcover and millions more in paperback editions, revolutionized the publishing industry in terms of opportunities for popular fiction aimed at African-American audiences. While recognizing her accomplishments as an author, McMillan objects to the assertion that she has singlehandedly transformed the status of black women authors. "Many people came before me who had a lot to do with this—the ALICE WALKERs and TONI MORRISONs—women who I really admire and who paved the way for me," she explained in a 2001 interview with *Ebony* magazine.

Further Reading

Hill, Patricia Liggins, ed. *Call and Response: The Riverside Anthology of the African American Tradition.* Boston: Houghton Mifflin Co., 1998.

McMillan, Terry. *A Day Late and a Dollar Short.* New York: Viking Press, 2001.

———. *Waiting to Exhale.* New York: Viking Press, 1992.

Whitaker, Charles. "Exhaling!" *Ebony*, April 2001, p. 154.

McPherson, James Alan

(1943–) *short story writer, essayist, autobiographer, editor, educator*

Short fiction writer and essayist James Alan McPherson was the first African-American writer to win the Pulitzer Prize for fiction, awarded for his short story collection *Elbow Room* (1978). His stories and essays have appeared in numerous periodicals, including the *Harvard Advocate,* the *New York Times Magazine, Ploughshares,* and the *Atlantic Monthly,* where he has been a regular contributor since 1969. The recipient of several prestigious literary fellowships, McPherson is also a distinguished professor at the University of Iowa's Writers' Workshop.

James Alan McPherson was born on September 16, 1943, to James and Mable McPherson, in Savannah, Georgia. "I grew up in a segregated world," McPherson said of his childhood in a 2002 interview. "I tried to keep my imagination alive by reading." McPherson attended Morgan State University and finished his bachelor's degree at Morris Brown College in 1965. He also earned a bachelor of laws (LL.B.) degree from Harvard University (1968) and a master of fine arts (M.F.A.) degree from the University of Iowa (1971). His first short story, "Gold Coast," published in the *Atlantic Monthly* in 1968, won a fiction award as the best story to appear in the magazine in 1968. "Gold Coast" was later included by John Updike in *The Best Short Stories of the Century* (1999).

In 1969 McPherson published *Hue and Cry,* a widely acclaimed collection of 10 short stories. Like "Gold Coast," which is included in the volume, the stories in *Hue and Cry* often portray characters who are separated by generational and racial divides that are ultimately unbridgeable. While concerned with issues of race in his stories, McPherson prefers to focus on characters whose problems are universal. "Certain of these people happen to be black, and certain of them happen to be white," explains McPherson, "but I have tried to keep the color part of them far in the background, where these things should rightly be kept."

McPherson's second collection of short stories, *Elbow Room,* was published in 1977 and won the Pulitzer Prize for fiction in 1978, the first to be awarded to an African American. Also nominated for the National Book Award, *Elbow Room* secured McPherson's reputation as one of the great short fiction writers of the 20th century. In stories marked by subtle humor ("Why I Love Country Music") and despair ("A Loaf of Bread"), McPherson explores racial and cultural dimensions of American life, and concludes, more optimistically than in his previous stories, that the hope for a more equitable society is not a futile one.

Apart from his short story collections, McPherson coedited *Railroad: Trains and Train People in American Culture* (1976, with Miller Williams) and *Fathering Daughters: Reflections by Men* (1998, with DeWitt Henry), and two collections of essays, *Crabcakes: A Memoir* (1998) and *A Region Not Home: Reflections from Exile* (2000). He has taught writing and literature at several universities, including the University of California at Santa Cruz, Harvard University, and the University of Virginia. Since 1981 he has been a faculty member at the University of Iowa's renowned Writers' Workshop. Commended for his brilliant craftsmanship as a writer by his literary mentor, RALPH ELLISON, with whom he cowrote an article for the *Atlantic Monthly*, James Alan McPherson continues to educate new generations of readers with his writing and teaching.

Further Reading

Beavers, Herman. *Wrestling Angels into Song: The Fictions of Ernest J. Gaines and James Alan McPherson*. Philadelphia: University of Pennsylvania Press, 1995.

McPherson, James Alan. *Elbow Room*. New York: Fawcett Books, 1989.

———. *Hue and Cry*. New York: Ecco Press, 2001.

———. *A Region Not Home: Reflections from Exile*. New York: Simon & Schuster, 2000.

Reid, Calvin. "James Alan McPherson: A Theatre of Memory." *Publishers Weekly* 244 (December 15, 1997): 36.

Miller, May
(Mary Millar, May Sullivan)
(1899–1995) *poet, playwright, short story writer, educator*

The most prolific female dramatist of the Harlem Renaissance, May Miller also distinguished herself as a poet and short fiction writer. In addition to her work as a writer, Miller was an accomplished actress with the Howard University Players and

W. E. B. DuBois's Krigwa Players. In her commitment to the African-American theater as a teacher, writer, and performer, Miller played an essential role in defining the direction of African-American drama in the early years of its development.

May Miller was born on January 26, 1899, in Washington, D.C. She was the daughter of Kelly Miller, an esteemed professor of sociology at Howard University, and Annie May Butler. As a child, Miller met many of the leading African-American artists, writers, and activists who frequently visited her father's home. Among them were the famed sociologist and intellectual W. E. B. DuBois, educator BOOKER T. WASHINGTON, and the poets WILLIAM BRAITHWAITE and PAUL LAURENCE DUNBAR.

As a student at Paul Laurence Dunbar High School in Washington, D.C., Miller studied with poet ANGELINA WELD GRIMKÉ. Miller later attended Howard University as a drama major, where she collaborated with the influential scholar ALAIN LOCKE as a member of the theatrical group Howard University Players. Her one-act play *Within the Shadows* was awarded a literary prize from Howard University as an outstanding drama. Following her graduation in 1920, Miller taught speech and drama at Frederick Douglass High School in Baltimore, Maryland, and founded the Negro Little Theatre Movement in Baltimore's junior high schools. Stressing the important role that drama can play in effecting social change, Miller wrote numerous historical dramas that depicted important events in African-American history.

Miller's most prolific years as a playwright occurred during the 1920s and 1930s. *The Bog Guide* (1925) was awarded third place in an annual contest sponsored by the National Urban League's journal *Opportunity*. A year later, she earned honorable mention in *Opportunity* for *A Cuss'd Thing*. Miller's drama, unlike many of her contemporaries, often featured white characters in major roles, and her plays were set in such varied places as Haiti and Africa. She also drew attention to important historical and social issues in her drama. *Stragglers in the Dust* (1930) focused on the contributions of African-American soldiers during World War I, while *Nails and Thorns* (1933) addressed the issue of lynching. It was her contribution of four plays to WILLIS RICHARD-SON's anthology *Negro History, in Thirteen Plays* (1935), however, that brought Miller national recognition as a playwright.

Miller wrote 15 plays, nine of which were staged. Her last, *Freedom's Children on the March* (1943), was performed at that year's Frederick Douglass High School commencement. Miller had married John Sullivan, a high school principal, in 1940. Following her retirement from teaching in 1943, the two settled in Washington, D.C. There she began writing poetry. Her seven volumes of poetry include *Into the Clearing* (1959); *Poems* (1962); *Lyrics of Three Women: Katie Lyle, Maude Rubin, and May Miller* (1964); *Not That Far* (1973); *The Clearing and Beyond* (1974); *Dust of Uncertain Journey* (1975); and *The Ransomed Wait* (1983). She also wrote a book of children's verse, *Halfway to the Sun*, published in 1981. Miller's poems are included in numerous anthologies, and she performed her works at the Smithsonian Institution, the Library of Congress, and at the presidential inauguration of Jimmy Carter. May Miller died in Washington, D.C., on February 8, 1995.

Along with her close friend and fellow playwright GEORGIA DOUGLAS JOHNSON, May Miller was considered one of the greatest dramatists of the Harlem Renaissance. A regular for many years at Johnson's famed S Street Salon in Washington, D.C., Miller was an intimate of such esteemed literary figures as LANGSTON HUGHES, JESSIE RED-MON FAUSET, and ZORA NEALE HURSTON, to name only a few.

Further Reading

Andrews, William L., Frances Smith Foster, and Trudier Harris, eds. *The Concise Oxford Companion to African American Literature.* New York: Oxford University Press, 2001.

Hatch, James V., and Leo Hamalian, eds. *The Roots of African American Theatre.* Detroit: Wayne State University Press, 1991.

Miller, May. *Collected Poems.* East Lansing, Mich.: Lotus Press, 1989.

Morrison, Toni
(Chloe Anthony Wofford)
(1931–   ) novelist, children's fiction writer, playwright, essayist, editor, educator

Few authors, American or African-American, have matched the success of Toni Morrison. The literary and cultural significance of her writings extends well beyond the sphere of American and African-American culture. Morrison has earned the highest national and international honors available to a writer, including the Pulitzer Prize for fiction and the Nobel Prize in literature. In the Swedish Academy's press release announcing her Nobel Prize in 1993, Morrison is praised as an author "who, in novels characterized by visionary force and poetic import, gives life to an essential aspect of American reality."

Toni Morrison was born Chloe Anthony Wofford on February 18, 1931, in Lorain, Ohio, a small steel mill town on Lake Erie, in a mixed racial community that she has described as "neither plantation nor ghetto." By working three jobs simultaneously, including a demanding position as a shipyard welder, Chloe's father, George Wofford, helped his family weather the Great Depression. Chloe grew up in a family of storytellers, hearing the folklore and family history of her parents and grandparents, who left their lives as sharecroppers in Alabama to find a better life in the North.

She learned to read at an early age, and much of her childhood and teenage years was spent reading the classic texts of American and European literature. After graduating from Lorain High School, she completed her bachelor's degree in English at Howard University, in Washington,

D.C., in 1953, and received a master's degree in 1955 from Cornell University, in New York, where she wrote her thesis on the theme of suicide in the works of William Faulkner and Virginia Woolf.

After spending two years as an instructor in English at Texas Southern University, in Houston, she returned to Howard University in 1957 to teach English. There she began to attend a writing workshop with another aspiring writer, GLORIA NAYLOR, and completed a short story about a young African-American girl who wished for blue eyes. (This story would later become the foundation for her first novel.) In 1958 she met and married a Jamaican architect, Harold Morrison, with whom she had two children. When her marriage ended in 1964, Morrison returned briefly to Lorain with her two children before accepting a senior editorial position with Random House in New York, where she helped promote the works of other African-American writers such as TONI CADE BAMBARA and GAYL JONES.

While devoting her days to her job and children, Morrison spent her evenings working on her first novel. In 1970, after many rejections, *The Bluest Eye* was published. Based on Morrison's early short story, the novel chronicled the tragic life of Pecola Breedlove, a young black girl whose lack of self-esteem, reinforced by racism, sexual abuse, and the emotional and physical neglect of her community in Lorain, Ohio, leads her to self-loathing and madness. In the spirit of ZORA NEALE HURSTON's *Their Eyes Were Watching God* (1937) and PAULE MARSHALL's *Brown Girl, Brownstones* (1959), *The Bluest Eye* emphasized how racism can subvert the identity of individuals and communities by upholding false cultural standards, symbolized by Pecola's obsessive desire for blue eyes. The novel received generally positive reviews.

Morrison established herself as a major new voice in American and African-American literature with *Sula* (1973), for which she received a National Book Award nomination. Set in a small community of Medallion, Ohio, known as "the Bottom," *Sula* depicts the turbulent relationship between two friends, Sula Peace and Nel Wright, whose contrasting natures illustrate the complexity and richness of African-American life, particularly in the relationships between women. While Nel embraces a conventional life of marriage, children, and social responsibility, Sula adopts a more unconventional and rebellious attitude toward life. Morrison has said of Sula and Nel that "the two of them together could have made a wonderful single human being."

Morrison continued to earn wide critical and popular acclaim with her next two novels. *Song of Solomon* (1977), Morrison's first novel to feature a male protagonist, tells the story of Macon "Milkman" Dead's rediscovery of his cultural heritage through his connection to ancestors, particularly his aunt, who serves as a spiritual and familial guide. The novel, which won the National Book Critics Circle Award, is rich in supernatural and mythic imagery, characteristics that would increasingly characterize Morrison's fiction. In *Tar Baby* (1981), Morrison charts the painful transformation of Jadine Childs from an aspiring model and well-educated professional woman, whose personal and racial identity have been stifled by cultural and familial forces, to an individualized and independent woman who chooses to face life on her own terms.

In 1987 Morrison published her best-known novel, *Beloved,* for which she received the Pulitzer Prize for fiction. Based on a true story of a slave, Margaret Garner, who murdered one of her children rather than have her sold into slavery, *Beloved* is set in rural Ohio in the years following the American Civil War. The novel chronicles the life of a former slave, Sethe, who reunites with the ghost of Beloved, the daughter she killed years earlier instead of allowing her to be sold into slavery. Unlike traditional slave narratives, *Beloved* articulated explicitly the unparalleled horrors of life under slavery for Sethe and her family, while also demonstrating the haunting legacy of slavery for all African Americans. In 1998 *Beloved* was adapted to the screen in a successful film that starred Oprah Winfrey and Danny Glover.

When *Beloved* won neither the National Book Award nor the National Book Critics Circle Award, several contemporary African-American authors, including MAYA ANGELOU, ALICE WALKER, and JOHN EDGAR WIDEMAN, signed a letter to the editor of the *New York Times*, which concluded with a tribute to Morrison that illustrated her considerable influence on her contemporaries. "For all of America, for all of American letters," the tribute read, "you have advanced the moral and artistic standards by which we must measure the daring and the love of our national imagination and our collective intelligence as a people."

By 1992 Morrison had achieved great success as an author of several best-selling novels and the recipient of a Pulitzer Prize. She continued to explore her unique vision of African-American life in her sixth novel, *Jazz* (1992), the story of Joe Trace, a 50-year-old married man who "fell for an eighteen-year-old girl with one of those deepdown, spooky loves that made him so sad and happy he shot her just to keep the feeling going." Morrison also wrote *Playing in the Dark: Whiteness and the Literary Imagination* (1992), a collection of literary criticism, and she edited *Race-ing Justice, Engendering Power: Essays on Anita Hill, Clarence Thomas, and the Construction of Social Reality* (1992).

In 1994 Morrison achieved what no other African American has accomplished: She won the Nobel Prize in literature. In her lecture to the Swedish Academy upon receiving the award, which was subsequently published as *The Dancing Mind* (1997), Morrison described the importance of language to her life and work in the context of a fable about an old, wise, and blind woman. "Word-work is sublime, she thinks, because it is generative; it makes meaning that secures our difference, our human difference—the way in which we are like no other." The old woman continues her meditation on language: "We die. That may be the meaning of life. But we do language. That may be the measure of our lives."

Morrison published her seventh novel, *Paradise*, in 1998; and though some critics felt it suf-

One of America's most acclaimed authors, Toni Morrison is the recipient of the Pulitzer Prize for fiction (1988) and the Nobel Prize in literature (1993). *(Maria Mulas)*

fered in comparison to *Beloved,* the novel became a commercial success. Set in the fictional and idyllic town of Ruby, Oklahoma, and in a former convent just outside of town, the novel depicts the struggle of a black community to preserve its manufactured harmony in the face of changing social, political, and sexual climates. The convent, which is home to a group of women who share a common bond of emotional and physical abuse, stands in contrast to the town of Ruby. While Ruby claims to be a haven against the evils of the outside world, the convent is the real refuge, a place without judgments where all are accepted as equals. The convent eventually becomes the object of the townspeople's wrath in their attempt to preserve Ruby from outside influences.

In addition to her award-winning novels, Morrison also wrote a play, *Dreaming Emmett* (1986), about the tragic murder of Emmett Till, an African-American teenager killed in Mississippi in 1955 for allegedly whistling at a white woman. In 1999 she collaborated with her son Slade Morrison on *The Big Box*, the first of her books for children, which include *I See You, I See Myself: The Young Life of Jacob Lawrence* (2001, coauthored with Deba Leach and Suzanne Wright), a children's biography of artist Jacob Lawrence, and *The Book of Mean People* (2002), Morrison's second collaboration with her son Slade. In 2003 Morrison was commissioned by the Michigan Opera Theater to write an opera based on the life of Margaret Garner, the escaped slave from Kentucky whose experiences inspired Morrison's novel *Beloved*. In late 2003 Morrison published her eighth novel, *Love*, in which she explores the complex nature of love as it manifests in the lives of Bill Cosey, a wealthy and enigmatic resort owner, and the six women obsessed by him.

Acclaimed by readers and critics throughout the world, Toni Morrison has achieved unparalleled success among contemporary American and African-American authors. In addition to the Pulitzer Prize and the Nobel Prize for literature, Morrison has also received the National Book Foundation Medal for Distinguished Contribution to American Letters (1996) and the National Humanities Medal (2001). As an educator, Morrison has taught literature at several prestigious institutions, including the State University of New York in Albany, Yale University, Harvard University, and Princeton University, where she served as the Robert F. Goheen Professor of Humanities.

Further Reading

Conner, Marc C., ed. *The Aesthetics of Toni Morrison: Speaking the Unspeakable.* Jackson: University Press of Mississippi, 2000.

David, Ron. *Toni Morrison Explained: A Reader's Road Map to the Novels.* New York: Random House, 2000.

Harris, Trudier. *Fiction and Folklore: The Novels of Toni Morrison.* Knoxville: University of Tennessee Press, 1991.

Peterson, Nancy J. *Toni Morrison: Critical and Theoretical Approaches.* Baltimore, Md.: Johns Hopkins University Press, 1997.

Morrison, Toni. *Beloved.* New York: Knopf, 1987.

———. *Playing in the Dark: Whiteness and the Literary Imagination.* Cambridge, Mass.: Harvard University Press, 1992.

Mosley, Walter

(1952–   ) *novelist, short story writer, essayist, editor*

An internationally acclaimed author of mystery and detective fiction, Walter Mosley has transformed the traditional detective genre by using it as a vehicle for chronicling African-American social history, particularly the post–World War II era in Los Angeles. Mosley's novels depict the everyday lives of working-class African Americans whose experiences reflect the moral and philosophical dilemmas of contemporary urban American life. "What I write about are black, male heroes," Mosley explained in a 2002 interview. The many heroes in Mosley's fiction include perhaps his best-known character, the streetwise detective Ezekiel "Easy" Rawlins.

Walter Mosley was born on January 12, 1952, in the Watts section of southeast Los Angeles. The only son of a biracial family, Mosley grew up amid the divergent though equally rich family traditions of his African-American father, LeRoy Mosley, who hailed from the Deep South, and his Jewish mother, Ella Mosley, whose family came to the United States from eastern Europe. Mosley's unique family background instilled a strong sense of social justice and equality. The Watts riots of 1965, during which 34 people—mostly African Americans—were killed, made a deep impression on Mosley, who witnessed firsthand the violence and the social conditions that led to its outbreak.

Mosley attended Goddard College, and later enrolled at Johnson State College in Vermont, from which he received his bachelor's degree in 1977. For several years Mosley supported himself with odd jobs. In 1982 he and Joy Kellman, whom he would marry in 1987, moved to New York. Mosley worked for much of the 1980s as a computer programmer, though he spent most of his free time reading the works of such classic mystery writers as Raymond Chandler and Dashiell Hammett. It was a critically acclaimed novel, *The Color Purple* (1982) by ALICE WALKER, however, that convinced Mosley to become a writer.

By the mid-1980s, Mosley had decided to quit his job as a programmer. He began to take writing classes at the City College of New York. His first novel, *Devil in a Blue Dress,* was published in 1990. Set in Los Angeles during the 1940s, *Devil in a Blue Dress* introduced one of Mosley's most enduring and acclaimed characters. Easy Rawlins turns to the life of a detective reluctantly, when he loses his job at an aircraft factory. After a friend encourages him to assist in an investigation of a young woman's disappearance, Rawlins soon finds himself enmeshed in the complicated and dangerous underworld of Los Angeles.

Mosley's first novel was highly regarded by critics and earned an Edgar Award nomination from the Mystery Writers of America. Easy Rawlins, whose outlook and experiences were based in part on the life of Mosley's father, became a frequently recurring character in Mosley's later novels, each of which chronicled a different period in Rawlins's life. *A Red Death* (1991) finds Easy Rawlins blackmailed by the FBI to assist in the investigation of a suspected communist during the early 1950s. In *White Butterfly* (1992), Los Angeles police refuse to investigate the deaths of several black women until a white woman dies under similar circumstances. Set in the early 1960s, *Black Betty* (1994), the fourth novel in the Easy Rawlins series, depicts Rawlins's search for a missing Beverly Hills maid.

In 1992 Mosley received unexpected support from president-elect Bill Clinton, who claimed that

Mosley's mysteries were among his favorite books. Despite the immense popularity of the Easy Rawlins novels, Mosley changed his artistic direction with the publication of *R. L.'s Dream* (1995), a moving portrait of the friendship between an aging blues guitarist, Soupspoon Wise, and Kiki, a young white woman from the South who has fled an abusive family. Through their unconventional friendship, Soupspoon and Kiki begin to heal their considerable emotional wounds.

Mosley resumed his chronicle of the life of Easy Rawlins in *A Little Yellow Dog* (1996), in which Easy has given up the dangerous life of private investigation for a job as a maintenance supervisor at a Los Angeles junior high school. When the brother-in-law of Idabell Turner, a young woman with whom Rawlins is involved, is murdered, Rawlins becomes a primary suspect. In an effort to clear his name, he must combat shadowy figures within Los Angeles's criminal underground, a suspicious police investigator, and a little, though menacing, yellow dog named Pharaoh. Other novels in Mosley's Easy Rawlins series include *Gone Fishin'* (1997), a prequel to *Devil in a Blue Dress* that depicts Rawlins's life prior to settling in Los Angeles, *Bad Boy Brawly Brown* (2002), set in the politically volatile climate of 1960s Los Angeles, and the short story collection *Six Easy Pieces* (2003).

In his 1997 short story collection *Always Outnumbered, Always Outgunned,* for which he received the Anisfield-Wolf Book Award from the Cleveland Foundation, Mosley introduced Socrates Fortlow, a troubled but compassionate ex-convict and street philosopher struggling to survive the moral and physical challenges of life in Watts. Like Easy Rawlins, Fortlow becomes an indispensable source of assistance to many in his community, while also trying to overcome his violent past. Socrates Fortlow returns in *Walkin' the Dog* (1999), another collection of interrelated short stories that depicts Fortlow's continued efforts to improve his life and his community.

Mosley continued to explore new creative ground with the publication of two works of science fiction: *Blue Light* (1998), about an unexplained blue light that confers supernatural abilities on all who see it, and *Futureland* (2001), a collection of related stories that address the marginalized and the poor in a future dominated by multinational corporations. Though Mosley's forays into science fiction have received decidedly cool reviews, *Blue Light* was named a *New York Times* Notable Book of the Year. Mosley also completed another work of science fiction, *Whispers in the Dark,* about Ptolemy "Popo" Bent, a child genius whose uncle, the quick-tempered ex-convict Chill Bent, tries to protect him from government agents seeking to exploit Popo's intellectual gifts. *Whispers in the Dark* was released in 2000 as an eBook.

In 2001 Mosley introduced a new protagonist in the novel *Fearless Jones,* set in 1950s Los Angeles. Similar in plot to his Easy Rawlins series, *Fearless Jones* introduces a new cast of compelling characters, from the meek Paris Minton, the owner of a used bookstore, to a ruthless ex-convict with a compassionate side, Fearless Jones. In 2003 Time Warner published Mosley's second installment of the Fearless Jones series, *Fear Itself.* Mosley's other publications include *Workin' on the Chain Gang: Contemplating Our Chains at the End of the Millennium* (1999), his critique of American capitalism, and *What Next: An African American Initiative toward World Peace* (2002), an African-American reaction to terrorism in light of the events of September 11, 2001.

An internationally best-selling author of mysteries, science fiction, and essays, Walter Mosley is one of few African-American authors to write predominantly in the genres of mystery and detective fiction, and his novels have been translated into more than 20 foreign languages. "Mysteries, stories about crime, about detectives," Mosley explained in a 2000 interview with the *New York Times,* "are the ones that really ask the existential questions such as 'How do I act in an imperfect world when I want to be perfect?'" Mosley has also adapted two of his works successfully to film: *Devil in a Blue Dress* in 1995, starring Denzel Washington, and *Always Outnumbered, Always Outgunned* in 1998, with Laurence Fishburne.

Further Reading

Mosley, Walter. *Always Outnumbered, Always Outgunned: The Socrates Fortlow Stories.* New York: W. W. Norton, 1998.

———. *Devil in a Blue Dress.* New York: W. W. Norton, 1990.

Wilson, Charles E. *Walter Mosley: A Critical Companion.* Westport, Conn.: Greenwood Publishing Group, 2003.

Walter Mosley is one of few African-American authors to write predominantly in the genres of mystery and detective fiction. *(AP/Wide World Photos)*

Murray, Albert
(Albert Lee Murray)
(1916–   ) *novelist, essayist, poet, critic, biographer, educator*

A versatile writer of novels, poetry, essays, literary and cultural criticism, and biography, Albert Murray has influenced generations of African-American writers and critics with his unique perspective on African-American culture. "Any fool can see," Murray wrote in his collection of essays *The Omni-Americans* (1970), "that the white people are not really white, and that black people are not black." In his fiction and nonfiction writing, Murray explores the vitality and complexity of African-American culture and its impact on American society, particularly through the mediums of music and literature.

Albert Lee Murray was born on June 12, 1916, in Nokomis, Alabama, to John Lee and Sudie Young Murray. He attended the renowned Tuskegee Institute, where he met RALPH ELLISON, at the time a music major in his junior year. Murray earned his bachelor's degree in 1939 and became an instructor at Tuskegee in 1940. Three years later, Murray joined the air force and earned the rank of major before his retirement in 1962. During his years in the service, Murray also completed his master's degree at New York University in 1948 and studied at the University of Michigan, Northwestern University, and the University of Paris.

Murray published his first book, *The Omni-Americans: New Perspectives on Black Experience and American Culture,* in 1970. In reviews, essays, and commentaries, Murray condemned what he called the "social science fiction" of prevailing theories of race, substituting what he called the "folklore of white supremacy and the fakelore of black pathology" with the idea that all Americans are multicolored. Murray located the root of African-American culture in the American South, and his second book, *South to a Very Old Place* (1971), emphasized unity among black communities in the South.

In his later works, Murray applied elements of jazz and blues musical theory to African-American literature and culture. In *The Hero and the Blues* (1973), based on a series of lectures Murray gave at the University of Missouri, Murray examines the musical principles of improvisation and

collaboration and what he calls the blues idiom. These ideas would inform his first novel, *Train Whistle Guitar* (1974), a coming-of-age story about a young boy's childhood in the segregated South. Scooter, intelligent and inquiring, is supported by a family and community that reinforce positive values of integrity and endurance, and he draws inspiration from a legendary blues musician, Luzana Cholly, who becomes an example of manhood and a symbol of the transformational quality of blues music, which creates art from the hardships of life. *Train Whistle Guitar* was awarded the Lillian Smith Award for Southern fiction.

Murray wrote two more novels that featured the character of Scooter. *Spyglass Tree,* published in 1991, follows Scooter through his young adult years, and in *The Seven League Boots* (1996), Scooter becomes an internationally successful jazz musician. Murray's depiction of Scooter reflects the broader cultural theories of his nonfiction works. Scooter realizes his potential as a man by incorporating all of his experience, in America and Europe, and among white and black communities.

Murray's other published works include *Good Morning Blues: The Autobiography of Count Basie* (1985, cowritten with Count Basie), and the essay collections *The Blue Devils of Nada* (1996), *Conjugations and Reiterations* (2001), and *From the Briarpatch File: On Context, Procedure, and American Identity* (2001). In 2000 Murray coedited *Trading Twelves: The Selected Letters of Ralph Ellison and Albert Murray.*

A respected and award-winning novelist, Albert Murray is perhaps better known for his brilliant analyses of the jazz and blues idioms and for his incorporation of these musical forms in a unique and influential perspective on African-American culture. His model of the blues hero, explained in numerous essays and given form in his novels, draws on the roots of black folk tradition and affirms the vitality and strength of African-American culture, embodied in the music and language of jazz and blues. The legendary jazz composer Duke Ellington described Murray as an "authority on soul from the days of old" and called him "the unsquarest person I know."

Further Reading

Murray, Albert. *Conjugations and Reiterations.* New York: Pantheon, 2001.

———. *From the Briarpatch File: On Context, Procedure, and American Identity.* New York: Pantheon, 2001.

———. *The Hero and the Blues.* New York: Vintage Books, 1996.

———. *Train Whistle Guitar.* New York: Pantheon, 1998.

Murray, Albert, and John F. Callahan, eds. *Trading Twelves: The Selected Letters of Ralph Ellison and Albert Murray.* New York: Modern Library, 2000.

N

Naylor, Gloria
(1950–   ) *novelist, essayist, screenwriter, editor, educator*

A critically acclaimed author of novels, essays, and screenplays, Gloria Naylor has earned two American Book Awards as well as fellowships from the National Endowment for the Arts and the Guggenheim Foundation. Naylor's novels focus predominantly on the challenges to black female identity within and outside of the African-American community. However, Naylor also achieves a universal perspective with richly symbolic narratives that seek to undermine traditional stereotypes of black culture.

Gloria Naylor was born on January 25, 1950, in New York City, to Roosevelt Naylor, a transit worker, and Alberta Naylor, a telephone operator. Naylor's parents had migrated from Mississippi to rear their children in the North. From her mother, Naylor inherited a love of literature, and she spent much of her childhood reading. She graduated from high school in 1968, the year that Martin Luther King, Jr., was assassinated. His death caused Naylor considerable personal and emotional turmoil.

Naylor turned to the Jehovah's Witnesses sect, working as a missionary for the next seven years in New York, North Carolina, and Florida. In 1975 she left the Jehovah's Witnesses and returned to New York. As she explained in the *New York Times*, "I had used that religion as a straightjacket—for my budding sexuality, for my inability to accept the various shadings of life—while doing it and myself an injustice."

After a brief enrollment at Medgar Evers College, where she studied nursing, Naylor transferred to Brooklyn College to pursue a degree in literature. Having written poetry since her high school years, Naylor credited her reading of TONI MORRISON's *The Bluest Eye* in 1977 for giving her the courage to adopt a more serious and personal approach to writing. Naylor graduated from Brooklyn College in 1981 and completed her master's degree at Yale University in 1983.

Naylor's first novel, *The Women of Brewster Place: A Novel in Seven Stories* (1982), established her reputation as a gifted young writer and won the American Book Award for first fiction in 1983. Set on a dead-end street in an unspecified northern urban ghetto, the novel depicts the lives of seven women, chronicling the physical and emotional hardships that brought each woman to Brewster Place as well as the strengths that allow each to overcome her suffering. Naylor adapted the novel to the screen, and *The Women of Brewster Place* was released as a television miniseries in 1989, produced by and starring Oprah Winfrey.

Following the critical and popular success of *The Women of Brewster Place*, Naylor published

Linden Hills (1985), an ambitious story of an upscale African-American community whose inhabitants have, in differing ways, sacrificed their humanity and cultural identity in the pursuit of increased wealth and social position, values that they have assimilated from white society. Naylor's novel features obvious parallels to Dante Alighieri's 14th-century poem *Inferno* in her representation of the community of Linden Hills as a kind of hell, presided over by the odious Luther Nedeed, the community's mortician and principal landowner. Two wandering poets, Lester and Willie, arrive at Linden Hills in search of work, only to discover a community of people who suffer the malevolent influence of Luther Nedeed.

In her third novel, *Mama Day* (1988), Naylor fashioned one of her most unusual narratives. The story is set in Willow Springs, a fictitious island off the U.S. East Coast. It is a location that has been all but forgotten, except by those who live there, since the early 19th century. Ophelia "Cocoa" Day, who lives in New York City, returns to her ancestral home in Willow Springs, and with the assistance of her great-aunt Miranda, a powerful conjurer and prophet who presides over the island's matriarchal society, Cocoa rediscovers her family heritage and reclaims her cultural identity. Based loosely on Shakespeare's 17th-century play *The Tempest*, the novel was praised by critics for its brilliantly conceived characters, particularly Miranda "Mama" Day.

In *Bailey's Café* (1992), Naylor again creates a timeless, placeless setting, using the structure of a jazz performance for the novel's organization. Narrated by Bailey, the owner of a café and a World War II veteran, the novel depicts the lives of several physically and emotionally destitute individuals who seek a safe haven within Bailey's Café, an establishment that has no fixed location, but which appears when anyone "hanging on to the edge" needs a place "to take a breather for a while." The novel's characters, which include the madam of a bordello, an aging prostitute, and a

host of others whose lives have been shattered by abuse and neglect, find some measure of redemption in the café, which provides a refuge against spiritual annihilation and death. Naylor adapted the novel for the stage in 1994.

Naylor has also edited *Children of the Night: The Best Short Stories by Black Writers, 1967 to the Present* (1995), and written *The Men of Brewster Place* (1998), a return to the themes and locales of her first novel, but from a male perspective, and for which Naylor won a second American Book Award. She has published essays and articles in several periodicals, including *Southern Review* and *Essence*, and she has served as a contributing editor to *Callaloo*. Naylor has also founded One Way Productions, an independent film company established as a vehicle for promoting positive images of the black community in film.

Recalling the influence of Toni Morrison on her decision to become a writer, Gloria Naylor discovered that for "a young black woman, struggling to find a mirror to her worth in this society, not only is your story worth telling but it can be told in words so painstakingly eloquent that it becomes a song." Naylor's novels provide an intimate portrait of everyday African-American women and men, whose lives are sometimes reduced merely to the struggle for survival, but which reveal the inherent strengths of the black community and the richness of black culture.

In addition to her writing career, Naylor has also taught literature and African-American studies at George Washington University, New York University, Princeton University, and Boston University, among others. In 1985 she served as cultural exchange lecturer in India as a member of the U.S. Information Agency.

Further Reading

Naylor, Gloria, ed. *Children of the Night: The Best Short Stories by Black Writers, 1967 to the Present.* Boston: Little, Brown and Co., 1995.

———. *The Women of Brewster Place.* New York: Viking, 1982.

Stave, Shirley A. *Gloria Naylor: Strategy and Technique, Magic and Myth*. Newark: University of Delaware Press, 2000.

Neal, Larry
(Lawrence Paul Neal)
(1937–1981) *poet, playwright, essayist, editor, educator*

Largely responsible for defining the aims and principles of the Black Arts Movement during the 1960s, a literary movement that he described as "concerned with the cultural and spiritual liberation of Black America," Larry Neal was also an accomplished poet, essayist, and playwright. In his collaborations with fellow poet AMIRI BARAKA, known at the time as LeRoi Jones, and in his own writings, Neal helped redirect the literary focus of African-American writers during a period of social and political upheaval.

Larry Neal was born Lawrence Paul Neal on September 5, 1937, in Atlanta, Georgia. His parents, Woodie and Maggie Neal, soon relocated to Philadelphia, and Larry grew up there with his four brothers. Neal graduated from Lincoln University in 1961 and earned his master's degree from the University of Pennsylvania in 1963. Two years later, he married Evelyn Rodgers, a chemist, and settled in New York City with his wife and son, Avatar.

In 1965 Neal and Baraka cofounded the Black Arts Repertory Theatre/School (BARTS) in Harlem, designed to provide an artistic and political forum for African Americans to experience and create art that was culturally and aesthetically relevant to their lives. Neal believed that black writers, and black artists in general, "carry the past and future memory of the race, of the Nation." This racial memory, combined with a political activism aligned with the Black Power movement, became a defining element of the new black aesthetic promoted by the Black Arts Movement.

Collaborating again with Baraka in 1968, Neal edited *Black Fire: An Anthology of Afro-American Writing*. The anthology collected poems, stories, essays, and plays that embodied the artistic principles promoted by the Black Arts Movement. Neal also edited numerous periodicals in the 1970s, including *Journal of Black Poetry* and *Liberator Magazine*. He further distinguished himself as a professor of English at the City University of New York, writer-in-residence at Wesleyan University in Connecticut, and as a Fellow of Yale University from 1970 to 1975. Recipient of a Guggenheim Fellowship in 1971, Neal also served as the executive director of the D.C. Commission on the Arts and Humanities from 1976 to 1979.

In 1969 Neal published his first volume of poetry, *Black Boogaloo: Notes on Black Liberation*. A second volume, *Hoodoo Hollerin' Bebop Ghosts*, was published in 1974. His poetry incorporated traditional folk themes, jazz rhythms, and street dialect. He also wrote two plays, *The Glorious Monster in the Bell of the Horn*, produced off-Broadway at the New Federal Theatre in 1979, and *In an Up-State Motel: A Morality Play*, produced at St. Mark's Playhouse in New York City in 1981. Larry Neal died following a massive heart attack on January 6, 1981.

At the time of his death, Neal had been working on an analytical study of African-American culture in the 1960s, a period that he helped transform artistically and politically. He inspired younger writers such as NIKKI GIOVANNI and CAROLYN M. RODGERS to celebrate African-American consciousness on all of its numerous levels, and his work with the Black Arts Repertory Theatre/School became a pattern for the establishment of similar theaters and schools across the country. Also a music critic, an accomplished musician, and screenwriter, Larry Neal displayed his considerable talents and innovative artistic vision in a variety of creative media.

Further Reading
Andrews, William L., Frances Smith Foster, and Trudier Harris, eds. *The Concise Oxford Companion*

to *African American Literature*. New York: Oxford University Press, 2001.

Gates, Henry Louis, Jr., and Nellie Y. McKay, eds. *The Norton Anthology of African American Literature*. New York: W. W. Norton, 1997.

Neely, Barbara

(1941–   ) *novelist, short story writer, social activist*

An award-winning novelist, short story writer, and one of the few African Americans who write predominantly in the genre of mystery and detective fiction, Barbara Neely has earned international acclaim with a series of novels featuring the amateur sleuth Blanche White. Neely has also been recognized for her social activism, having won several community service awards for her efforts on behalf of numerous women's organizations, including Women for Economic Justice and Women of Color for Reproductive Freedom, which Neely helped found.

The oldest of three children, Barbara Neely was born in 1941 in the rural Pennsylvania Dutch community of Lebanon, Pennsylvania, to Ann and Bernard Neely. She attended Lebanon's private Catholic schools, where she was the only African-American student in her junior and senior high school classes. In 1971 Neely earned her master's degree in urban and regional planning from the University of Pittsburgh. Initially drawn to a life of public service, Neely organized a community-based program in the Pittsburgh suburb of Shady Side to provide support for women upon their release from jail. Neely also became involved in the Massachusetts-based group Women for Economic Justice, for which she served as director until 1992, and worked as a radio producer for the Africa News Service.

Neely published her first short story, "Passing the Word," in *Essence* in 1981. Other stories have appeared in the journal *Southern Exposure* and in numerous literary anthologies, including *Test Tube Women* (1984), *Things That Divide Us* (1985), *Angels of Power* (1986), and *Breaking Ice: An Anthology of Contemporary African American Literature* (1990).

In 1992 Neely published her first novel, *Blanche on the Lam*, which introduced the character of Blanche White, a middle-aged housekeeper who is reluctantly drawn into the family intrigues of her wealthy employers. A proud, articulate, and intelligent working-class woman, Blanche is well suited for the work of a detective. Set in fictional Farleigh, North Carolina, *Blanche on the Lam* opens with Blanche in a courtroom, facing charges for passing bad checks. She takes refuge from the law in the household of the Carters, a wealthy and eccentric white family, where she uncovers a murder and eventually identifies the culprit.

Neely's debut novel won the Agatha, Macavity, and Anthony awards for best first mystery novel in 1993. Following her celebrated first novel, Neely published the second book in the Blanche White series, *Blanche among the Talented Tenth* (1994), which finds Blanche embroiled in another mystery, this time in the wealthy black community of Amber Cove, Massachusetts. The other books in the series include *Blanche Cleans Up* (1998) and *Blanche Passes Go* (2000).

Though celebrated for her compelling mystery novels, Neely's work has also been recognized for its valuable social commentary. Large portions of her novels focus on Blanche's observations on issues of race, class, and gender, and each one reveals new depths in Blanche's character. *Blanche among the Talented Tenth* addresses the class and intraracial prejudices among an elite African-American community in Massachusetts, while *Blanche Passes Go* depicts Blanche's confrontation with a man who had raped her years before.

Barbara Neely has earned international critical and popular success with her Blanche White mysteries. Books in the series have been translated into French, German, and Japanese, and they are regularly included in university curricula. Despite her enormous success as a writer, Neely remains devoted to social and community activism. She has won numerous service awards, including a Community Works Social Action Award for Leadership and Activism for Women's Rights and Economic Justice, and the Fighting for Women's Voices Award from the Coalition for Basic Human Needs. A resident of Boston, Massachusetts, Neely hosts a weekly radio interview program, *Commonwealth Journal*, and serves as a member of the Jamaica Plain Neighborhood Arts Council.

Further Reading

Andrews, William L., Frances Smith Foster, and Trudier Harris, eds. *The Concise Oxford Companion to African American Literature*. New York: Oxford University Press, 2001.

Neely, Barbara. *Blanche among the Talented Tenth*. New York: St. Martin's Press, 1994.

———. *Blanche Cleans Up*. New York: Viking, 1998.

———. *Blanche on the Lam*. New York: St. Martin's Press, 1992.

———. *Blanche Passes Go*. New York: Viking, 2000.

Nell, William Cooper
(1816–1874) *historian, journalist*

William Cooper Nell was one of the first African-American writers to document the historical contributions of blacks to American society. He worked aggressively as an abolitionist in Boston, Massachusetts, and assisted other African-American writers, like the autobiographer HARRIET JACOBS, to find publishers for their work.

Born on December 20, 1816, in Boston, Massachusetts, Nell grew up in a middle-class abolitionist family. His father, William Guion Nell, was a prominent leader in Boston's black community, serving as a founding member of the Massachusetts General Colored Association. He was also an associate of the abolitionist and writer DAVID WALKER. Nell attended a segregated school for blacks in the basement of the African Baptist Church, and he later graduated from Boston's Smith School. An

excellent student, Nell experienced early the racial prejudices of the free North when the customary medal and an invitation to an awards dinner, supposedly given to all Boston public school students who distinguish themselves academically, was denied to him by the governor because of his race.

Following his graduation from school, Nell worked with the white abolitionist leader William Lloyd Garrison, first as secretary of the Juvenile Garrison Independent Society, and later as a messenger for Garrison's publication the *Liberator*, where he was also apprenticed as a printer. Nell's first published piece was the text of a speech delivered at the second anniversary celebration of the Juvenile Garrison Independent Society, which appeared in the *New England Telegraph* in 1833. Nell also studied law briefly, worked as a clerk in a law office, and held several positions in various antislavery organizations.

In 1840 Nell began a long campaign to end segregation in Boston's public schools. He organized petition drives on a city and state level, and he supported lawsuits filed on behalf of African-American students who objected to the quality of education they received in the city's only black school. The Massachusetts legislature finally ended school segregation in 1855, becoming the only state to do so prior to the Civil War. Nell was recognized by the leading white and African-American abolitionists of Boston for his tireless efforts on behalf of desegregation.

Nell had joined the staff of the *North Star*, published by the celebrated autobiographer and abolitionist FREDERICK DOUGLASS, in 1847. Following the passage of the Fugitive Slave Act in 1850, which allowed slavers to track and capture fugitive slaves residing in free northern cities, Nell assisted runaway slaves by providing food and protection. He also made an unsuccessful attempt at election to the Massachusetts legislature as a member of the Free-Soil Party.

In 1851 Nell wrote a pamphlet, *Services of Colored Americans in the Wars of 1776 and 1812*, that was one of the first publications to address the experiences of African Americans in the context of their historical contributions. Nell published a larger work, *The Colored Patriots of the American Revolution,* in 1855, which included an introduction by the celebrated white author and abolitionist Harriet Beecher Stowe. Considered the first comprehensive work of African-American history, *Colored Patriots* included a tribute to Crispus Attucks, a former slave and the first man killed during a demonstration against British troops in 1770, an event that came to be known as the Boston Massacre.

During the early years of the Civil War, Nell contributed columns to Garrison's *Liberator* in support of using African-American troops in the Union army. In 1861, defying a legal restriction that prohibited the federal government from hiring African Americans, Boston's postmaster, John G. Palfrey, appointed Nell a postal clerk, making him one of the first African Americans to hold a federally appointed civilian position. Nell married in 1869, fathered two children, and remained a postal employee until his death. William Cooper Nell died in 1874.

Known primarily as the first African-American historian, Nell devoted his life to the abolition of slavery and to greater civil rights for freeborn and emancipated blacks in the North. As an activist, he helped end school segregation in Boston, and as a historical biographer, he celebrated the achievements of African-American patriots in an era when white historians ignored or suppressed such achievements.

Further Reading

Andrews, William L., Frances Smith Foster, and Trudier Harris, eds. *The Concise Oxford Companion to African American Literature.* New York: Oxford University Press, 2001.

Horton, James Oliver. *Free People of Color: Inside the African American Community.* Washington, D.C.: Smithsonian Institution Press, 1993.

Oliver, Diane
(Diane Alene Oliver)
(1943–1966) *short story writer*

At the age of 22, Diane Oliver was killed in an automobile accident, cutting short what promised to be a bright literary future. A student at the renowned University of Iowa Writers' Workshop, Oliver demonstrated a remarkable ability for storytelling. Her 1966 story "Neighbors" was selected for publication in *Prize Stories 1967: The O. Henry Awards* and remains one of her best-known and most anthologized works.

Diane Alene Oliver was born on July 28, 1943, in Charlotte, North Carolina. William Oliver, her father, was a teacher and school administrator, and her mother, Blanche, taught piano. Oliver's childhood coincided with many key events in the Civil Rights movement. She was a grade school student in 1954 when the landmark Supreme Court ruling in *Brown v. Board of Education* stated that segregation in public schools was unconstitutional. Oliver attended segregated grade schools and graduated from West Charlotte High School, before enrolling in 1960 at the University of North Carolina at Greensboro.

As a college student, Oliver became the managing editor of the student newspaper *The Carolinian* and began writing short stories. She also studied under poet Randall Jarrell, one of many

influences on Oliver's writing. Other literary influences included JAMES BALDWIN, RALPH ELLISON, and James Agee. In 1964, following her graduation from college, Oliver won a guest editorship at *Mademoiselle* magazine, which allowed her to travel to England. She also spent part of that year participating in the Experiment in International Living, an eight-week program in Switzerland.

Oliver published only five stories during her lifetime. (Another appeared posthumously in 1967.) Her first published story, "Key to the City," appeared in the *Red Clay Reader* in 1965 and depicted a young woman's frustrated ambitions when she and her family migrate from the South to Chicago to join her father, only to discover that he has abandoned the family. Oliver's stories emphasize the strength of African-American women in their struggle to maintain family unity despite a racially intolerant society that consistently challenges family loyalties.

In "Health Service" (1965), Libby, a young mother whose husband has abandoned the family, tries to get medical treatment for her children at a country clinic but is refused because of her race. Libby is also the protagonist of "Traffic Jam" (1966), in which she confronts her husband, who has returned home unexpectedly after a long period of abandonment. In 1966 Oliver published her best-known work, "Neighbors," which received third prize in that year's O. Henry Awards. Based on a true story of school integration during the 1960s, "Neighbors" describes the violent backlash against an African-American family's decision to send their young son to a white school. Oliver's other stories include "The Closet on the Top Floor" (1966) and "Mint Juleps Not Served Here" (1967), published posthumously in the anthology *Southern Writing in the Sixties.*

Oliver earned a scholarship to the renowned Writers' Workshop at the University of Iowa in 1965. Just prior to her graduation, she was killed in an automobile accident on May 21, 1966, ending what promised to be an acclaimed career as an author. Despite her relatively small body of work, Oliver is considered by many critics to be an important predecessor to such notable contemporary figures in African-American literature as TONI MORRISON and ALICE WALKER.

Further Reading

Alvarez, Joseph A. "Diane Oliver." *Cyclopedia of World Authors,* Second Revised Edition. Hackensack, N.J.: Salem Press, 2003.

Andrews, William L., Frances Smith Foster, and Trudier Harris, eds. *The Concise Oxford Companion to African American Literature.* New York: Oxford University Press, 2001.

Naylor, Gloria, ed. *Children of the Night: The Best Short Stories by Black Writers, 1967 to the Present.* Boston: Little, Brown and Co., 1995.

P

Parks, Suzan-Lori
(1963–) *playwright, screenwriter, educator*

Hailed by critics and peers as a leading playwright of her generation, Suzan-Lori Parks has distinguished herself as a versatile and innovative writer in the tradition of ADRIENNE KENNEDY and NTOZAKE SHANGE. Her unique dramatizations, which incorporate elements of jazz improvisation, have garnered two Obie Awards (the off-Broadway equivalent of the Tony Award), and numerous fellowships and grants. In 2002 Parks became only the fourth African-American playwright to win the Pulitzer Prize.

The daughter of an army officer, Suzan-Lori Parks was born in Fort Knox, Kentucky, on May 10, 1963. She grew up in numerous cities in the United States and spent four years in Germany, where she attended German schools and studied in German. At Mount Holyoke College, in South Hadley, Massachusetts, she studied creative writing with JAMES BALDWIN, who soon recognized her remarkable talent for dialogue. She had written stories since her childhood, but Baldwin encouraged her to explore drama, a medium that had never before attracted her.

Prior to her graduation with a degree in English and German, Parks completed her first play, *The Sinner's Place*, though Mount Holyoke's drama department refused to produce it. Despite this early rejection, Parks's next play, *Imperceptible Mutabilities in the Third Kingdom* (1989), received wide critical acclaim and earned her an Obie Award in 1990. Displaying a complex and musical use of language, *Imperceptible Mutabilities* comprises multiple stories rather than traditional acts, including the imaginative retelling of a slave ship's journey from Africa to America, and a reworking of Homer's epic poem *The Odyssey.*

In *The Death of the Last Black Man in the Whole Entire World* (1990), Parks's characters include Black Man with Watermelon and Black Woman with Fried Drumstick, figures who seem to exist as much on a linguistic level as they do a physical one. In her production notes for the play, Parks describes the struggle of these two central characters as an effort to remain present. "Heroism is being there and seeing through it. I guess I have a greater understanding of the small gesture, or the great act that is also very small—like being present."

In *The America Play* (1993) and *Venus* (1996), for which she received a second Obie, Parks continued to explore the boundaries of history and language with two of her most unusual characters. In *The America Play,* The Foundling Father, a black man who becomes infatuated with Abraham Lincoln after being told frequently that he bears a striking resemblance to him, leaves his family to reenact Lincoln's assassination in a circus sideshow. In *Venus,* Parks confronts the racial

Outside the Ambassador Theater in New York, Suzan-Lori Parks reacts to the news that she has won the 2002 Pulitzer Prize for drama, the first to be awarded to an African-American woman. *(AP/Wide World Photos)*

and sexual stereotypes of African-American women in her depiction of the Hottentot Venus. The play is based loosely on the life of an African woman, Saartje Baartman, who was taken from her home in South Africa in 1810 and displayed across Europe as a freak because of her unusual anatomy. Even after her death, her brain and sexual organs were displayed in the Museé de l'Homme in France until 1985.

Parks's recent plays, including *In the Blood* (1999) and *Fucking A* (2000), both of which incorporate characters and themes from Nathaniel

Hawthorne's novel *The Scarlet Letter,* and *Topdog/Underdog* (2002), feature more conventional characters, though Parks's signature linguistic complexities remain. *Topdog/Underdog* is a two-character play that depicts the sibling rivalry between two brothers, Lincoln and Booth. The brothers explore their past and future as each remembers their family's history differently, and as each tries to get the upper hand. Shortly after *Topdog/Underdog* debuted on Broadway in April of 2002, Parks was awarded the Pulitzer Prize for drama, making her only the fourth African-American playwright, and the first female African-American playwright, to receive the award. She has also been the recipient of a MacArthur Foundation grant and a Guggenheim Fellowship, as well as numerous grants from the National Endowment for the Arts.

Apart from her success as a playwright, Parks has also produced and written for the big screen. In 1990 she cowrote and coproduced an independent film, *Anemone Me,* released in New York, and she wrote the script for Spike Lee's 1996 film *Girl 6.* Parks has studied acting in London, and she has taught at the New School for Social Research in New York (now New School University) and the Yale School of Drama. In 2003 Parks published her first novel, *Getting Mother's Body,* in which a young woman, Billy Beede, attempts to recover a fortune in jewels that may have been buried with the body of her mother, the raucous blues singer Willa Mae Beede. Currently, Parks is the director of the Audrey Skirball Kernis Theatre Projects Writing for Performance Program at the California Institute for the Arts.

Further Reading

Garrett, Shawn-Marie. "The Possession of Suzan-Lori Parks." *American Theatre* 17, no. 8 (October 2000): 22.

Parks, Suzan-Lori. *Red Letter Plays.* New York: Theatre Communications Group, 2000.

———. *Topdog/Underdog.* New York: Theatre Communications Group, 2002.

Petry, Ann
(Ann Lane Petry, Arnold Petry)
(1908–1997) *novelist, short fiction writer, children's fiction writer*

Published in 1946, Ann Petry's *The Street* sold more than a million copies, the first novel by an African-American woman to become a best-seller. Petry's books, which include novels, short stories, and children's fiction and biography, reveal her concern for the challenges that confront African Americans in a prejudiced society, particularly women, who face both racial and gender discrimination.

Ann Lane Petry was born Ann Lane on October 12, 1908 (some sources say 1911), in Old Saybrook, Connecticut, the second daughter of Peter Lane and Bertha James Lane. Her father owned a drugstore and worked as a pharmacist, and her mother was a chiropodist. The Lane family enjoyed a comfortable middle-class existence, and Ann grew up in a predominantly white neighborhood.

Raised on stories of her ancestors, four generations of which had settled in New England, she developed an early love for reading and storytelling. As a student at Old Saybrook High School, she began to write stories and one-act plays. She graduated in 1929 and enrolled in the Connecticut College of Pharmacy. She completed her Ph.D in pharmacology at the University of Connecticut in 1934 and joined her father in the family drugstore in Old Saybrook and later in Old Lyme.

In 1938 she married George Petry, a mystery writer, and moved with him to New York City, where she began to pursue a career as a writer. She found work at two Harlem newspapers, the *Amsterdam News* and *People's Voice,* for which she edited the women's page and wrote a weekly column about Harlem social life called "The Lighter Side." Petry's first short story, "Marie of the Cabin," published under the pseudonym Arnold Petry, appeared in Baltimore's *Afro-American* newspaper. Under her own name, Petry published "On Saturday the Siren Sounds at Noon" in the *Crisis,* the literary magazine published by the National Association for the Advancement of Colored People (NAACP). "The Winding Sheet," Petry's second story to appear in the *Crisis,* was collected in *Best American Stories of 1946* and brought her to the attention of critics and publishers.

While Petry struggled to make her way as a writer, she also devoted much of her time to community programs in Harlem. She founded a consumer advocacy group for African-American women, and she initiated an after-school program at a Harlem elementary school to assist children in Harlem's crime-ridden neighborhoods, an experience that proved to be a rich source of material for her first novel.

With the help of a writing fellowship, Petry published *The Street,* her first and most acclaimed work of fiction, in 1946. Written in the protest tradition of RICHARD WRIGHT's *Native Son* (1940), the novel depicts a young mother's struggle against racial, social, and economic forces that combine to ensure her failure. When Lutie Johnson, an

Ann Petry, shown here in New York in 1946, was one of the first African-American authors to address the particular challenges of urban life for black women in her 1946 novel *The Street.* *(AP/Wide World Photos)*

aspiring singer, seeks the assistance of her bandleader, Boots Smith, to hire a lawyer to defend her son, who has been arrested for theft, she discovers that Smith's only interest is in seducing her. In a fit of rage against her powerlessness, Lutie kills Boots Smith and flees New York, leaving her son and her dreams of a better future behind.

Petry's first novel was an overwhelming success, becoming the first best-seller by an African-American woman and making Petry an overnight literary sensation. The critical and popular attention, however, soon compelled Petry to leave New York and return to the relative tranquility of Old Saybrook, Connecticut. There, she published her second novel, *Country Place,* in 1947.

A significant departure from her first novel, *Country Place* is set in a small New England town and features a cast of predominantly white characters. Through the experiences of Johnnie Roane, a young World War II veteran who returns home to discover that his wife has been unfaithful, Petry explores the moral ambiguities and the prejudices of race and class that exist beneath the surface of life in Lennox, Connecticut. Though decidedly less popular than her first novel, *Country Place* revealed Petry's effort to expand the narrative scope of her writing.

Petry continued to break new ground with her third and final novel, *The Narrows,* published in 1953. The novel depicts an ill-fated romance between a well-educated young black man, Lincoln Williams, and a wealthy white heiress, Camilo Sheffield, in the small community of Monmouth, Connecticut. When Lincoln discovers that Camilo has deceived him and that she is actually the wife of Capt. Bunny Sheffield, he breaks off the relationship, only to be accused by Camilo of rape. With the help of her husband, Camilo kidnaps and murders Lincoln, but is later discovered by the police as she tries to get rid of his body.

In her later years, Petry explored other genres besides the novel. Her first work for young readers, *The Drugstore Cat,* was published in 1949. She followed this with a well-received young adult biography, *Harriet Tubman: Conductor on the Underground Railroad* (1955), and *Tituba of Salem Village* (1964), the story of a Barbadian slave girl's experiences during the 1692 Salem witch trials. In 1970 Petry collected many of her short stories in *Lives of the Saints*. After a brief illness, Ann Lane Petry died in a convalescent home in Old Saybrook, Connecticut, on April 28, 1997.

Despite her landmark success with the publication of *The Street* in 1946, Ann Petry was a relatively obscure literary figure in the final decades of her life. If only on the basis of her first novel, Ann Petry occupies an important position in the African-American literary tradition. The first best-seller to be written by an African-American woman, the novel is also widely regarded as a classic of social realism and protest fiction. Petry explained the goal of her children's writing in a speech published in 1965 in the *Horn Book Magazine*, using words that could apply equally to all of her fiction. "Remember for what a long, long time black people have been in this country, have been a part of America: a sturdy, indestructible, wonderful part of America, woven into its heart and into its soul."

Further Reading

Hill, Patricia Liggins, ed. *Call and Response: The Riverside Anthology of the African American Literary Tradition*. Boston: Houghton Mifflin Co., 1998.

Holladay, Hilary. *Ann Petry*. New York: Twayne Publishers, 1996.

Petry, Ann. *The Street*. Boston: Houghton Mifflin Co., 1946.

Poston, Ted
(Theodore Roosevelt Augustus Major Poston)
(1906–1974) *journalist, short story writer*

Ted Poston was one of the first African Americans to work for a major New York daily newspaper. His distinguished career as a journalist and writer included a position as speechwriter for New York governor Alfred E. Smith in Smith's presidential campaign of 1928 and coverage of several controversial legal actions against African Americans, including the notorious Scottsboro trial, in which nine African-American youths were falsely accused of rape in 1931. Poston also published several short stories in the *New Republic*, some of which later appeared in anthologies of African-American literature, including LANGSTON HUGHES's *The Best Short Stories by Negro Writers: An Anthology from 1899 to Present* (1967).

Theodore Roosevelt Augustus Major Poston was born on July 4, 1906, in Hopkinsville, Kentucky, to Ephraim Poston, a newspaper publisher, and Mollie Cox Poston. At the age of 22, Poston began his career in journalism as a copy clerk for his father's newspaper, *The Contender*. Poston attended segregated schools in Hopkinsville before graduating from Tennessee Agricultural and Industrial State College in 1928. Later that year, Poston joined his brother Ulysses in New York City, who helped him get a position as speechwriter for the presidential campaign of New York governor Alfred E. Smith. After a short stint as a columnist for the *Pittsburgh Courier*, Poston accepted his first full-time position, as a writer for the *Amsterdam News* in 1929.

Having ascended to the position of city editor with the *Amsterdam News* in 1934, Poston was fired two years later for supporting a strike by employees who wanted to unionize. He found employment with the Works Progress Administration, a federal employment program initiated by President Franklin D. Roosevelt as part of his New Deal. He returned to journalism in the late 1930s as a writer for the *New York Post*, where he remained employed until 1972. He was assigned to cover city hall, earning the respect of white colleagues who initially rejected him for his ability to gain access to leading political figures like Huey Long and Republican presidential candidate Wendell Willkie.

During a five-year leave from the *New York Post*, Poston was invited to Washington, D.C., as a special assistant to President Truman. He served as a public relations consultant during World War II for several government offices, including the War Production Board and the War Manpower Commission. He also ran the Negro News Desk in the Office of War Information.

Poston returned to work at the *New York Post* in 1945 and took several politically and racially explosive assignments in the South. While covering the Scottsboro trial in Alabama, Poston disguised himself as a traveling preacher to protect himself from the violence of angry white mobs during his coverage of the bus boycott in Montgomery, Alabama, in 1955. He narrowly escaped death a few years later at the home of civil rights activist Daisy Bates in Little Rock, Arkansas, when gunshots were fired into the house.

During the 1950s, Poston earned numerous awards for his coverage of civil rights stories, including the Heywood Braon Award from the American Newspaper Guild in 1950. With his success as a pioneering African-American journalist, Poston opened up many opportunities for black writers. When he retired from the *New York Post* in 1972, the city of New York awarded him its distinguished service medal. While Poston was visiting the Virgin Islands in 1973 to work on his autobiography, his health began to fail. He returned to New York and made a brief recovery. On January 11, 1974, Theodore Roosevelt Augustus Major Poston died suddenly in his home at the age of 67.

Further Reading

Andrews, William L., Frances Smith Foster, and Trudier Harris, eds. *The Concise Oxford Companion to African American Literature.* New York: Oxford University Press, 2001.

Notable Black American Men. Detroit, Michigan: Gale Research, 1998, pp. 949–951.

Poston, Ted. *The Dark Side of Hopkinsville: Stories by Ted Poston.* Athens University of Georgia Press, 1991.

Prince, Nancy
(Nancy Gardner Prince)
(1799–unknown) *autobiographer*

In her 1850 autobiography, *Narrative of the Life and Travels of Mrs. Nancy Prince*, Nancy Gardner Prince contributed an important historical record of life among freeborn blacks in the antebellum North, a life characterized by poverty, hard work, and racial prejudice. Prince's *Narrative* describes her years as a domestic in Massachusetts, her travels through Europe, and her residency in the court of the Russian Emperor Alexander I (1777–1825) and his successor, Nicholas I (1796–1855), as the wife of a palace guard. She also includes a detailed historical sketch of the West Indies and the volatile conditions under which newly emancipated slaves lived in Jamaica.

Nancy Gardner Prince was born Nancy Gardner on September 15, 1799, in Newburyport, Massachusetts. A freeborn African American and the second of her mother's eight children, Gardner never knew her father, Thomas Gardner, who died when she was three months old. Her grandfather, Tobias Wornton, served in the Continental Army during the Revolutionary War and fought at the battle of Bunker Hill, and he became something of a surrogate father to Prince. Compelled to work at a young age to help support her family after the death of her stepfather, Gardner had little time for formal schooling, save for some religious instruction from her grandfather. As a teenager, she worked in Essex and Salem as a domestic until the strain of a severe workload and poor living conditions, similar to those later described by HARRIET E. WILSON in her novel *Our Nig* (1859), affected her health and forced her to return home.

Between 1817 and 1824, Gardner continued to provide for her family while also learning the trade of seamstress. In 1824 she married a Mr. Prince on his return voyage from Russia. Mr. Prince, also born free in Marlborough, served as an attendant in Emperor Alexander I's court in St. Petersburg, Russia. Gardner, now Mrs. Prince, accompanied her husband on his voyage back to Russia. After a brief stay in Copenhagen, Denmark, Prince and her husband arrived in St. Petersburg, Russia, on June 21, 1824.

Prince noted the equitable relations between different ethnic groups in Alexander I's court. "There was no prejudice against color," she writes. "There were there all castes, and the people of all nations, each in their place." Prince prospered in Russia, establishing a successful business as a seamstress and founding an asylum for orphaned children in St. Petersburg. After 10 years in Russia, Prince was compelled to return to America for health reasons. Her husband had assumed the position of sentry in the court of the new emperor, Nicholas I, and decided to remain for a time. He died, however, before he was able to leave.

Upon her return to Boston, Prince devoted herself to numerous social causes. She established a short-lived orphanage for African-American children and later became involved in the growing antislavery movement. In 1840 she volunteered to assist in missionary work in Jamaica and taught school in St. Ann Harbor and Kingston until 1841. She returned a year later, but civil unrest and corruption among the country's British administrators compelled her to leave after three months. Her return to America was a difficult and harrowing experience, during which she nearly lost her freedom during a stop in Key West, where free blacks could be taken captive as slaves, and where most of her belongings were stolen.

After she arrived home, Prince struggled to support herself financially. In an effort to "obtain the means to help supply my necessities," as she wrote in the preface to her autobiography, Prince published her *Narrative of the Life and Travels of Mrs. Nancy Prince* in 1850, with two reprints in 1853 and 1856. Providing a compelling account of her childhood struggles to hold her family together despite economic and racial oppression, and her travels in distant lands, Prince's *Narrative* also reveals her years of humanitarian service. Among the many fascinating historical details included in her *Narrative*, Prince discusses the culture and geography of Russia and gives a chilling account of the Decembrist Revolt of 1826. Few facts are known about Nancy Gardner Prince's life following the third printing of her *Narrative*, published in 1856, and the date of her death is uncertain.

Further Reading

Appiah, Kwame Anthony, and Henry Louis Gates, Jr., eds. *Africana: The Encyclopedia of the African and African American Experience*. New York: Basic Civitas Books, 1999.

Prince, Nancy Gardner. *Narrative of the Life and Travels of Mrs. Nancy Prince*. Reprinted as *A Black Woman's Odyssey through Russia and Jamaica*. Princeton, N.J.: Markus Wiener Publishers, 1990.

Rampersad, Arnold

(1941–　) *biographer, essayist, literary critic, editor, educator*

An acclaimed author, educator, and literary critic, Arnold Rampersad is best known for his biographies of LANGSTON HUGHES and W. E. B. DuBOIS. Also the author of essays and literary studies, Rampersad has been awarded numerous honors and has maintained a distinguished teaching career at such universities as Stanford, Rutgers, and Princeton.

Born on November 13, 1941, in Trinidad, West Indies, Arnold Rampersad was educated in the United States. After completing bachelor's and master's degrees at Bowling Green State University, in Kentucky, Rampersad finished a second master's degree and his Ph.D. at Harvard University in 1973. He first gained prominence as a scholar and author with his groundbreaking study of American author Herman Melville, *Melville's Israel Potter: A Pilgrimage and Progress* (1969), a critical analysis of Melville's little-known short novel *Israel Potter: His Fifty Years of Exile*, published during the 1850s.

In 1976 Rampersad published his first biographical work, *The Art and Imagination of W. E. B. DuBois*. A compelling and meticulously researched study of the life and writing of one of the 20th century's most influential African-American intellectuals and social leaders, Rampersad's biography earned wide critical acclaim for its imaginative and literary approach to its subject matter.

Describing himself as a "literary historian, someone concerned with the combination of history and literature," Rampersad brought a unique literary sensibility to his later biographical works. After six years of research, Rampersad published *The Life of Langston Hughes: Volume 1: 1902–1941, I, Too, Sing America* (1986), the first of two volumes on the life of poet Langston Hughes. Winner of the Anisfield-Wolf Book Award for Race Relations in 1987, and nominated for the New York Book Critics Circle Award for biography, *I, Too, Sing America* was hailed by critics for its revealing look at the creative and ideological influences on Hughes's early life. In 1988 Rampersad published *The Life of Langston Hughes: Volume 2: 1941–1967, I Dream a World*, which won the American Book Award in 1990. *The Life of Langston Hughes* is widely considered the authoritative text on the life of a seminal figure in the African-American literary tradition.

Rampersad continued to explore literary topics in many of his later works, including *Slavery and the Literary Imagination*, coedited with Deborah E. McDowell in 1989; the two-volume *Richard Wright: Works*, edited by Rampersad for the Library of America in 1991; *Richard Wright: A Collection of Critical Essays*, edited in 1995; and *The Collected Poems of Langston Hughes*, edited with David Roessal in 1995.

Rampersad also published two acclaimed sports biographies: *Days of Grace: A Memoir* (1993, coauthored with African-American tennis great Arthur Ashe), and *Jackie Robinson: A Biography* (1997), about the life and challenges of Major League Baseball's first African-American player.

Arnold Rampersad has become one of America's premier biographers, praised for his exhaustive research as well as his ability to depict the lives of his subjects within the complex cultural contexts of their time. "Mr. Rampersad offers a compelling interpretation of a significant chunk of American cultural history," poet RITA DOVE wrote in her review of *I Dream a World*, "which makes this biography not only entertaining but essential reading." In addition to his award-winning biographical writing, Rampersad has published essays in such periodicals as *American Literature, Yale Review,* and *Southern Review.* Rampersad has also served as a professor of English at Stanford, Rutgers, Columbia, and Princeton Universities. In 2003 Rampersad returned to Stanford to serve as the cognizant dean for the humanities.

Further Reading

Andrews, William L., Frances Smith Foster, and Trudier Harris, eds. *The Concise Oxford Companion to African American Literature.* New York: Oxford University Press, 2001.

Rampersad, Arnold, ed. *The Life of Langston Hughes: Volume 1: 1902–1941, I, Too, Sing America.* New York: Oxford University Press, 1986.

———. *The Life of Langston Hughes: Volume 2: 1941–1967, I Dream a World.* New York: Oxford University Press, 1988.

Reed, Ishmael
(Emmett Coleman, Ishmael Scott Reed)
(1938–   ) *novelist, poet, essayist, playwright, editor, educator*

Twice nominated for the National Book Award for poetry and fiction, Ishmael Reed was also a finalist for the Pulitzer Prize for poetry in 1973 for *Conjure: Selected Poems, 1963–1970* (1972). A prolific author of novels, poetry, essays, and plays, Reed has also edited numerous literary anthologies. His unorthodox approach to characterization and plot has led some critics to identify Reed as the preeminent, and often most controversial, postmodern novelist among contemporary African-American authors.

Ishmael Reed was born Emmett Coleman on February 22, 1938, in Chattanooga, Tennessee, but he grew up in Buffalo, New York, with his mother, Thelma Coleman, and Bennie Reed, his stepfather. In grade school, Reed began composing stories, and by the age of 14, he contributed a regular column on jazz to the *Empire State Weekly,* a local black newspaper. After graduating from high school in 1956, Reed studied briefly at Millard Fillmore College before transferring to the University of Buffalo, where he received encouragement from his professors to pursue a career in writing.

Due to limited financial means and a growing disinterest in school, Reed left the University of Buffalo in 1960 to focus more fully on his writing. That year he also married Priscilla Rose, with whom he had a daughter. Reed moved to New York City in 1962 and joined the Umbra Workshop, a Black Arts–inspired poetry collective. While Reed's early years as a writer coincided with the emergence of the Black Arts Movement, in which he tacitly participated as a member of the Umbra Workshop, Reed transcended, and frequently criticized, the efforts of those who sought to impose a mutually exclusive aesthetic on black writing. To support his family, Reed wrote for the weekly *Newark Advance,* eventually becoming the editor in 1965. He also cofounded his first publication, the underground newspaper *East Village Other.*

In 1967 Reed published his first novel, *The Free-Lance Pallbearers,* a sweeping critique of American politics, religion, and culture, and the impact that these structures have made on the

Ishmael Reed speaks during an interview at his home in Oakland, California, in 1998. *(AP/Wide World Photos)*

black community. In his second novel, *Yellow Back Radio Broke-Down* (1969), Reed articulated more explicitly the philosophical and artistic foundations of his writing, a concept that he called Neo-HooDooism. Drawn from a combination of African, Caribbean, and African-American folk and religious traditions, Reed's Neo-HooDooism operates on what some scholars have identified as two primary principles: syncretism, the adoption of divergent religious and cultural traditions, and a synchronistic concept of time in which past and future events can occur contemporaneously in the present.

In his later novels, which include *Mumbo Jumbo* (1972), nominated for the National Book Award, *The Last Days of Louisiana Red* (1974), *Flight to Canada* (1976), *The Terrible Twos* (1982), *Reckless Eyeballing* (1986), *The Terrible Threes*

(1989), and *Japanese by Spring* (1993), Reed continued to expand the application of his Neo-HooDoo aesthetic. He also satirized a multitude of ideological elements in American and African-American culture, from the politics of Ronald Reagan to what Reed considered the misrepresentation of African-American males in the works of black feminist authors.

Like his novels, Reed's poetry further advanced his Neo-HooDoo aesthetic, particularly in works such as *Catechism of D Neoamerican Hoodoo Church* (1971) and *Conjure: Selected Poems, 1963–1970* (1972). Reed's aim in his fiction and poetry is an alternative view of history, one that recognizes America's multicultural origins and rescues history from the revisionism created by racism. "i am outside of / history. i wish / i had some peanuts, it / looks hungry there in / its cage," Reed writes in his poem "Dualism" from *Conjure*. Reed's other volumes of poetry include *Chattanooga: Poems* (1973), *A Secretary to the Spirits* (1977), and *New and Collected Poems* (1988).

Reed has often generated controversy for the iconoclastic and satirical nature of his fiction and poetry. No less vexing to Reed's detractors have been his numerous collections of essays. Reed defended his unconventional approach to writing in his first essay collection, *Shrovetide and Old New Orleans* (1978). "Many people have called my fiction muddled, crazy, incoherent," he wrote, "because I've attempted in fiction the techniques and forms painters, dancers, filmmakers, musicians in the West have taken for granted for 50 years, and the artists of many other cultures, for thousands of years."

In other essay collections, which include *God Made Alaska for the Indians: Selected Essays* (1982), *Writin' Is Fightin': Thirty-seven Years of Boxing on Paper* (1988), *Airing Dirty Laundry* (1993), *Multi America: Essays on Cultural Wars and Cultural Peace* (1997), *The Reed Reader* (2000), and *Another Day at the Front: Dispatches from the Race War* (2003), Reed has continued to bring his acerbic wit and penetrating insight to bear on a host of contemporary and historical issues regarding black culture in America.

During a prolific writing career that has spanned more than four decades, Ishmael Reed has distinguished himself as an innovative and compelling author in numerous genres. In addition to novels, poetry, and essays, Reed has written several plays: *The Lost State of Franklin* (1976, with his second wife, Carla Blank, and Suzushi Hanayaga); *The Ace Boons* (1980); and *Mother Hubbard* (1982). Reed also cofounded two independent publishing companies, Yardbird Publishing Company in 1971 and Reed, Cannon and Johnson Communications in 1973. With novelist and poet AL YOUNG, Reed founded the literary magazine *Quilt* in 1980, a periodical devoted to minority and student writings, and he has served for many years as a distinguished lecturer at the University of California at Berkeley. The recipient of numerous literary grants and two National Book Award nominations, Ishmael Reed is widely regarded as a provocative and original voice among contemporary African-American authors.

Further Reading

Boyer, Jay. *Ishmael Reed.* Boise, Idaho: Boise State University Press, 1993.

Dick, Bruce Allen, and Amritjit Singh, eds. *Conversations with Ishmael Reed.* Jackson: University Press of Mississippi, 1995.

Dick, Bruce Allen, and Pavel Zemliansky. *The Critical Response to Ishmael Reed.* Westport, Conn.: Greenwood Publishing Group, 1999.

Reed, Ishmael. *The Reed Reader.* New York: Basic Books, 2000.

Richardson, Willis
(ca. 1889–1977) *playwright, essayist, editor, educator*

A pioneer of African-American drama during the 1920s, Willis Richardson became the first black playwright to debut a nonmusical play on Broadway when *The Chip Woman's Fortune* opened at the Frazee Theatre in 1923. During an era in which American theater reinforced racial stereotypes in the limited and one-dimensional roles available for black actors, Richardson depicted in his dramas the richness and complexity of African-American culture. His efforts to create drama that entertained and educated black audiences prefigured the Black Aesthetic Movement of the 1960s.

Though sources differ as to the details of his place and date of birth, as well as the identity of his biological parents, Willis Richardson is thought to have been born on November 5, 1889, in Wilmington, North Carolina, to Willis and Agnes Ann Richardson. In the wake of racial riots in Wilmington in 1898, the Richardson family moved to Washington, D.C., where young Richardson attended public elementary school before graduating from the prestigious M Street High School (later renamed Dunbar High School) in 1910. Turning down a scholarship to Howard University, Richardson began work at the U.S. Bureau of Engraving and Printing in 1911, where he remained employed until his retirement in 1954, and where he met Mary Ellen Jones. The two were married in 1914 and had three children.

Encouraged to pursue drama by Mary Burrill, one of his high school teachers, and inspired by a 1916 production of ANGELINA WELD GRIMKÉ's play *Rachel*, Richardson began studying drama and poetry through a correspondence course. In 1919 he published an essay, "The Hope of a Negro Drama," in the *Crisis*, a monthly periodical published by the National Association for the Advancement of Colored People (NAACP) and edited by the eminent sociologist and critic W. E. B. DuBOIS. In the essay, Richardson wrote of his desire for drama that would reveal "the soul of a people." He published his first plays, one-act historical sketches of influential African Americans designed for children, in *The Brownie's Book*, a children's periodical published by W. E. B. DuBois and edited by JESSIE REDMOND FAUSET.

Richardson's first staged play, *The Deacon's Awakening*, was produced in St. Paul, Minnesota, in 1921. Encouraged in his writing by several early figures of the Harlem Renaissance, including DuBois, ALAIN LOCKE, a professor at Howard University and cofounder of the theatrical group Howard University Players, and the prominent educator Carter Woodson, Richardson began to generate interest in his drama. In 1923 *The Chip Woman's Fortune* was performed at the Frazee Theatre by the Ethiopian Art Players, an African-American theatrical company from Chicago. It was the first production of a serious drama by a black playwright to appear on Broadway.

During the 1920s and 1930s, Richardson became the preeminent African-American dramatist, winning first prize in drama in a *Crisis* literary contest for two plays, *Broken Banjo, A Folk Tragedy* (1925) and *The Bootblack Lover* (1926), both published in the *Crisis*. In the years that followed, Richardson wrote dozens of plays, many of which were mounted regularly in high school, university, and community productions throughout the United States. He also edited three groundbreaking anthologies of drama: *Plays and Pageants from the Life of the Negro* (1930), *Negro History in Thirteen Plays* (1935), and *The King's Dilemma and Other Plays for Children* (1956).

As he expressed in "The Hope of a Negro Drama," Richardson believed that "plays written by African Americans should focus on the black community and not on racial tension and differences." His plays were rooted in African-American folk traditions and depicted the social and familial struggles of everyday African Americans from all levels of society. At the height of his popularity as a playwright, Richardson joined an influential circle of leading Harlem Renaissance artists and writers, including LANGSTON HUGHES,

JEAN TOOMER, and ZORA NEALE HURSTON, with whom he regularly associated. In later years Richardson's plays fell out of fashion as trends in African-American drama became progressively more political. Willis Richardson died in 1977 in relative obscurity.

The author of more than 50 published and unpublished plays, and the first African-American dramatist to have a serious play produced on Broadway, Willis Richardson made significant contributions to the early development of African-American drama. His many awards included two Amy Spingarn prizes for drama in 1925 and 1926, and the Edith Schwarb Cup from Yale University in 1928. Modern scholars have shown a renewed interest in Richardson's drama, and recent publications of his plays and anthologies have brought his work to the attention of a new generation of readers.

Further Reading

Andrews, William L., Frances Foster, and Trudier Harris, eds. *The Concise Oxford Companion to African American Literature*. New York: Oxford University Press, 2001.

Gray, Christine Rauchfuss. *Willis Richardson, Forgotten Pioneer of African-American Drama*. Westport, Conn.: Greenwood Press, 1999.

Richardson, Willis. "The Broken Banjo." In *The Crisis Reader*, edited by Sondra Kathryn Wilson. New York: Random House, 1999.

Rodgers, Carolyn M.
(Carolyn Marie Rodgers)
(1945–   ) *poet, novelist, editor, educator*

During the Black Arts Movement of the 1960s, Carolyn M. Rodgers emerged as one of the most committed and controversial advocates of the so-called New Black Aesthetic, an artistic approach that sought to define and address the immediate social and political needs of the black community. Her aggressive style of writing, which often incorporated inflammatory and explicit language, resonated with women, whose perspectives within the Black Arts Movement were often overshadowed by those of their male counterparts. Known primarily as a poet and as cofounder with HAKI R. MADHUBUTI (then known as Don L. Lee) of Third World Press, Rodgers has also published a novel and contributed articles to Chicago's *Daily News* and Milwaukee's *Courier.*

Carolyn Marie Rodgers was born on December 14, 1945, in Chicago, Illinois, to Bazello and Clarence Rodgers. Her parents had moved north from Little Rock, Arkansas, shortly before her birth. The youngest of four children, Rodgers grew up on Chicago's South Side, where her attendance at the local African Methodist Episcopal Church was strictly enforced by her mother. Rodgers graduated from Hyde Park High School and briefly attended the University of Illinois in Urbana before transferring to Chicago's Roosevelt University. She later completed her bachelor's degree in English (1981) and a master's degree (1984) at Chicago State University.

Though she had started writing poetry as a teenager, Rodgers began to write seriously during the 1960s. With HOYT FULLER, Rodgers helped found the Organization of Black American Culture, which sponsored numerous writing workshops. "One night a week we came together to read our work to each other, to criticize and support each other, and to learn from our wonderful mentor, Hoyt W. Fuller," Rodgers later recalled. She also received early inspiration for her writing by attending workshops led by GWENDOLYN BROOKS, where she met other young writers like Don L. Lee (later known as Haki R. Madhubuti) and Johari Amini, with whom Rodgers founded Third World Press.

In 1968 Third World Press published Rodgers's first collection of poetry, *Paper Soul,* for which she received the Conrad Kent Rivers Memorial Award.

These early poems, which included such well-known works as "A Non Poem About Vietnam or Try Black," "Testimony," and "Now Ain't That Love," explored issues of revolution, religion, and relationships between men and women, themes that would remain central to her later writing. In the poem "One," Rodgers also revealed a vulnerable side, which would become increasingly visible in her later publications.

The poems in her second major collection, *Songs of a Blackbird* (1969), also demonstrated Rodgers's commitment to the principles of the Black Arts Movement. In poems such as "Breakthrough," however, Rodgers also expressed a need to indulge her creative freedom and to distinguish herself within the group of Black Arts authors. "How do I put myself on paper," she writes, "The way I want to be or am and be / Not like any one else in this / Black world but me." *Songs of a Blackbird* also contains two poems, "Jesus Was Crucified" and "It Is Deep," about the complicated but deeply influential relationship Rodgers had with her mother. In 1970 Rodgers received the Poet Laureate Award from the Society of Midland Authors.

Rodgers received a National Book Award nomination for her next collection of poems, *How I Got Ovah* (1975), her first book to be released by a major publisher. Taking its title from a Negro spiritual made popular by the legendary African-American gospel and opera singer Mahalia Jackson, *How I Got Ovah* and Rodgers's 1978 collection *The Heart As Ever Green* move further away in theme and tone from her early militant poems to explore issues of personal and spiritual identity.

Though her critical reputation as an author rests primarily on her early poetry collections, Rodgers has continued to publish numerous volumes through her own Eden Press, including *Translation* (1980), *Eden and Other Poems* (1983), *Morning Glory* (1989), *We're Only Human* (1994), *A Train Called Judah* (1996), *The Girl with Blue Hair* (1996), and *Salt* (1998). In addition to her poems, Rodgers has published a novel, *A Little Lower Than the Angels* (1984), and her short stories and poems have appeared in *Black Digest, Ebony,* and *Black Arts Anthology.*

During the 1960s and 1970s, Carolyn M. Rodgers helped define the principles of the Black Arts Movement with her emotionally raw and unconventional verse. Her later collections of poetry, conditioned by her conversion to Christianity, reveal a less militant though equally committed voice for racial and gender equality. In addition to her writing, Rodgers has taught English and African-American literature at Chicago State University, Columbia College, and Harold Washington College.

Further Reading

Evans, Mari, ed. *Black Women Writers (1950–1980): A Critical Evaluation.* Garden City, N.Y.: Doubleday, 1984.

Gates, Henry Louis, Jr., and Nellie Y. McKay, eds. *The Norton Anthology of African American Literature.* New York: Norton, 1997.

Hill, Patricia Liggins, ed. *The Riverside Anthology of the African American Literary Tradition.* Boston: Houghton Mifflin Co.: 1998.

S

Sanchez, Sonia
(Sonia Benita Sanchez, Wilsonia Benita Driver)

(1934–) *poet, playwright, children's fiction writer, short fiction writer, essayist, editor, educator*

Winner of the American Book Award for her poetry collection *Homegirls and Handgrenades* (1984), Sonia Sanchez has received wide acclaim for combining political activism with personal experience in a distinguished body of work that includes poetry, plays, children's fiction, short stories, and essays. A celebrated figure in the Black Arts Movement, Sanchez has remained a vital force in contemporary African-American poetry, performing her works on stages and in universities throughout North America, Europe, Africa, and Asia.

Sonia Sanchez was born Wilsonia Benita Driver in Birmingham, Alabama, on September 9, 1934, to Wilson Driver, a musician and teacher, and Lena Driver, who died when Sonia was still a baby. During her early childhood, Driver and her sister Pat lived with several relatives, including their paternal grandmother, who played an important role in Driver's early emotional development. When Driver was nine, her father moved the family to Harlem, where she attended public schools. She enrolled at Hunter College and completed her bachelor's degree in 1955. As a graduate stu-dent at New York University, Driver studied under the poet Louise Bogan, who encouraged her to write poetry.

During the 1950s and early 1960s, Driver became active in the Civil Rights movement as a member of the Congress of Racial Equality (CORE), founded in 1942 in Chicago, and which by 1961 had 53 chapters throughout the United States. Under the influence of poets AMIRI BARAKA (then known as LeRoi Jones) and LARRY NEAL, both early architects of the Black Arts Movement, she began to write poetry steeped in the politics and street vernacular of urban African-American communities. Driver also helped form the Broadside Quartet, a group of radical young poets that included HAKI R. MAD-HUBUTI, NIKKI GIOVANNI, and ETHERIDGE KNIGHT, whom she married in 1968 and later divorced. She was also briefly married to Albert Sanchez, a Puerto Rican immigrant.

In her early poetry, collected in *Homecoming* (1969) and *We a BaddDDD People* (1970), Sanchez celebrated icons of black culture, from Malcolm X to Billie Holiday. She also decried the physical brutality of racial oppression as well as the self-destructive elements of drug use and intraracial violence within the black community. One of the first African-American poets to employ the unconventional syntax and punctuation that characterized the work of many Black Arts poets, Sanchez also used the complex rhythms and black idioms of the street so effectively that fellow poet Haki R. Madhubuti credited Sanchez in *Black Women Writers, 1950–1980: A Critical Perspective* (1984) for "legitimizing the use of urban Black English in written form" more substantially than any other poet of the time.

In 1972 Sanchez joined the Nation of Islam (NOI). "The Nation was the one organization that was trying to deal with the concepts of nationhood, morality, small businesses, schools," Sanchez explained in Claudia Tate's *Black Women Writers at Work* (1983). However, the limitations placed on women by the NOI eventually compelled Sanchez to leave. Her poetry of this period, in such works as *Love Poems* (1973), *A Blues Book for Blues Black Magical Women* (1973), and *I've Been a Woman: New and Selected Poems* (1978), reflected a growing concern for the role of black women in society and her own evolving sense of what it meant to be a woman. "*Blues Book* is about my motions and observations as a child," Sanchez explained in Tate's *Black Women Writers at Work,* "as a young black woman, and about how society does not prepare young black women, or women period, to be women."

Throughout her career as a poet, Sanchez has remained committed to the political and creative principles of her early writing, particularly in her 1984 collection *Homegirls and Handgrenades,* for which she received an American Book Award. Her later collections, which include *Under a Soprano Sky* (1987), *Wounded in the House of a Friend* (1995), *Does Your House Have Lions?* (1997), *Like the Singing Coming Off Drums* (1998), and *Shake Loose My Skin: New and Selected Poems* (1999), have continued to honor black cultural heroes of the past and present, while also highlighting the urgency of contemporary issues such as AIDS.

Though known primarily as a poet, Sanchez has published in a variety of genres, including children's literature, drama, and essays, and she has edited several literary anthologies. Her works for children include *It's a New Day: Poems for Young Brothas and Sistuhs* (1971) and two collections of children's stories, *The Adventures of Fat Head, Small Head, and Square Head* (1973) and *A Sound Investment and Other Stories* (1979). Sanchez has also published and produced numerous plays: *The Bronx Is Next* (1968), about a plot to burn down a Harlem ghetto; *Sister Son/ji* (1969), in which a black woman rediscovers her cultural roots; *Uh, Huh, But How Do It Free Us?* (1974), which dramatizes the urgent need for sexual as well as racial equality; *Malcolm Man/Don't Live Here No Mo'* (1979), about the civil rights leader Malcolm X; *I'm Black When I'm Singing, I'm Blue When I Ain't* (1982); and *Black Cats Back and Uneasy Landings* (1995).

In her more than 30 years as a poet, Sanchez has earned the acclaim of peers and critics for the clarity of her poetic vision and her mastery of language, nowhere more apparent than in her spoken performances of her work. Sanchez has performed her poetry throughout the United States, as well as in Europe, Africa, Cuba, China, and the West Indies. She has also released numerous recordings of her readings, sometimes with the accompaniment of jazz musicians.

Throughout her distinguished career as an author, Sanchez has maintained a strong commitment to her role as an educator. As a professor at San Francisco State University from 1967 to 1969, Sanchez was instrumental in the establishment of a black studies department. She has also taught at the University of Pittsburgh, Amherst College in Massachusetts, and Temple University.

Widely regarded as one of the most respected poets to emerge from the Black Arts Movement, Sonia Sanchez has earned numerous literary and community service honors, including the American Book Award, the Lucretia Mott Award, and the Pennsylvania Governor's Award for Excellence in the Humanities. An innovative and influential voice among contemporary African-American poets and authors, Sanchez has for more than three decades occupied an essential place within American and African-American literature.

Further Reading

Joyce, Joyce Ann. *Ijala: Sonia Sanchez and the African Poetic Tradition*. Chicago, Ill.: Third World Press, 1996.

Sanchez, Sonia. *Homegirls and Handgrenades*. Detroit, Mich.: Third World Press, 1984.

Tate, Claudia, ed. *Black Women Writers at Work*. New York: Continuum Publishing Group, 1983.

Schuyler, George
(George Samuel Schuyler, Samuel I. Brooks, Rachel Call, Edgecombe Wright, John Kitchen, William Stockton, Verne Caldwell, D. Johnson)
(1895–1977) *journalist, novelist, short story writer*

George Schuyler was the preeminent African-American journalist of the early 20th century and considered one of the finest newsmen of any period. Called the "Black Mencken," Schuyler is the first African American to be known primarily as a satirist and the first to serve as a foreign correspondent for a major metropolitan newspaper.

George Samuel Schuyler was born on February 25, 1895, in Providence, Rhode Island, and was raised in Syracuse, New York. His father, George Francis Schuyler, was a chef in a local hotel, and the family lived in a racially mixed middle-class neighborhood. From his mother, Eliza Jane Fischer, George learned to read and write at a young age and developed a love of books from the modest library that she had collected.

Schuyler was quick to distinguish himself as a descendent of free blacks as far back as pre-revolutionary times, and that self-confidence informs much of his fictional and journalistic work. He attended public school in New York until the age of 17, when he left to enlist in the U.S. Army. From 1912 to 1919 he served in the black 25th U.S. Infantry, earning the rank of first lieutenant and fighting in France during World War I.

In 1921 Schuyler joined the Socialist Party, where he met Asa Philip Randolph, editor of the *Messenger,* a radical black magazine based in Harlem. Schuyler began his long and prolific career in journalism in 1923 as an assistant editor under Randolph at the *Messenger,* and then as a columnist, contributing a monthly piece entitled "Shafts and Darts: A Page of Calumny and Satire." The following year, he became the New York correspondent for the *Pittsburgh Courier,* a relationship that would endure for more than 40 years. In that time, he wrote a weekly column, "Views and Reviews," several investigative pieces, including a series on race relations in Mississippi in 1925–26, and served as a foreign correspondent in South America, Portugal, the Caribbean, and Africa.

Though Schuyler's work dominated the pages of such esteemed newspapers and journals of the African American community as the *Messenger,* the *Crisis,* and the *Pittsburgh Courier,* Schuyler also published essays in such notable mainstream publications as the *New York Evening Post,* the *Washington Post,* H. L. Mencken's the *American Mercury,* and the *Nation.* Schuyler's essay "The Negro Art Hokum," published in the *Nation* 1926, caused many of his contemporaries, writers of the Harlem Renaissance, to criticize him for his perceived assimilationist views.

His assertion that literature should be judged by literary standards and not on the basis of race prompted a reply by the poet LANGSTON HUGHES, a central figure in the Harlem Renaissance. In his famous essay "The Negro Artist and the Racial Mountain," Hughes criticizes those black writers "who would surrender racial pride in the name of a false integration." Schuyler's marriage to a white artist, Josephine Cogdell, in 1928, and his rigorous criticisms of fellow African-American artists and activists contributed to the growing perception among some that Schuyler was an enemy of his race.

In 1931 Schuyler further distanced himself from his contemporaries with the publication of his most successful work, the satirical novel *Black No More.* In the story, Dr. Junius Crookman makes a landmark discovery of a method to convert black people to white. The novel examines the ramifications of such a change and exposes the myth of racial purity on both sides of the color line. Schuyler includes thinly disguised parodies of many leading African-American figures, including W. E. B. DuBois (Dr. Shakespeare Agamemnon Beard), Marcus Garvey (Santop Licorice), and Madame C. J. "Sarah" Walker (Madame Sisseretta Blandish).

While Schuyler's reputation has rested primarily on his contributions to journalism and his novel *Black No More,* recent scholarship has revealed that between 1933 and 1939, he published some 54 short stories and four serialized novels in the pages of the *Pittsburgh Courier* under various pseudonyms. These works include *The Black Internationale* and *Black Empire,* published together in 1991 by Northeastern University Press under the title *Black Empire.* The nationalist tone of this work, in which the charismatic and diabolical Dr. Belsidus leads a worldwide revolt against white society to reclaim Africa and establish a dominant black society, contrasts sharply with his negative characterization of other nationalist leaders such as Marcus Garvey.

In his later years, Schuyler became increasingly conservative, eschewing his former ties to the Socialist Party and becoming something of a red-baiter in his militant stance against communism, which he perceived was misleading African Americans with a false sense of solidarity. He published his autobiography *Black and Conservative* in 1966 and continued to stir up yet more controversy with his criticism of Martin Luther King, Jr., and the Civil Rights movement as a whole, prompting the *Pittsburgh Courier* to disavow any agreement with his editorial opinions and eventually to drop him as a correspondent.

Schuyler ended his long and distinguished career in journalism with the ultraconservative *Manchester Union Leader,* a New Hampshire–based

daily. His daughter Philippa, an accomplished concert pianist and also a correspondent for the *Union Leader,* died on May 9, 1967, in a helicopter crash while on assignment in Vietnam, and his wife died two years later. George Samuel Schuyler died in 1977.

Despite the alienation he suffered as a result of his extreme political and racial views, Schuyler remains an intriguing and influential figure in African-American literature. He was a pioneer in the genre of science fiction, leading the way for later authors like SAMUEL R. DELANY and OCTAVIA BUTLER, and certainly one of the finest journalists of the early 20th century.

Further Reading

Gates, Henry Louis, Jr. "A Fragmented Man: George Schuyler and the Claims of Race." *New York Times Book Review,* September 20, 1992, pp. 42–43.

Schuyler, George S. *Black and Conservative: The Autobiography of George S. Schuyler.* Boston: Northeastern University Press, 1991.

———. *Black Empire.* New Rochelle, N.Y.: Arlington House Publishers, 1966.

———. "The Negro Art Hokum." *Within the Circle: An Anthology of African American Literary Criticism from the Harlem Renaissance to the Present.* Durham, N.C.: Duke University Press, 1994.

Séjour, Victor
(Juan Victor Séjour Marcou et Ferrand)
(1817–1874) *short story writer, playwright, poet*

Known primarily for his extravagantly staged dramas, which were immensely popular in Paris during the mid-19th century, Victor Séjour is also credited with publishing the earliest known short story by an African-American writer. *Le Mulâtre* ("The Mulatto") appeared in a Paris journal, *La revue des colonies,* in 1837. Séjour was a friend of several European literary luminaries, including the distinguished novelist Alexandre Dumas *père,* and his dramas enjoyed wide popular support in Europe and the United States.

Juan Victor Séjour Marcou et Ferrand was born on June 2, 1817, in New Orleans, Louisiana, to François Marcou, a free black from Santo Domingo, and Eloisa Ferrand, a woman of mixed-race parentage from New Orleans. Séjour was educated at the respected Sainte Barbe Academy in New Orleans and showed an early interest in literature. Following his graduation, his family sent him to Paris to continue his education, where he remained after completing his studies to pursue a literary career.

In 1837 Séjour published his short story *Le Mulâtre* ("The Mulatto") in the French journal *La revue des colonies,* published by the French abolitionist Cyrille Bisette. Set in the Haitian town of St.-Domingue, the story depicts a slave's murder of his master, whom he discovers later to be his father. Written in French, *Le Mulâtre* ("The Mulatto") first appeared in translation in the *Norton Anthology of African American Literature* (1997).

Séjour published his next work, the heroic ode *Le retour de Napoléon,* in 1841. Nationalist in tone, the poem celebrated the return of Napoléon's remains to France and secured Séjour his first literary success. He earned the respect of several leading French writers, including Alexandre Dumas *pére,* also of mixed African descent, and the playwright Émile Augier. *Le retour de Napoléon* was later published in the United States in Armand Lanusse's *Les Cenelles,* an anthology of African-American poetry published in 1845.

With the production of his first play, *Diégarias* (1844), Séjour began a 25-year career as one of France's leading dramatists. His early plays were historical dramas written in verse. During the 1850s, Séjour earned national popularity for prose melodramas and comedies that featured elaborate sets and costumes. Among his most popular were *Richard III* (1852), *Le fils de la nuit* (1856), and *Les volontaires de 1814,* his only play with an American theme, the defense of New Orleans against the English. By the late 1860s, after the production of 21 plays, Séjour found no market for his

work. He suffered several years of poverty and privation, during which his health began to fail. In 1874 Juan Victor Séjour Marcou et Ferrand was admitted to the charity ward of a Paris hospital, where he died of consumption (tuberculosis).

During his most successful years as a dramatist in Paris, Victor Séjour was relatively unknown in the United States. His impact on African-American and American writers, however, remains significant. His short story *Le Mulâtre* ("The Mulatto") was one of the first literary works to explore the psychological traumas inflicted by slavery. Séjour's expatriation in Paris, where he was free of the constraints imposed by a racially oppressive society, set an example for such later writers as CHESTER HIMES, RICHARD WRIGHT, and JAMES BALDWIN, all of whom sought refuge in France to pursue their literary careers.

Further Reading

Andrews, William L., Frances Smith Foster, and Trudier Harris, eds. *The Concise Oxford Companion to African American Literature.* New York: Oxford University Press, 2001.

Gates, Henry Louis, Jr., and Nellie Y. McKay, eds. *The Norton Anthology of African American Literature.* New York: W. W. Norton, 1997.

O'Neill, Charles E. *Séjour: Parisian Playwright from Louisiana.* Lafayette: University of Southwestern Louisiana, 1996.

Séjour, Victor. *The Jew of Seville.* Translated by Norman R. Shapiro. Urbana-Champaign: University of Illinois Press, 2002.

Shange, Ntozake (Paulette Linda Williams) (1948–   ) *playwright, poet, novelist*

An innovative and award-winning author of plays, poetry, and novels, Ntozake Shange became only the second African-American woman (LORRAINE HANSBERRY was the first) to have a play produced on Broadway when *for colored girls who have considered suicide/when the rainbow is enuf* opened at the Booth Theatre in New York in 1976. The play transformed Shange from a relatively unknown poet and dancer to an internationally celebrated author.

Ntozake Shange was born Paulette Linda Williams on October 18, 1948, in Trenton, New Jersey. Her father, Paul Williams, was a surgeon, and her mother, Eloise Williams, worked as a psychiatric social worker and educator. Raised in a comfortable middle-class home, she enjoyed a culturally rich childhood. "My parents have always been especially involved in all kinds of Third World culture," Shange explained in Claudia Tate's *Black Women Writers at Work* (1983). "We used to go to hear Latin music, jazz and symphonies, to see ballets." Frequent guests to her parents' home included such legendary musicians as Josephine Baker, Charlie Parker, and Miles Davis, as well as the renowned sociologist and critic W. E. B. DuBOIS.

Ntozake Shange became an overnight success with her 1976 Broadway production of *for colored girls who have considered suicide/when the rainbow is enuf.* *(Jules Allen)*

In 1953 Williams moved with her family to St. Louis, Missouri, where she was one of the first African-American students in that city to integrate the public school system. She returned to New Jersey in 1961 and attended Morristown High School. She began to rebel against her middle-class upbringing and explored her changing perspective in poetry as a high school student. Though she published some of her work in her high school literary magazine, she was often criticized by teachers and fellow students for her Afrocentric themes.

Following the end of her first marriage, Williams enrolled at Barnard College in 1966, marking a difficult transitional period in her life. Despite her emotional turmoil, which led to several suicide attempts, she completed her bachelor's degree and graduated with honors in 1970. She moved to California and enrolled in graduate studies at the University of Southern California in Los Angeles, and completed her master's degree in 1973. Adopting the name Ntozake Shange (a Zulu name meaning "she who comes with her own things" and "one who walks with lions"), Shange began to write in earnest.

Shange participated in the Third World Women's Cooperative during the early 1970s, where she joined women writers and dancers of many different cultural backgrounds in performing poetry, drama, and dance throughout the San Francisco Bay area. "We did our work for our own people," she explained in 1983, "and all of my work just grew from there." Shange also taught humanities and women's studies courses at Mills College and Sonoma State College, and she starred in a theatrical production of *The Evolution of Black Dance*, which toured public schools in Oakland and Berkeley in 1973 and 1974. Shange's early theatrical experiences helped shape the themes and structure of her first major dramatic work.

Shange's first play, *for colored girls who have considered suicide/when the rainbow is enuf,* was produced off-Broadway in New York in 1975. The play opened on Broadway the following year. Shange has been credited with defining a new genre, the choreopoem, with her blend of drama, poetry, and dance in *for colored girls*. In the voices of seven women, named according to the color of their respective dresses, the play decried the physical, sexual, and racial exploitation of black women in American society. *for colored girls* earned Obie and Outer Critics Circle Awards, and was nominated for Tony, Grammy, and Emmy Awards in 1977; but some critics faulted Shange for what was perceived as an unfairly negative portrait of black men. "My job as an artist," Shange responded, "is to say what I see."

Shange continued to explore the themes of identity and personal renewal in later plays, while also continuing to blur the distinctions between drama and poetry. Her later dramatic works include *A Photograph: Still Life with Shadows* (1977), *Where the Mississippi Meets the Amazon* (1977), and *Spell #7* (1979). In 1980 Shange produced an adaptation of Bertolt Brecht's play *Mother Courage and Her Children,* for which she received a second Obie Award. *The Love Space Demands,* a performance piece in which Shange read her poetry to the accompaniment of guitarist Bill Patterson, was produced in 1992.

A prolific author whose works cross multiple genres, Shange has also published novels, poetry, and essays. *Sassafras: A Novella* appeared in 1976, followed by her first novel, *Sassafras, Cypress, and Indigo* (1982). In 1985 Shange published *Betsey Brown,* a semiautobiographical novel about a young woman's struggle to break with her family's middle-class values and discover her own identity. Shange's other novels include *Liliane: Resurrection of the Daughter* (1994) and three works for young adults, *Whitewash* (1997), *Float Like a Butterfly* (2002), and *Daddy Says* (2003).

Much of Shange's poetry has formed the foundation of her drama. Her earliest poems informed the creation of her first drama, *for colored girls,* in 1975. Shange published her first collection of poetry, *Nappy Edges,* in 1978. Like her plays, Shange's poetry addresses the physical and emotional development of African-American women and emphasizes the vital role that Shange

feels women play in combating the violence and hatred of contemporary society. Shange's other volumes of poetry include *Natural Disasters and Other Festive Occasions* (1979), *A Daughter's Geography* (1983), in which Shange chronicles her extensive travel in the South Pacific and Central and South America, *From Okra to Greens* (1984), *Ridin' the Moon in Texas: Word Paintings* (1987), and *I Live in Music* (1994).

Though Ntozake Shange has distinguished herself in several genres, she is recognized particularly for her contributions to American and African-American drama. Her use of what she calls the choreopoem, an amalgam of drama, poetry, and dance, has had an important impact on contemporary dramatists, particularly in the work of Pulitzer Prize–winning dramatist SUZAN-LORI PARKS. Shange's unconventional use of grammar and punctuation reveal her abiding interest in the ability of language to express personal truths. "I listen to words," Shange explained in a 1976 interview in the *New Yorker,* "and when people can't say what they mean they are in trouble."

Further Reading

Gates, Henry Louis, Jr., and Nellie Y. McKay, eds. *The Norton Anthology of African American Literature.* New York: W. W. Norton, 1997.

Hill, Patricia Liggins, ed. *Call and Response: The Riverside Anthology of the African American Literary Tradition.* Boston: Houghton Mifflin and Co., 1998.

Lester, Neal A. *Ntozake Shange: A Critical Study of the Plays.* New York: Garland, 1995.

Shange, Ntozake. *for colored girls who have considered suicide/when the rainbow was enuf.* San Lorenzo, Calif.: Shameless Hussy Press, 1975.

Spencer, Anne
(Annie Bethel Scales Bannister)
(1882–1975) *poet, educator, social activist*

One of the most innovative poets of the Harlem Renaissance, Anne Spencer published fewer than

30 poems during her lifetime. Her small body of published work appeared in numerous anthologies of African-American poetry, during and after the Harlem Renaissance, and she was only the second African-American poet to be included in the *Norton Anthology of Modern Poetry*. Her distinctive style and artistic vision brought her national attention as a poet of considerable depth, even eliciting comparisons to the white American poet Emily Dickinson.

Spencer was born Annie Bethel Scales Bannister on February 6, 1882, in Henry County, Virginia. Her father, Joel Cephus Bannister, was of African and Native American ancestry, and her mother, Sarah Louise Scales, was the daughter of a former slave and her white owner. Bannister's parents separated when she was six, and she moved with her mother to the coal mining community of Bramwell, West Virginia. Unable to support her daughter without assistance, Sarah Scales placed Annie with a foster family and contributed to her support by working as a cook.

With little formal education as a child, Bannister learned to read from the books and magazines that her foster father read. To avoid the limited educational opportunities available in the local free black school in Bramwell, she was enrolled in the Virginia Seminary, an all-black academy, in 1892. Demonstrating an early independence of thought, she wrote her first poem, "The Skeptic," in 1896, in opposition to the prevailing religious dogma of the school. She excelled as a student, graduating as the valedictorian of her class in 1899. She married Edward Spencer, a fellow graduate of Virginia Academy, in 1901 and settled in Lynchburg, Virginia. Her husband's job as a postal worker afforded the couple a prosperous middle-class life in which to raise their three children.

To spare his wife the duties of maintaining the household and rearing their three children, Edward engaged domestic servants. He also designed and built an elaborate garden and small cottage to provide inspiration for his wife's writing and a place for her to work in seclusion. The cottage was named Edankraal, which combined their two names with the Afrikaans word *kraal* meaning "refuge." Spencer devoted her time to tending the garden, writing poetry, and working at a library on the campus of the all-black Dunbar High School, where she was employed from 1923 to 1943.

On a visit to Lynchburg to establish a local chapter of the National Association for the Advancement of Colored People (NAACP), JAMES WELDON JOHNSON, an accomplished poet and civil rights activist, learned of Spencer's writings. He convinced her to publish her poetry, and the poem "Before the Feast of Shushan" appeared in the *Crisis*, the monthly periodical published by the NAACP, in 1920. Johnson was the first of many leading African-American intellectuals, artists, and activists to visit the Spencer home. Others included W. E. B. DUBOIS, LANGSTON HUGHES, and in the early 1960s, Martin Luther King, Jr. The appearance of her poetry in the *Crisis* earned her the admiration of many Harlem Renaissance artists, and her poems appeared in numerous anthologies, including Johnson's *The Book of American Negro Poetry* in 1922, ALAIN LOCKE's *The New Negro* in 1925, and COUNTEE CULLEN's *Caroling Dusk: An Anthology of Verse by Black Poets*, in 1927.

"Before the Feast of Shushan" and the frequently anthologized "At the Carnival," first published in 1927, are representative of the recurring themes of female identity and gender bias in much of her poetry. Both poems address the objectification of women and the limitations placed on them by a corrupt world. In "Before the Feast of Shushan," the drunken king views his wife merely as a tool for the fulfillment of his pleasure. The king muses angrily, "How says Vashti, love is both bread and wine," while his own opinion of love provides the final lines of the poem. "Love is but desire and thy purpose fulfillment / I, thy King, so say!"

In "At the Carnival," Spencer contrasts the innocence of a young woman, the "Girl-of-the-Diving-Tank," who exists "amid the malodorous / Mechanics of this unlovely thing," with those around her, whom life and circumstance has corrupted. Spencer concludes that the young woman's death as an innocent is preferable to life's long, slow decay, wherein "Years may seep into your soul." Spencer's exploration of gender and the unique attributes of female identity was characteristic of her highly individualized poetry, setting her apart from most of her contemporaries by its general lack of overtly political or racial protest and its focus on universal themes of existence.

Fiercely independent in her life and in her poetry, Spencer resisted any attempt to compromise the integrity of her work. She refused the assistance of the acclaimed critic and editor H. L. Mencken, who helped further the careers of numerous African-American writers. She defied her editors by publishing poems that directly attacked the prevailing notions of racial and gender inequality, and she differed with many of her African-American contemporaries within the NAACP by her opposition to the integration of schools.

Following the death of her husband in 1964, Spencer retired from society and suffered frequent illness. She continued to write, producing hundreds of poems, essays, and the beginning of a novel. Many of her writings were scribbled on whatever scrap of paper was at hand. Following her hospitalization shortly before her death, friends who did not understand their worth apparently discarded most of her papers, and her garden cottage was vandalized. Anne Spencer died on July 27, 1975.

More than any other writer of the Harlem Renaissance era, Spencer focused less on racial issues than on broader, existential themes. In J. Lee Greene's *Time's Unfading Garden: Anne Spencer's Life and Poetry,* she is quoted as saying that she "react[s] to life more as a human being than as a Negro being." In her life, however, Spencer often took radical steps to protest racial prejudice. She helped organize her local chapter of the NAACP, wrote inflammatory newspaper articles challenging the superiority of whites, and boycotted the local transit department in opposition to segregation. Her unique vision as a poet secured her an enduring reputation as one of the most complex and innovative African-American writers of the 20th century.

Further Reading

Cullen, Countee. *Caroling Dusk: An Anthology of Verse by Black Poets.* New York: Carol Publishing Group, 1993.

Gates, Henry Louis, Jr., and Nellie Y. McKay, eds. *The Norton Anthology of African American Literature.* New York: W. W. Norton, 1997.

Greene, J. Lee. *Time's Unfolding Garden: Anne Spencer's Life and Poetry.* Baton Rouge: Louisiana State University Press, 1977.

T

Taylor, Mildred D.
(Mildred Delois Taylor)
(1943–) *children's and young adult fiction writer*

In her award-winning novels for children and young adults, Mildred Taylor celebrates the strength and unity of African-American families and communities, particularly in the face of overwhelming social and racial prejudice. In her acceptance speech for a 1997 award from the *ALAN Review,* which focuses on literature for adolescents, Taylor described the narrative focus of her writing: "I envisioned presenting a family united in love and self-respect, and parents, strong and sensitive, attempting to guide their children successfully without harming their spirits, through the hazardous maze of living in a discriminatory society."

Mildred Delois Taylor was born on September 13, 1943, in Jackson, Mississippi, the second daughter of Wilber Lee Taylor and Deletha Marie Taylor. Taylor's parents relocated shortly after her birth to Toledo, Ohio, where they hoped to find a less violent and racist community in which to raise their two daughters. During her childhood, Taylor's home was filled with aunts, uncles, and other extended family members, whose stories of family history and folklore provided an early influence on her creative aspirations.

As a student at Scott High School, Taylor edited the school newspaper and became the only African American from her school to be named to the National Honor Society. Following her graduation in 1961, Taylor enrolled at the University of Toledo. She intended to major in creative writing, but to satisfy her parents, who preferred that she study something more practical, Taylor completed her bachelor's degree in English, with a minor in history, in 1965.

Taylor spent the next two years teaching English in Ethiopia as a member of the Peace Corps. She also served as a Peace Corps recruiter for a year prior to her enrollment at the University of Colorado in Boulder, where she completed a master's degree in journalism in 1969. Taylor was an active member of the Black Student Alliance, and following her graduation she worked with the University of Colorado to improve the black studies department. In 1971 Taylor moved to Los Angeles, California, to devote more time to her writing.

Though she had written numerous stories and completed the manuscript of a novel during the 1960s, Taylor achieved her first success as a writer with the story "Song of the Trees," which won a literary contest sponsored by the Council on Interracial Books in 1973, and was subsequently published as an illustrated children's book by Dial Press in 1975. *Song of the Trees,* the story of an African-American man's battle to save his land from an unscrupulous white logger, introduced the Logan family, whose various members would serve as the narrators for Taylor's later books.

In 1976 Taylor published *Roll of Thunder, Hear My Cry,* her most successful and best-known work of fiction. The novel chronicles the struggles of the Logan family, and in particular the novel's narrator, Cassie Logan, as they suffer the devastating effects of racial oppression and violence in the South during the 1930s. The novel earned Taylor the 1977 Newbery Medal, awarded by the American Library Association, and a nomination for the National Book Award. The critical and popular success of the novel established Taylor as a nationally respected author for young adults and brought her the financial wherewithal to devote herself exclusively to writing.

In subsequent years, Taylor published several more books about the Logan family, each of which explored various aspects of the African-American struggle for equality and justice in the overwhelmingly hostile society of the pre–civil rights South. *Let the Circle Be Unbroken* (1981), in which a Logan family friend unjustly stands trial for murder, depicts young Cassie's growing awareness of how segregation impacts her life. The novel earned an American Book Award nomination and won the Coretta Scott King Award in 1982. Other books in the Logan family series include *The Road to Memphis* (1990), *The Well: David's Story* (1995), and *The Land* (2001), a prequel to *Roll of Thunder, Hear My Cry.* Taylor has also published several novels that, though not exclusively focused on the Logan family, feature various family members. These works include *The Friendship* (1987), *The Gold Cadillac* (1987), and *Mississippi Bridge* (1990).

Mildred Taylor has earned numerous honors for her young adult fiction, including National Book Award and American Book Award nominations, four Coretta Scott King Awards, and the National Council of Teachers of English's Assembly on Literature for Adolescents' ALAN Award for Significant Contributions to Young Adult Literature in 1997. In her acceptance speech for the ALAN Award, Taylor credited the stories told to her during her childhood for her literary inspiration. "From *Song of the Trees* to *The Well,*" she explained, "I have attempted to present a true picture of life in America . . . as I remember it in the days before the Civil Rights movement." While her novels document the intense racial hatred suffered by African Americans, Taylor's books also emphasize the love among black families and communities, whose unity provided the strength to persevere.

Further Reading

Andrews, William L., Frances Smith Foster, and Trudier Harris, eds. *The Concise Oxford Companion to African American Literature.* New York: Oxford University Press, 2001.

Crowe, Chris. *Presenting Mildred Taylor.* New York: Twayne Publishers, 1999.

Taylor Mildred D. *Roll of Thunder, Hear My Cry.* New York: Dial Press, 1976.

Terry, Lucy
(Lucy Terry Prince)
(ca. 1730–1821) *poet*

Lucy Terry is best known as the author of the first poem written by an African-American woman. She also distinguished herself as a woman of remarkable intelligence with a gift for public speaking that was eulogized following her death for its ability "to captivate all around her."

Lucy Terry was born in Africa, probably in 1730. She was kidnapped by slave traders as a child and brought to Newport, Rhode Island, in 1735, where she was sold to Ebenezer Wells. She spent the next 20 years with the Wells family in Deerfield, Massachusetts, as a domestic slave. She converted to Christianity and was baptized during the Great Awakening that swept across New England in the middle 1700s under the leadership of Jonathan Edwards and George Whitefield.

In 1746, at the age of 16, Lucy witnessed an Indian ambush of two white families in a Deerfield meadow known as The Bars. She recorded the event in her poem "Bars Fight," written in rhymed tetrameter couplets and preserved orally by local residents for more than a century before it was published in Josiah Holland's *History of Western Massachusetts* in 1855. The poem relates in great detail the slaughter of the two families, including the names of the slain, and conveys sympathy for their deaths.

In 1756 Lucy married Abijah Prince, a soldier and former slave who had inherited land from his former master and who had spent 10 years saving the money required to buy Lucy's freedom. The Princes settled in Deerfield and reared six children. In 1770 they relocated to Guilford, Vermont, where Abijah had acquired additional land. Abijah Prince died in 1794, and Lucy remained in Guilford with her children until 1803, after which she settled in Sunderland, Vermont.

An early advocate for civil rights, Lucy Prince encouraged her oldest son to attend Williams College. When his application was refused, she is reputed to have traveled to Williamstown, Massachusetts, and delivered a three-hour address to the college trustees decrying their policy of racial discrimination. Though she failed to convince the trustees to admit her son, Prince gained a reputation as a gifted orator. She further demonstrated her eloquence and erudition as a speaker and advocate when a land dispute with a neighbor went before the U.S. Circuit Court. When she became dissatisfied with her lawyer, Isaac Ticknor (a future governor of Vermont), she argued her own case before the judge, who praised her arguments for being better than any he had heard from the Vermont bar and decided the case in her favor.

Lucy Terry Prince remained in Sunderland, Vermont, until her death in 1821, at the age of 91. Her place in African-American literary history rests primarily on "Bars Fight," her one surviving poem. Apart from the literary merits of this work, the poem stands as the first to be composed by an African-American woman. In addition, Prince's efforts to defend her civil and legal rights

in the face of oppression establish her as a forerunner of the leaders and movements that would shape the literature and history of African Americans in the decades that followed.

Further Reading

Andrews, William L., Frances Smith Foster, and Trudier Harris, eds. *The Oxford Companion to African American Literature.* New York: Oxford University Press, 1997.

Kaplan, Sidney. *The Black Presence in the Era of the American Revolution.* Sidney Kaplan and Emma Nogrady Kaplan, eds. Amherst: University of Massachusetts Press, 1989.

Lauter, Paul, ed. *The Heath Anthology of American Literature.* Vol. 1. Lexington, Mass.: D. C. Heath and Company, 1994.

Thomas, Joyce Carol
(1938–   ) *poet, novelist, young adult fiction writer, playwright, editor, educator*

In her novels, poetry, and plays, Joyce Carol Thomas celebrates the healing power of community and draws heavily on African-American folk traditions. Also a distinguished professor of creative writing, black studies, and literature, she has led seminars and workshops on writing and cultural studies in Nigeria and Haiti.

The fifth of eight children, Joyce Carol Thomas was born Joyce Carol Haynes on May 25, 1938, in Ponca City, Oklahoma, to Floyd and Leona Haynes. Her father was a bricklayer, and her mother worked as a hairstylist. In the small agricultural community of Ponca City, Haynes developed a special bond to her hometown, and she would draw on its people and atmosphere in her later fiction. At the age of 10, she moved to rural Tracy, California, where she harvested crops alongside Mexican migrant workers during the summers and became interested in the Spanish language.

Haynes married Gettis Withers in 1959 and raised her four children while working as a telephone operator during the day and studying Spanish and French at San Jose State University in the evenings. In 1967 she finished her master's degree in education at Stanford University and began teaching French and Spanish in the Ravenwood School District of Palo Alto, California. In 1968, Haynes's marriage to Gettis Withers ended. That same year she married Roy Thomas, Jr., a college professor. Between 1969 and 1980, Thomas taught black studies, creative writing, and literature in many local California colleges, published three volumes of poetry, and wrote four two-act plays.

With a growing reputation as a poet and dramatist, Thomas published her first novel, *Marked by Fire,* in 1981. The book won the National Book Award for young adult fiction as well as the Before Columbus American Book Award, and it became a classic of adolescent fiction, appearing frequently on high school reading lists. Set in the author's hometown of Ponca City, Oklahoma, *Marked by Fire* tells the story of Abyssinia Jackson, who was born in a cotton field and marked by an ember from a fire. A local healer predicts that she has been "marked for unbearable pain and unspeakable joy." Experiencing profound tragedies in her childhood, particularly her rape at the age of 10, Abyssinia draws on the strength of her family and Mother Barker, the town's spiritual healer, to regain her emotional strength and a spiritual faith that was badly damaged by her suffering.

Bright Shadow, Thomas's second novel, was published in 1983, and picks up Abyssinia's story during her college years. Once again enmeshed in difficult circumstances following the brutal murder of her aunt, Abyssinia learns that pain and beauty are constant and dynamic elements of life. Two other novels, *The Golden Pasture* and *Water Girl,* both published in 1986, explore the lives of characters introduced in her first two works. Though not received with the critical attention given to *Marked by Fire,* Thomas's young adult novels found an eager audience among children and adults.

In 1990 Thomas edited the critically acclaimed *A Gathering of Flowers: Stories about Being Young in America,* a collection of stories that depict the life and culture of various ethnic groups, including African-American, Native American, and Hispanic. She also published *Brown Honey and Broomwheat Tea,* a collection of children's verse about love and family that won the Coretta Scott King Honor Book Award for 1994. Collaborating with illustrator Frank Cooper, Thomas produced two more volumes of children's verse, *Ginger-bread Days* in 1995, and *I Have Heard of a Land* in 1998.

With the publication of *House of Light* in 2001, Thomas shifted her literary focus toward adult fiction, while also returning to Ponca City, Oklahoma, and Abyssinia Jackson, who in this novel was married and practicing medicine. Thomas's familiar themes of redemptive suffering and the influence of family, community, and home in the shaping of personal identity, dominate the novel.

The winner of many literary awards and fellowships and the author of numerous volumes of poetry, Joyce Carol Thomas was named Poet Laureate for Life in 1996 by the University of Oklahoma Center for Poets and Writers. In her poetry, fiction, and drama, Thomas draws on her roots in Oklahoma and California to portray the hardships and joys of life in rural African-American communities as well as to document the influences of African Americans on the history and culture of the western United States. Her writing also explores the process of cultural and emotional self-discovery. In a 1998 interview with *African American Review,* Thomas expressed the hope that readers of all ethnic backgrounds will "gain at least a little awareness of the lives of black Americans while also finding those universal needs and concerns that transcend the very special circumstances of a particular group."

Further Reading

Andrews, William L., Frances Smith Foster, and Trudier Harris, eds. *The Concise Oxford Companion to African American Literature.* New York: Oxford University Press, 2001.

Henderson, Darwin L. and Anthony L. Manna. "Evoking the "Holy and the Horrible": Conversations with Joyce Carol Thomas." *African American Review*, 32 (spring 1998): 139–147.

Thomas, Joyce Carol. *A Mother's Heart, a Daughter's Love: Poems for Us to Share*. New York: Avon Books, 2001.

———. *Marked by Fire*. New York: Avon Books, 1999.

Thurman, Wallace
(Wallace Henry Thurman, Patrick Casey, Ethel Belle Mandrake)
(1902–1934) *novelist, playwright, essayist, screenwriter, editor*

The versatile author of fiction, drama, and essays, Wallace Thurman never satisfied the high standard that he set for himself as a writer. At the age of 23, he joined the ranks of LANGSTON HUGHES, GWENDOLYN BENNETT, COUNTEE CULLEN, and others in New York at the height of the Harlem Renaissance, becoming a celebrated leader and bohemian icon of a generation of brilliant young African-American authors and artists.

Thurman was born in Salt Lake City, Utah, in 1902, the son of Oscar and Beulah Thurman. A sickly child, Thurman spent his early years reading and watching movies. He attended the University of Utah from 1920 to 1922 before moving to Los Angeles to resume his studies in journalism at the University of Southern California. After leaving school in 1923 to pursue a career in writing, he wrote a column called "Inklings" for a local black newspaper and founded a literary magazine, *Outlets*, which failed after six months. He also worked as a postal clerk, where he met ARNA BONTEMPS.

Thurman left Los Angeles for Harlem in 1925, living briefly with Bontemps, who had come to New York a year earlier. First as a reporter and editor for *The Looking Glass* in 1925, and then as managing editor of the *Messenger* in 1926, Thurman soon earned the respect of writers and publishers alike as an editor of uncommon expertise.

Under his influence, readers of the *Messenger* were introduced to the works of Langston Hughes, Countee Cullen, ZORA NEALE HURSTON, and ALICE DUNBAR-NELSON. In autumn 1926, Thurman joined the staff of a white religious publication, the *World Tomorrow*, before landing a job as a reader for McFadden Publications, the first African American to hold such a position at a major New York publishing firm.

Also in 1926, Thurman joined Langston Hughes, Gwendolyn Bennett, and artists Richard Bruce Nugent and Aaron Douglas as the editor of an experimental literary journal called *Fire!!* Intended to provide a forum for young African-American artists that was "purely artistic in intent and conception," the journal folded after its first issue and left Thurman with debts that took him four years to satisfy. In 1928 he created another journal, *Harlem: A Forum of Negro Life*. Less radical than *Fire!!*, *Harlem* featured writing by Hughes, Dunbar-Nelson, GEORGE SCHUYLER, and ALAIN LOCKE. Like the previous attempt, however, *Harlem* ended after its premiere issue.

Thurman's artistic vision put him at odds with other writers of the Harlem Renaissance. He viewed much of the writing of this era as political and propagandistic, concerned with presenting a favorable portrait of black culture and art that would be embraced by white society. As he described it in his essay "Negro Artists and the Negro," he was interested in "people who still retained some individual race qualities and who were not totally white American in every respect save for skin color." His writing would reflect this desire in its presentation of a range of characters from all levels of black society.

In 1928 Thurman married Louise Thompson, a teacher and writer. Citing her husband's homosexual tendencies and excessive drinking, Louise separated from Thurman shortly after their marriage.

With the debut of his first play, *Harlem*, at the Apollo Theater on February 20, 1929, Thurman enjoyed an almost overnight success. The play tells the story of the Williams family, which migrates to

New York to escape the hardships of life in the South. Instead of finding a land of promise and opportunity, they discover a New York that is beset with its own problems, including unemployment, generational tensions, alcohol abuse, and sexual promiscuity. Thurman collaborated on the play with a white writer, William Jourdan Rapp, who remained a lifelong friend, and the play ran for 93 performances before traveling to the Midwest, the West Coast, and Canada.

Also in 1929, Thurman published his first novel, *The Blacker the Berry*. The title is taken from a folk saying: "The blacker the berry, the sweeter the juice." The novel, largely autobiographical, examines racial prejudice within the black community. It relates the struggles of Emma Lou Morgan to flee the racial biases of her Midwestern home and to find acceptance among the black community in Harlem. The novel received largely positive reviews, particularly for its exploration of themes that were considered taboo in African-American literature, which included intraracial prejudices and homosexuality. Some, however, criticized Thurman for depicting negative images of Harlem life.

Thurman's second novel, *Infants of the Spring*, was published in 1932. A thinly disguised parody of many leading figures in the Harlem Renaissance, the novel examines the social, artistic, and intellectual lives of several artists and writers who live in Niggerati Manor, a rooming house in Harlem. In his fiction and editorial writing, Thurman became increasingly critical of the Harlem Renaissance movement, and his dissipated lifestyle began to affect his health. Later in 1932, he collaborated with the white writer Abraham L. Furman on the publication of his final novel, *The Interne*, which addresses the unethical treatment of patients at New York's City Hospital on Welfare Island (later Roosevelt Island).

In the final years of his life, Thurman continued to publish essays and reviews, and he completed three unpublished plays: *Jeremiah the Magnificent*, cowritten with W. J. Rapp, editor of *True Story* magazine, (1930); *Savage Rhythm*; and *Singing the Blues* (both 1932). He also ghostwrote numerous stories for *True Story* under the pseudonyms of Patrick Casey and Ethel Belle Mandrake. In 1934 Thurman returned to California and wrote two screenplays for Bryan Foy Productions: *Tomorrow's Children*, produced in 1934, and *High School Girl*, released in 1935. Upon his return to New York City later in 1934, he was admitted to City Hospital, ironically the same facility that he had criticized in his novel *The Interne*. Wallace Thurman died there of complications from tuberculosis and alcoholism.

Praised by his contemporaries for his formidable abilities as an editor, Thurman also provided an important perspective on the lives of Harlem Renaissance intellectuals and writers. He was critical of artists whom he judged as more concerned with creating an acceptable image of African-American culture for white audiences than with creating art, and though he never achieved the personal standards that he set for his own work, he embodied the aspirations of the younger generation of Harlem Renaissance writers who struggled to find their own, unique voices.

Further Reading

Thurman, Wallace. *Infants of the Spring*. Boston: Northeastern University Press, 1992.

———. *The Blacker the Berry*. New York: Simon and Schuster, 1996.

Van Notten, Eleonore. *Wallace Thurman's Harlem Renaissance*. New York: Editions Rodopi, 1994.

Watson, Steven. *The Harlem Renaissance: Hub of African-American Culture, 1920–1930*. New York: Pantheon Books, 1995.

Tolson, Melvin B.
(Melvin Beaunorus Tolson)
(ca. 1900–1966) *poet, novelist, playwright, essayist, journalist, editor*

A complex poet whose works have been compared to those of the modernist poets T. S. Eliot and Hart Crane, Melvin Tolson received wide critical acclaim for his challenging and erudite verse. Also the author of numerous novels, only one of which has been published, as well as several original and adapted plays, Tolson is known chiefly for his poetry. In her introduction to *Harlem Gallery and Other Poems of Melvin B. Tolson* (1999), former U.S. Poet Laureate RITA DOVE characterized Tolson's impact as a poet in this way: "A glance at nearly any passage will confirm that one is in the presence of a brilliantly eclectic mind. Tolson contained multitudes."

Melvin Beaunorus Tolson was born in about 1900 in Moberly, Missouri. His father, Alonzo Tolson, was a Methodist minister whose duties took the family to numerous cities throughout the Midwest during Tolson's childhood. His mother, Lera Hurt Tolson, worked as a seamstress. Tolson had been fond of painting as a child, but his creative interests soon turned toward writing. He published his first poem, "The Wreck of the Titanic," in an Oskaloosa, Iowa, newspaper in 1912. Later, as a student at Lincoln High School in Kansas City, Missouri, he served as the senior class poet and published two poems and two short stories in the school yearbook.

In 1918 Tolson attended Fisk University, in Nashville, Tennessee, before transferring a year later to Lincoln University in Oxford, Pennsylvania. There, he met Ruth Southall, and the two were married in 1922. Tolson graduated with honors in 1923 and moved with his wife to Marshall, Texas, to teach English and speech at Wiley College. During the next 17 years, apart from his duties as a teacher and the father of four children, Tolson also coached several college athletic teams and organized a debating club, the Wiley Forensic Society, which competed nationally with great success.

A fellowship from Columbia University in 1931 allowed Tolson to spend a year in New York to work on a master's degree in comparative literature. He chose as his thesis a study of Harlem Renaissance writers, and he began writing poems that would later appear in his acclaimed collection *Harlem*

Gallery, published in 1965. Tolson published fragments of this work in several journals, including *Arts Quarterly* and *Modern Monthly,* during the 1930s.

Tolson's first critical success as a poet came with the publication of "Dark Symphony" in 1939, which won a national poetry contest sponsored by Chicago's American Negro Exhibition. Published in 1941 in the *Atlantic Monthly,* the poem drew the attention of an editor at the publishing house Dodd, Mead, and Company, who persuaded Tolson to complete a volume of poetry. His first collection of poems, *Rendezvous with America,* was published in 1944 and went through three editions.

During the 1930s and 1940s, Tolson also contributed articles to the *Pittsburgh Courier* and the *Washington Tribune,* which published his weekly column "Caviar and Cabbages" from 1937 to 1944. In his column Tolson criticized those in the African-American community, particularly the black middle classes, whose attitudes he felt reflected apathy toward the political and social challenges facing blacks in America. He also wrote several novels, none of which have been published, and adapted novels by other authors for the stage, including GEORGE SCHUYLER's *Black No More* and RICHARD WRIGHT's *Black Boy.*

Tolson left Wiley College in 1947 to teach at Langston University, in Langston, Oklahoma. That same year, he was appointed the poet laureate of the Republic of Liberia by William V. S. Tubman, the president of Liberia. To celebrate the centennial anniversary of the founding of the West African nation, Tolson published his most ambitious work, the *Libretto for the Republic of Liberia,* in 1953, a task that took six years to complete. During this period, he also found time to serve four consecutive terms as mayor of Langston, Oklahoma.

Tolson described his objective in writing *Libretto* in this way: "I, as a black poet, have absorbed the Great Ideas of the Great White World and interpreted them in the melting-pot idiom of my people." In lyrical, sometimes surreal verse, Tolson traced African culture from its early grandeur to its captivity, and ultimately to the promise of its liberation. Tolson's modernist approach to the composition of *Libretto* invited comparisons to the poetry of such modernist masters as T. S. Eliot and Ezra Pound.

After nearly 40 years of neglect, Tolson returned to his unfinished manuscript of *Harlem Gallery.* He intended to write an epic history of African-American life in five volumes but completed only the first, *Harlem Gallery: Book One, The Curator,* published in 1965. In 24 cantos characterized by a surreal blend of unusual characters, unorthodox imagery, and complex language informed by the rhythms of jazz and blues, Tolson explored the nature of African-American art from the perspective of a museum curator. In recognition of his literary accomplishment with *Harlem Gallery,* Tolson was awarded grants from the National Institute and American Academy of Arts and Letters as well as the Rockefeller Foundation. He was also named to the Avalon Chair in humanities at Tuskegee Institute. Less than a year later, Melvin Beaunorus Tolson died of abdominal cancer on August 29, 1966.

To many of his contemporaries, Melvin Tolson was a controversial poet. Some critics recognized his aesthetic connection to modernism but overlooked the ways in which he transcended and augmented that tradition. Others, particularly those of the Black Arts Movement, distrusted the complexity of Tolson's verse and charged him with accommodating a white readership by focusing on artistic rather than overtly political themes. Out of fashion and out of print for several years, Tolson's poetry has drawn renewed critical interest with the publication of *Harlem Gallery and Other Poems of Melvin B. Tolson* (1999), which includes his three previously published books of poetry. Modern scholars have noted that while Tolson was influenced by modernist aesthetics, he adapted them to a uniquely African-American perspective. In doing so, he broadened the scope and influence of African-American literature.

Further Reading

Gates, Henry Louis, Jr. and Nellie Y. McKay, eds. *The Norton Anthology of African American Literature.* New York: W. W. Norton, 1997.

Lenhart, Gary. "Caviar and Cabbage: The Voracious Appetite of Melvin Tolson." *American Poetry Review* 29, no. 2 (March/April 2000): 35.

Tolson, Melvin. *Harlem Gallery and Other Poems of Melvin B. Tolson.* Charlottesville: University Press of Virginia, 1999.

Tolson, Melvin, Jr. "The Poetry of Melvin B. Tolson (1898–1966)." *World Literature Today* 64, no. 3 (summer 1990): 398.

Toomer, Jean
(Nathan Eugene Pinchback Toomer)
(1894–1967) *poet, novelist, short story writer, playwright, literary critic, essayist, educator*

An innovative and gifted writer, Jean Toomer is best known for his groundbreaking novel *Cane,* published in 1923. Toomer was hailed as the voice of a new generation of Harlem Renaissance writers and held the promise, in the view of many contemporary critics and writers, of great works to come. Though he never again equaled the critical success of *Cane* in his later writings, Toomer's novel has remained a remarkable addition to the African-American literary canon.

Jean Toomer was born Nathan Pinchback Toomer in Washington, D.C., on December 26, 1894. When his father, Nathan Toomer, abandoned the family, Toomer and his mother, Nina Pinchback, moved in with her father, the former Reconstructionist politician Pinckney Benton Stewart Pinchback. They lived in the affluent and predominantly white Bacon Street neighborhood of Washington, D.C., until 1906, when Nina married her second husband and the family moved to New York. Following her death in 1909, Toomer returned to Washington, D.C., where his grandparents had suffered financial setbacks and had relocated to a black section of the city.

Light-skinned enough to pass for white, Toomer preferred to describe himself as an American rather than an African American. "In my body were many bloods," he wrote, "some dark blood, all blended in the fire of six or more generations." Following his graduation from M Street High School (later renamed Dunbar High School) Toomer attended several universities and colleges, including the University of Wisconsin, the American College of Physical Training in Chicago, and the City College of New York, though he never completed a degree. To support himself during these years, he worked as a car salesman, a physical education teacher, a shipyard worker, and a welder.

As a boy in New Rochelle, New York, Toomer had read avidly in the public library, consuming volumes of Arthurian romances. In high school and college, William Shakespeare, George Bernard Shaw, Charles Dickens, and Johann Wolfgang von Goethe were among his favorite writers. In 1919, through his friendship with the white author Waldo Frank, Toomer met a number of leading white literary figures of his day, including the poets Edward Arlington Robinson and Witter Bynner, and members of Greenwich Village's younger literary set, among them the writers Hart Crane and Malcolm Cowley. Frank later became a close friend and literary mentor. Toomer also met Sherwood Anderson, with whom he maintained a lengthy correspondence, and whose collection of related short stories, *Winesburg, Ohio* (1919), has been cited by critics as a possible source of inspiration for the unusual structure of *Cane*.

Toomer's early literary works included numerous poems, short stories, and dramas, written primarily between 1918 and 1923, and many of which were later revised or incorporated into larger works. In 1921 Toomer met the principal of a small rural school in Sparta, Georgia. At the time, Toomer had been struggling to write while also caring for his aging grandparents. Losing confidence and unable to find his voice as a writer, Toomer accepted an invitation from the Sparta Agricultural and Industrial Institute, which was modeled after Booker T. Washington's Tuskegee Institute, to serve as a substitute principal. Though he stayed in Sparta only two months, his experience there changed the course of his writing career and resulted in his masterpiece, *Cane*, published in 1923.

For two months Toomer lived and worked among Sparta's rural poor, listening to the songs of African-American women preparing meals for their families, absorbing the folklore and the feel of the region, and witnessing both the degradation and the dignity of a people with whom he initially struggled to identify on a personal level. He began writing sketches and poems on his return to Washington, D.C., and by 1923, he had completed his manuscript. On the advice of Waldo Frank, Toomer decided to combine the various sketches, poems, and drama into a cohesive whole, in what has been called an experimental, lyrical novel. Though *Cane* sold fewer than 1,000 copies in two editions, critics praised its innovative structure and compelling imagery.

In the first section of *Cane*, Toomer creates six literary portraits in prose and poetry that depict the lives of women in rural Georgia. "Karintha," which opens the novel, relates the struggles of a young black girl whose beauty captivates the men of her town. "Karintha is a woman," writes Toomer. "Men do not know that the soul of her was a growing thing ripened too soon." Toomer shifts the narrative in the second section of *Cane* to the urban North, where transplanted southerners cut off from their cultural roots struggle to maintain their identity. The urban settings, ranging from Chicago to New York, represent a stifling influence on African Americans as an oppressive white society and intraracial strife create obstacles to a fully enfranchised position in urban life. The final section, entitled "Kabnis," blends prose, poetry, and drama in its depiction of Ralph Kabnis's journey from New York to rural Georgia. He has returned to the South as a teacher, hoping to improve the lives of his people and to discover his roots. At the novel's end, however, Kabnis failed to achieve his goal.

Cane received enormous critical acclaim. Toomer's ability to create an authentic and unique African-American vision within the context of experimental modernist literary forms appealed to white and African-American audiences alike. His depiction of the spiritual and cultural fragmentation of African-American life in modern society mirrored in some respects the work of such esteemed modernist authors as T. S. Eliot and James Joyce. In later publications Toomer moved away from specifically African-American themes. He had long held an interest in Eastern religions, and in 1924 he began a rigorous study of the teachings of Russian mystic George Gurdjieff.

Toomer's later writings reflected his philosophical shift from the exploration of African-American cultural roots to the investigation of a more universal cultural identity. Perhaps as a result, critics and publishers gave him little consideration. Among these later writings were the novels *The Gallonwerps* (1927) and *York Beach* (1929). He also wrote a play, *The Sacred Factory* (1927); *Essentials* (1931), a collection of philosophical and religious aphorisms; and the lengthy poem "Blue Meridian" (1936), which expresses his vision of a future America where racial divisions are obliterated in the development of what he called a "universal human being."

While attending a workshop on the teachings of Gurdjieff in 1931, Toomer met Margery Latimer, also a writer. The two soon married and moved to Carmel, California, where they lived in an artists' colony until Margery's death in 1932 during childbirth. Toomer recorded these experiences, particularly the controversy surrounding his interracial marriage to Margery, in an unpublished novel, *Colomb* (1932). In 1934 he married Marjorie Content, also white, with whom he would remain until his death. The couple settled in Doylestown, Pennsylvania, in 1936, where Toomer established a center for Gurdjieff studies and later joined the Society of Friends, or Quakers. He continued to

Jean Toomer was one of the most innovative authors of the Harlem Renaissance era. *(Yale University, Beinecke Rare Book and Manuscript Library)*

write monographs and poems, usually related to philosophical or religious issues, until 1952, after which his health began to decline. Following several years of invalidism and crippling arthritis, Jean Toomer died on March 30, 1967.

Some scholars have argued that the Harlem Renaissance began with the publication of *Cane* in 1923. In the African-American literary canon, it ranks with RICHARD WRIGHT's *Native Son* (1940) and RALPH ELLISON's *Invisible Man* (1952) as one of the most significant achievements in the development of the African-American novel. Toomer's later works, though generally dismissed by critics, reveal a passionate exploration of personal and spiritual identity that is not wholly absent from *Cane*. His contributions as a writer gave direction to a burgeoning tradition of African-American literature in the 1920s, and his influence can be traced in the generations of African-American writers that followed him.

Further Reading

Gates, Henry Louis, Jr., and Nellie Y. McKay, eds. *The Norton Anthology of African American Literature.* New York: W. W. Norton, 1997.

Pardlo, Gregory A. "The Trick of Transcending Race." *Black Issues Book Review* 3, no. 1 (January/February 2001): 12.

Rusch, Frederik L., ed. *A Jean Toomer Reader: Selected Unpublished Writings.* New York: Oxford University Press, 1993.

Toomer, Jean. *Cane.* New York: Liveright, 1923. Reprint, New York: Modern Library, 1994.

Watson, Steven. *The Harlem Renaissance: Hub of African-American Culture, 1920–1930.* New York: Pantheon Books, 1995.

Troupe, Quincy
(Quincy Thomas Troupe, Jr.)
(1943–   ) *poet, biographer, editor, educator*

A two-time American Book Award winner, Quincy Troupe has distinguished himself as a poet, biographer, editor, and university professor. He has collaborated on anthologies of African-American and developing-world poetry and on documentary screenplays. His writings have also appeared in more than 200 publications around the world. In 2002 Troupe was named the first official poet laureate of the state of California.

Quincy Thomas Troupe, Jr., was born in New York City on July 23, 1943, the son of Dorothy Troupe and Quincy Troupe, Sr., a celebrated catcher for the St. Louis Stars baseball team in the Negro Leagues. During his early childhood, Troupe and his family moved to St. Louis, Missouri. Troupe attended Louisiana's Grambling College (now Grambling University) on a basketball scholarship and received his bachelor's degree in political science in 1963.

Troupe lived in Europe from 1963 to 1965, during which time he met philosopher and novelist Jean-Paul Sartre and received encouragement from him to write. The works of Spanish poet Pablo Neruda, and the poetry of African-American authors such as PAUL LAURENCE DUNBAR, LANGSTON HUGHES, JEAN TOOMER, and STERLING BROWN also influenced Troupe's growing interest in writing. His first published poem, "What Is a Black Man?," appeared in the journal *Paris Match* in 1964.

Following his return from Europe, Troupe settled in Los Angeles, California, and in 1966 began teaching creative writing at the Watts Writers Workshop, a literary collective organized in response to the Watts riot of 1965. Troupe completed an associate's degree in journalism at Los Angeles City College in 1967. His first book-length publication, *Watts Poets: A Book of New Poetry and Essays,* appeared in 1968 and featured poetry and nonfiction by local authors.

Troupe published his first collection of poetry, *Embryo Poems,* in 1972. Employing African-American dialects and influenced heavily by jazz and blues, Troupe's early poetry grew out of his experiences in Watts. "When I first started writing, I didn't know anything about poetry," he explained in a 1999 interview. "Then I moved to Watts, in Los Angeles. It was the first time I had been around African-American poets. They were writing poems that came right out of the African-American experience—the church, the barbershop, the street."

Snake-Back Solos: Selected Poems 1969–1977 (1979), Troupe's second collection of poetry, earned an American Book Award. Deriving its title from a regional nickname for the Mississippi River, *Snake-Back Solos* revealed a poetic voice steeped in the oral and musical traditions of African-American culture. In the title poem, "swimming up river / up the river of rain satchmo breaking the darkness," Troupe writes "his trumpet & grin polished overpain speaking / to the light flaming off the river's back / at sunset snake river's back." Troupe explained his deep appreciation of the blues in a 1993 interview as a way of honoring "the continuum of African spirituality, where the music comes from."

Troupe married Margaret Porter, also a poet, with whom he has four children. Many of Troupe's later collections of poetry address his role as a father and husband. "I write about connections between myself and other people more—the whole idea of constructing an interior life, my interior life," Troupe explained in *The Before Columbus Foundation Poetry Anthology* (1992). In the collections *Skulls along the River* (1984), *Weather Reports: New and Selected Poems* (1991), *Avalanche: Poems* (1996), *Choruses: Poems* (1999), and *Transcircularities: New and Selected Poems* (2002), Troupe further displayed his ability to infuse his poetry with the rhythms of blues and jazz, while also continuing to focus on issues of race and culture.

Known primarily for his poetry, Troupe has earned considerable accolades for his prose. He won a second American Book Award for his collaboration with Miles Davis on *Miles: The Autobiography of Miles Davis* (1989), widely regarded as the finest study of Davis's life and music. In 1991 Troupe coproduced and wrote for the *Miles Davis Radio Project* on PBS, for which he received a Peabody Award. Troupe explored the more personal side of his friendship with Miles Davis in *Miles and Me: A Memoir* (2000).

Troupe's other works include *The Inside Story of T.V.'s "Roots"* (1978, with David L. Wolper) and *James Baldwin: The Legacy* (1989). Troupe has also edited the literary anthology *Giant Talk: An Anthology of Third World Writing* (1975) and

Quincy Troupe laughs with a group of schoolchildren following his appointment as California's first poet laureate in Sacramento, California, on June 11, 2002. *(AP/Wide World Photos)*

served as a founding editor of *Confrontation: A Journal of Third World Literature and American Rag.* Troupe has also held faculty positions at numerous colleges and universities, including Columbia University, the University of California at Berkeley, and the University of California at San Diego, where he currently serves as professor of creative writing and American and Caribbean literature.

In 2002 Quincy Troupe was selected by the California Arts Council and Governor Gray Davis to serve as the state's first official poet laureate. "Beyond his many awards and accomplishments," said California first lady Sharon Davis, who announced Troupe's appointment, "Quincy is simply a gifted poet with the rare ability to make words come alive." From his early involvement with the Watts Writers Workshop to his role as artistic director of the celebrated literary program *Artists on the Cutting Edge: Cross Fertilizations* for the Museum of Contemporary Art in San Diego, Quincy Troupe has served as an eloquent and passionate ambassador for the arts and its ability to transform individuals and communities.

Further Reading

Hill, Patricia Liggins, ed. *Call and Response: The Riverside Anthology of the African American Literary Tradition.* Boston: Houghton Mifflin Co., 1998.

Keita, Nzade Zimele. "Quincy Troupe." *American Visions* 8 (February-March 1993): 30.

Troupe, Quincy. *Snake-Back Solos: Selected Poems 1969–1977.* New York: I. Reed Books, 1979.

———. *Transcircularities: New and Selected Poems.* Minneapolis, Minn.: Coffee House Press, 2002.

Walker, Alice
(Alice Malsenior Walker)

(1944–   ) *novelist, poet, short story writer, literary critic, children's fiction writer, editor, educator*

Celebrated for her poignant depictions of racial and gender inequality, rooted in the culture and traditions of the American South, Alice Walker gained international critical and popular acclaim with her 1983 novel *The Color Purple,* for which she received the Pulitzer Prize for fiction. Walker has also published numerous volumes of poetry, short fiction, children's fiction, and essays. "We black women writers know very clearly that our survival depends on trust," Walker explained in Claudia Tate's *Black Women Writers at Work* (1983). "We will not have or cannot have anything until we examine what we do to and with each other."

Alice Malsenior Walker was born on February 9, 1944, in Eatonton, Georgia, the eighth daughter of Willie Lee Walker, a sharecropper, and Minnie Tallulah Walker, a part-time domestic. From an early age, Walker learned the importance of family and community, particularly from the influence of her mother, whom Walker has described as a "walking history of our community." A childhood injury left Walker partially blind in one eye for several years. During this period, she retreated into the world of books and became a keen observer of her sur-

roundings. The people and places of her southern heritage would later inform all of her literary works.

Walker excelled as a student and won a scholarship to Atlanta's Spelman College in 1961. She later transferred to Sarah Lawrence College, in Bronxville, New York, and completed her bachelor's degree in 1965. As a student at Sarah Lawrence, Walker spent a summer in Africa, where she fell in love with a local man and wrote many of the poems that would later appear in *Once* (1968), her first published book. Upon her return, Walker discovered that she was pregnant and struggled with thoughts of suicide. After long consideration, Walker chose to abort the pregnancy, a procedure that, at that time, was illegal.

Following her graduation in 1965, Walker began working in New York City's Welfare Department. Two years later, she married Melvyn Roseman Leventhal, a white civil rights lawyer. The couple later moved to Jackson, Mississippi, where Walker devoted herself to writing and to an increased involvement with civil rights activities. She served as writer in residence at Jackson State College (1968–69) and Tougaloo College (1970–71). Walker also gave birth to her only child, Rebecca Leventhal, in 1969. Walker and Leventhal divorced in 1977, in part because of pervasive racial prejudice against interracial marriage.

Walker's 10-year marriage was a fertile creative period in her writing career. In addition to

Alice Walker poses at her home in Berkeley, California, in 2000. *(AP/Wide World Photos)*

her first volume of poetry, *Once* (1968), and her short story "To Hell with Dying," published a year earlier, Walker published two additional volumes of poetry, *Five Poems* (1972) and *Revolutionary Petunias and Other Poems* (1973), nominated for a National Book Award, and a collection of short stories, *In Love and Trouble: Stories of Black Women* (1974), which chronicled in 13 stories the struggle of women against gender inequality and sexism, and for which she earned an American Academy and Institute of Arts and Letters Award. Walker also published two novels: *The Third Life of Grange Copeland* (1973), a multigenerational portrait of an African-American family torn apart by internal conflicts, and *Meridian* (1976), the story of a young woman's spiritual and emotional maturity during the turbulent Civil Rights movement in the South.

In her poetry and fiction, Walker has emphasized the lives of black women—their power to effect social change, their response to the dual challenges of racism and sexism, and their role in uniting and strengthening communities. This approach, for which Walker has coined the term *womanist,* has led her to devote much of her career to the discovery and preservation of the works of female African-American authors. In 1973 Walker traveled to Florida to research the life of ZORA NEALE HURSTON, eventually discovering her neglected grave site and erecting a headstone. Largely through Walker's efforts, contemporary scholars have renewed their interest in Hurston's writing and her significance as an early and important literary ancestor for a new generation of female authors.

Walker paid further tribute to Hurston by editing *I Love Myself When I'm Laughing . . . and Then Again When I Am Looking Mean and Impressive: A Zora Neale Hurston Reader* (1979). Following the publication of her second collection of stories, *You Can't Keep a Good Woman Down* (1981), and the essay collection *In Search of Our Mother's Gardens: Womanist Prose* (1983), Walker published her most acclaimed and controversial work, the novel *The Color Purple* (1983).

Comprising letters written by the novel's protagonist, Celie, to God, as well as letters exchanged with her sister, Nettie, *The Color Purple* portrays the transformation of a young African-American woman from a physically and emotionally abused child to a woman of strength and grace. Celie's struggle to overcome the crippling effects of her rape as a child and an oppressive and abusive marriage resonated among readers of all ethnic backgrounds.

The Color Purple earned Walker the Pulitzer Prize for fiction and the American Book Award, though the novel was criticized by some scholars, as many of her previous works had been, for its perceived negative depictions of black males. Walker's incorporation of the themes of incest and lesbianism also generated considerable controversy. *The Color Purple* has since become an international classic and one that *Newsweek* magazine reviewer Peter S. Prescott has called "an American novel of permanent importance." *The Color Purple* was adapted to film in 1985 by director Steven Spielberg, earning 11 Academy Award nominations.

Walker continued to explore the complex and poignant struggles of African-American women in novels such as *The Temple of My Familiar* (1989), a nonlinear narrative that spans multiple times and regions; *Possessing the Secret of Joy* (1992), the story of a young African woman's struggle with her tribal custom of female genital mutilation; and *By the Light of My Father's Smile* (1998).

A diverse and prolific author, Walker has published numerous other works, including *Warrior Marks: Female Genital Mutilation and the Sexual Blinding of Women* (1993, with Pratibha Parmar); the short story collection *The Way Forward Is with a Broken Heart* (2000); and *Absolute Trust in the Goodness of Earth: New Poems* (2003). Walker has also published several essay collections, including *Living by the Word* (1988), *Alice Walker Banned* (1996), *Anything We Love Can Be Saved: A Writer's Activism* (1997), and *Sent by Earth: A Message from the Grandmother Spirit after the Bombing of the World Trade Center and the Pentagon* (2001).

Alice Walker has achieved international acclaim as an author, poet, activist, and educator. During her distinguished career, she has held teaching positions at such institutions as Brandeis University and the University of California at Berkeley, and she has given lectures and readings on campuses throughout the United States. A powerful voice against racial and gender discrimination, Walker has consistently emphasized the creative and spiritual legacy of black women to American and African-American culture.

Further Reading

Dieke, Ikenna, ed. *Critical Essays on Alice Walker.* Westport, Conn.: Greenwood Press, 1999.

Gates, Henry Louis, Jr., and K. A. Appiah, eds. *Alice Walker: Critical Perspectives Past and Present.* New York: Penguin, 1993.

Walker, Alice. *The Color Purple.* New York: Harcourt, 1982.

———. *Her Blue Body Everything We Know: Earthling Poems, 1965–1990 Complete.* New York: Harcourt, 1991.

———. *In Search of Our Mothers' Gardens: Womanist Prose.* New York: Harcourt, 1983.

Walker, David
(1785–1830) *essayist, abolitionist*

During the early 19th century, David Walker shocked abolitionists in the North and terrified slaveholders in the South with the publication of his *Appeal to the Colored Citizens of the World* in 1829. His vehement denunciation of slavery and his encouragement of violent rebellion to achieve emancipation set him apart from other antislavery writers such as OLAUDAH EQUIANO and FREDERICK DOUGLASS, whose autobiographical narratives advocated more peaceful and political methods to end slavery.

David Walker was born on September 28, 1785, in Wilmington, North Carolina, the free son of an enslaved father and freeborn mother. Few details about his early life are known. He learned to read and write at a young age, and his writing reflects a considerable knowledge of the Bible and history. Walker left the South and settled in Boston, Massachusetts, in 1826. He married a fugitive slave and raised three children, supporting his family by working in a secondhand clothing store. In Boston, Walker became involved in the abolitionist movement as an agent for *Freedom's Journal,* the first African-American newspaper published in the United States. He also gave speeches and published articles, which he collected in 1829 and published in pamphlet form under the title *David Walker's Appeal, in Four Articles; Together with a Preamble, to the Coloured Citizens of the World, but in Particular, and Very Expressly, to Those of the United States.*

Walker's *Appeal* is patterned on the U.S. Constitution, with a preamble that introduces his argument and articles that cover the historical and moral arguments against slavery. Citing biblical and historical sources, Walker condemns slavery and chastises the hypocrisy of a nation founded on the principles of liberty and freedom that would sanction such an institution. He also warns slaveholders to expect judgment. Encouraging his brethren in bondage to use violence if necessary to effect their emancipation, Walker predicts that slavery will eventually divide the nation. "Yet the Lord our God will bring other destructions upon them—for not unfrequently will he cause them to rise up one against another, to be split and divided . . . and sometimes to open hostilities with sword in hand."

Though many of Walker's contemporaries in the antislavery movement, including William Lloyd Garrison and others, objected to the use of violence to end slavery, Walker's *Appeal* was circulated in the North and South, with portions appearing in William Lloyd Garrison's otherwise conservative abolitionist periodical *Liberator.* When copies of the pamphlet turned up in Georgia, the state legislature enacted a bill that made the dissemination of materials designed to incite rebellion among slaves a capital offense. The legislature also offered a reward for Walker's capture. Between 1829 and 1830, Walker revised and expanded his *Appeal* and continued to encourage rebellion. On June 28, 1830, David Walker died in Boston under mysterious circumstances, allegedly the victim of poison.

Though unabashedly militant in his advocacy of violence to effect the emancipation of slaves, he also encouraged forgiveness for slaveholders who willingly freed their slaves. In 1848 the abolitionist writer Henry Highland Garnet, whose own writings spoke eloquently in support of the mass rebellion of slaves, published a new edition of Walker's *Appeal,* including a brief biography of the author. Walker's revolutionary zeal, and his commitment to the freedom of all African Americans by any means necessary, prefigured the work of 20th century radical activists, particularly the Black Power movement of the 1960s. His writing remains relevant to the continued struggle for racial equality.

Further Reading

Finseth, Ian. "David Walker, Nature's Nation, and Early African American Separatism." *Mississippi Quarterly* 54, no. 3 (summer 2001): 337.

Gates, Henry Louis, Jr., and Nellie Y. McKay, eds. *The Norton Anthology of African American Literature.* New York: W. W. Norton, 1997.

Walker, David. *David Walker's Appeal, in Four Articles; Together with a Preamble, to the Colored Citizens of the World, but in Particular, and Very Expressly, to Those of the United States of America.* New York: Hill and Wang, 1995.

Walker, Margaret
(Margaret Abigail Walker, Margaret Walker Alexander)
(1915–1998) *poet, novelist, essayist, biographer, educator*

A celebrated author, Margaret Walker emerged after the Harlem Renaissance era and before the Black Arts Movement as an eloquent and influential voice in American and African-American literature. Walker is known primarily as a versatile and gifted poet whose sonnets, ballads, and free verse pay tribute to the rich history, spirituality, and folk traditions of African-American culture and demonstrate a passionate commitment to racial equality and civil rights.

Margaret Abigail Walker was born on July 7, 1915, in Birmingham, Alabama, the daughter of Sigismund Walker, a Methodist minister, who immigrated to the United States from Buff Bay, Jamaica, and Marion Walker, a music teacher. From her parents, Walker received early encouragement in her academic and literary goals. She read widely as a child in the classics of English and American literature, as well as the works of celebrated African-American authors such as COUNTEE CULLEN, ZORA NEALE HURSTON, and LANGSTON HUGHES, who was an important influence on her decision to become a writer. Walker also grew up hearing stories of life under slavery from her grandmother. "My grandmother talked about it all the time," Walker recalled in a 1992 interview, "and when I was a little girl, I told her, 'When I grow up I'm going to write that story.'"

Walker graduated from Gilbert Academy at the age of 14 in New Orleans, Louisiana, where she and her family had relocated in 1925. Walker attended New Orleans University (now Dillard University) until her sophomore year, when she was encouraged by Langston Hughes, whom Walker met when he visited the university, to attend a more prestigious school outside the South. Walker moved to Chicago, Illinois, to complete her bachelor's degree at Northwestern University in 1935. Following her graduation, Walker found work with the Works Progress Administration's Federal Writers' Project, where she met other aspiring young writers such as GWENDOLYN BROOKS, FENTON JOHNSON, and RICHARD WRIGHT, with whom Walker developed a close friendship.

Walker published her first poem, "Daydreaming," in 1935 in the *Crisis*, a literary periodical published by the National Association for the Advancement of Colored People (NAACP). During this period, Walker began to define the direction of her later poetry. While rooted in the early traditions of African-American culture, Walker's poetry also addressed the immediate political and social needs of black communities, a creative focus that she found lacking in much of the literature from the Harlem Renaissance period. "They lacked social perspective," Walker explained in a 1950 interview, "and suffered from a kind of literary myopia."

In 1939 Walker moved to Iowa City, Iowa, and enrolled at the University of Iowa Writers' Workshop, where she completed her master's degree in 1940. Her thesis was a collection of poems that would later be published by Yale University Press as *For My People* (1942), and which earned Walker the Yale University Younger Poet's Award. The title poem, "For My People," had appeared earlier in 1937 in *Poetry* magazine, and would later be anthologized in STERLING BROWN's influential anthology *The Negro Caravan* (1941). In his introduction to *For My People*, Stephen Vincent Benét praised Walker for her "controlled intensity of emotion and language that, at times, even when it is most modern, has something of the surge of biblical poetry." *For My People* established Walker's reputation as a nationally known poet.

Walker married Firnist James Alexander in 1943 while teaching at Livingston College in North Carolina, and she gave birth to the first of four children in 1944. For the next several years, Walker balanced her duties as a mother with her teaching career. In 1949 she joined the faculty of Jackson State College (later Jackson State University), in Mississippi, where she remained until her retirement in 1979. There, she resumed research on a novel that she had begun as a student at Northwestern University. Walker's research, which included extensive genealogical records of her mother's roots in Alabama and Georgia, provided the foundation for her celebrated novel *Jubilee* (1966).

In 1962 Walker returned to the Writers' Workshop at the University of Iowa to complete her Ph.D. in English and used the manuscript of *Jubilee* as her dissertation. Walker completed her degree requirements in 1965 and published *Jubilee* in 1966, following 30 years of research and writing and fulfilling her promise to her grandmother, whose life inspired the character of the novel's protagonist, Vyry Ware Brown. *Jubilee* chronicles Vyry's life, from her early childhood as a plantation slave, through her teenage years during the Civil War, and to her maturity as a mother and freedwoman during the Reconstruction era.

Jubilee sought to present an accurate portrait of life in the South for slaves before and following the Civil War, in part to counter inaccuracies and stereotypes common to an immensely popular genre, the Civil War romance. Walker's novel was highly regarded by critics and has remained a frequently assigned text in schools and universities because of its rich historical detail, and the novel has remained in print continuously since its publication.

Though she achieved her greatest literary success with her first two books, Walker continued to write poetry. She published several additional volumes, including *Prophets for a New Day* (1970), which honors the heroes of the struggle for civil rights in America; *October Journey* (1973), a collection of more personal poems and poetic portraits of contemporaries such as Gwendolyn Brooks and ROBERT HAYDEN; *For Farish Street Green* (1986), which depicts life in the Farish Street community of Jackson, Mississippi; and *This Is My Century: New and Collected Poems* (1989).

Walker also published several nonfiction works. In *How I Wrote "Jubilee"* (1972, expanded as *How I Wrote "Jubilee" and Other Essays on Life and Literature,* 1990), Walker chronicled the 30 years of research that went into the making of her celebrated novel. *A Poetic Equation: Conversations with Nikki Giovanni and Margaret Walker* (1974), a literary exchange between Walker and the celebrated Black Arts poet NIKKI GIOVANNI, demonstrated Walker's influence on the rising generation of young poets in the 1960s and 1970s. Walker also published a second collection of essays, *On Being Female, Black, and Free* (1997), and her controversial biography *Richard Wright, Daemonic Genius: A Portrait of the Man, a Critical Look at His Work* (1988), in which she documents her close friendship with the celebrated novelist.

At the time of her death, Walker was working on several manuscripts, including "God Touched My Life," a biography of Sister Thea Bowman, a black nun in Mississippi, and her own autobiography. Margaret Abigail Walker died on November 30, 1998, in Chicago, Illinois.

In her dual roles as author and educator, Margaret Walker was committed to the principles of social justice and racial equality for African Americans. The Institute for the Study of History, Life and Culture of Black People, founded by Walker in 1968, was later renamed the Margaret Walker Alexander National Research Center. Housed on the campus of Jackson State University, the center is dedicated to the preservation of African-American history and culture, a fitting legacy to Walker's life and writing.

Further Reading

Graham, Maryemma, ed. *Fields Watered with Blood: Critical Essays on Margaret Walker.* Athens: University of Georgia Press, 2001.

———. *Conversations with Margaret Walker.* Jackson: University of Mississippi Press, 2002.

Walker, Margaret. *On Being Female, Black, and Free: Essays by Margaret Walker, 1932–1992.* Athens: University of Georgia Press, 1997.

———. *This Is My Century: New and Selected Poems.* Athens: University of Georgia Press, 1989.

Walrond, Eric
(Eric Derwent Walrond)
(1898–1966) *short fiction writer, journalist, essayist, editor*

Born in the British West Indies, Eric Walrond became an important and influential voice of the Harlem Renaissance movement in New York in the 1920s. His collection of short stories, *Tropic Death* (1926), remains a classic of the Harlem Renaissance period and earned the praise of such notable African-American literary figures as LANGSTON HUGHES, W. E. B. DuBOIS, and ALAIN LOCKE. Walrond's fiction brought a new perspective on the issues of race and identity by providing a glimpse of the struggles of black communities in the West Indies.

Eric Derwent Walrond was born in Georgetown, British Guiana (now known as Guyana), in 1898, the son of a Guyanese father and a Barbadian mother. When Eric was eight, his father abandoned the family, and his mother moved with him to a rural village near Black Rock in Barbados. He attended St. Stephen's Boys School until 1910, when he and his mother moved to Colón, Panama. The building of the Panama Canal drew thousands of men looking for work from the West Indies and Guyana. Walrond's mother hoped to reconcile with her husband, whom she believed was in Panama. She was ultimately unsuccessful, but she and Eric remained in Colón. Walrond attended public schools and finished his secondary education with the assistance of private tutors.

Walrond began work as a journalist in 1916 for the *Panama Star and Herald,* covering court cases and sporting events. In 1918 he arrived in New York City and struggled to find work as a journalist. While continuing his education at the City College of New York (now City University) and at Columbia University, Walrond became co-owner, editor, and staff reporter for the *Brooklyn and Long Island Informer,* an African-American weekly newspaper, from 1921 to 1923, after which he joined Marcus Garvey's *Negro World* as an associate editor.

The early and mid-1920s marked the most prolific period of Walrond's writing career. His short stories began to appear in numerous literary periodicals, including the National Urban League's *Opportunity* and the National Association for the Advancement of Colored People's *Crisis* magazine. His story "The Voodoo's Revenge" (1925) won third prize in *Opportunity* magazine's annual literary contest. Walrond also published numerous essays and reviews in *New Age, New Republic, Saturday Review of Literature,* and *Vanity Fair.*

Like some of his contemporaries, including the poet CLAUDE MCKAY and Marcus Garvey, head of the Universal Negro Improvement Association (UNIA), Walrond brought an international perspective to the cultural revival taking place during the Harlem Renaissance. In his most celebrated work, the short story collection *Tropic Death* (1926), Walrond displayed a highly impressionistic

literary style, often compared to the writing of JEAN TOOMER in *Cane,* in his perceptive and detailed depictions of life among Afro-Caribbean communities in the West Indies, whose lives were shaped by the contrasting colonial influences of the British Empire and the Catholic Church.

The 10 stories comprising *Tropic Death* capture in vivid detail the physical and emotional landscape of life in the West Indies. In the title story, "Drought," and "The Wharf Rats," Walrond exposes the poverty, racism, and violence that characterized the lives of those in the Caribbean's African diaspora. Though commercially unsuccessful, Walrond's *Tropic Death* was a sensation among critics and peers. He became a minor literary celebrity and a leading figure within social and intellectual circles in Harlem, befriending several of the leading figures of the early Harlem Renaissance era, including Langston Hughes, WALLACE THURMAN, and ZORA NEALE HURSTON.

Walrond left New York in 1927 and traveled in Europe and the West Indies, where he conducted research on a new book about the Panama Canal. Largely completed by 1928, *The Big Ditch* was never published. Though he returned to the United States briefly in the early 1930s, Walrond lived abroad for the rest of his life, mainly in London and Paris, where he lived briefly with fellow expatriate COUNTEE CULLEN. The literary production of Walrond's later years included only a handful of stories and essays in various European journals. He was working on a new book about the Panama Canal at the time of his death in London in 1966.

Eric Derwent Walrond achieved considerable renown as one of the most promising young authors of the early Harlem Renaissance era. Despite his critical success, however, Walrond was largely forgotten in the decades leading up to and following his death. The publication of *"Winds Can Wake Up the Dead": An Eric Walrond Reader* (1998), an anthology of Walrond's fiction, essays, and reviews, has renewed scholarly interest in Walrond's legacy as an author and brought his works to a new generation of readers.

Further Reading

Parascandola, Louis J. *"Winds Can Wake Up the Dead":*
    An Eric Walrond Reader. Detroit: Wayne State Uni-
    versity Press, 1998.
Wade, Carl A. "African-American Aesthetics and the
    Short Fiction of Eric Walrond: Tropic Death and the
    Harlem Renaissance." *CLA Journal* 42 (1999): 429.
Walrond, Eric. *Tropic Death.* New York: Boni and Liv-
    eright, 1926. Reprint, New York: Macmillan, 1972.

Waniek, Marilyn Nelson
(Marilyn Nelson)
(1946–   ) *poet, literary critic, educator*

A poet, professor, and literary critic, Marilyn Nelson Waniek was named the state poet laureate of
Connecticut in 2001. Her poetry has been praised
for its ability to "bring alive the most rarified and
subtle of experiences," and she has been a finalist
three times for the National Book Award, in 1991,
1997, and 2001.

Marilyn Nelson was born on April 26, 1946,
in Cleveland, Ohio. The daughter of a career air
force officer, Melvin M. Nelson, who also wrote
poetry and plays, and a teacher, Johnnie
Mitchell Nelson, Marilyn grew up on air bases
throughout the United States. She exhibited an
early talent for poetry, writing her first poem in
elementary school at the age of 11. She earned
her bachelor of arts degree from the University
of California at Davis, and postgraduate degrees
from the University of Pennsylvania (M.A.,
1970) and the University of Minnesota (Ph.D.,
1978).

Waniek has held several teaching positions
in the United States and Europe, including a vis-
iting professorship at Nissum Seminarium in
Denmark, and has been writer-in-residence at
Vanderbilt University. Since 1978, she has been a
professor of creative writing and Aframerican and
American Ethnic Literature at the University of
Connecticut in Storrs. Her work as a writer and
teacher has garnered two fellowships from the
National Endowment for the Arts and a Fulbright
Teaching Fellowship.

Waniek's first volume of poetry, *For the Body,*
appeared in 1978 and was followed by a collaborative translation with Pamela Espeland of the
Danish poet Halfdan Rasmussen's *Hundreds of
Hens and Other Poems for Children* in 1982. This
work gave rise to her own volume of children's
verse, *The Cat Walked through the Casserole and
Other Poems for Children* in 1984, also with Pamela
Espeland. With the publication of *The Homeplace*
in 1990, Waniek attracted national attention as a
finalist for the 1991 National Book Award.

The Homeplace is a collection of poems about
family history that Waniek calls "my mother's gift
to me and mine to her memory." Much of Waniek's
poetry explores her ancestral roots. The sense of
identity, familial and racial, is particularly strong in
"The House on Moscow Street," the first poem in
the collection, which she calls "the ragged source of
memory." These poems recover and preserve memories, giving a new kind of life to the stories of her
past and celebrating, as she put it, the "generations
lost to be found."

Following the success of *The Homeplace,* which
earned the Anisfield-Wolf Book Award in 1992,
Waniek published *Magnificat* in 1994 and *The Fields
of Praise: New and Selected Poems* in 1997, earning
a second nomination for the National Book Award.
In *Carver: A Life in Poems,* published in 2001,
Waniek creates a lyrical biography of the scientist
and educator George Washington Carver. As in
The Homeplace, she includes photographs to create
a framework for her words, enlivening the images
with her spare but powerful language.

An award-winning poet and respected professor, Marilyn Nelson Waniek continues to break new
ground with her poetry and remains one of the most
dynamic and respected contemporary African-
American poets. In 2001 she was named the state
poet laureate of Connecticut and she received a
Guggenheim Fellowship. In 2003 she was working
on a book that she described as an "African-
American take on Chaucer's *Canterbury Tales.*"

Further Reading

Andrews, William L., Frances Smith Foster, and Trudier Harris, eds. *The Concise Oxford Companion to African American Literature*. New York: Oxford University Press, 2001.

Hacker, Marilyn. "Double Vision." *Women's Review of Books* 15, no. 8 (May 1998): 17.

Waniek, Marilyn Nelson. *The Homeplace*. Baton Rouge: Louisiana State University Press, 1990.

———. *Magnificat*. Baton Rouge: Louisiana State University Press, 1994.

———. *The Fields of Praise*. Baton Rouge: Louisiana State University Press, 1997.

———. *Carver: A Life in Poems*. Asheville, N.C.: Front Street Press, 2001.

Washington, Booker T.
(Booker Taliaferro Washington)
(ca. 1856–1915) *autobiographer, biographer, educator*

Known primarily as the founder and chief administrator of the renowned Tuskegee Institute, Booker T. Washington became an influential voice among late 19th- and early 20th-century African-American cultural leaders. The author of some 20 books, including two autobiographies, a biography of FREDERICK DOUGLASS, and numerous educational texts, Washington earned international acclaim for his 1901 autobiography, *Up from Slavery*, which chronicled his ascent from slavery to celebrated educator and social leader.

Booker Taliaferro Washington was born into slavery in 1856, on a plantation in Franklin County, Virginia. His mother, Jane, was a slave cook in the household of James Burroughs, a small planter, and his father may have been a member of the Burroughs family. As soon as he was old enough, Washington was sent into the fields of the Burroughs plantation, carrying water to other slaves and doing other menial chores. Emancipated at the conclusion of the Civil War, Washington's mother joined Washington Ferguson, whom she had married during the war, in Malden, West Virginia. Booker's stepfather found employment in a salt-packing plant, and the boy soon began work there to help support the family.

Desiring an opportunity to receive an education, Booker taught himself to read and spent his evenings studying with a teacher from the local school for blacks. He decided to attend the Hampton Institute, established by the Virginia legislature for the education of blacks. He traveled the nearly 300 miles to Hampton, Virginia, by walking and hitching rides when he could. He arrived at the institute penniless and exhausted in 1872.

Booker T. Washington, who founded the celebrated Tuskegee Institute in Mississippi, was one of the most respected African-American cultural leaders of the 19th century. *(Library of Congress)*

Washington graduated from Hampton in 1875 and returned to West Virginia briefly as a schoolteacher. On the recommendation of the Hampton Institute's head administrator, General Armstrong, Washington was invited to create a new school for African Americans in Tuskegee, Mississippi. With only a $2,000 federal grant, Washington built the Tuskegee Normal and Industrial Institute literally from the ground up. His first class of students met in a small shanty. After borrowing money to purchase an old plantation, Washington began the long process of developing a permanent site for the school. Its original name was the Normal School for Colored Teachers.

The Tuskegee Institute would remain the focal point of Washington's life. He served as its president from 1881 to 1915. Rooted in the educational philosophy of the Hampton Institute, Washington's focus as an educator was the economic independence and progress of African Americans. Unlike his contemporary W. E. B. DuBOIS, whose strident political objections to American racism created fear and resentment among many whites, Washington's nonpolitical, or as DuBois characterized it, accommodationist, approach drew widespread federal and local support from white political leaders. An 1895 address at the Cotton States and International Convention in Atlanta, during which Washington expressed his agenda of economic cooperation between blacks and whites in what became known as the "Atlanta Compromise," secured his position as a national representative for the interests of African Americans. "In all things purely social we can be as separate as the fingers," he told the congregation of agriculturalists, political leaders, and delegates, "yet one as the hand in all things essential to mutual progress."

In addition to his achievements as the head of the Tuskegee Institute and his broader role as an important social leader within the black community, Washington also wrote numerous books. Most notable of these was his 1901 autobiography, *Up from Slavery*. Considered a classic work of early 20th-century African-American literature, *Up from Slavery* played an important role in shaping racial attitudes in the post-Reconstruction South. At a time when the lynching of blacks was a frequent event, and southern white society perceived African Americans as a social and economic threat, Washington presented his own personal triumph in *Up from Slavery* as an example of cooperation between the races and the advantages of his educational and social approach. However, Washington's book also provided African Americans with a heroic example of a black man's success against enormous odds, and a program for their own liberation through hard work and self-discipline.

Though hailed for much of his life as the preeminent social and educational spokesman for progress among African Americans, Washington was eventually eclipsed by more politically aggressive leaders such as W. E. B. DuBois, who, during his affiliation with the National Association for the Advancement of Colored People (NAACP), founded in 1909, and the Niagara Movement, its predecessor, called for a more radical approach to black equality and progress. Washington also received criticism from some who questioned his political motives, citing his use of manipulative methods to silence critics and retain his political power. Booker Taliaferro Washington died on November 14, 1915, in his home in Tuskegee, Mississippi.

Washington was sharply criticized in the years following his death for, among other things, his accommodationist stance on race relations. Recent scholarship, however, has revealed that Washington maintained a more aggressive opposition to segregation and violence against blacks, at least in private. Funding for the Tuskegee Institute required a great deal of compromise on Washington's part, though in private he worked steadfastly for social and judicial reforms for African Americans. Washington's legacy as an educator continues to inform the mission of the Tuskegee Normal and Industrial Institute, which in 1985 was granted university status and remains committed to the improvement of African-American life. It is now known as Tuskegee University.

Further Reading

Baker, Houston A. *Turning South Again/Re-thinking Modernism/Re-reading Booker T.* Durham, N.C.: Duke University Press, 2001.

Harlan, Louis R. *Booker T. Washington: The Making of a Black Leader, 1856–1901.* New York: Oxford University Press, 1972.

Washington, Booker T. *Up from Slavery: An Autobiography.* New York: A. L. Burt Company, 1901. Reprint, New York: Penguin, 1986.

West, Cornel
(Cornel Ronald West)
(1953–   ) *literary critic, essayist, editor, educator*

The author of numerous works of literary, political, and cultural criticism, Cornel West is widely recognized as one of America's leading intellectuals. Characterized by HENRY LOUIS GATES, JR., a former colleague at Harvard University, as "our black Jeremiah," West explained in a 1993 interview that his enduring goal as an author and activist is "to uphold the moral character of the black freedom struggle in America."

Cornel West was born on June 2, 1953, in Tulsa, Oklahoma, the son of Clifton West, a civilian administrator in the U.S. Air Force, and Irene West, an educator. West credits the stability of his early life to "my closely knit family and overlapping communities of church and friends." West and his family moved frequently during his childhood, eventually settling in a middle-class black neighborhood of Sacramento, California. There, West participated in his first civil rights demonstration and joined high school students from surrounding areas to demand the addition of black studies courses to the curriculum.

Author and educator Cornel West has become one of the most celebrated cultural and literary critics of the late 20th century. *(Harvard University)*

West graduated magna cum laude from Harvard University in 1973 with a bachelor's degree in Near Eastern languages and literature. He later completed his master's (1975) and Ph.D. (1980) degrees at Princeton University. West began his distinguished teaching career in 1977 as an assistant professor at Union Theological Seminary in New York City. In 1984 he joined the faculty of Yale University's Divinity School. From 1989 to 1994 West served as the director of the African-American Studies program and as a professor of religion at Princeton University. He began his long tenure at Harvard University in 1994, where he joined fellow scholars Henry Louis Gates, Jr., and Kwame Anthony Appiah.

West's early works, such as *Black Theology and Marxist Thought* (1979) and *Prophecy Deliverance! An Afro-American Revolutionary Christianity* (1982), sought to achieve a synthesis of traditional religious and philosophical systems with more radical marxist thought in opposing racial prejudice and oppression. West continued to explore the philosophical and religious dimensions of racial protest in works such as *The Ethical Dimensions of Marxist Thought* (1991) and *Keeping Faith: Philosophy and Race in America* (1993).

In 1993 West published his most acclaimed work to date, *Race Matters*, a collection of essays on a variety of subjects, including the Los Angeles riots of 1992, sparked by the verdict in the Rodney King beating; Malcolm X; and the sexual harassment lawsuit brought against U.S. Supreme Court nominee Clarence Thomas by Anita Hill in 1991. West's unique and persuasive approach to matters of race and culture appealed to a broad segment of society, and *Race Matters* brought him wide popularity outside the academic circles in which he had almost exclusively been previously known. West followed this success with several collaborative works, including *Jews and Blacks: Let the Healing Begin* (1995, with Michael Lerner), *The Future of the Race* (1996, with Henry Louis Gates, Jr.), and the critically acclaimed *The Future of American Progressivism: An Initiative for Political and Economic Reform* (1998, with Roberto Mangabeira Unger). West's other works include *Breaking Bread: Insurgent Black Intellectual Life* (1991, with BELL HOOKS), and *The Cornel West Reader* (2001), an expansive compendium of original and previously published essays.

West's considerable contributions to philosophical, religious, and racial discourse have been characterized by his willingness to engage widely divergent points of view. "One of Professor West's great gifts," explained former colleague Henry Louis Gates, Jr., "is that he can engage in conversation with almost anyone, whatever their ideology." West has also been quick to embrace new mediums for his creative pursuits. In 2001 he collaborated with his brother, Clifton, and others on a spoken word and rap recording entitled *Sketches of My Culture*. West's involvement drew criticism from Larry Summers, president of Harvard University, who suggested that West was neglecting his teaching for the sake of nonscholarly work. Summers also alleged that West might be inflating student grades. After several months of speculation, during which West and his colleagues defended his academic reputation, West announced in 2002 that he would leave his post at Harvard and return to Princeton University as the Class of 1943 University Professor of Religion.

One of the leading American intellectuals, and perhaps the most significant African-American intellectual of his generation, Cornel West has devoted his life as an author and educator to the struggle for social and racial justice. His writings reveal a remarkable breadth of interests, from the philosophical and religious to the political and literary, that continue to augment and enliven the expanding discourse on race and culture in America. West's essays have been published in numerous scholarly and popular periodicals, including *Monthly Review*, the *Nation, Tikkun, Critical Quarterly*, and the *New York Times*.

Further Reading

Andrews, William L., Frances Smith Foster, and Trudier Harris, eds. *The Concise Oxford Companion to African American Literature*. New York: Oxford University Press, 2001.

Nichols, John. "Cornel West." *The Progressive*, January 1997, p. 26.

West, Cornel. *The Cornel West Reader*. New York: Basic Civitas Books, 2001.

———. *Race Matters*. Boston: Beacon Press, 1993.

West, Dorothy
(Mildred Augustine Wirt Benson, Mildred A. Wirt, Frank Bell, Joan Clark, Don Palmer, Ann Wirt, Helen Louise Thorndyke)
(1907–1998) *short story writer, essayist, novelist*

Commenting on her years as a writer during the Harlem Renaissance, Dorothy West observed that she was the "best-known unknown writer of the time." She was a friend and contemporary of virtually every major writer of that era, including LANGSTON HUGHES, ZORA NEALE HURSTON, and WALLACE THURMAN. The author of novels, short stories, and essays, West surprised the literary world with the publication of her second novel, *The Wedding*, in 1995, after nearly 50 years of relative obscurity as a writer.

Dorothy West was born on June 2, 1907, in Boston, Massachusetts. The only daughter of Isaac West, a former slave who became a prosperous Boston businessman, and Rachel West, Dorothy grew up in a comfortable upper-middle-class household. She studied with private tutors as a child and graduated from the Girl's Latin School (now the Boston Latin Academy). She later studied philosophy at Boston University and attended the Columbia School of Journalism, in New York City.

In 1926 West shared second prize in a literary contest sponsored by the National Urban League's *Opportunity* magazine for her short story "The Typewriter." She moved later that year to live in New York City with her cousin, HELENE JOHNSON, a poet and popular literary personality during the Harlem Renaissance. West soon became a favorite among Harlem's leading literary figures, with many of whom she traveled to Russia in 1932 to work on *Black and White*, a film about the oppression of African Americans in the United States. When the project was canceled later that year, she remained in Russia until news of her father's death reached her.

During the 1930s West founded the magazine *Challenge*, in which she published works by ARNA BONTEMPS, CLAUDE MCKAY, and many others. The magazine failed in 1937, but it enjoyed a brief revival under the editorship of RICHARD WRIGHT, who managed to release one more issue with the title *New Challenge*. West worked as a welfare investigator during the late 1930s and joined the swelling ranks of African-American authors who worked for the Federal Writers' Project, part of President Franklin D. Roosevelt's Works Progress Administration (1936–40). She also published stories and essays in the *New York Daily News*.

West left New York City in 1945 to live in her family's summer home in the Oak Bluff community of Martha's Vineyard, where she wrote her first novel, *The Living Is Easy* (1948). Some critics praised the novel for its satirical depiction of social and political strife within black middle-class society and its effects on family relationships, while others faulted the book's absence of racial protest themes. West also became a regular columnist for the *Vineyard Gazette*. She began work on a second novel during the 1950s, but the rise of black militant groups like the Black Panthers, and their literary counterparts in the Black Arts Movement, convinced West that her work would not be well received.

Decades later, West resumed work on the novel when former first lady Jacqueline Kennedy Onassis, an editor at Doubleday and fellow resident of Martha's Vineyard, encouraged her to finish the manuscript. *The Wedding*, West's long-anticipated second novel, about a group of aristocratic black families living in Martha's Vineyard, was finally published by Doubleday in 1995 and dedicated to the memory of Onassis. The book drew wide critical acclaim and generated renewed interest in West's earlier works. Doubleday also released *The Richer, The Poorer: Stories, Sketches, and Reminiscences* (1995), which included material originally published between 1926 and 1987. *The Wedding* was later adapted for television with the help of Oprah Winfrey and aired in 1998. After more than 70 years as a writer and journalist, Dorothy West, the last surviving member of the Harlem Renaissance, died on August 16, 1998, in Boston, Massachusetts.

A gifted and insightful storyteller, Dorothy West became an important voice among Harlem Renaissance writers. She joined such distinguished contemporaries as Zora Neale Hurston, JESSIE REDMON FAUSET, and NELLA LARSEN in establishing a strong female presence within modern African-American literature.

Further Reading

Bascom, Lionel C., ed. *A Renaissance in Harlem: Lost Essays of the WPA by Ralph Ellison, Dorothy West and Other Voices of a Generation.* New York: Amistad Press, 2000.

Gates, Henry Louis, Jr., and Nellie Y. McKay, eds. *The Norton Anthology of African American Literature.* New York: W. W. Norton, 1997.

West, Dorothy. *The Richer, The Poorer: Stories, Sketches, and Reminiscences.* New York: Doubleday, 1995.

———. *The Wedding.* New York: Doubleday, 1995.

Wheatley, Phillis
(Phillis Wheatley Peters)
(ca. 1753–1784) *poet*

Since the publication of *Poems on Various Subjects, Religious and Moral by Phillis Wheatley, Negro Servant to Mr. John Wheatley, of Boston, in New England* in 1773, the first book published by an African-American author, Phillis Wheatley has remained one of the most controversial yet celebrated figures in African-American literature. In Wheatley's lifetime, the significance of her achievements was debated by scientists, abolitionists, and even the future U.S. president Thomas Jefferson. In the centuries that followed, scholars questioned the relevance of her poetry to the broader political and racial issues affecting African Americans in their struggle for freedom. No African-American author of any century, however, has contributed more than Wheatley to the creation and development of the African-American literary tradition.

Phillis Wheatley is thought to have been born in about 1753 in what is now Senegal, in West Africa. Kidnapped by slave traders at the age of seven or eight, she was brought to America and sold to a prominent Boston merchant, John Wheatley, who desired a personal servant for his wife Suzanna. Given the name Phillis, Wheatley was required to perform only light duties, due to her delicate health, and enjoyed a prominent place within the Wheatley household. Though never formally educated, Wheatley learned English, Latin, and Greek, and she began reading the Bible as well as classical Latin and Greek literature and British poetry. Influenced by the strong religious beliefs of her master's family, Wheatley was baptized in 1771.

Wheatley's remarkable facility for language and literature made her a favorite among some of Boston's literary elite. Mather Byles, a Harvard-educated poet and minister, corresponded frequently with Wheatley and may have served as a tutor to the young prodigy. His uncle, Cotton Mather, had bequeathed to him an enormous library, which included ancient Latin and Greek texts as well as books by Alexander Pope, with all of which Wheatley was to become completely familiar.

Wheatley became a member of the Old South Church, a rare occurrence for a slave. In addition to providing her access to some of the most renowned religious and literary minds of colonial Boston, Wheatley's membership placed her in the middle of the growing political crisis between England and the colonies. On March 5, 1770, British soldiers opened fire on a crowd in what became known as the Boston Massacre. Following the event, a town meeting was convened at the Old South Church. Wheatley is believed to have written about the events in her poem "On the Affray in King-Street, on the Evening of the 5th of March," though no copies of the poem have survived.

Though it is not known when Wheatley first began to write poetry, she published her first poem, "On Messrs. Hussey and Coffin," about two local hurricane survivors, on December 21, 1767, in the *Newport Mercury*. She earned wide popular acclaim three years later with the publication of "An Elegaic Poem, on the Death of that Celebrated, Divine, and Eminent Servant of Jesus Christ, the Reverend and Learned George Whitefield" in 1770. These and other early poems exhibited the influence of the English poets Alexander Pope and John Milton, both of whom were among Wheatley's favorite authors.

By 1772 Wheatley had completed enough poems for a published volume, though she was unable to find a publisher in Boston. Her poem on George Whitefield, an internationally known Methodist evangelist, brought her to the attention of the English philanthropist Selina Hastings, countess of Huntingdon. Suffering a decline in her health in 1773, Wheatley accompanied Nathaniel Wheatley, her master's son, to London, where she was received by the countess and became a favorite of London society.

During her six weeks in London, Wheatley became acquainted with the colonial statesman Benjamin Franklin and earned the praise of the celebrated French philosopher and poet Voltaire. With the help of the countess of Huntingdon, Wheatley also secured a publisher for her collection of poetry, *Poems on Various Subjects, Religious and Moral by Phillis Wheatley, Negro Servant to Mr. John Wheatley, of Boston, in New England*, published first in London in 1773, and later appearing in Boston.

Consisting of 38 poems written in the neoclassical style and mostly religious in theme, *Poems on Various Subjects* contains elegies written to memorialize the deaths of several eminent clergymen and to mark the loss of husbands, wives, and children of her acquaintance, verse adaptations of biblical stories, a brief translation of a text by the Roman poet Ovid, and a meditation on her capture in Africa as a child.

The social and literary implications of Wheatley's book, the first to be published by an African American, and only the second published by a woman in the American colonies, were enormous. Upon its release in Boston, *Poems on Various Subjects* contained prefatory materials that included a letter from her master, which attested to the fact that she was indeed an African slave, and a short biography of the poet. In addition, a group of 18 prominent Boston political and religious leaders signed a public statement included in the preface to "assure the World, that the POEMS specified . . . were (as we verily believe) written by PHILLIS, a young Negro Girl." Among the signatures included were those of Thomas Hutchinson, governor of Massachusetts, and John Hancock.

The space given to establishing Wheatley's identity as a slave attested to the almost universal unwillingness of white society to acknowledge that African Americans possessed the faculties required to write poetry, considered the highest form of artistic and intellectual expression in the 18th century. Wheatley's poetry contradicted the basic justifications for slavery, which relied on the belief that slaves were incapable of civilization and therefore fit only for enslavement.

When Wheatley returned from England in 1773, John Wheatley granted her freedom, though she remained in his household until his death. In 1775 Wheatley wrote a letter to George Washington, then the leader of the American Revolutionary Army, and enclosed a poem. She later visited him by his invitation at his headquarters in Cambridge, Massachusetts. After John Wheatley's death in 1778, Wheatley married a free black man, John Peters, about whom little is known. She published only a few poems during the final years of her life, which were marked by extreme poverty, and she tried unsuccessfully to publish a second book of poetry. The mother of three children, none of whom survived her, Phillis Wheatley died on December 5, 1784.

Phillis Wheatley occupies a preeminent position among African-American writers. Described by the eminent literary critic and educator HENRY LOUIS GATES, JR., as the "progenitor of the black literary tradition," Wheatley was the first African-American to publish a book and the first to earn her manumission on the basis of her writing. Though some scholars have criticized her poetry as irrelevant to the broader political and racial issues of African Americans in the 20th century, modern critics have noted the presence of strong political and antislavery themes in Wheatley's poems and letters. "How well the cry for liberty," Wheatley wrote in a letter to Samuel Occam in 1774, "and the reverse disposition for the exercise of oppressive power over others agree—I humbly think it does not require the penetration of a philosopher to determine."

Further Reading

Andrews, William L., Frances Scott Smith, and Trudier Harris, eds. *The Concise Oxford Companion to African American Literature*. New York: Oxford University Press, 2001.

Balkin, Mary McAleer. "Phillis Wheatley's Construction of Otherness and the Rhetoric of Performed Ideology." *African American Review* 36, no. 1 (spring 2002): 121.

Gates, Henry Louis, Jr., and Nellie Y. McKay, eds. *The Norton Anthology of African American Literature*. New York: W. W. Norton, 1997.

Wheatley, Phillis. *Complete Writings*. New York: Penguin, 2001.

Whitehead, Colson

(1970–) *novelist, essayist*

The author of two award-winning novels, Colson Whitehead has earned wide critical acclaim as one of the most gifted young African-American authors of his generation. His subtle and intelligent writing style has elicited comparisons to RALPH ELLISON, while critics also praise Whitehead for his unique plots and compelling characters.

Colson Whitehead was born in New York City in 1970, and spent his childhood living in several areas of Manhattan. "All of these different neigh-borhoods—the East Side, the Upper West Side, Harlem—they've left their mark on me." Whitehead discovered his desire to write in his childhood, after reading his first Stephen King novel. He graduated from Harvard University in 1991 and returned to New York, where he worked for several years at the *Village Voice* as a television critic.

Whitehead's first novel, *The Intuitionist* (1998), received nationwide critical attention for its unique blend of detective fiction and metaphysical inquiry, and for Whitehead's intelligent and compelling narrative. Lila Mae Watson, an elevator inspector, is the first African-American woman to be employed by the Guild of Elevator Inspectors. Lila is further marginalized by her association with the more esoteric branch of elevator inspectors, the intuitionists, whose methodology is considered primitive by the opposing school of elevator inspection, the empiricists, despite the intuitionists' better safety record.

When one of Lila Mae's elevators inexplicably malfunctions, she begins to investigate the cause of the failure, a search that puts her in the middle of a power struggle within the Guild of Elevator Inspectors and which leads her to a mysterious blueprint created by James Fulton, the founder of the intuitionist school. The blueprint contains Fulton's design for the perfect elevator, a black box built on intuitionist principles that would accommodate the highest skyscraper.

In her pursuit of the coveted blueprint, Lila Mae discovers that Fulton was an African American who passed for white, and that his theoretical design for the black box masks a larger goal for an improved society. The excerpts from Fulton's principal work, *Theoretical Elevators*, appear throughout the novel and reveal Fulton's elevator as a metaphor for humanity's quest for cultural and spiritual elevation. *The Intuitionist* was a finalist in 1999 for the Hemingway/PEN Award for first fiction and won the Whiting Writers' Award in 2000.

In his second novel, *John Henry Days* (2001), Whitehead explores the myth of John Henry, the legendary railroad worker who, according to a celebrated folk ballad, challenged and defeated a steam drill in a race to lay track, only to die from exhaustion in the process. J. Sutter, a freelance and freeloading journalist, arrives in Talcott, West Virginia, the site of the John Henry Days festival, to cover the event for a travel website. As Sutter unravels the myths and facts surrounding the figure of John Henry, Whitehead contrasts the industrial age that ultimately destroyed John Henry with the age of information and consumer culture that threatens the future of J. Sutter.

Like Whitehead's first novel, *John Henry Days* presents a plot with multiple layers. "I was trying, over the course of the book, to explore the idea of John Henry," Whitehead explained in an interview in 2001, "to attack it from different angles, different ways people interact with the myth." Among his unusual cast of characters are a blues singer; an employee at the Tin Pan Alley music publishers, which popularized the John Henry ballad; the celebrated African-American actor Paul Robeson, who played John Henry on Broadway; and the historical figure of John Henry himself. *John Henry Days* was named a *New York Times* Editor's Selection in 2001 and earned the New York Public Library's Young Lions Fiction Award in 2002. In 2003 Whitehead published *The Colossus of New York: A City in Thirteen Parts,* a collection of essays in which he provides a compelling and unconventional portrait of the sights, sounds, and people of the city of New York.

Colson Whitehead has garnered enormous critical acclaim for a young novelist and earned the respect of fellow writers such as the novelist WALTER MOSLEY. Critics have compared *The Intuitionist* to such landmark works as Ralph Ellison's *The Invisible Man* and TONI MORRISON's *The Bluest Eye,* citing Whitehead's unique approach to racial allegory. With literary influences that include JEAN TOOMER and ISHMAEL REED, as well as postmodern novelists such as Don DeLillo and Thomas Pynchon, Whitehead identifies with the traditional themes and methods of African-

American literature while also attempting to expand them. "I'm dealing with serious race issues," he explained in a 1999 interview, "but I'm not handling them in a way that people expect."

Further Reading

Hill, Logan. "Whitehead Revisited." *New York,* May 7, 2001, p. 38.

Porter, Evette. "Writing Home." *Black Issues Book Review* 4, no. 3 (May/June 2002): 36.

Whitehead, Colson. *The Intuitionist.* New York: Anchor Books, 1998.

———. *John Henry Days.* New York: Doubleday, 2001.

Whitfield, James Monroe
(1822–1871) *poet*

An accomplished poet whose antislavery poetry earned the respect of abolitionist and autobiographer FREDERICK DOUGLASS and fellow poet WILLIAM WELLS BROWN, James Monroe Whitfield struggled for most of his life to balance his activities as a writer with his need to support his family. Little is known about his private life, but his poetry, suffused with anger against the institution of slavery, speaks to his powerful command of language and earned him a reputation as the leader among African-American antislavery poets.

James Monroe Whitfield was born free in Exeter, New Hampshire, in 1822. He married and fathered two sons and a daughter. While working in Buffalo, New York, in 1850, he met Frederick Douglass, who took an interest in his poetry. Whitfield's first published poems appeared in Douglass's newspapers, the *North Star* and *Fredrick Douglass' Paper,* as well as William Lloyd Garrison's *Liberator.* In 1853 Whitfield published his only volume of poetry, *America and Other Poems,* released by the James L. Leavitt Company in Buffalo, New York.

With a fiery cynicism that stops just shy of complete despair, Whitfield condemns the moral and political hypocrisy of slavery in a nation founded on the principles of liberty and equality for all men. In the title poem, "America," written in the fashion of a nationalistic hymn, he contrasts the sacrifices of African Americans for the sake of freedom during the Revolutionary War with the bondage of slavery that became their children's legacy: "They never thought, when thus they shed / Their heart's best blood, in freedom's cause / That their own sons would live in dread / Under unjust, oppressive laws." "Sing not to me of landscapes bright," Whitfield writes in the poem "Yes! Strike Again That Sounding String," but rather "the awful waste of human life."

In 1854 Whitfield joined Martin R. Delaney, one of the leading proponents of black emigration from the United States, in organizing the National Emigration Convention in Cleveland, Ohio. Whitfield continued to advocate emigration and black separatism throughout the decade leading up to the Civil War, even spending two years in Central America looking for a suitable location for colonization. In 1861 Whitfield moved to San Francisco, where he continued his trade as a barber and published his poetry and letters in the *San Francisco Elevator,* an African-American newspaper.

Following the Civil War, Whitfield broke with the black emigration movement, and the tone of his poetry became more optimistic. His last published poem, an untitled piece on the theme of liberty, appeared in the *Elevator* in 1870. He called America the "One favored land" and emphasized his hope for racial equality under the law and a fully integrated black citizenship. James Monroe Whitfield died of heart disease in San Francisco in 1871.

Further Reading

Andrews, William L., Frances Smith Foster, and Trudier Harris, eds. *The Concise Oxford Companion to African American Literature.* New York: Oxford University Press, 2001.

Gates, Henry Louis, Jr., and Nellie Y. McKay, eds. *The Norton Anthology of African American Literature.* New York: W. W. Norton, 1997.

"James Monroe Whitfield." In *Dictionary of Literary Biography, Volume 50: Afro-American Writers Before the Harlem Renaissance,* edited by Trudier Harris. Detroit: The Gale Group, 1986, pp. 260–263.

Wideman, John Edgar

(1941–   ) *novelist, short story writer, literary critic, autobiographer, essayist, educator*

A Rhodes scholar and an award-winning author of novels, short fiction, essays, and autobiography, John Edgar Wideman is the only American author to win the PEN/Faulkner Award for literature twice. Much of Wideman's fiction is informed by his upbringing in the economically depressed urban Pittsburgh neighborhood of Homewood, the setting of many of his works, as well as overwhelming personal tragedies that highlight the difficulties that confront black communities in a society deeply divided by social and racial injustice. Wideman also addresses the emotional and spiritual dimensions of black life. "I want to trace the comings and goings of my people on the invisible plane of existence," Wideman explained in an interview with the *New York Times Book Review,* "where so much of the substance of black life resides."

John Edgar Wideman was born on June 14, 1941, in Washington, D.C., the eldest of Edgar and Betty French Wideman's five children, but he grew up in the Homewood community of Pittsburgh, Pennsylvania, in which his great-great-great grandmother, a runaway slave, was among the original settlers. A gifted student, Wideman graduated from the prestigious Peabody Academy at the top of his class in 1959 and earned a scholarship to the University of Pennsylvania. There he also served as the captain of the university basketball team and initially hoped to pursue a career as a professional player. He graduated Phi Beta Kappa in 1963.

Wideman ultimately chose to continue his education. He won a Rhodes scholarship to

Oxford University, becoming only the second African American to earn that distinction (the first was ALAIN LOCKE). Wideman graduated Oxford with a degree in 18th-century literature in 1966. After his return to the United States, Wideman and his wife, Judith Goldman, whom he had married in 1965, moved to Iowa City, Iowa, where Wideman served as a Kent Fellow at the University of Iowa Writers' Workshop.

Despite his upbringing in Homewood, Wideman felt alienated from the black community in later years. During his student years in predominantly white schools, Wideman learned to suffer the racial taunts of his classmates in silence. "Speaking out, identifying myself with the group being slurred by these expressions, was impossible," he recalled in an interview with the *New York Times Book Review.* "I had neither the words nor the heart." Through his writing, much of which focuses on Homewood, Wideman reconnected with his cultural roots through characters who struggle against overwhelming pressure to preserve their identities.

At the age of 26, Wideman published his first novel, *A Glance Away,* which depicts a day in the life of a recovering drug addict, Eddie Lawson, who struggles to put his life back together with the help of an unlikely friend, Robert Thurley. The novel generated considerable critical acclaim for its depiction of characters who contend with the alienation and suffering of their respective pasts.

Wideman taught literature and Afro-American studies at the University of Pennsylvania from 1967 to 1974, a period that saw the publication of his next two novels, *Hurry Home* (1970) and *The Lynchers* (1973), both of which return to the themes of isolation and cultural alienation. In *Hurry Home,* an upwardly mobile lawyer, Cecil Otis Braithwaite, leaves his relatively comfortable but unfulfilling life to reconnect with his past during a three-year sojourn in Europe. *The Lynchers,* set in a nondescript urban neighborhood in the Northeast, depicts a plot hatched by four disenchanted African-American

working-class men who decide to sway the cultural balance of power by kidnapping and lynching a white police officer.

In 1973 Wideman suffered the death of his grandmother, an event that would serve as a catalyst for his best-known works of fiction. Wideman relocated to Laramie, Wyoming, in 1974, and began a long residence as professor of English at the University of Wyoming. Tragedy struck Wideman again in 1976 when his younger brother, Robbie, was sentenced to life in prison for his participation in a robbery that ended in murder. Fueled by his brother's imprisonment and the memories of his family's long history in Homewood, Wideman published what has come to be known as the Homewood Trilogy during the early 1980s.

A celebrated novelist, critic, and Rhodes scholar, John Edgar Wideman originally hoped for a career as a professional basketball player. *(Fred Vuich, Courtesy of Pantheon Books)*

In *Damballah* (1981), a collection of 12 inter-related stories, Wideman traces the history of Homewood, from its founding by a runaway slave through five succeeding generations. In the novel *The Hiding Place* (1981), Tommy Lawson, a street-wise Homewood youth, tries to evade the police after being falsely accused of murder during a robbery in which he participated. Wideman uses Tommy's story, which resembles in some respects the fate of his own brother, to highlight the divisions between generations and family members in Homewood. The third installment of the Homewood Trilogy, the novel *Sent for You Yesterday* (1983), follows the lives of several residents of Homewood, each of whom endeavor to avoid the mistakes of their predecessors. *Sent for You Yesterday* earned Wideman the first of his two PEN/Faulkner awards in 1984.

In his next book, Wideman examined the circumstances and wider implications of his brother's imprisonment for murder. *Brothers and Keepers* (1984), Wideman's first work of nonfiction, was widely acclaimed for its blend of poignant autobiography and stringent social criticism. Wideman documents his personal response to his brother's fate and his outrage at the deep racial divisions within American society that have ravaged the black community. *Brothers and Keepers* was nominated for the National Book Critics Circle Award in 1984, and Wideman was later featured on a segment of the television program *60 Minutes*.

Wideman suffered another personal crisis when, in 1986, his 16-year-old son Jacob, the second of his three children, pleaded guilty to the murder of a classmate and received a life sentence in prison. Wideman has made few public comments about his son's trial and imprisonment, but his subsequent writing has reflected the profound and conflicting emotions engendered by the loss of his son.

In the novel *Reuben* (1987), a young lawyer offers legal aid to residents of Homewood, whose various personal conflicts, including a young black prostitute's struggle for custody of her son, form the basis of the narrative. *Philadelphia Fire* (1990) depicts the bombing by the city of Philadelphia of the headquarters of the militant African-American organization MOVE in 1985. Referred to by some critics as "docufiction," the novel blends a fictional narrative with Wideman's own reactions to the bombing and subsequent fire that consumed a Philadelphia city block. Wideman also includes some thoughts on his son's life sentence for murder. "Few pages of prose," wrote a reviewer from the *Chicago Tribune*, "carry as much pain as do Wideman's thoughts on his son, his words to him in prison, his feelings of confusion as a father." Wideman won his second PEN/Faulkner Award and an American Book Award for *Philadelphia Fire* in 1991.

In fiction and nonfiction, Wideman continued to explore the social and cultural implications of African-American life in his later works, among them *The Stories of John Edgar Wideman* (1992); *Fatheralong: A Meditation on Fathers and Sons, Race and Society* (1994); the novels *Cattle Killing* (1996) and *Two Cities: A Love Story* (1998); and the memoir *Hoop Roots: Basketball, Race, and Love* (2001). Wideman has also edited *My Soul Has Grown Deep: Classics of Early African-American Literature* (2001). In 2003 Wideman published *The Island*, a travel memoir that documents his visit to Martinique and his reaction to the rich history and culture of the island nation.

The author of more than 20 books of fiction and nonfiction, John Edgar Wideman has achieved international acclaim for his penetrating depictions of contemporary African-American life. His works have been translated into more than a dozen languages. In 2001 Wideman was named Distinguished Professor of English at the University of Massachusetts in Amherst, where he began teaching in 1986. Though rooted in the history and culture of black America, Wideman's writing addresses the challenges and tragedies common to all human beings, and the ways in which individuals confront injustice and suffering. "Things happen, situations repeat themselves," he wrote in the memoir *Fatheralong.* "You perform as you must . . . and the unthinkable subsides to a kind of numbed persistence, familiar after a while, not better, not easier, as you repeat what must be done."

Further Reading

Baker, Lisa. "Storytelling and Democracy (in the Radical Sense)." *African American Review* 34 (summer 2000): 263.

Tusmith, Bonnie, ed. *Conversations with John Edgar Wideman.* Jackson: University Press of Mississippi, 1998.

Wideman, John Edgar. *Fatheralong: A Meditation on Fathers and Sons, Race and Society.* New York: Pantheon Books, 1994.

———. *The Homewood Trilogy.* New York: Avon Books, 1985.

Williams, John Alfred
(J. Dennis Gregory)
(1925–   ) *novelist, essayist, poet, biographer, historian, educator*

A founding member of the Black Arts Movement in the 1960s, as well as one of the most prolific and esteemed novelists of his generation, John Alfred Williams was also a distinguished professor of literature. He taught at numerous universities, including the City University of New York, the University of California at Santa Barbara, and Rutgers University, prior to his retirement in 1994. A two-time winner of the American Book Award in 1983 for his novel !*Click Song,* and in 1998 for his collection of poetry *Safari West,* Williams remains an aggressive and insightful critic of the lingering presence of racial inequality in modern society.

John Alfred Williams was born on December 5, 1925, in Hinds County, Mississippi, and grew up in Syracuse, New York. Following his graduation from Central High School, he served in the U.S. Navy during World War II. In 1947 he married Carolyn Clopton, with whom he had two sons prior to their divorce. He also enrolled in Syracuse University, from which he graduated in 1950. During the 1950s, Williams worked for a public

John A. Williams, shown here in 1962, published more than 20 novels and garnered international acclaim for the imaginative and artistic range of his writing. *(Library of Congress)*

relations firm, the CBS television network, and two small publishing firms. He also worked as a European correspondent for *Jet* and *Ebony,* and served as an African correspondent for *Newsweek.*

In 1960 Williams published the first of three largely autobiographical novels, *The Angry Ones,* in which Steve Hill, a publicity director for a small publishing firm, confronts racial prejudice in his personal and professional life. *Night Song* (1961), a pioneering work in the area of jazz fiction, depicts the struggles of a self-destructive jazz musician, a former college professor, and a preacher, all of whom suffer the debilitating effects of racial prejudice. In *Sissie* (1963), Williams created a more complex narrative in his depiction of the lives of Sissie Joplin and her two children, Iris and Ralph. Williams traces the legacy of hardship and disappointment among Joplin family members whose alienation from each other mirrors the cultural and artistic disenfranchisement of blacks in an oppressive white society.

Drawing enthusiastic critical attention with his early novels, Williams was set to receive the prestigious Prix du Rome, a fellowship awarded by the American Academy of Arts and Letters. Having announced Williams the winner in 1961, the academy inexplicably rescinded the award. Williams suspected that racial discrimination prompted the academy's action. When the poet Alan Dugan was later announced as the winner, Dugan courageously voiced those suspicions in his acceptance speech. The controversy would have a lasting influence on Williams's writing.

Williams married his second wife, Lorrain Isaac, in 1965. After working numerous jobs to support himself and his family, Williams settled in to a life of writing and teaching. In *The Man Who Cried I Am*, published in 1967, Williams created an enduring and bleak portrait of race relations on a global scale. Considered his masterpiece, the novel depicts the life of the celebrated writer and journalist Max Redding, who uncovers an international conspiracy to prevent African Americans from uniting politically and socially. When he tries to expose the plot, government agents assassinate him. Against the background of international intrigue, Williams addresses pivotal moments in African-American history, from the beginnings of slavery among Dutch traders to key events and leaders in the Civil Rights movement in the United States during the 1960s. Reminiscing about his past through much of the novel, Redding, who is dying of colon cancer, examines the politically and racially oppressive forces that shaped his life as he attempts to uncover his true identity.

The relationship between inner conflicts and outer political realities, and the struggle to understand and confront history, continued to inform Williams's later novels. In *Sons of Darkness, Sons of Light* (1969), Eugene Browning is driven to violence when he concludes that civil rights marches and protests will not eliminate the injustices

committed against blacks. Following the release of his biography of RICHARD WRIGHT, *The Most Native of Sons: The Life of Richard Wright*, in 1970, Williams published *Captain Blackman* (1975), in which Abraham Blackman, a Vietnam veteran and professor of military history, travels back in time to witness the historical contributions of African-American soldiers during America's early wars. The novel captures the paradoxical position of black soldiers, whose heroism in defense of a nation that oppresses them is both ironic and tragic. Williams also makes use of historical letters in the novel, which reveal the little-known racist beliefs of American presidents Abraham Lincoln and Theodore Roosevelt.

Following the publication of *Mothersill and the Foxes* (1975) and *The Junior Bachelor Society* (1975), Williams wrote *!Click Song*, published in 1982, for which he received his first American Book Award. The novel documents the struggles of a writer, Cato Douglass, to overcome racism within the publishing industry, while also reconnecting with his three children, all from different marriages to women of various ethnicities. Williams continued to explore racial dynamics in the United States and beyond in *The Berhama Account* (1985) and *Jacob's Ladder* (1987), both of which confront questions of intraracial prejudice and the lasting traces of colonialism in Caribbean and African nations.

Williams retired from a long and distinguished teaching career in 1994. During the early 1990s he edited several nonfiction works on literature, and he wrote his second biography, *If I Stop I'll Die: The Comedy and Tragedy of Richard Pryor*. In 1998 Williams earned his second American Book Award for *Safari West: Poems*, a collection of poetry Williams had written intermittently over 30 years. He published *Clifford's Blues* in 1999, in which he depicts the life of a homosexual black jazz musician confined by the Nazis in the concentration camp at Dachau during World War II. The novel documents Clifford Pepperidge's attempt to stay alive by performing for his captors. Heavily researched, *Clifford's Blues* provides a unique glimpse of the suffering of African Americans under the Nazi regime.

Known primarily as a novelist, John Alfred Williams has authored volumes of poetry, essays, biography, and history. He has also written two plays, an operatic libretto, and several television scripts. In an interview published in John O'Brien's *Interviews with Black Writers* (1973), Williams discussed his approach to writing novels: "What I try to do with novels is to deal in forms that are not standard, to improvise as jazz musicians do with their music, so that a standard theme comes out looking brand new."

Further Reading

Gates, Henry Louis, Jr., and Nellie Y. McKay, eds. *The Norton Anthology of African American Literature.* New York: W. W. Norton, 1997.

Williams, John. *Clifford's Blues.* Minneapolis, Minn.: Coffee House Press, 1999.

———. *Sons of Darkness, Sons of Light.* Boston: Northeastern University Press, 1999.

Williams, Sherley Anne

(1944–1999) *novelist, poet, children's fiction writer, short fiction writer, playwright, literary critic, educator*

A renowned scholar, critic, and author of novels, poetry, plays, short stories, and children's fiction, Sherley Anne Williams emphasized the same ideals in her writing that she brought to her distinguished teaching career. Her goal as a writer was to educate her readers about the culture and history of African Americans and to instill a sense of hope for the future. Her own elevation from extreme poverty to international acclaim as a literary figure testifies to the strength of her creative vision.

Born on August 25, 1944, in Bakersfield, California, Sherley Anne Williams grew up with her three sisters in the housing projects of Fresno, California. Her parents, Jessee and Lily Marie Williams, earned their meager living picking fruit and cotton, and Sherley joined them in the fields during much of her childhood. Williams's father died of tuberculosis prior to her eighth birthday, and her mother died eight years later. To cope with the poverty and isolation of her early life, Williams soon turned to literature. Her early influences included RICHARD WRIGHT's *Black Boy* (1945) and Eartha Kitt's *Thursday's Child* (1956). "It was largely through these autobiographies I was able to take heart in my life," Williams said in a 1986 interview.

Unlike many of her peers, Williams graduated high school. She enrolled at Fresno State University, completing her bachelor's degree in history in 1966. The following year, she published her first short story, "Tell Martha Not to Moan," in the *Massachusetts Review.* Williams later attended Howard University as a graduate student before transferring to Brown University, where she taught in the black studies department and completed her master's degree in 1972. That year Williams also published her first book, *Give Birth to Brightness: A Thematic Study of Neo-Black Literature*, a highly regarded collection of essays on contemporary African-American literature, in particular the works of AMIRI BARAKA, JAMES BALDWIN, and ERNEST J. GAINES.

Williams published her first collection of poetry, *The Peacock Poems*, in 1975 to wide critical acclaim. The recipient of a National Book Award nomination, *The Peacock Poems* depicted the hardships of her early life in Bakersfield and the joys of motherhood inspired by the birth of her son John Malcolm. In her second collection of poetry, *Some One Sweet Angel Chile* (1982), also nominated for a National Book Award, Williams drew on her abiding interest in African-American history and culture in her poetic depiction of women from different historical periods. Also in 1982, Williams wrote a play, *Letters from a New England Negro*, adapted from her poem of the same name.

Despite her considerable success as a poet, Williams returned to fiction writing with her 1986 novel *Dessa Rose,* inspired by historical characters that Williams had discovered in Herbert Aptheker's *American Negro Slave Revolts* (1947) as a graduate student at Brown University. Written in the style of traditional slave narratives, the novel is a fictionalized account of the life of Dessa Rose, a pregnant slave who leads an Alabama revolt in the early 19th century. After her capture, she is sentenced to death, pending the birth of her child. She escapes imprisonment, however, and takes refuge with Miss Rufel (Ruth Sutton), a white plantation owner who provides refuge for escaped slaves.

The novel chronicles Dessa Rose's struggle to keep her family free and the unlikely bond of friendship that grows between Dessa and Ruth. *Dessa Rose* was widely acclaimed by critics and earned Williams national recognition as a writer. The *New York Times* listed the novel among its notable books of 1986. Williams was also commissioned to prepare a screenplay of the novel for a film adaptation that was later canceled.

In subsequent fictional works, Williams produced two highly acclaimed works for children. *Working Cotton* (1992) was based on her childhood experiences in the cotton fields of Bakersfield, California. The book was awarded the American Library Association's Caldecott Medal and the Coretta Scott King Award. In 1999, just prior to her death, Williams published her second children's book, *Girls Together,* about the friendships among a group of young girls who dream of escaping the poverty and isolation of their decaying urban neighborhood.

In addition to her success as an author, Williams maintained a lifelong commitment to teaching. From 1969 to 1970 she lectured in ethnic studies at California State University at Fresno. In 1972 she served as an associate professor of English at Fresno. Later, Williams joined the faculty of the University of California at San Diego, where she became a full professor of English in 1982, a position she held for more than 17 years. Williams also taught at the University

of Ghana in 1984 as a Fulbright lecturer. Sherley Anne Williams died of cancer on July 6, 1999, in San Diego, California.

Employing language that was steeped in the blues and jazz musical traditions and the patterns of African-American dialect, Sherley Anne Williams created a unique and compelling vision of African-American life in her poetry, fiction, drama, and essays. She was influenced early in her life by the works of LANGSTON HUGHES and STERLING BROWN, writers to whom Williams has sometimes been compared. "They were the earliest influences on my work," she explained in a 1986 interview in the *Los Angeles Times Magazine.* "I was totally captivated by their language, their speech and their character because I've always loved the way black people talk."

Further Reading

Gates, Henry Louis, Jr., and Nellie Y. McKay, eds. *The Norton Anthology of African American Literature.* New York: W. W. Norton, 1997.

Hill, Patricia Liggins, ed. *Call and Response: The Riverside Anthology of the African American Literary Tradition.* Boston: Houghton Mifflin Co., 1998.

Tate, Claudia, ed. *Black Women Writers at Work.* New York: Continuum Publishing Co., 1983.

Williams, Sherley Anne. *Dessa Rose.* New York: William Morrow and Co., 1986.

———. *The Peacock Poems.* Middletown, Conn.: Wesleyan University Press, 1975.

Wilson, August
(Frederick August Kittell)
(1945–   ) *playwright, poet, essayist*

One of the most acclaimed American playwrights of the 20th century, August Wilson is also among the most frequently produced dramatists in America. His plays have won two Pulitzer Prizes, seven New York Drama Critics Circle Awards, and Broadway's highest honor, the Tony Award. Part of a 10-play cycle, Wilson's eight produced plays chronicle the history of African-American culture in the United States, with each play set in a different era and focusing on a particular social issue. "What I am trying to do," Wilson has explained, "is put Black culture on stage and demonstrate to the world—not to white folks, not to Black folks, but to the world—that it exists and that it is capable of sustaining you."

August Wilson was born Frederick August Kittel in Pittsburgh, Pennsylvania, in 1945, the son of a German baker, Frederick Kittel, and an African-American cleaning woman, Daisy Wilson Kittel. One of four children, Wilson grew up in a two-bedroom apartment in a racially mixed region of Pittsburgh known as The Hill. His father had little contact with the family, and Wilson's parents eventually divorced. His mother later married

Peter Bedford, a white man, and the family relocated to a white suburb, where Wilson began to experience increased racial prejudice. He attended Gladstone High School until 1961, when he was unjustly accused of plagiarism. He dropped out of high school, eventually joined the army for a year, and finally settled in a Pittsburgh boardinghouse in 1965 to pursue a career in writing.

Largely self-educated, Wilson spent much of his time as a teenager in the public library and on the streets of The Hill, where he listened to the stories of older African-Americans. Wilson became interested in the Black Power movement in the late 1960s and began writing poetry and short fiction. His first published poem, "For Malcolm X and Others," appeared in *Negro World* in 1969. Wilson was also deeply influenced by Bessie

August Wilson, left, poses with director Lloyd Richards on the set of *The Piano Lesson* in 1990. *(AP/Wide World Photos)*

Smith, a celebrated blues singer of the 1920s, about whom he wrote the poem "Bessie," which appeared in *Black Lines* in 1971.

After cofounding the Black Horizons Theatre Company, a black nationalist organization, with Rob Penny in 1969, Wilson began his first attempts at writing drama. That year he also married Brenda Burton, a Muslim. Their daughter, Sakina Ansari, was born in 1970. Though initially inspired by the Black Power and Black Arts Movements, particularly the works of AMIRI BARAKA (formerly known as LeRoi Jones), Wilson never fully embraced Black Nationalism, a factor that contributed to the failure of his marriage in 1972.

In 1978 Wilson left Pittsburgh for Minneapolis, Minnesota, at the suggestion of a friend, director Claude Purdy. Wilson worked as a scriptwriter for children's plays staged by the Science Museum of Minnesota in order to support his writing. *Black Bart and the Sacred Hills*, a musical satire set in the Old West and a work that many critics consider his first major drama, was produced in St. Paul, Minnesota, in 1977. Wilson's two-act play *Jitney*, produced at the Allegheny Repertory Theatre in Pittsburgh in 1980, brought Wilson his first public recognition as a playwright. *Jitney* would later open on Broadway in 1999 in a revised form. Wilson was invited to the 1982 National Playwrights Conference, an event that bolstered his confidence as a writer. Wilson married Judy Oliver, a white social worker, in 1981, and she provided financial support during these early years of his playwriting career.

Wilson made his Broadway debut in 1984 when celebrated director Lloyd Richards decided to produce his play *Ma Rainey's Black Bottom.* Set in Chicago during the 1920s, the play depicts the exploitation of black singers by whites who profited more from their work than the singers did themselves. The play opened at Broadway's Cort Theatre in 1984 and ran for 275 performances. The play also earned a New York Drama Critics' Circle Award (1985) and was nominated for the prestigious Tony Award.

Wilson's next play, *Fences,* opened on Broadway in 1987, following a successful production at the Yale Repertory Theatre the previous year. *Fences* portrayed the life of Troy Maxson, a man hardened by his struggle for racial and economic justice who cannot understand or embrace the shifting racial climate of the 1950s and 1960s. Maxson's inability to change creates barriers, or fences, that obstruct the hopes of his wife and children for the future. An enormous success, the play earned Wilson his second New York Drama Critics' Circle Award and the Pulitzer Prize for drama. The play also earned four Tony Awards for Wilson, the director, and two of the actors.

Before *Fences* had ended its run on Broadway, Wilson's next play, *Joe Turner's Come and Gone,* opened at the Ethel Barrymore Theatre in 1988, making him the only African-American playwright to have two plays on Broadway at the same time. Set in a Pittsburgh boardinghouse in 1911, the play, which won a New York Critics' Circle Award in 1988, focuses on the negative aspects of the black migration from the rural South to the urban North.

In 1989 Wilson became only the seventh playwright to win a second Pulitzer Prize for drama, for his play *The Piano Lesson.* Produced on Broadway at the Walter Kerr Theatre in 1990, the play, set in the 1930s, centers on a family crisis that arises over the ownership of an heirloom piano. The piano holds significant sentimental value for the family, whose enslaved ancestors had been traded for it, and whose images were later carved into the piano's surface. The piano also represents an opportunity for the family's future as a means of purchasing land. In 1995 Wilson adapted the play as a television movie starring Charles Dutton and Alfre Woodard.

At the height of his success, Wilson left New York and moved to Seattle, Washington, where he completed his next play, *Two Trains Running,* produced on Broadway at the Walter Kerr Theatre in 1992. The play is set in a coffee shop in The Hill section of Pittsburgh, where local residents congregate to discuss the plight of African Americans during the 1960s. *Two Trains Running* earned a Tony nomination and won the American Theatre Critics Association Award.

Wilson continued to build on his success in later plays. *Seven Guitars,* which opened on Broadway in 1996, is set in the post–World War II era and depicts the life of a murdered blues guitarist whose friends have assembled to reminisce about his life. In 2001 Wilson's eighth play in his 20th-century cycle, the highly acclaimed *King Hedley II,* opened on Broadway. The play, set during the 1980s in The Hill district, chronicles the struggle by King Hedley to overcome a difficult and painful past. A critical and popular success, *King Hedley II* earned six Tony nominations.

Known predominantly as a dramatist, Wilson wrote several poems during his early writing career. In 2002 he published *The Ground on Which I Stand,* a slim volume that contains an address made by Wilson during a visit to Princeton University and which previously appeared in the journal *Callaloo* in 1997. In his address, Wilson offers a broad look at the history of African-American theater and its relation to previous dramatic traditions.

August Wilson is one of the most decorated American playwrights in American theater. His plays continue to appear on Broadway and in community theaters throughout the United States. Wilson has frequently cited the impact of the works of African-American painter Romare Bearden (1912–88) on his writing, in words that could apply equally to his own plays. "What I saw was black life presented on its own terms, on a grand and epic scale," Wilson said of Bearden's collage paintings, "with all its richness and fullness, in a language that was vibrant and which, made attendant to everyday life, ennobled it, affirmed its value, and exalted its presence."

Further Reading

Gates, Henry Louis, Jr., and Alan Nadel, eds. *May All Your Fences Have Gates: Essays on the Drama of August Wilson.* Iowa City: University of Iowa Press, 1993.

Shannon, Sandra Garrett. *The Dramatic Vision of August Wilson.* Washington, D.C.: Howard University Press, 1995.

Wilson, August. *The Ground on Which I Stand.* New York: Theatre Communications Group, 2002.

———. *Fences.* New York: New American Library, 1986.

Wilson, Harriet E.
(Harriet E. Adams Wilson)
(ca. 1828–ca. 1870) *novelist*

With the rediscovery and republication in 1983 of *Our Nig; or, Sketches from the Life of a Free Black, in a Two-story White House, North. Showing That Slavery's Shadows Fall Even There. By "Our Nig"* (1859), Harriet E. Adams Wilson became recognized as the first female African American to publish a novel in English. Combining elements of the slave narrative and those of the popular sentimental novels of the 19th century, Wilson's autobiographical novel made her, in the opinion of HENRY LOUIS GATES, JR., the renowned literary and cultural theorist, "one of the first major innovators of American fictional narrative form."

Few biographical details are available about the tragic life of Harriet E. Adams Wilson prior to 1850, and most of what is known about her life comes from information in her novel, as verified by public records. She was born in about 1828 in New Hampshire. She is thought to have lived for several years with the white family of Samuel Boyles, a carpenter, in Milford, New Hampshire. In 1851 she married an alleged fugitive slave named Thomas Wilson, with whom she had one child, George Mason Wilson. Shortly before the birth of their son, Thomas abandoned the family and went to sea. Wilson's son was born in the County House in New Hampshire, an organization that provided assistance to destitute families. Thomas returned to his family briefly, but he soon disappeared again. A white family eventually adopted Wilson's son George, as she was unable to support him, and she moved to Boston in 1855 to find work.

In Boston, while working as a dressmaker, Wilson wrote her autobiographical novel, *Our Nig*, published in 1859. Her purpose for writing the novel, as inferred from the book's preface, was to earn the means of retrieving her child from his foster home. Six months after the publication of *Our Nig*, however, young George died of fever. Wilson is believed to have remained in Boston until 1863, after which she disappeared from public records. Though no record of her death has been discovered, Harriet E. Adams Wilson is thought to have died in about 1870.

Wilson's novel depicts the life of Alfrado, known as Frado, the daughter of an interracial marriage who is abandoned by her mother, Mag Smith, at the home of a white middle-class family, the Bellmonts, in Massachusetts. At the age of seven, Frado becomes an indentured servant to the Bellmonts, and she suffers severe physical and psychological abuse at the hands of Mrs. Bellmont and her daughter Mary. The male members of the Bellmont family sympathize with Frado's situation, though they are not able to intervene. Eventually, Frado stands up to her tormentors by threatening to quit working if they continue to harass her.

At the age of 18, after years of beatings and sleeping in unhealthy quarters, Frado leaves the Bellmonts to find work as a servant. Her poor health prevents her from finding stable employment until she is taken in by Mrs. Moore, who teaches her to sew. Frado supports herself by making straw hats until she meets and marries Samuel, a con artist who earns his living from abolitionists by giving lectures about his supposed life as a slave. When Frado becomes pregnant, Samuel abandons her, and she is forced to rely on the charity of the poorhouse. Samuel returns briefly after the birth of her son, but he leaves again and eventually dies of fever. Frado places her son in a foster home, and the novel ends with the writing of her story, in the hope that she can earn enough money to retrieve her son.

Our Nig received few critical responses following its publication in 1859. The events and people it so vividly depicted—racial bigotry and abuse in northern free states, interracial marriage, and gullible abolitionists who were frequently duped by enterprising con men passing as former slaves—were not likely to find acceptance among white readers. In 1983, after more than a century in obscurity, Wilson's novel was republished with an introduction by Henry Louis Gates, Jr., who had discovered the novel two years earlier in a Manhattan bookstore.

Modern critics have hailed Wilson's novel as a pivotal work in the history of the American and African-American novel. Renewed critical interest has led many scholars to verify more autobiographical details in the novel, revealing further biographical details about the life of one of America's most innovative yet obscure African-American writers.

Further Reading

Stern, Julia. "Excavating Genre in *Our Nig*." *American Literature* 67, no. 3 (September 1995): 439–466.

White, Barbara A. "Our Nig and the She-Devil: New Information about Harriet Wilson and the 'Bellmont' Family." *American Literature* 65, no. 1 (March 1993): 19.

Wilson, Harriet E. Adams. *Our Nig; Or, Sketches from the Life of a Free Black, in a Two-Story White House, North. Showing That Slavery's Shadows Fall Even There. By "Our Nig."* Edited by Henry Louis Gates, Jr. New York: Vintage, 1983.

Wright, Jay
(ca. 1935–)   *poet, playwright*

Hailed by many critics as a unique and powerful voice among American and African-American contemporary poets, Jay Wright has earned numerous awards for his writing, including

Guggenheim and MacArthur fellowships and an American Academy and Institute of Arts and Letters Literary Award. In 1996 he was named a fellow of the Academy of American Poets. Deeply influenced by the cultural and spiritual traditions of Native American and African peoples, among many others, Wright's poetry explores the impact that these traditions have on the creation of individual and cultural identity.

Jay Wright was born on May 25, 1935 (some sources say 1934), in Albuquerque, New Mexico, to Leona Dailey, a woman of African and Native American descent, and Mercer Murphy Wright, a construction worker who also claimed a mixed African and Native American ancestry. During his early childhood, Wright lived mostly with foster parents. He moved to San Pedro, California, as a teenager to live with his father. In high school Wright played minor league baseball and developed a passion for jazz and the bass.

From 1954 to 1957 Wright served in the U.S. Army medical corps in Germany, which allowed him to travel extensively throughout Europe. He enrolled at the University of California at Berkeley following his discharge and completed his bachelor's degree in comparative literature. Wright also attended Union Theological Seminary in New York for a semester and pursued his Ph.D. in comparative literature at Rutgers University, in New Jersey.

While living and working in Harlem during the 1960s, Wright came into contact with several young African-American poets, including LARRY NEAL, HENRY DUMAS, and LeRoi Jones (later known as AMIRI BARAKA). Wright's cross-cultural approach to the social, spiritual, and intellectual dimensions of African-American life, however, put him at odds with many of his contemporaries, who rejected any such influences outside of the African-American experience.

Wright has described his early collections of poetry as "an octave progression," with certain volumes in the sequence bearing a closer thematic relationship to others. His first collection, *The Homecoming Singer* (1971), was, as he later characterized it, "the record of my developing black American life in the United States." In *Soothsayers and Omens* (1976), Wright continued to explore "black people acting in history," a common thread in all of his poetry.

Wright has adopted several poetic personas in his works, from a Bambaran religious initiate in West Africa in *The Double Invention of Komo* (1980) to a Scotsman in the poem "MacIntyre, the Captain and the Saints" from *Explications/Interpretations* (1984). Wright's other volumes of poetry include *Elaine's Book* (1986), *Selected Poems of Jay Wright* (1987), *Boleros* (1991), and *Transfigurations: Collected Poems* (2000). Characterized by a complex blend of cultural and religious traditions, Wright's poetry celebrates the rich diversity of African and African-American life.

Jay Wright's poetry has often been compared to the work of ROBERT HAYDEN and MELVIN B. TOLSON, particularly with regard to the complexity of its themes and language as well as its incorporation and transformation of Western literary traditions. The breadth of Wright's poetic vision is enhanced by his adoption of American, African, European, Native American, and South American dialects, creating a cosmopolitan, uniquely symbolic language that reflects his belief in the interconnections between cultures. In recognition of his contributions to American and African-American literature, Wright was awarded the Anisfield-Wolf Lifetime Achievement Award from the Cleveland Foundation in 2002.

Further Reading

Andrews, William L., Frances Smith Foster, and Trudier Harris, eds. *The Concise Oxford Companion to African American Literature*. New York: Oxford University Press, 2001.

Okpewho, Isidore. "Prodigal's Progress: Jay Wright's Focal Center." *MELUS* 23 (fall 1998): 187.

Wright, Jay. *Transfigurations: Collected Poems*. Baton Rouge: Louisiana State University Press, 2000.

Wright, Richard
(Richard Nathaniel Wright)
(1908–1960) *novelist, short story writer, autobiographer, playwright, essayist, poet*

One of the earliest African-American authors to gain national prominence in the 20th century, Richard Wright provided an important link between the Harlem Renaissance of the 1920s and 1930s and the emergence of the Black Arts Movement in the 1960s. His novel *Native Son* became a national best-seller when it was published in 1940 and inspired a generation of authors, such as RALPH ELLISON and JAMES BALDWIN. In 1945 Wright's *Black Boy* was published, which has since become a classic of American autobiography. Also the author of essays, short stories, and plays, Wright created a brutal and realistic portrait of the devastating effects of racial oppression in American society.

Richard Nathaniel Wright was born on September 4, 1908, on a plantation near Natchez, Mississippi, the first child of Nathaniel Wright, a sharecropper, and Ella Wilson Wright, a schoolteacher. In 1912 the Wright family moved to Memphis, Tennessee, where Wright's father eventually abandoned the family to a life of increasing poverty. "When I felt hunger," Wright later wrote in his autobiography, "I thought of [my father] with a deep biological bitterness." While living with his grandmother, Wright accidentally set the house on fire, an event that he would later recount in his autobiography, and which haunted him for most of his life. Through much of his early years, Wright and his mother and brother lived with various relatives.

Though his education was often interrupted as a child, Wright eventually graduated as the valedictorian of the Smith-Robinson Public School in Jackson, Mississippi, in 1925. His life in Mississippi, where he lived under the strict religious rule of his Seventh-day Adventist grandmother, began to alienate Wright from his family. Unable to afford college, Wright began working odd jobs and even-

Richard Wright, shown here in 1939, was one of the first African-American authors to achieve national recognition for his contributions to American literature. *(Library of Congress)*

tually saved enough money to return to Memphis. There he began to devote himself to reading, even forging a note that gained him access to the all-white public library. He was drawn early to the works of naturalist authors Stephen Crane, Theodore Dreiser, and Sinclair Lewis.

Wright moved north to Chicago, Illinois, in 1927 to escape the racial hostility of the South. His mother and brother soon joined him in a cramped apartment on Chicago's South Side. To support his family, Wright took a series of jobs, including positions as a postal clerk and an insurance agent. In 1932 Wright joined the John Reed Society, a radical communist organization, and received encouragement from fellow members to pursue a career as a writer. Wright explained his interest in communism in an essay published in Richard Crossman's *The God That Failed* (1949). "It seemed to me that here at last, in the realm of revolutionary expression," he wrote, "Negro experience could find a home." Wright published several poems and articles in radical publications such as *Left Front*. His poem "I Have Seen Black Hands" appeared in *New Masses* in 1934. "I am black and I have seen black hands / Raised in fists of revolt, side by side with the white fists / Of white workers."

In 1936 Wright found work with the Works Progress Administration's Federal Writers' Project, part of President Franklin D. Roosevelt's New Deal program that employed out-of-work writers. During this period, he met several aspiring black authors, including ARNA BONTEMPS, FRANK YERBY, and MARGARET WALKER. Assigned to work on the *Illinois Guidebook* for the Federal Writers' Project, Wright also completed several manuscripts, including the stories that would later comprise the posthumously published *Lawd Today* (1963).

By 1937 Wright's involvement in the Communist Party began to conflict with his writing. Though communism would remain an influential force in his life and writing, Wright questioned what he perceived as an inherent paranoia within the organization that frequently resulted in the expulsion of members for disloyalty. Wright moved to New York in 1937 and became the Harlem editor of the *Daily Worker*, at the time the largest communist newspaper in the United States, and continued to pursue his writing.

In 1938 Wright published his first book, the short story collection *Uncle Tom's Children,* and quickly began to attract critical and popular acclaim. Based on his childhood in Mississippi, the stories in *Uncle Tom's Children* expressed outrage over the endemic violence against blacks in the South. "His purpose was to force open closed eyes," Arna Bontemps wrote of Wright's book in

1966, "to compel America to look at what it had done to the black peasantry in which he was born."

Wright married Rose Dhima Meadman in 1939, and with the assistance of a Guggenheim fellowship and an award for *Uncle Tom's Children* from *Story* magazine, he completed *Native Son,* his first novel. Published in 1940, *Native Son* became an instant best-seller, with more than 250,000 copies sold in the first six months. A militant condemnation of the degrading forces of racism and capitalism on the black community in America, *Native Son* chronicles the life of Bigger Thomas, an illiterate and violent young black man whose life is transformed after he accidentally kills a young white woman. Wright contrasts Bigger's brutality, which is manifest throughout the novel as he flees the scene of his initial crime, to the broader cultural influences of hatred and racial oppression in which Bigger's rage and violence was born.

Native Son secured Wright's reputation as one of the most accomplished authors in American literature. Wright received the Spingarn Medal from the National Association for the Advancement of Colored People. The acclaimed author JAMES BALDWIN later described Wright's novel as "the most powerful and celebrated statement we have had yet of what it means to be a Negro in America." *Native Son* has influenced the direction of African-American narratives in the generations that followed its publication by serving as a blueprint of sorts for social protest fiction. In contrast to his overwhelming success as a writer, Wright's marriage to Rose Meadman ended in 1940. In 1941 Wright married Ellen Poplar, and their daughter, Julia, was born the following year.

In 1941 Wright collaborated on an illustrated history of African Americans, *Twelve Million Voices: A Folk History of the Negro in the United States.* He also cowrote with Paul Green a stage adaptation of *Native Son* for Orson Welles's Mercury Theatre. In 1945 Wright published *Black Boy,* the first volume of his autobiography. Like *Native Son, Black Boy,* which spans the first 19 years of his life, was an immediate critical and popular success. Wright purchased a home in Greenwich Village in 1945, and later that year he traveled with his wife and daughter to France.

During his three-month stay in France, Wright witnessed the vast differences in the treatment of blacks in the United States and Europe. Upon his return, Wright sold his house and relocated to France permanently in 1947. For decades, Paris had been a popular destination for African-American authors and artists seeking a less prohibitive and oppressive society. Wright settled in an apartment in the Left Bank region of Paris and soon became a central figure among the celebrated authors of Paris's literary circles, which included writers such as existentialist philosophers Jean-Paul Sartre and Simone de Beauvoir. In addition to his membership in the literary group Les Temps Modernes, Wright also became active in the Pan-Africanist organization Presence Africaine.

While he would never match the success of his early publications, Wright continued to write during his expatriation and traveled widely in Europe, Africa, and Asia. His later works included the novels *The Outsider* (1953), *Savage Holiday* (1954), and *The Long Dream* (1958), all of which reveal the considerable influence of Sartre's existentialism. Most of Wright's later writings documented his growing interest in political activism and his extensive travels. In *Black Power* (1954), Wright describes his experiences in Ghana, a West African nation. *The Color Curtain* (1956) was published following Wright's involvement in the Bandung Conference in Indonesia. His other non-fiction works include *Pagan Spain* (1956) and *White Man Listen!* (1957).

During his final years, Wright lectured widely in Europe and made frequent television appearances. In 1959 he sold the farm in Normandy that had been his home since 1955 and traveled to London. Unable to obtain a permanent visa, he returned to Paris. Richard Nathaniel Wright died of apparent heart failure on November 28, 1960.

Several manuscripts that he had been working on at the time of his death have been published in recent years. These posthumous works include a short story collection, *Eight Men* (1961); the novel *Lawd Today* (1963), written primarily during the 1930s; and the novella *The Man Who Lived Underground* (1971).

Widely considered the most important writer of his generation, Richard Wright has remained an essential figure in 20th-century American and African-American literature, drawing comparisons to such celebrated authors as John Steinbeck and Theodore Dreiser. Wright was one of the earliest black authors to make a living on the proceeds of his writing. Deeply committed to the principles of racial and economic justice for African Americans, Wright set the standard for black social-protest fiction and paved the way for the social and political activism that characterized works by authors of the Black Arts Movement during the 1960s. In an essay published in Richard Crossman's *The God That Failed* (1949), Wright described the aim of his writing, which was "to hurl words into the darkness and wait for an echo . . . no matter how faintly."

Further Reading

Gates, Henry Louis, Jr., and K. A. Appiah, eds. *Richard Wright: Critical Perspectives Past and Present.* New York: Amistad, 1993.

Kinnamon, Keneth, and Michel Fabre, eds. *Conversations with Richard Wright.* Jackson: University of Mississippi Press, 1993.

Rampersad, Arnold, ed. *Richard Wright: A Collection of Critical Essays.* Englewood Cliffs, N.J.: Prentice Hall, 1995.

Rowley, Hazel. *Richard Wright: The Life and Times.* New York: Henry Holt and Co., 2001.

Wright, Richard. *Black Boy.* New York: Harper and Brothers, 1945. Reprint, New York: HarperCollins, 1993.

———. *Native Son.* New York: Harper and Brothers, 1940. Reprint, New York: HarperCollins, 1993.

Yerby, Frank
(Frank Garvin Yerby)
(1916–1991) *novelist, short story writer, poet, essayist*

Widely considered the best-selling author in the history of African-American literature, Frank Yerby published 33 novels during his lifetime. He also contributed short stories and poems to numerous periodicals in the United States and Europe. Despite the commercial success of his books, Yerby never earned the critical attention of many of his literary contemporaries, such as JAMES BALDWIN, LANGSTON HUGHES, and RICHARD WRIGHT. Yerby's novels were often dismissed by critics for their reliance on popular rather than protest themes.

Frank Garvin Yerby was born on September 5, 1916, in Augusta, Georgia, to Rufus and Wilhelmina Yerby. He graduated from Haines Institute, a respected secondary school for African Americans established by Lucy Laney, a graduate of Atlanta University and a pioneering educator whose curriculum emphasized classical languages, algebra, and music, to prepare her students for college. Yerby later received his bachelor's degree from Payne College in 1937 and a master's degree from Fisk University in Atlanta, Georgia, in 1938.

Yerby began writing poetry as an undergraduate and received encouragement from the poet JAMES WELDON JOHNSON while at Fisk University. Yerby enrolled briefly at the University of Chicago and worked in the Federal Writers' Project, part of President Franklin D. Roosevelt's Works Progress Administration, where he met aspiring African-American authors ARNA BONTEMPS, Richard Wright, and MARGARET WALKER.

After teaching English from 1939 to 1941 at Florida Agricultural and Mechanical College in Tallahassee and Southern University in Baton Rouge, Louisiana, Yerby worked as a technician at Ford Motor Company in Michigan and later at Ranger Aircraft in Jamaica, New York. During this period, he began writing his first novel, a work of protest fiction about an African-American steelworker turned professional boxer. When he could find no publisher for his book, Yerby began writing short stories. His first story, "Health Card," appeared in *Harper's Magazine* in 1944 and won the O. Henry Memorial Prize for best first short story.

Yerby continued to seek a publisher for his protest novel, but after repeated rejections, he turned his attention to the genre of historical fiction, popularized by such works as Margaret Mitchell's *Gone with the Wind* (1936). Yerby's first published novel, *The Foxes of Harrow* (1946), became an instant commercial success, selling more than 2 million copies. The novel was also adapted for the screen, and despite Yerby's objections to major changes in his story, the film was released in 1947 starring Rex Harrison and Maureen O'Hara. Two of Yerby's subsequent novels, *The Golden Hawk* (1948) and *The Saracen Blade* (1952) were also made into successful films.

Set in the South, *The Foxes of Harrow* traces the fortunes and misfortunes of its white protagonist, Stephen Fox, an outsider of Irish descent seeking his fortune in aristocratic southern society. With its fast-paced narrative and vivid depictions of 19th-century New Orleans, the novel received mixed reviews. Critics acknowledged Yerby's gift for writing a compelling story, but many regarded the work as little more than a popular novel with a predictable plot and one-dimensional characters.

The author of more than 30 novels, Frank Yerby, shown here in 1947, was perhaps the best-selling African-American author of his time. *(Library of Congress)*

Following the success of *The Foxes of Harrow*, Yerby went on to publish 32 more novels between 1947 and 1985. Among his most popular were *Griffin's Way* (1962), *An Odor of Sanctity: A Novel of Medieval Moorish Spain* (1965), and *The Dahomean: An Historical Novel* (1971), which portrays the life of an African man, Nyasanu, prior to his enslavement in America. While Yerby used familiar plot devices in many of his novels, he excelled in his depiction of historical settings and often included social commentary on the lives of his African-American characters of the type that was studiously avoided by popular white authors of historical fiction.

Like fellow African-American expatriates James Baldwin and CHESTER HIMES, Yerby left the United States to escape the physical and psychological constraints of racism. He moved to France in 1952 and eventually settled in Madrid, Spain, where he remained until his death. Yerby's novels sold more than 55 million copies during his lifetime. His enormous popular success, however, did little to dispel the criticism of some African-American scholars and critics who praised his pioneering work in popular fiction but faulted his reluctance to address more specific racial themes. Frank Garvin Yerby died on November 29, 1991, in Madrid.

Having failed to achieve success as a writer of social protest novels, Frank Yerby used the vehicle of popular historical fiction to address issues of race and to correct historical and racial misconceptions, particularly with regard to the antebellum and postbellum American South. Though many of his protagonists were white, Yerby used their status as social, and sometimes racial, outcasts to critique the injustices of particular historical periods and cultures.

Further Reading

Andrews, William L., Frances Smith Foster, and Trudier Harris, eds. *The Concise Oxford Companion to African American Literature.* New York: Oxford University Press, 2001.

Glasrud, Bruce A., and Laurie Champion. "'The Fishes and the Poet's Hand': Frank Yerby, a Black Author in White America." *Journal of American and Comparative Culture* 23, no. 4 (winter 2000): 15.

Metzger, Linda, and Deborah A. Straub, eds. *Contemporary Authors.* New Revision Series. Detroit, Mich.: Gale Research, 1986, pp. 466–471.

Yerby, Frank. *The Foxes of Harrow.* New York: Doubleday, 1986.

Young, Al
(Albert James Young)

(1939–   ) novelist, poet, screenwriter, short fiction writer, essayist, editor, educator

An internationally renowned author of novels, poetry, screenplays, and essays, Al Young has lectured and performed his poetry in cities across America, Europe, the Middle East, and Asia. Music plays an essential role in Young's writing, influencing the language and rhythm of his poems and shaping the characters of his novels. A musician for much of his life, Young has also written several musical memoirs in which he explores the impact of music on his life and work.

Albert James Young was born on May 31, 1939, in Ocean Springs, Mississippi, the son of Ernest Albert Young, a professional musician and autoworker, and Mary Campbell Young. Ocean Springs, a Gulf Coast city near Biloxi, provided Young with a unique blend of cultural and musical influences during his early childhood. He listened to jazz and blues on the radio and learned of his family's history in stories told by his father.

Young's father later relocated the family to Detroit, Michigan. Young attended public schools and later enrolled at the University of Michigan in Ann Arbor to pursue a degree in literature. Inspired by poetry readings that he heard aired on Canadian radio as a youth, Young began to consume volumes of poetry from the local library. "All the energy and little nuances and secret meanings and things that the voice transmits and conveys," Young has explained about his discovery of poetry, "I could hear all that for the first time. It came

alive for me." He began to write and publish poems as an undergraduate at the University of Michigan, where he also coedited *Generation,* the campus literary magazine.

In 1961 Young left the University of Michigan and moved to Berkeley, California, where he worked as a disc jockey, a medical photographer, and a musician to support himself and his writing. He eventually returned to college, graduating from the University of California at Berkeley in 1969 with a degree in Spanish, and began a distinguished career as a creative writing instructor. From 1969 to 1976 he served as the Edward B. Jones Lecturer in Creative Writing at Stanford University in Palo Alto, California. Young has taught and lectured at numerous universities throughout the United States, including Rice University, the University of Washington at Seattle, and the University of Arkansas.

Young sees the function of poetry not as a weapon, as many of his contemporaries have articulated, but rather as a tool for unity. "Besides being as necessary as food, water, air, sunlight, and sleep," Young explained in *Contemporary Poets* (2001), "poetry is my way of celebrating spirit, in all of its infinite forms (charted and uncharted), as the central, unifying force in creation." Young's first volume of poetry, *Dancing: Poems* (1969), revealed the strong influence of jazz and blues in its use of varied linguistic rhythms.

Young continued to experiment with rhythm and structure in *The Song Turning Back into Itself* (1971), *Some Recent Fiction* (1974), and *Geography of the Near Past* (1976), in which he includes a cycle of five poems dictated by the fictional O. O. Gabugah, a militant proponent of the oral tradition in African-American literature. O. O. Gabugah is a thinly disguised parody of the politically revolutionary Black Arts poets of the 1960s and 1970s. Young's other works of poetry include *The Blues Don't Change: New and Selected Poems* (1982), *Heaven: Collected Poems, 1956–1990* (1989), the chapbook *Conjugal Visits* (1996), and *The Sound of Dreams Remembered: Poems 1990–2000* (2001).

Like his poetry, Young's novels reflect his abiding interest in the artistic and philosophical dimensions of music. His first novel, *Snakes* (1970), depicts the life of a young aspiring jazz musician, MC, who discovers a sense of personal freedom in his music. In *Who Is Angelina?* (1975), Young addresses the theme of personal liberation as a young woman comes to terms with her family roots and begins to see herself as an individual.

In *Sitting Pretty* (1976), Young presents one of his most engaging characters, Sidney J. Prettymon, known as Sitting Pretty, or Sit for short. Like LANGSTON HUGHES's Jesse B. Semple stories, *Sitting Pretty* presents the unique wisdom of a man whose life reads like a jazz improvisation, as he tries to live a life without harming others but without compromising his own principles. The character of O. O. Gabugah, introduced in the poems of *Geography of the Near Past,* makes a brief appearance in the novel. Young's published novels also include *Ask Me Now* (1980), which received the *New York Times* Outstanding Book of the Year citation, *Seduction by Light* (1988), and *Straight No Chaser* (1994).

Young described his interest in music more directly in a series of musical memoirs, through which he articulates what he perceives as the profound link between music and everyday life. These include *Bodies & Soul* (1981), winner of the American Book Award; *Kinds of Blue* (1984); *Things Ain't What They Used to Be* (1987); *Mingus/Mingus: Two Memoirs* (1991, with Janet Coleman); and *Drowning in the Sea of Love* (1995).

Young has also written several screenplays, including the script for Richard Pryor's film *Bustin' Loose* (1981). With novelist and poet ISHMAEL REED, Young edited two anthologies of poetry, *Yardbird Lives!* (1978) and *Califa: The California Poetry* (1979). In 1995 Young edited *African American Literature: A Brief Introduction and Anthology.*

Al Young has lectured and performed his poetry throughout the United States, Europe, and Asia, and his works have been translated into more than a dozen languages. "I see my poetry as being essentially autobiographical in subject matter and detail," he explained in *Contemporary Poets* (2001), "characterized by a marked personal and lyrical mysticism as well as a concern with social and spiritual problems of contemporary man in a technological environment that grows hourly more impersonal and unreal." While concerned particularly with the personal renewal of black culture and life, Young's writing addresses spiritual and philosophical issues that continue to appeal to a broad and international audience.

Further Reading

Lee, Don. "About Al Young: A Profile." *Ploughshares* 19 (spring 1993): 219.

Young, Al. *Heaven: Collected Poems, 1956–1990.* Berkeley, CA: Creative Arts Book Co., 1992.

———. *Snakes.* New York: Holt, Rinehart, Winston, 1970.

———. *The Sound of Dreams Remembered: Poems, 1990–2000.* Berkeley, Calif.: Creative Arts Book Co., 2001.

BIBLIOGRAPHY AND RECOMMENDED SOURCES

LITERARY ANTHOLOGIES

Chapman, Abraham, ed. *Black Voices: An Anthology of African American Literature*. New York: Signet, 2001.

Donalson, Melvin, ed. *Cornerstones: An Anthology of African American Literature*. New York: St. Martin's Press, 1996.

Gates, Henry Louis, Jr., and Nellie Y. McKay, eds. *The Norton Anthology of African American Literature*. New York: W. W. Norton, 1997.

Goss, Linda, and Marian E. Barnes, eds. *Talk That Talk: An Anthology of African-American Storytelling*. New York: Simon and Schuster, 1994.

Hamalian, Leo, and James Hatch. *The Roots of African American Drama: An Anthology of Early Plays, 1858–1938*. Detroit: Wayne State University Press, 1991.

Harper, Michael S., and Anthony Walton, eds. *The Vintage Book of African American Poetry*. New York: Vintage Books, 2000.

Hill, Patricia Liggens, ed. *Call and Response: The Riverside Anthology of the African American Literary Tradition*. Boston: Houghton Mifflin, 1998.

Johnson, James Weldon, ed. *The Book of American Negro Poetry*. New York: Harcourt, 1922. Reprint, New York: Harvest Books, 1983.

Killens, John Oliver, and Jerry W. Ward, eds. *Black Southern Voices: An Anthology of Fiction, Poetry, Drama, Nonfiction, and Critical Essays*. New York: Meridian, 1992.

Major, Clarence, ed. *Calling the Wind: Twentieth-Century African-American Short Stories*. New York: HarperCollins, 1993.

McMillan, Terry, ed. *Breaking Ice: An Anthology of Contemporary African-American Fiction*. New York: Viking, 1990.

Medina, Tony, Samiya Bashir, and Quarishi Ali Lansana, eds. *Role Call: A Generational Anthology of Social and Political Black Art and Literature*. Chicago: Third World Press, 2002.

Perkins, Kathy A., ed. *Black Female Playwrights: An Anthology of Plays before 1950*. Bloomington: Indiana University Press, 1989.

Smith, Rochelle, and Sharon L. Jones, eds. *The Prentice Hall Anthology of African American Literature*. New York: Prentice Hall, 1999.

Wilson, Sondra K., ed. *The Crisis Reader: Stories, Poetry, and Essays from the N.A.A.C.P's Crisis Magazine*. New York: Modern Library, 1999.

———. *The Opportunity Reader: Stories, Poetry, and Essays from the Urban League's Opportunity Magazine*. New York: Modern Library, 1999.

Young, Al. *African American Literature: A Brief Introduction and Anthology*. Edited by Ishmael Reed. New York: HarperCollins, 1996.

BIOGRAPHICAL SOURCES

Andrews, William L., Frances Scott Smith, and Trudier Harris, eds. *The Concise Oxford Companion to African American Literature*. New York: Oxford University Press, 2001.

————. *The Oxford Companion to African American Literature*. New York: Oxford University Press, 1997.

Appiah, Kwame Anthony, and Henry Louis Gates, Jr., eds. *Africana: The Encyclopedia of the African and African American Experience*. New York: Basic Civitas Books, 1999.

Bryant, Jerry H. *"Born in a Mighty Bad Land": The Violent Man in African American Folklore and Fiction*. Bloomington: Indiana University Press, 2003.

Fabre, Michael. *From Harlem to Paris: Black American Writers in Paris, 1840–1980*. Urbana: University of Illinois Press, 1991.

Harris, Trudier. *Saints, Sinners, Saviors: Strong Black Women in Black Literature*. New York: Palgrave Macmillan, 2001.

Nelson, Emmanuel S. *Contemporary African American Novelists*. Westport, Conn.: Greenwood Press, 1999.

Rasmussen, R. Kent, ed. *The African American Encyclopedia*. 2d rev. ed. New York: Marshall Cavendish, 2001.

Sherman, Joan R. *Invisible Poets: Afro-Americans of the Nineteenth Century*. Urbana: University of Illinois Press, 1989.

Smith, Valerie, ed. *African American Writers*. New York: Charles Scribner's Sons, 2000.

Tate, Claudia, ed. *Black Women Writers at Work*. New York: Continuum, 1983.

CRITICISM AND THEORY

Adell, Sandra. *Double-Consciousness/Double Bind: Theoretical Issues in Twentieth-Century Black Literature*. Urbana: University of Illinois Press, 1994.

Auger, Philip. *Native Sons in No Man's Land: Rewriting Afro-American Manhood in the Novels of Baldwin, Walker, Wideman, and Gaines*. New York: Garland Publishing, 2000.

Bassard, Katherine Clay. *Spiritual Interrogations: Culture, Gender, and Community in Early African American Women's Writing*. Princeton, N.J.: Princeton University Press, 1999.

Benston, Kimberly W. *Performing Blackness: Enactments of African-American Modernism*. New York: Routledge, 2000.

Boan, Devon. *The Black "I": Author and Audience in African-American Literature*. New York: Peter Lang, 2002.

Carroll, Rebecca. *I Know What the Red Clay Looks Like: The Voice and Vision of Black Women Writers*. New York: Random House, 1994.

De Weever, Jacqueline. *Mythmaking and Metaphor in Black Women's Fiction*. New York: St. Martin's, 1992.

Diedrich, Maria, Henry Louis Gates, Jr., and Carl Pedersen. *Black Imagination and the Middle Passage*. New York: Oxford University Press, 1999.

Dixon, Melvin. *Ride Out the Wilderness: Geography and Identity in Afro-American Literature*. Urbana: University of Illinois Press, 1987.

Ervin, Hazel Arnett. *African American Literary Criticism, 1773–2000*. New York: Twayne, 1999.

Foster, Frances S. *Written by Herself: Literary Production by African American Women, 1746–1892*. Bloomington: Indiana University Press, 1993.

Fox, Robert Elliot. *Conscientious Sorcerers: The Black Postmodernist Fiction of LeRoi Jones/Amiri Baraka, Ishmael Reed, and Samuel R. Delany*. Westport, Conn.: Greenwood Publishing, 1987.

Johnson, Charles. *Being and Race: Black Writing Since 1970*. Bloomington: Indiana University Press, 1988.

McDowell, Deborah E. *The Changing Same: Black Women's Literature, Criticism, and Theory*. Bloomington: Indiana University Press, 1995.

Napier, Winston, ed. *African American Literary Theory: A Reader*. New York: New York University Press, 2000.

Normant, Nathaniel. *Readings in African American Language: Aspects, Features, and Perspectives*. New York: Peter Lang, 2002.

Posnock, Ross. *Color and Culture: Black Writers and the Making of the Modern Intellectual.* Cambridge, Mass.: Harvard University Press, 1998.

Simawe, Saadi. *Black Orpheus: Music in African American Fiction from the Harlem Renaissance to Toni Morrison.* New York: Garland Publishing, 2000.

Smethurst, James Edward. *The New Red Negro: The Literary Left and African American Poetry, 1930–1946.* New York: Oxford University Press, 1999.

Sundquist, Eric J. *To Wake the Nations: Race in the Making of American Literature.* Cambridge, Mass.: Harvard University Press, 1993.

Warren, Kenneth W. *Black and White Strangers: Race and American Literary Realism.* Chicago: University of Chicago Press, 1993.

Wetmore, Kevin J., Jr. *Black Dionysus: Greek Tragedy and African American Theatre.* Jefferson, N.C.: McFarland and Company, 2003.

GENRES AND LITERARY MOVEMENTS

Ammons, Elizabeth. *Short Fiction by Black Women, 1900–1920.* New York: Oxford University Press, 1991.

Andrews, William L., ed. *African American Autobiography: A Collection of Critical Essays.* Englewood Cliffs, N.J.: Prentice Hall, 1993.

Bailey, Frankie Y. *Out of the Woodpile: Black Characters in Crime and Detective Fiction.* Westport, Conn.: Greenwood Press, 1991.

Baker, Houston A. *Modernism and the Harlem Renaissance.* Chicago: University of Chicago Press, 1987.

Bascom, Lionel C., ed. *A Renaissance in Harlem: Lost Essays of the WPA by Ralph Ellison, Dorothy West, and Other Voices of a Generation.* New York: Amistad Press, 2000.

Bassett, John Earl. *Harlem in Review: Critical Reactions to Black American Writers.* Selinsgrove, Penn.: Susquehanna University Press, 1992.

Beaulieu, Elizabeth Ann. *Black Women Writers and the American Neo-Slave Narrative: Femininity Unfettered.* Westport, Conn.: Greenwood Press, 1999.

Bell, Bernard. *The Afro-American Novel and Its Tradition.* Amherst: University of Massachusetts Press, 1987.

Bland, Sterling Lecater. *Voices of the Fugitives: Runaway Slave Stories and Their Fictions of Self-Creation.* Westport, Conn.: Greenwood Press, 2000.

Dubey, Madhu. *Black Women Novelists and the Nationalist Aesthetic.* Bloomington: Indiana University Press, 1994.

Early, Gerald, ed. *Speech and Power: The African-American Essay and Its Cultural Content from Polemics to Pulpit.* New York: Ecco Press, 1992.

Favor, J. Martin. *Authentic Blackness: The Folk in the New Negro Renaissance.* Durham, N.C.: Duke University Press, 1999.

Frankovich, Nicholas, and David Larzelere, eds. *The Columbia Granger's Index to African-American Poetry.* New York: Columbia University Press, 1999.

Gates, Henry Louis, Jr., ed. *The Schomburg Library of Nineteenth-Century Black Women Writers.* 30 vols. New York: Oxford University Press, 1988.

Knopf, Marcy, ed. *The Sleeper Wakes: Harlem Renaissance Stories by Women.* New Brunswick, N.J.: Rutgers University Press, 1993.

Kutenplon, Deborah, and Ellen Olmstead. *Young Adult Fiction by African American Writers, 1968–1993: A Critical and Annotated Guide.* New York: Garland, 1996.

Lewis, David L., ed. *The Portable Harlem Renaissance Reader.* New York: Viking Press, 1994.

Major, Clarence, ed. *Calling the Wind: Twentieth-Century African-American Short Stories.* New York: HarperCollins, 1993.

Marsh-Lockett, Carol P., ed. *Black Women Playwrights: Vision on the American Stage.* New York: Garland Publishing, 1999.

Perkins, Kathy A., and Judith L. Stephens, eds. *Strange Fruit: Plays on Lynching by American*

Women. Bloomington: Indiana University Press, 1998.

Roses, Lorraine Elena, and Ruth Elizabeth Randolph, eds. *Harlem's Glory: Black Women Writing, 1900–1950.* Cambridge, Mass.: Harvard University Press, 1996.

Schwarz, A. B. Christa. *Gay Voices of the Harlem Renaissance.* Bloomington: Indiana University Press, 2003.

Smith, Karen Patricia, ed. *African-American Voices in Young Adult Literature: Tradition, Transition, Transformation.* Metuchen, N.J.: Scarecrow Press, 1994.

Soitos, Stephen S. *The Blues Detective: A Study of African American Detective Fiction.* Amherst: University of Massachusetts Press, 1996.

Stepto, Robert. *From Behind the Veil: A Study of African-American Narrative.* Urbana: University of Illinois Press, 1991.

Wall, Cheryl A. *Women of the Harlem Renaissance.* Bloomington: Indiana University Press, 1995.

Witalec, Janet, ed. *The Harlem Renaissance: A Gale Critical Companion.* Detroit, Mich.: Gale Research, 2003.

ENTRIES BY LITERARY GENRE

AUTOBIOGRAPHY
Angelou, Maya
Bibb, Henry Walton
Brooks, Gwendolyn
Brown, Claude
Clifton, Lucille
Derricotte, Toi
Douglass, Frederick
Equiano, Olaudah
Giovanni, Nikki
Himes, Chester
Hurston, Zora Neale
Jacobs, Harriet Ann
Lorde, Audre
McElroy, Colleen
McKay, Claude
McPherson, James Alan
Prince, Nancy
Washington, Booker T.
Wideman, John Edgar

BIOGRAPHY
Chesnutt, Charles W.
Gayle, Addison, Jr.
Griggs, Sutton
Haley, Alex
Jordan, June
Killens, John Oliver
Locke, Alain
Murray, Albert
Rampersad, Arnold

Troupe, Quincy
Walker, Margaret
Washington, Booker T.
Williams, John Alfred

CHILDREN'S/YOUNG ADULT
Angelou, Maya
Clifton, Lucille
Evans, Mari
Everett, Percival
Guy, Rosa Cuthbert
Hamilton, Virginia
Jordan, June
Killens, John Oliver
Petry, Ann
Sanchez, Sonia
Taylor, Mildred
Thomas, Joyce Carol
Walker, Alice
Williams, Sherley Anne

DETECTIVE/MYSTERY
Fisher, Rudolph
Himes, Chester
Mosley, Walter
Neely, Barbara
Schuyler, George
Thomas, Joyce Carol

DIARIST/JOURNAL
Dunbar-Nelson, Alice
Grimké, Charlotte Forten

DRAMA
Angelou, Maya
Attaway, William
Baldwin, James
Baraka, Amiri
Bonner, Marita Odette
Brown, William Wells
Bullins, Ed
Childress, Alice
Cleage, Pearl
Cooper, J. California
Dodson, Owen
Dove, Rita
DuBois, W. E. B.
Evans, Mari
Fuller, Charles
Grimké, Angelina Weld
Guy, Rosa Cuthbert
Hansberry, Lorraine
Hopkins, Pauline Elizabeth
Hughes, Langston
Johnson, Fenton
Jordan, June
Kennedy, Adrienne
Killens, John Oliver
Miller, May
Morrison, Toni
Neal, Larry
Parks, Suzan-Lori
Richardson, Willis
Sanchez, Sonia

Séjour, Victor
Shange, Ntozake
Thomas, Joyce Carol
Thurman, Wallace
Tolson, Melvin B.
Toomer, Jean
Williams, Sherley Anne
Wilson, August
Wright, Jay

EDITOR

Bambara, Toni Cade
Bontemps, Arna
Brown, Sterling
Childress, Alice
Cleage, Pearl
Cullen, Countee
Danticat, Edwidge
DuBois, W. E. B.
Evans, Mari
Forrest, Leon
Fuller, Hoyt
Gates, Henry Louis, Jr.
Gayle, Addison, Jr.
Giovanni, Nikki
Hansberry, Lorraine
Harper, Michael S.
Hemphill, Essex
Johnson, Charles
Johnson, James Weldon
Kincaid, Jamaica
Knight, Etheridge
Komunyakaa, Yusef
Locke, Alain
Mackey, Nathaniel
Madhubuti, Haki R.
Major, Clarence
McKay, Claude
McMillan, Terry
McPherson, James Alan
Morrison, Toni
Mosley, Walter
Naylor, Gloria
Neal, Larry

Petry, Ann
Rampersad, Arnold
Reed, Ishmael
Richardson, Willis
Rodgers, Carolyn M.
Sanchez, Sonia
Thomas, Joyce Carol
Thurman, Wallace
Tolson, Melvin B.
Troupe, Quincy
Walker, Alice
Walrond, Eric
West, Cornel
Young, Al

ESSAY

Angelou, Maya
Baldwin, James
Bambara, Toni Cade
Baraka, Amiri
Bonner, Marita Odette
Bradley, David
Brooks, Gwendolyn
Brown, Claude
Bullins, Ed
Chesnutt, Charles W.
Childress, Alice
Cleage, Pearl
Cliff, Michelle
Clifton, Lucille
Cooper, Anna Julia
Cooper, J. California
Delany, Samuel R.
Dove, Rita
DuBois, W. E. B.
Dunbar, Paul Laurence
Ellison, Ralph
Evans, Mari
Fauset, Jessie Redmon
Forrest, Leon
Fuller, Hoyt
Gayle, Addison, Jr.
Giovanni, Nikki
Griggs, Sutton

Grimké, Charlotte Forten
Guy, Rosa Cuthbert
Harper, Frances Ellen Watkins
Hayden, Robert
Hemphill, Essex
Hopkins, Pauline Elizabeth
Hughes, Langston
Hurston, Zora Neale
Johnson, Charles
Johnson, Fenton
Johnson, James Weldon
Jordan, June
Kelley, William Melvin
Kennedy, Adrienne
Killens, John Oliver
Kincaid, Jamaica
Knight, Etheridge
Komunyakaa, Yusef
Locke, Alain
Lorde, Audre
Mackey, Nathaniel
Madhubuti, Haki R.
Major, Clarence
Marshall, Paule
McPherson, James Alan
Morrison, Toni
Mosley, Walter
Murray, Albert
Naylor, Gloria
Neal, Larry
Rampersad, Arnold
Reed, Ishmael
Richardson, Willis
Sanchez, Sonia
Shange, Ntozake
Thurman, Wallace
Tolson, Melvin B.
Toomer, Jean
Walker, David
Walker, Margaret
Walrond, Eric
Washington, Booker T.
West, Cornel
West, Dorothy

Whitehead, Colson
Wideman, John Edgar
Williams, John Alfred
Wilson, August
Wright, Richard
Yerby, Frank
Young, Al

JOURNALISM/TRAVEL
Bennett, Gwendolyn
Cleage, Pearl
Corrothers, James
Douglass, Frederick
Gardner, Nancy
Haley, Alex
Hopkins, Pauline Elizabeth
Hughes, Langston
Marshall, Paule
Matthews, Victoria Earle
Nell, William Cooper
Petry, Ann
Poston, Ted
Schuyler, George
Tolson, Melvin B.
Walrond, Eric

LITERARY CRITICISM
Braithwaite, William
Brown, Sterling
Delany, Samuel R.
DuBois, W. E. B.
Ellison, Ralph
Fuller, Hoyt
Gates, Henry Louis, Jr.
Gayle, Addison, Jr.
hooks, bell
Johnson, James Weldon
Jones, Gayl
Locke, Alain
Rampersad, Arnold
Toomer, Jean
Walker, Alice
Waniek, Marilyn Nelson
West, Cornel

Wideman, John Edgar
Williams, Sherley Anne

NOVEL
Ai
Andrews, Raymond
Angelou, Maya
Attaway, William
Baldwin, James
Bambara, Toni Cade
Beckham, Barry
Bontemps, Arna
Bradley, David
Brooks, Gwendolyn
Brown, William Wells
Bullins, Ed
Butler, Octavia
Chesnutt, Charles W.
Childress, Alice
Cleage, Pearl
Cliff, Michelle
Coleman, Wanda
Cooper, J. California
Cullen, Countee
Danticat, Edwidge
Delany, Samuel R.
Demby, William
Dodson, Owen
Dove, Rita
DuBois, W. E. B.
Dunbar, Paul Laurence
Ellison, Ralph
Everett, Percival
Fauset, Jessie Redmon
Fisher, Rudolph
Forrest, Leon
Gaines, Ernest J.
Griggs, Sutton
Guy, Rosa Cuthbert
Haley, Alex
Hamilton, Virginia
Harper, Frances Ellen Watkins
Himes, Chester
Hopkins, Pauline Elizabeth

Hughes, Langston
Hurston, Zora Neale
Johnson, Charles
Johnson, James Weldon
Jones, Gayl
Jordan, June
Kelley, William Melvin
Killens, John Oliver
Kincaid, Jamaica
Larsen, Nella
Mackey, Nathaniel
Major, Clarence
Marshall, Paule
McKay, Claude
McMillan, Terry
Morrison, Toni
Mosley, Walter
Murray, Albert
Naylor, Gloria
Neely, Barbara
Petry, Ann
Reed, Ishmael
Rodgers, Carolyn M.
Schuyler, George
Shange, Ntozake
Thomas, Joyce Carol
Thurman, Wallace
Tolson, Melvin B.
Toomer, Jean
Walker, Alice
Walker, Margaret
West, Dorothy
Whitehead, Colson
Wideman, John Edgar
Williams, John Alfred
Williams, Sherley Anne
Wilson, Harriet E.
Wright, Richard
Yerby, Frank
Young, Al

POETRY
Ai
Angelou, Maya

Baldwin, James
Baraka, Amiri
Bennett, Gwendolyn
Bontemps, Arna
Braithwaite, William
Brooks, Gwendolyn
Brown, Sterling
Brown, William Wells
Cleage, Pearl
Cliff, Michelle
Clifton, Lucille
Coleman, Wanda
Corrothers, James
Cortez, Jayne
Cullen, Countee
Derricotte, Toi
Dodson, Owen
Dove, Rita
DuBois, W. E. B.
Dumas, Henry
Dunbar, Paul Laurence
Dunbar-Nelson, Alice Ruth
      Moore
Evans, Mari
Fauset, Jessie Redmon
Forrest, Leon
Forten, Sarah Louise
Giovanni, Nikki
Grimké, Angelina Weld
Hammon, Jupiter
Harper, Frances Ellen Watkins
Harper, Michael S.
Hayden, Robert
Hemphill, Essex
hooks, bell
Horton, George Moses
Hughes, Langston
Johnson, Fenton
Johnson, Georgia Douglas
Johnson, Helene
Johnson, James Weldon
Jones, Gayl
Jordan, June
Kaufman, Bob

Knight, Etheridge
Komunyakaa, Yusef
Lorde, Audre
Mackey, Nathaniel
Madhubuti, Haki R.
Major, Clarence
McElroy, Colleen
McKay, Claude
Miller, May
Murray, Albert
Neal, Larry
Reed, Ishmael
Rodgers, Carolyn M.
Sanchez, Sonia
Shange, Ntozake
Spencer, Anne
Terry, Lucy
Thomas, Joyce Carol
Tolson, Melvin B.
Toomer, Jean
Troupe, Quincy
Walker, Alice
Walker, Margaret
Waniek, Marilyn Nelson
Wheatley, Phillis
Whitfield, James Monroe
Williams, John Alfred
Williams, Sherley Anne
Wilson, August
Wright, Jay
Wright, Richard
Yerby, Frank
Young, Al

SCIENCE FICTION/FANTASY
Butler, Octavia
Delany, Samuel R.
Mosley, Walter
Reed, Ishmael
Schuyler, George

SCREENWRITING
Angelou, Maya
Attaway, William

Bambara, Toni Cade
Baraka, Amiri
Childress, Alice
Demby, William
Fuller, Charles
Killens, John Oliver
McMillan, Terry
Naylor, Gloria
Parks, Suzan-Lori
Thurman, Wallace
Young, Al

SHORT STORY
Attaway, William
Bambara, Toni Cade
Baraka, Amiri
Bonner, Marita Odette
Bontemps, Arna
Butler, Octavia
Chesnutt, Charles W.
Cleage, Pearl
Cliff, Michelle
Coleman, Wanda
Cooper, J. California
Danticat, Edwidge
Delany, Samuel R.
Dove, Rita
Dumas, Henry
Dunbar, Paul Laurence
Dunbar-Nelson, Alice Ruth
      Moore
Ellison, Ralph
Evans, Mari
Everett, Percival
Fisher, Rudolph
Fuller, Hoyt
Gaines, Ernest J.
Grimké, Angelina Weld
Hamilton, Virginia
Harper, Frances Ellen Watkins
Himes, Chester
Hopkins, Pauline Elizabeth
Hughes, Langston
Hurston, Zora Neale

Johnson, Charles
Johnson, Fenton
Jones, Gayl
Kelley, William Melvin
Kennedy, Adrienne
Kincaid, Jamaica
Larsen, Nella
Marshall, Paule
Matthews, Victoria Earle
McElroy, Colleen
McKay, Claude
McMillan, Terry
McPherson, James Alan

Miller, May
Neely, Barbara
Oliver, Diane
Petry, Ann
Poston, Ted
Sanchez, Sonia
Schuyler, George
Séjour, Victor
Toomer, Jean
Walker, Alice
West, Dorothy
Wideman, John Edgar
Williams, Sherley Anne

Wright, Richard
Yerby, Frank
Young, Al

SLAVE NARRATIVE
Bibb, Henry Walton
Brown, William Wells
Douglass, Frederick
Equiano, Olaudah
Jacobs, Harriet Ann
Washington, Booker T.

ENTRIES BY LITERARY MOVEMENT/ SUBJECT MATTER/STYLE

AFRICAN-AMERICAN FOLKLORE
Brown, Sterling
Chesnutt, Charles W.
Gaines, Ernest J.
Hamilton, Virginia
Hughes, Langston
Hurston, Zora Neale
Thomas, Joyce Carol
Tolson, Melvin B.
Whitehead, Colson
Williams, Sherley Anne

ANTISLAVERY MOVEMENT
Bibb, Henry Walton
Brown, William Wells
Douglass, Frederick
Forten, Sarah Louise
Grimké, Charlotte Forten
Harper, Frances Ellen Watkins
Horton, George Moses
Jacobs, Harriet Ann
Nell, William Cooper
Prince, Nancy
Walker, David
Washington, Booker T.
Wilson, Harriet E.

BLACK ARTS MOVEMENT
Baraka, Amiri
Brooks, Gwendolyn
Bullins, Ed

Clifton, Lucille
Fuller, Charles
Fuller, Hoyt
Gayle, Addison, Jr.
Giovanni, Nikki
Hansberry, Lorraine
Johnson, Fenton
Kelley, William Melvin
Kennedy, Adrienne
Madhubuti, Haki R.
Marshall, Paule
Neal, Larry
Rodgers, Carolyn M.
Sanchez, Sonia

COLONIAL AND EARLY NATIONALIST ERAS
Equiano, Olaudah
Hammon, Jupiter
Terry, Lucy
Walker, David
Wheatley, Phillis

CULTURAL AND LITERARY STUDIES
Braithwaite, William
Brown, Sterling
Childress, Alice
DuBois, W. E. B.
Gates, Henry Louis, Jr.
hooks, bell

Jordan, June
Locke, Alain
Matthews, Victoria Earle
McPherson, James Alan
Morrison, Toni
Rampersad, Arnold
West, Cornel

EXPATRIATES
Baldwin, James
Bennett, Gwendolyn
Cullen, Countee
Demby, William
DuBois, W. E. B.
Fauset, Jessie Redmon
Himes, Chester
Hughes, Langston
Kelley, William Melvin
Locke, Alain
McKay, Claude
Yerby, Frank

FEMINIST ISSUES
Ai
Angelou, Maya
Bambara, Toni Cade
Childress, Alice
Cleage, Pearl
Clifton, Lucille
Coleman, Wanda
Cooper, Anna Julia

Cooper, J. California
Cortez, Jayne
Derricotte, Toi
Evans, Mari
Harper, Frances Ellen Watkins
hooks, bell
Jones, Gayl
Jordan, June
Matthews, Victoria Earle
McMillan, Terry
Morrison, Toni
Naylor, Gloria
Sanchez, Sonia
Shange, Ntozake
Thomas, Joyce Carol
Walker, Alice
Waniek, Marilyn Nelson

GAY AND LESBIAN ISSUES

Baldwin, James
Delany, Samuel R.
Hemphill, Essex
Lorde, Audre

HARLEM RENAISSANCE

Bennett, Gwendolyn
Bonner, Marita Odette
Bontemps, Arna
Braithwaite, William
Cullen, Countee
DuBois, W. E. B.
Fauset, Jessie Redmon
Fisher, Rudolph
Grimké, Angelina Weld
Guy, Rosa Cuthbert
Himes, Chester
Hughes, Langston
Hurston, Zora Neale
Johnson, Georgia Douglas
Johnson, Helene
Johnson, James Weldon
Larsen, Nella
Locke, Alain
Miller, May

Petry, Ann
Richardson, Willis
Schuyler, George
Spencer, Anne
Thurman, Wallace
Tolson, Melvin B.
Toomer, Jean
West, Dorothy

JAZZ AND BLUES AESTHETICS

Baldwin, James
Baraka, Amiri
Brown, Sterling
Coleman, Wanda
Cortez, Jayne
Dodson, Owen
Ellison, Ralph
Evans, Mari
Harper, Michael S.
Hayden, Robert
Hughes, Langston
Kaufman, Bob
Knight, Etheridge
Komunyakaa, Yusef
Mackey, Nathaniel
Major, Clarence
Marshall, Paule
McElroy, Colleen
Murray, Albert
Parks, Suzan-Lori
Rampersad, Arnold
Reed, Ishmael
Sanchez, Sonia
Tolson, Melvin B.
Troupe, Quincy
Williams, Sherley Anne
Wilson, August
Young, Al

MODERN, POSTMODERN, AND EXPERIMENTAL LITERATURE

Dodson, Owen
Ellison, Ralph
Everett, Percival

Forrest, Leon
Harper, Michael S.
Hayden, Robert
Johnson, Charles
Mackey, Nathaniel
Major, Clarence
McPherson, James Alan
Parks, Suzan-Lori
Reed, Ishmael
Tolson, Melvin B.
Toomer, Jean
Whitehead, Colson
Wideman, John Edgar
Williams, John Alfred
Wright, Jay

NEO-SLAVE NARRATIVE

Brown, William Wells
Butler, Octavia
Clifton, Lucille
Cooper, J. California
Dove, Rita
Gaines, Ernest J.
Haley, Alex
Hamilton, Virginia
Johnson, Charles
Jones, Gayl
Morrison, Toni
Naylor, Gloria
Reed, Ishmael
Walker, Alice
Walker, Margaret
Williams, Sherley Anne

NORTHERN MIGRATION

Attaway, William
Baldwin, James
Brooks, Gwendolyn
Ellison, Ralph
Haley, Alex
Hughes, Langston
Larsen, Nella
Marshall, Paule
Morrison, Toni

Petry, Ann
Toomer, Jean
Wright, Richard

SOCIAL PROTEST LITERATURE
Andrews, Raymond
Attaway, William
Baraka, Amiri
Beckham, Barry
Bradley, David
Brown, Claude
Childress, Alice
Coleman, Wanda
Corrothers, James
Dumas, Henry
Evans, Mari
Forrest, Leon
Grimké, Angelina Weld

Hopkins, Pauline Elizabeth
Kennedy, Adrienne
Killens, John Oliver
Marshall, Paule
McKay, Claude
Naylor, Gloria
Oliver, Diane
Poston, Ted
Taylor, Mildred
Whitfield, James Monroe
Wideman, John Edgar
Williams, John Alfred
Wright, Richard

TRANSCULTURAL AND IMMIGRANT ISSUES
Ai
Bambara, Toni Cade

Cliff, Michelle
Danticat, Edwidge
Dunbar-Nelson, Alice Ruth
    Moore
Gaines, Ernest J.
Jones, Gayl
Kincaid, Jamaica
Komunyakaa, Yusef
Lorde, Audre
Mackey, Nathaniel
Marshall, Paule
McElroy, Colleen
McKay, Claude
Séjour, Victor
Walrond, Eric
Williams, Sherley Anne
Wright, Jay

Entries by Year of Birth

1700s
Equiano, Olaudah
Hammon, Jupiter
Horton, George Moses
Prince, Nancy
Terry, Lucy
Walker, David
Wheatley, Phillis

1800–1819
Bibb, Henry Walton
Brown, William Wells
Douglass, Frederick
Forten, Sarah Louise
Jacobs, Harriet Ann
Nell, William Cooper
Séjour, Victor

1820–1849
Grimké, Charlotte Forten
Harper, Frances Ellen Watkins
Whitfield, James Monroe
Wilson, Harriet E.

1850–1879
Braithwaite, William
Chesnutt, Charles W.
Cooper, Anna Julia
Corrothers, James
DuBois, W. E. B.
Dunbar, Paul Laurence

Dunbar-Nelson, Alice Ruth
  Moore
Griggs, Sutton
Hopkins, Pauline Elizabeth
Johnson, James Weldon
Matthews, Victoria Earle
Washington, Booker T.

1880–1899
Bonner, Marita Odette
Fauset, Jessie Redmon
Fisher, Rudolph
Grimké, Angelina Weld
Hurston, Zora Neale
Johnson, Fenton
Johnson, Georgia Douglas
Larsen, Nella
Locke, Alain
McKay, Claude
Miller, May
Richardson, Willis
Schuyler, George
Spencer, Anne
Toomer, Jean
Walrond, Eric

1900–1909
Bennett, Gwendolyn
Bontemps, Arna
Brown, Sterling
Cullen, Countee

Himes, Chester
Hughes, Langston
Johnson, Helene
Petry, Ann
Poston, Ted
Thurman, Wallace
Tolson, Melvin B.
West, Dorothy
Wright, Richard

1910–1919
Attaway, William
Brooks, Gwendolyn
Childress, Alice
Dodson, Owen
Ellison, Ralph
Hayden, Robert
Killens, John Oliver
Murray, Albert
Walker, Margaret
Yerby, Frank

1920–1929
Angelou, Maya
Baldwin, James
Demby, William
Evans, Mari
Fuller, Hoyt
Guy, Rosa
Haley, Alex
Kaufman, Bob

Marshall, Paule
Williams, John Alfred

1930–1939
Andrews, Raymond
Bambara, Toni Cade
Baraka, Amiri
Brown, Claude
Bullins, Ed
Clifton, Lucille
Cortez, Jayne
Dumas, Henry
Forrest, Leon
Fuller, Charles
Gaines, Ernest J.
Gayle, Addison, Jr.
Hamilton, Virginia
Hansberry, Lorraine
Harper, Michael S.
Jordan, June
Kelley, William Melvin
Kennedy, Adrienne
Knight, Etheridge
Lorde, Audre
Major, Clarence
McElroy, Colleen
Morrison, Toni

Neal, Larry
Reed, Ishmael
Sanchez, Sonia
Thomas, Joyce Carol
Wright, Jay
Young, Al

1940–1949
Ai
Beckham, Barry
Butler, Octavia
Cleage, Pearl
Cliff, Michelle
Coleman, Wanda
Delany, Samuel R.
Derricotte, Toi
Giovanni, Nikki
Johnson, Charles
Jones, Gayl
Kincaid, Jamaica
Komunyakaa, Yusef
Mackey, Nathaniel
Madhubuti, Haki R.
McPherson, James Alan
Neely, Barbara
Oliver, Diane
Rampersad, Arnold

Rodgers, Carolyn M.
Shange, Ntozake
Taylor, Mildred
Troupe, Quincy
Walker, Alice
Waniek, Marilyn Nelson
Wideman, John Edgar
Williams, Sherley Anne
Wilson, August

1950–1959
Bradley, David
Dove, Rita
Everett, Percival
Gates, Henry Louis, Jr.
Hemphill, Essex
hooks, bell
McMillan, Terry
Mosley, Walter
Naylor, Gloria
West, Cornel

1960–1970
Danticat, Edwidge
Parks, Suzan-Lori
Whitehead, Colson

INDEX

Boldface locators indicate main entries. *Italic* locators indicate photographs.